McDOUGAL LITTELL

Discovering FRENCH Nouveau!

Workbook

Jean-Paul Valette
Rebecca M. Valette

Overview

The *Discovering French, Nouveau!–Bleu* Workbook is an integrated workbook that provides additional practice to allow students to build their control of French and develop French proficiency.

The activities provide guided communicative practice in meaningful contexts and frequent opportunity for self-expression.

C, 2

ISBN-13: 978-0-618-29825-9 ISBN-10: 0 - 618 - 29825 - 8

31 32 33 34 0868 15 14 13 12
4500369752

BLEU

Table of Contents

Table of Contents

To the Student

The Workbook is divided into eight units. Each unit has three sections:

Listening Activities

The Listening Activities have the pictures you will need to complete the recorded activities. The lessons correspond to the lessons in the student text.

Writing Activities

The Writing Activities will give you the chance to develop your writing skills and put into practice what you have learned in class. The lessons correspond to the lessons in the student text. The exercises are coded to correspond to a particular part of the lesson. For example, **A** at the beginning of an exercise or group of exercises means that the material is related to the structures or vocabulary presented in Section A of that lesson. The last activity is called *Communication* and encourages you to express yourself in various additional communicative situations.

Reading and Culture Activities

The Reading and Culture Activities contain realia (illustrations and objects from real life) from French-speaking countries and various kinds of cultural activities. Each unit includes one set of Reading and Culture Activities.

Nom ____________________

Classe ____________________ Date ____________________

Discovering FRENCH Nouveau!

BLEU

Unité 1. Faisons connaissance

LEÇON 1 Bonjour Vidéo-scène A. La rentrée

LISTENING ACTIVITIES

Section 1. Je m'appelle . . .

A. Compréhension orale Listening comprehension

▶ (a) François
b. Frank

1. a. Nathalie
b. Nicole

2. a. Sylvie
b. Cécile

3. a. Jean-Claude
b. Jean-Paul

4. a. Lucie
b. Juliette

B. Compréhension orale

Antoine
David
Guillaume
Marc
Maxime
Nicolas
Philippe
Vincent

Caroline
Céline
Charlotte
Émilie
Julie
Marie
Monique
Pauline

Nom ______________________________

Classe ____________________ Date ____________

Discovering FRENCH Nouveau!

BLEU

Section 2. L'alphabet

C. Écoutez et répétez. Listen and repeat.

A	B	C	D	E	F	G	H	I	J	K	L	M
N	O	P	Q	R	S	T	U	V	W	X	Y	Z

D. Écoutez et écrivez. Listen and write.

1. ___ ___ ___ ___
2. ___ ___ ___ ___ ___ ___
3. ___ ___ ___ ___ ___ ___
4. ___ ___ ___ ___ ___ ___ ___
5. ___ ___ ___ ___ ___ ___

Section 3. Les signes orthographiques

E. Écoutez et regardez. Listen and look.

´ accent aigu **Cécile**

¨ tréma **Noël**

` accent grave **Michèle**

¸ cédille **François**

^ accent circonflexe **Jérôme**

F. Écoutez et écrivez. Listen and write.

1. Aur<u>e</u>lie 2. Myl<u>e</u>ne 3. Jér<u>o</u>me 4. Jo<u>e</u>lle 5. Fran<u>c</u>oise 6. Mich<u>e</u>le

Section 4. Les nombres de 0 à 10 (Numbers from 0 to 10)

G. Écoutez et répétez. Listen and repeat.

0 (zéro)	**1** (un)	**2** (deux)	**3** (trois)	**4** (quatre)	**5** (cinq)
	6 (six)	**7** (sept)	**8** (huit)	**9** (neuf)	**10** (dix)

H. Écoutez et écrivez. Listen and write.

Modèle	a.	b.	c.	d.	e.	f.	g.	h.	i.	j.	k.
8											

Section 5. Dictée

I. Écoutez et écrivez. Listen and write.

— __________! Je m'appelle Thomas. Et ___?

— ___, ___ m'appelle Céline.

Nom ______________________________

Classe ____________________ Date ____________

Discovering FRENCH Nouveau!

BLEU

WRITING ACTIVITIES

1. Au Club International

You have met the following young people at the Club International. Six of them have names of French origin. Circle these names. Then write them in the box below, separating the boys and the girls.

(Note: Don't forget the accent marks!)

Carlos Suárez	Tatsuya Matsumoto
Birgit Eriksen	Jérôme Dupuis
Hélène Rémy	Janet Woodford
Jean-François Petit	Maureen Stewart
Michiko Sato	Marie-Noëlle Laîné
Frédéric Lemaître	Svetlana Poliakoff
Heinz Mueller	Stéphanie Mercier

FLASH culturel

French is spoken not only in France. Today about thirty countries use French as their official language (or one of their official languages). Which continent has the largest number of French-speaking countries?

❑ Europe ❑ Africa ❑ Asia ❑ South America

→page 4

Nom ______________________________

Classe ______________________ Date ______________

Discovering FRENCH Nouveau!

BLEU

2. Allô!

First write down your phone number and the numbers of two friends or relatives. Then write out the numbers as you would say them in French.

1. Moi

☐ ☐ ☐ - ☐ ☐ ☐ ☐

______________________ - ______________________

2. Nom *(name)*: ______________________

☐ ☐ ☐ - ☐ ☐ ☐ ☐

______________________ - ______________________

3. Nom *(name)*: ______________________

☐ ☐ ☐ - ☐ ☐ ☐ ☐

______________________ - ______________________

3. Communication: En français!

On the bus you meet a new French student. Write out what you would say — in French!

1. *Say hello.*

____

2. *Give your name.*

____

3. *Ask the French student his/her name.*

____

FLASH culturel

French is the official language in about 20 African countries. The largest of these countries is the Democratic Republic of Congo in central Africa. Other countries where French is spoken by many of the citizens are: Algeria, Tunisia, and Morocco in North Africa; Senegal and the Ivory Coast in West Africa; and the island of Madagascar off the coast of East Africa.

Vidéo-scène B. Tu es français?

LISTENING ACTIVITIES

Section 1. Quelle nationalité?

A. Compréhension orale Listening comprehension

Modèle: Tu es anglaise?

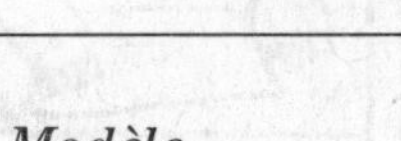

Modèle ____ ✓

1. ____ ____

2. ____ ____
3. ____ ____
4. ____ ____
5. ____ ____
6. ____ ____
7. ____ ____
8. ____ ____

B. Compréhension orale

French flag

A

British flag

B

US flag

C

Canadian flag

D

1				
2				
3				
4				
5				
6				

Nom ______________________________

Classe ____________________ Date ____________________

BLEU

Section 2. Les nombres de 10 à 20

C. Écoutez et répétez. Listen and repeat.

10 (dix) **11** (onze) **12** (douze) **13** (treize) **14** (quatorze) **15** (quinze)

16 (seize) **17** (dix-sept) **18** (dix-huit) **19** (dix-neuf) **20** (vingt)

D. Écoutez et écrivez. Listen and write.

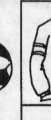

► **Philippe**

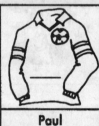

Paul

François

Marc

Jérôme

Jean-Michel

Frédéric

Patrick

Robert

Thomas

Section 3. Dictée

E. Écoutez et écrivez.

—Tu ____ française ____ anglaise?

—Je ____ américaine.

—Moi _____!

WRITING ACTIVITIES

1. Présentations *(Introductions)*

The following people are introducing themselves, giving their names and their nationalities. Complete what each one says.

Je m'appelle Cédric.

Je suis ____________________.

Je m'appelle Liz.

Je suis ____________________.

Je m'appelle Tina.

Je suis ____________________.

Je m'appelle Pierre.

Je suis ____________________.

Je m'appelle Bob.

Je suis ____________________.

Je m'appelle Véronique.

Je suis ____________________.

FLASH culturel

Martinique and Guadeloupe are two French-speaking islands in the Caribbean. In which other Caribbean country is French spoken?

❑ Cuba ❑ Puerto Rico ❑ Haiti ❑ The Dominican Republic

→page 8

Nom ______________________________

Classe ______________________ Date ______________

Discovering FRENCH Nouveau!

BLEU

2. Les maths

Write out the answers to the following arithmetic problems.

▶ 4 + 7 = onze

1. 9 + 3 = __________
2. 8 + 6 = __________
3. 10 + 7 = __________
4. 17 + 2 = __________
5. 5 × 3 = __________
6. 2 × 10 = __________

3. Communication: En français!

You are at a party and have just met two French-speaking students: Philippe and Marie-Laure.

1. *Say hello to them.*

____

2. *Give your name.*

____

3. *Say that you are American.*

____

4. *Ask Philippe if he is French.*

____

5. *Ask Marie-Laure if she is Canadian.*

____

BOSTON HAÏTI COURRIER

FLASH culturel

Haiti is a former French colony. Toward the end of the eighteenth century, the black slaves who worked in the sugar cane plantations revolted against their French masters. In 1804, Haiti became an independent country. It is the first republic established by people of African origin.

Today French, which is the official language of Haiti, is spoken by many Haitians, along with Creole. Many people of Haitian origin live in the United States, especially in Florida, New York, and Boston. If you meet young Haitians, you might want to speak French with them.

Nom ______________________________________

Classe ______________________ Date ______________________

Discovering FRENCH Nouveau!

BLEU

Vidéo-scène C. Salut! Ça va?

LISTENING ACTIVITIES

Section 1. Salutations

A. Compréhension orale Listening comprehension

Modèle: Au revoir, madame.

Modèle	____	✓
1.	____	____
2.	____	____
3.	____	____
4.	____	____
5.	____	____
6.	____	____

Section 2. Ça va?

B. Compréhension orale

Ça va bien!

a. ____

Ça va très bien!

b. ____

Ça va comme ci, comme ça.

c. ____

Ça va mal.

d. ____

Ça va très mal.

e. ____

Nom ______________________________

Classe ______________ Date ______________

C. Questions et réponses Questions and answers

▶ —Ça va?
—Ça va comme ci, comme ça.

Section 3. Les nombres de 20 à 60

D. Écoutez et répétez. Listen and repeat.

20	**21**	**22**	**23**	**24**	**25**	**26**
27	**28**	**29**	**30**	**31**	**32**	**33 . . .**
40	**41**	**42 . . .**	**44**	**45**	**46 . . .**	**50**
51 . . .	**57**	**58**	**59**	**60**		

E. Écoutez et écrivez. Listen and write.

Thomas ____ . ____ . ____ . ____ . ____

Caroline ____ . ____ . ____ . ____ . ____

Mathieu ____ . ____ . ____ . ____ . ____

Stéphanie ____ . ____ . ____ . ____ . ____

Section 4. Dictée

F. Écoutez et écrivez.

—______! Ça va?

—Oui, ______! Ça va très ______. Et toi?

—Ça va ______!

Nom ______________________________

Classe ____________________ Date ______________

WRITING ACTIVITIES

1. Loto *(Bingo)*

You are playing Loto in Quebec. The numbers below have all been called. If you have these numbers on your card, circle them.

seize **trente et un** **vingt-deux** **cinquante** **quarante-neuf** **quinze** **quarante** **trente-quatre** **vingt-neuf** **soixante** **quarante-huit** **douze** **cinquante-deux** **onze** **dix-sept** **vingt et un** **vingt** **trente-cinq** **trente-sept** **cinquante-six** **sept** **cinquante-quatre** **cinquante-neuf** **trois**

5	14	26	37	49
7	15	29	40	52
9	18	X	41	54
11	21	33	46	59
12	22	35	48	60

How many numbers did you circle? __________

How many rows of five did you score? __________

FLASH culturel

France is not the only European country where French is spoken. In which of the following countries do one fifth of the people speak French?

❑ Germany ❑ Italy ❑ Spain ❑ Switzerland

→page 12

Nom ______________________________

Classe ______________________ Date ______________________

2. Bonjour!

The following people meet in the street. How do you think they will greet each other? Fill in the bubbles with the appropriate expressions.

3. Ça va?

How do you think the following people would answer the question **Ça va?**

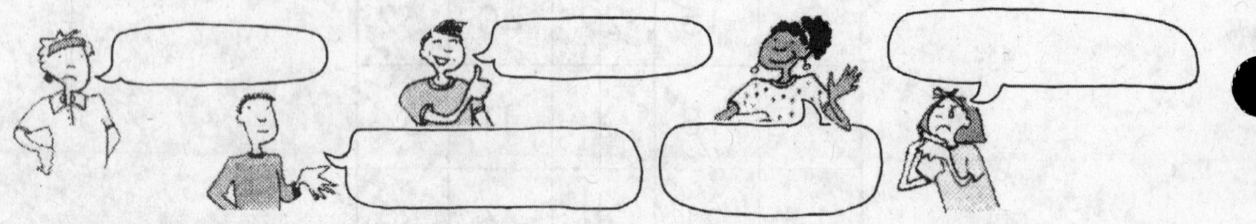

4. Communication: En français!

You have just enrolled in a French school as an exchange student.

1. On the way to school, you meet your friend Catherine.

   Say hello to her. ______________________

   Ask her how things are going. ______________________

2. Now you meet Mademoiselle Lebrun, your new music teacher.

   Say hello to her. ______________________

   Ask her how she is. ______________________

FLASH culturel

Although all of these countries border on France, only Switzerland has a sizeable French-speaking population. The main French-speaking city of Switzerland is Geneva **(Genève),** which is the headquarters of the International Red Cross and the seat of several other international organizations.

Nom ______________________________ **Discovering FRENCH** *Nouveau!*

Classe ____________________ Date ______________

BLEU

LEÇON 2 Famille et copains
Vidéo-scène A. Copain ou copine?

LISTENING ACTIVITIES

Section 1. Qui est-ce?

A. Compréhension orale Listening comprehension

Modèle: Voici une amie.

	A	B
Modèle	un ami	(une) amie
1.	un prof	une prof
2.	un journaliste	une journaliste
3.	un artiste	une artiste
4.	un photographe	une photographe
5.	un pianiste	une pianiste
6.	un secrétaire	une secrétaire

B. Écoutez et parlez. Listen and speak.

▶—Tiens, voilà Isabelle!
—Qui est-ce?
—C'est une copine.

1. un copain? une copine?
2. un copain? une copine?
3. un ami? une amie?
4. un ami? une amie?
5. un prof? une prof?
6. un prof? une prof?

Nom ___________________________________

Classe ____________________ Date ____________________

Section 2. Les nombres de 60 à 79

C. Écoutez et répétez. Listen and repeat.

60	61	62	63	64	65	66	67	68	69
70	71	72	73	74	75	76	77	78	79

D. Écoutez et écrivez. Listen and write.

Mélanie ____ . ____ . ____ . ____ . ____

Nicolas ____ . ____ . ____ . ____ . ____

Julie ____ . ____ . ____ . ____ . ____

Vincent ____ . ____ . ____ . ____ . ____

Section 3. Dictée

E. Écoutez et écrivez.

—________ Nathalie.

—________ est-ce?

—________ une ________.

Nom ______________________________

Classe ____________________ Date ______________

Discovering FRENCH Nouveau!

BLEU

Unité 1 Leçon 2

Workbook

WRITING ACTIVITIES

1. Pour détectives

You have found a notebook in which several people are mentioned only by their initials. Read the descriptions and determine who is male and who is female. Circle the corresponding letter.

▶	J.G. est un journaliste français.	(M)	F
▶	C.C. est une actrice italienne.	M	(F)
1.	B.H. est un musicien anglais.	M	F
2.	V.C. est un pianiste.	M	F
3.	S.F. est une photographe américaine.	M	F
4.	E.M. est une artiste française.	M	F
5.	P.N. est un excellent acteur.	M	F
6.	T.B. est un artiste américain.	M	F
7.	P.V. est un cousin de San Francisco.	M	F
8.	V.U. est une cousine de Montréal.	M	F

2. Descriptions

Describe the following people. For each one, write two sentences using two different nouns from the box. Be sure to use **un** or **une** as appropriate.

garçon	**ami**	**copain**	**monsieur**	**prof**
fille	**amie**	**copine**	**dame**	**prof**

▶ **Christine** ______________________________

____

Jean-François ______________________________

____

M. Martinot ______________________________

____

Mme Pichon ______________________________

____

FLASH culturel

The **Tour de France** is an international bicycle race that is held in France every summer. How long does it last?

❑ 10 hours ❑ 24 hours ❑ 10 days ❑ 3 weeks

→**page 16**

Nom ______________________________

Classe ____________________ Date ____________________

3. Les nombres

Fill in the six missing numbers in the grid. Then write out these numbers in French.

60		62	63	64
65	66	67		69
		72	73	74
75		77		79

- ______________________________
- ______________________________
- ______________________________
- ______________________________
- ______________________________
- ______________________________

4. Communication: En français!

1. You are walking in town with your French friend Catherine. Catherine waves hello to a girl on a bicycle.
   Ask Catherine who it is.
   ____
2. You see Jean-Louis who is sitting in a café.
   Point him out and tell Catherine that he is a friend.
   ____
3. You see your friend Juliette coming in your direction.
   Express your surprise and explain to Catherine who is approaching.
   ____

FLASH culturel

The **Tour de France** is the longest and most strenuous bicycle race in the world. It is divided into about 20 stages (or **étapes**) and lasts approximately three weeks. During the race, the participants cover about 3,000 kilometers, riding along the valleys and climbing the high mountains of France. The American cyclist Greg Lemond is a three-time winner of the **Tour de France**.

Nom ______________________________________

Classe ____________________ Date ____________

Discovering FRENCH Nouveau!

BLEU

Vidéo-scène B. Une coïncidence

LISTENING ACTIVITIES

Section 1. Qui est-ce?

A. Compréhension orale Listening comprehension

Modèle: Elle est de Paris?

Modèle	____	✓
1.	____	____
2.	____	____
3.	____	____
4.	____	____
5.	____	____
6.	____	____
7.	____	____
8.	____	____
9.	____	____
10.	____	____

B. Écoutez et répétez. Listen and repeat.

Isabelle

1. Marc

2. Philippe

3. Nathalie

4. Patrick

▶—Elle est française?
—Oui, elle est française.

—Comment s'appelle-t-elle?
—Elle s'appelle Isabelle.

Nom ______________________________

Classe ____________________ Date ____________________

Discovering FRENCH Nouveau!

BLEU

Section 2. Les nombres de 80 à 100

C. Écoutez et répétez. Listen and repeat.

80	81	82	83	84	85	86	87	88	89	
90	91	92	93	94	95	96	97	98	99	100

D. Écoutez et écrivez. Listen and write.

Florence	Juliette	Philippe	Laure

Delphine	Julien	Olivier	Caroline

Section 3. Dictée

E. Écoutez et écrivez.

—Tu connais ____ fille?

—Oui, ____ s'appelle Christine.

—Et ____ garçon?

—C'est ____ copain. ____ s'appelle Jean-Pierre.

Nom ______________________________

Classe ____________________ Date ____________________

WRITING ACTIVITIES

1. *Le, la ou l'?*

Write **le, la,** or **l'** in front of the following nouns, as appropriate.

▶ la copine

1. ____ garçon
2. ____ monsieur
3. ____ fille
4. ____ ami
5. ____ copain
6. ____ amie
7. ____ prof: M. Lenoir
8. ____ prof: Mme Dupin

2. Photos de vacances

Last summer you went on an international camping trip and took pictures of some of your friends. Give each person's name and nationality.

▶ Il s'appelle Jim.
Il est anglais.

FLASH culturel

In the United States, there are many places that have names of French origin. Which of the following states is named after a French king?

❑ Georgia ❑ North Carolina ❑ Louisiana ❑ Virginia

→page 20

Nom ______________________________

Classe ______________________ Date ______________________

3. Loto

Imagine that you are playing **Loto** in France. The following numbers have been called. Read them carefully and put an "X" on the numbers that appear on your **Loto** card.

soixante-treize **soixante-quatre** **quatorze** **cinquante-trois** **huit**
quatre-vingt-douze **vingt-trois** **quatre-vingt-neuf** **soixante-quinze**
cinquante-huit **trente-sept** **quarante-cinq** **soixante-quatorze** **seize**
vingt et un **quatre-vingt-six** **soixante-dix-huit** **quatre-vingt-un**

Which row did you complete to win **Loto**: the top, the middle, or the bottom?

____

Now write in digits the numbers that were not on your card.

____

		21		45			73	81	92
	17				53		74	86	95
8			39			64	78		99

4. Communication: Dialogues

Complete the following mini-dialogues by filling in the missing words.

1. —Philippe ____________ français?
   —Non, ____________ est canadien.
2. —Tu ____________ le garçon là-bas?
   —Oui, c'est ____________ copain.
3. —____________ s'appelle ____________ prof?
   —____________ s'appelle Madame Vallée.

FLASH culturel

Louisiana was named in honor of the French king Louis XIV (1638–1715). Louisiana was once a French colony and extended up the entire Mississippi basin. The U.S. purchased it from France in 1803. Today, French is still spoken in the state of Louisiana by some people in the "Cajun" areas.

Nom ______________________________

Classe ____________________ Date ______________

Discovering FRENCH Nouveau!

BLEU

Vidéo-scène C. Les photos d'Isabelle

LISTENING ACTIVITIES

Section 1. Qui est-ce?

A. Compréhension orale Listening comprehension

Modèle: Voici ma cousine.

Modèle	____	✓
1.	____	____
2.	____	____
3.	____	____
4.	____	____
5.	____	____
6.	____	____
7.	____	____
8.	____	____

Section 2. L'âge

B. Compréhension orale

1. Marc a ____ ans.
2. Mélanie a ____ ans.
3. Mon oncle a ____ ans.
4. Ma grand-mère a ____ ans.
5. Mon chat a ____ ans.
6. Mon chien a ____ ans.
7. Le prof a ____ ans.
8. La prof a ____ ans.

Nom ____
Classe ______________________ Date ______________

C. Écoutez et parlez. Listen and speak.

Section 3. Dictée

D. Écoutez et écrivez. Listen and write.

—Quel ____ as-tu?

—____ quatorze ____.

—Et ____ cousine Nathalie?

—Elle ____ seize ans.

Nom ______________________________

Classe ____________________ Date ____________

Discovering FRENCH Nouveau!

BLEU

WRITING ACTIVITIES

1. La famille de Catherine

Catherine has taken a picture of her family. Identify each of the people in the photograph.

▶ Suzanne est la soeur de Catherine.

1. M. Arnaud est ____________ de Catherine.
2. Jean-Michel est ____________ de Catherine.
3. Mme Laurent est ____________ de Catherine.
4. Mme Arnaud est ____________ de Catherine.
5. M. Laurent est ____________ de Catherine.
6. Hugo, c'est ____________.
7. Mimi, c'est ____________.

FLASH culturel

At what age can a French teenager drive a car?

❑ 15 ❑ 16 ❑ 17 ❑ 18

→page 24

Nom ____

Classe ____________________ Date ____________________

Discovering FRENCH Nouveau!

BLEU

2. *Mon ou ma?*

Philippe is talking about his friends and relatives, as well as other people he knows. Complete his statements with **mon** or **ma**, as appropriate.

1. __________ cousine s'appelle Christine.
2. __________ frère est à Paris.
3. __________ copine Susan est anglaise.
4. __________ amie Cécile a seize ans.
5. __________ ami Jean-Pierre a quinze ans.
6. __________ prof d'anglais est américaine.
7. __________ prof d'histoire est canadien.
8. __________ mère est journaliste.

3. Quel âge?

Look at the years in which the following people were born. Then complete the sentences below by giving each person's age.

1. (1991) Corinne ______________________________.
2. (1996) Jean-Philippe ______________________________.
3. (1982) Mademoiselle Richaume ______________________________.
4. (1969) Monsieur Lambert ______________________________.

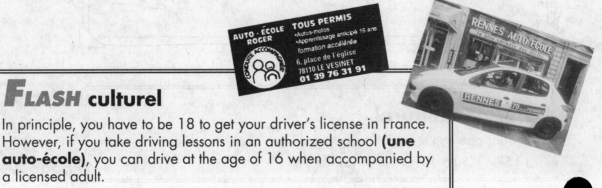

4. Communication: En français!

1. *Tell how old you are.*

____

2. *Ask a friend how old he/she is.*

____

3. *Ask a friend how old his/her brother is.*

____

FLASH culturel

In principle, you have to be 18 to get your driver's license in France. However, if you take driving lessons in an authorized school **(une auto-école)**, you can drive at the age of 16 when accompanied by a licensed adult.

UNITÉ 1 Reading and Culture Activities

A. En voyage *(On a trip)*

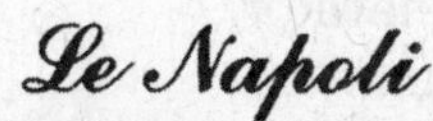

Restaurant - Pizzéria
Spécialités - Grillades

7, Av. des Poilus - Place Cavet ☎ 04 94 74 03 34
83110 Sanary-sur-mer

1. Why would you go to Le Napoli?
   - ❑ To shop for food.
   - ❑ To have dinner.
   - ❑ To see a movie.
   - ❑ To plan a trip to Italy.

RESTAURANT

BONAPARTE
CUISINE DE FRANCE
443, rue St-François-Xavier
Vieux-Montréal
Réservations 514-844-4368

2. In which country is the Bonaparte located?
   - ❑ In France.
   - ❑ In Canada.
   - ❑ In Switzerland.
   - ❑ In Belgium.

HOTEL LES CLEMATITES**
18 chambres
Télévision - Téléphone
Plein centre Ville
19, rue Vaugelas 74000 ANNECY
Tél. 04.50.52.84.33 - Fax 04.50.45.49.06

3. Why would you call the number shown in this ad?
   - ❑ To buy a train ticket.
   - ❑ To rent a video.
   - ❑ To have your phone repaired.
   - ❑ To reserve a room.

La COUVERTOIRADE
AVEYRON
MONUMENT HISTORIQUE
ADULTE
Conservez votre ticket.
№ 80810

4. Why did someone buy this ticket?
   - ❑ To visit a historical site.
   - ❑ To see a historical movie.
   - ❑ To listen to classical music.
   - ❑ To tour a battleship.

Nom ______________________

Classe ______________ Date ______________

5. If you were in France, where would you see this sign?
   - ❑ In a train.
   - ❑ In an elevator.
   - ❑ On a highway.
   - ❑ In a stadium.

6. If you were driving on this highway, you would exit to the right . . .
   - ❑ if you needed gas
   - ❑ if you wanted to take pictures
   - ❑ if you were looking for a campground
   - ❑ if you were meeting a flight

7. CEEL is a language school in Geneva. They teach four languages including German **(allemand),** which is one of the official languages of Switzerland. Which of the following languages do they NOT teach?
   - ❑ English.
   - ❑ French.
   - ❑ Spanish.
   - ❑ Italian.

CEEL 19 rue du Prieuré, 1202 Genève ■ Tél. 371 5612 - 371 5893
ANGLAIS
ALLEMAND
ESPAGNOL
FRANÇAIS
Tous niveaux de 2 à 20h par semaine

8. This is a card of phone numbers that was distributed in Strasbourg, France.
   - You would dial 15 if you had . . .
     - ❑ a medical emergency
     - ❑ a problem with your telephone
     - ❑ a fire to report
     - ❑ a burglary to report
   - To get a prescription filled, you would call . . .
     - ❑ 15
     - ❑ 18
     - ❑ 03.88.41.12.45
     - ❑ 03.88.61.54.13
   - If you needed transportation to get to the airport, you would call . . .
     - ❑ 15
     - ❑ 18
     - ❑ 03.88.41.12.45
     - ❑ 03.88.61.54.13

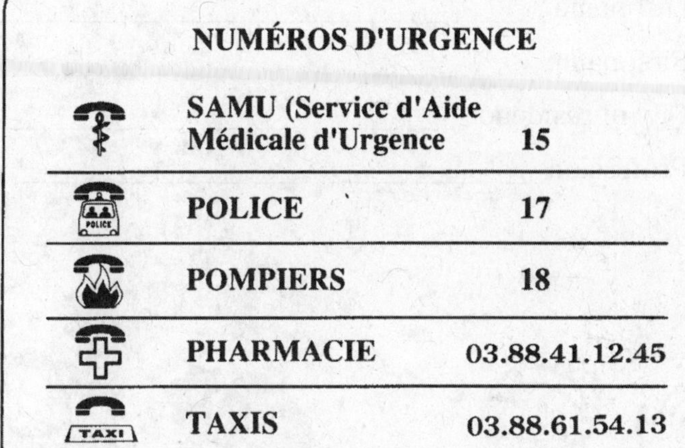

NUMÉROS D'URGENCE
SAMU (Service d'Aide Médicale d'Urgence 15
POLICE 17
POMPIERS 18
PHARMACIE 03.88.41.12.45
TAXIS 03.88.61.54.13
POLICE
TAXI

Nom ______________________________

Classe ______________________ Date ______________________

BLEU

B. Carte de visite

Marie-Françoise Bellanger
photographe

47, rue du Four
Paris 6e
Tél. 01.42.21.30.15

A friend of yours has given you the calling card of her cousin in France. Fill in the blanks below with the information that you can find out about this cousin by reading the card.

- Last name ______________________________
- First name ______________________________
- City of residence ______________________________
- Profession ______________________________

Nom ______________________________

Classe ____________________ Date ____________________

Discovering FRENCH *Nouveau!*

BLEU

Unité 2. La vie courante

LEÇON 3 Bon appétit! Vidéo-scène A. Tu as faim?

LISTENING ACTIVITIES

Section 1. Au café

A. Compréhension orale

a. ____ trois croissants

b. ____ une glace à la vanille

c. ____ un hot dog

d. ____ un sandwich

e. ____ un sandwich au jambon et un sandwich au pâté

f. ____ un steak-frites et une salade

B. Écoutez et répétez.

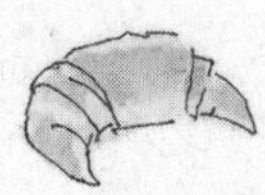

1. un croissant

2. un sandwich

3. un steak

4. un steak-frites

5. un hamburger

6. un hot dog

7. une salade

8. une pizza

9. une omelette

10. une crêpe

11. une glace

Nom ______________________________

Classe ____________________ Date ____________________

C. Questions et réponses

Je voudrais un sandwich.

1.

2.

3.

4.

5.

Section 2. Intonation

D. Écoutez et répétez.

Écoutez: **Voici un steak . . . et une salade.**

Répétez: **Je voudrais une pizza.**

Je voudrais une pizza et un sandwich.

Je voudrais une pizza, un sandwich et un hamburger.

Voici un steak.

Voici un steak et une salade.

Voici un steak, une salade et une glace.

Section 3. Dictée

E. Écoutez et écrivez.

—Oh là là! J'ai _______!

—Qu'est-ce que tu _______? Un steak ou _______ pizza?

—_______-moi un steak, s'il _______ plaît.

Nom ______________________________

Classe ________________ Date ____________

Discovering FRENCH *Nouveau!*

BLEU

Unité 2 Leçon 3

Workbook

WRITING ACTIVITIES

1. *Un ou une?*

Complete the names of the following foods with **un** or **une**, as appropriate.

1. ________ sandwich

2. ________ pizza

3. ________ steak

4. ________ crêpe

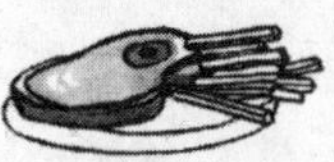

5. ________ steak-frites

6. ________ salade

7. ________ croissant

8. ________ omelette

2. Conversations

Complete the conversations with expressions from the box.

1. —Tu as faim?
   —Oui, ________________________ faim.

2. —Qu'est-ce que ________________________?
   —Je ________________________une glace.

3. —S'il te plaît, ________________________ un sandwich.
   —Voilà un sandwich.
   —________________________!

merci
tu veux
j'ai
voudrais
donne-moi

FLASH culturel

Camembert, Brie, and Roquefort are all products of French origin. What are they?

❑ pastries ❑ cheeses ❑ perfumes ❑ crackers

→page 32

Nom ______________________

Classe ______________ Date ______________

3. Communication: En français!

A. You have invited your French friend Philippe to your home.

1. *Ask Philippe if he is hungry.*

____

2. *Ask him if he wants a sandwich.*

____

3. *Ask him if he wants an ice cream cone.*

____

B. You are in a French restaurant with a friend.

1. *Tell your friend that you are hungry.*

____

2. *Tell her what type of food you would like to have.*

____

FLASH culturel

France produces over 400 varieties of cheese, among which **Camembert**, **Brie**, and **Roquefort** are the best known. In a traditional French meal, cheese is served as a separate course, after the salad and before the dessert. It is eaten with bread, and occasionally with butter.

Vidéo-scène B. Au café

LISTENING ACTIVITIES

Section 1. Au café

A. Écoutez et répétez.

1. un soda 2. un jus d'orange 3. un jus de pomme 4. un jus de tomate 5. un jus de raisin

6. une limonade 7. un café 8. un thé 9. un chocolat

Section 2. S'il te plaît, donne-moi . . .

B. Questions et réponses

▶—Tu veux un café ou un thé?
—S'il te plaît, donne-moi un café.

▶

1

2

3
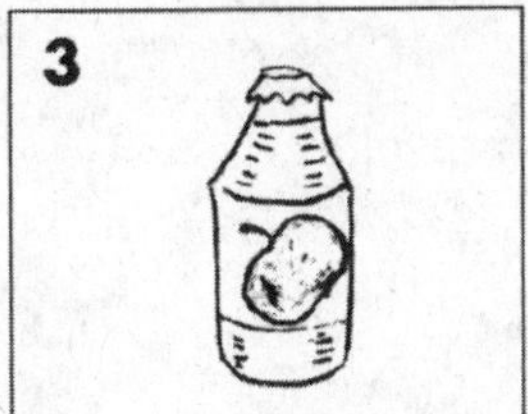

4

Nom ______________________________________

Discovering FRENCH Nouveau!

Classe ______________________ Date ______________ ______________

BLEU

Section 3. Je voudrais . . .

C. Questions et réponses

▶ —Vous désirez?
—**Je voudrais un thé, s'il vous plaît.**

1 

2 

3 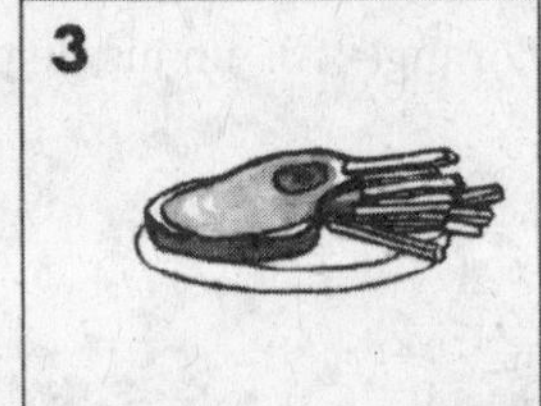

4 

Section 4. Conversations

D. Compréhension orale

1. How does the boy feel?
   a. tired
   b. thirsty
   c. hungry

2. What would the girl like?
   a. a soda
   b. a glass of orange juice
   c. a glass of grape juice

3. Where does the scene take place?
   a. in a café
   b. at a picnic
   c. at home

4. Where does the scene take place?
   a. in a café
   b. in a French restaurant
   c. at a picnic

Section 5. Dictée

E. Écoutez et écrivez.

—Vous __________, mademoiselle?

—Je __________ un chocolat.

—Et vous, monsieur?

—_______-moi un _______, s'il _______ plaît.

WRITING ACTIVITIES

1. Les boissons

Find the French names of eight beverages in the following grid. The names can be read horizontally, vertically, or diagonally. Then list these beverages, using **un** or **une**, as appropriate.

J	O	J	B	M	N	C	I	X	Y	A	Z
M	U	U	R	E	W	H	L	Q	B	C	F
J	U	S	D	E	T	O	M	A	T	E	R
K	V	D	D	L	G	C	C	U	K	N	Z
X	D	E	A	E	L	O	H	T	L	Z	C
Y	B	P	A	F	R	L	C	H	X	T	P
Z	S	O	D	A	C	A	F	É	J	M	B
O	N	M	C	K	B	I	I	N	K	A	Y
L	I	M	O	N	A	D	E	S	D	O	C
S	Q	E	T	F	I	P	D	V	I	G	L
H	T	W	M	R	O	S	Y	I	U	N	J

- ______________
- ______________
- ______________
- ______________
- ______________
- ______________
- ______________
- ______________

2. Mes préférences

In the chart below, list which three of the above beverages you like the best and which three you like the least.

1. ______________	4. ______________
2. ______________	5. ______________
3. ______________	6. ______________

FLASH culturel

Which of the following beverages is most likely to be served with a French meal?

❑ milk ❑ coffee ❑ iced tea ❑ mineral water

→page 36

Nom ______________________________

Classe ____________________ Date ____________________

3. Communication: En français!

A. Your French friend Marc has dropped by your house.

1. *Ask him if he is thirsty.*

____

2. *Ask him if he wants a soda or a glass of orange juice.*

____

B. You are in a French café with a friend.

1. *Tell your friend that you are thirsty.*

____

2. *Tell the waiter (or waitress) to bring you a beverage of your choice.*

____

FLASH culturel

The French drink a lot of mineral water. In fact, they have the highest consumption of mineral water in the world: about 60 liters per person per year. These mineral waters, some plain and some carbonated, come from natural springs in various parts of the country and are widely exported.

Vidéo-scène C. Ça fait combien?

LISTENING ACTIVITIES

Section 1. L'euro

A. Écoutez et répétez.

un euro	**six euros**
deux euros	**sept euros**
trois euros	**huit euros**
quatre euros	**neuf euros**
cinq euros	**dix euros**

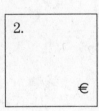

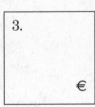

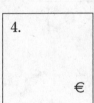

Section 2. C'est combien?

B. Compréhension orale

Modèle	1.	2.	3.	4.	5.
10 €	€	€	€	€	€

C. Questions et réponses

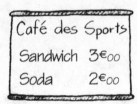

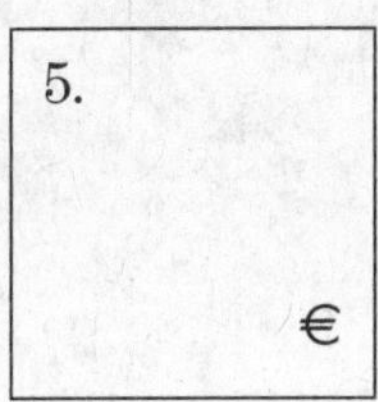

Café des Sports
Sandwich 3€00
Soda 2€00

1. 
2. 
3. 
4. 

Nom ______________________________________

Classe ____________________ Date ____________

Discovering FRENCH Nouveau!

BLEU

Section 3. Conversations

D. Compréhension orale Listening comprehension

1. What does the boy do?
   a. He orders a pizza.
   b. He asks the price of a pizza.
   c. He asks where the pizzeria is.
2. What does the woman want to do?
   a. pay the bill
   b. order food
   c. go to a café
3. What does the boy want to do?
   a. pay the bill
   b. borrow money
   c. leave a tip for the server

Section 4. Dictée.

E. Écoutez et écrivez.

—________ coûte l'omelette?

—______ coûte trois euros cinquante.

—Et la glace?

—Deux euros cinquante.

—Ça ______ six euros au total.

Dis, Mélanie, ______-moi six euros, s'il te plaît.

Nom ______________________________

Classe ____________________ Date ____________________

Discovering FRENCH Nouveau!

BLEU

Unité 2 Leçon 3

Workbook

WRITING ACTIVITIES

1. C'est combien?

Identify the items pictured and give their prices.

▶ 2€

Voici un sandwich.

Il coûte deux euros.

1.  1€

2.  3€50

3.  3€35

4.  6€45

5.  2€20

6.  4€60

FLASH culturel

The backs of the euro bills are illustrated with pictures of bridges. Which bill has the most modern bridge?

❑ 10 euro note ❑ 50 euro note ❑ 100 euro note ❑ 500 euro note

→page 40

Nom ______________________

Classe ______________ Date ______________

2.  Communication: En français!

Imagine that you are at Le Rallye with two French friends, Olivier and Valérie.

Use the menu to write out the following conversation (in French, of course!).

Le Rallye

Boissons		Sandwichs	
Café	2€	Sandwich au jambon	3€50
Thé	2€	Sandwich au fromage	3€50
Chocolat	2€50	**Et aussi:**	
Soda	2€50	Croissant	2€
Limonade	2€25	Pizza	8€
Jus d'orange	2€50	Salade	3€50
Eau minérale	1€50	Omelette	4€50
Glaces		Hamburger	4€
Glace au café	2€50	Steak	7€
Glace à la vanille	2€50	Steak-Frites	8€50

LE GARÇON: ______________________

May I help you?

TOI: ______________________

I would like [a food and a beverage].

VALÉRIE: ______________________

Please give me [a food and a beverage].

OLIVIER: ______________________

I would like a [a food and a beverage], please.

TOI: ______________________

How much does that come to?

LE GARÇON: ______________________

That comes to [the price of what was ordered].

TOI: ______________________

Hey, Olivier, loan me ten euros, please.

FLASH culturel

The bills are sequenced so that the styles of bridges go from the oldest (5 euro note) to the most modern (500 euro note).

Nom ______________________________ **Discovering FRENCH** *Nouveau!*

Classe ______________ Date ______________

BLEU

LEÇON 4 De jour en jour Vidéo-scène A. L'heure

LISTENING ACTIVITIES

Section 1. Quelle heure est-il? (Part 1)

A. Compréhension orale

▶

1.

2.

3.

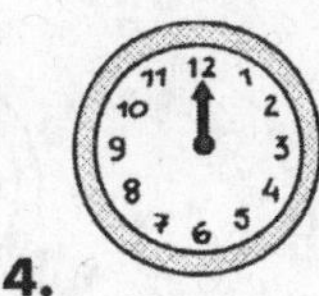

4.

5.

B. Questions et réponses

▶

1.

2.

3.

4.

▶

Quelle heure est-il?
Il est huit heures.

5.

6.

7.

Section 2. Quelle heure est-il? (Part 2)

C. Compréhension orale

▶

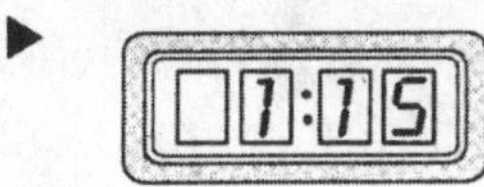

1.

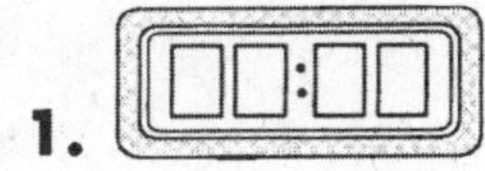

2.

3.

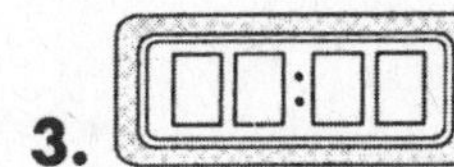

4.

Nom ______________________________

Classe ____________________ Date ____________

D. Questions et réponses

▶ 

1.

2.

3.

4.

5.

6.

Section 3. À quelle heure?

E. Compréhension orale

▶ le film 4 h 15

1. la classe de français ______
2. le dîner ______
3. le film ______
4. le train de Toulouse ______

Section 4. Dictée

F. Écoutez et écrivez.

—Dis, Philippe, quelle ______ est-il?

—Il ______ cinq heures ______ le quart.

—Et à quelle heure est le film?

—À sept heures et ______.

—Merci!

Nom ______________________________

Classe ______________________ Date ______________

Discovering FRENCH Nouveau!

BLEU

WRITING ACTIVITIES

1. Oui ou non?

Watches do not always work well. Read the times below and compare them with the times indicated on the watches. If the two times match, check **oui**. If they do not match, check **non**.

	oui	non
▶ Il est une heure dix.	☑	❑
▶ Il est une heure vingt-cinq.	❑	☑
1. Il est deux heures et demie.	❑	❑
2. Il est trois heures et quart.	❑	❑
3. Il est cinq heures moins vingt.	❑	❑
4. Il est sept heures moins le quart.	❑	❑
5. Il est huit heures cinq.	❑	❑
6. Il est onze heures cinquante-cinq.	❑	❑

FLASH culturel

In many French-speaking countries, official time is given using a 24-hour clock. For example, on this Canadian TV schedule, the movie *Driving Miss Daisy* begins at 22 h 40 (**vingt-deux heures quarante**). What would be the corresponding time on our 12-hour clock?

❑ 2:40 P.M. ❑ 8:40 P.M. ❑ 9:40 P.M. ❑ 10:40 P.M.

Super Écran

VENDREDI 22 MARS

14h50	Lawrence d'Arabie
18h20	Oncle Buck
20h05	Les Simpson
21h00	Tremors
22h40	Miss Daisy et Son Chauffeur

→page 44

Nom ______________________________

Classe ____________________ Date ____________________

Discovering FRENCH *Nouveau!*

BLEU

2. Quelle heure est-il?

Stéphanie's watch is not working. Tell her what time it is. Write out your responses.

1:00 1. ____________________________.

12:00 2. ____________________________.

3:15 3. ____________________________.

7:30 4. ____________________________.

8:45 5. ____________________________.

10:50 6. ____________________________.

3. Communication: En français!

A. *Conversation avec Caroline* You are in a café with your friend Caroline. You plan to see a movie together. Complete the dialogue.

CAROLINE: Quelle heure est-il?

YOU: ____________________________
(Look at your watch and tell her the time.)

CAROLINE: À quelle heure est le film?

YOU: ____________________________
(Name a time about half an hour from now.)

B. *Conversation avec Julien* You are in a hurry to keep an appointment with Mme Pascal, your math teacher. You meet your friend Julien. Complete the dialogue.

YOU: ____________________________
(Ask Julien what time it is.)

JULIEN: Il est onze heures dix. Pourquoi *(why)*?

YOU: ______________ avec Madame Pascal.
(Say you have an appointment with Madame Pascal.)

JULIEN: À quelle heure?

YOU: ____________________________
(Tell him at quarter past eleven, and say good-bye.)

FLASH culturel

With the 24-hour clock, times are expressed as follows:

- A.M. hours go from 0 h 01 (one minute after midnight) to 12 h 00 (noon).
- P.M. hours go from 12 h 01 to 24 h 00.

To calculate the P.M. equivalent of 24-hour clock times, simply subtract 12.

22 h 40 =
22:40–12 =
10:40 P.M.

Nom ____

Classe ______________________ Date ______________

Discovering FRENCH Nouveau!

BLEU

Vidéo-scène B. Le jour et la date

LISTENING ACTIVITIES

Section 1. Les jours de la semaine

A. Compréhension orale Listening comprehension

▶ Christine arrive mardi.

▶ Christine — b. mardi

1. Pauline
2. Bertrand
3. Céline
4. Didier
5. Agnès
6. Guillaume
7. Véronique

a. lundi
b. mardi
c. mercredi
d. jeudi
e. vendredi
f. samedi
g. dimanche

Section 2. La date

B. Compréhension orale

▶ C'est le 2 février.

1. C'est le ______ mars.
2. C'est le ______ juin.
3. C'est le ______ juillet.
4. C'est le ______ août.
5. C'est le ______ septembre.
6. C'est le ______ novembre.

Nom ______________________________

Classe ____________________ Date ______________

Discovering FRENCH Nouveau!

BLEU

C. Questions et réponses

▶ —Quel jour est-ce?

—C'est le 5 décembre.

1. 

2. 

3. 

4. 

5. 

6. 

7. 

Section 3. L'anniversaire

D. Compréhension orale

▶ Alice: le 18/7

1. Béatrice: le ______
2. Françoise: le ______
3. Julie: le ______
4. Delphine: le ______
5. Denis: le ______
6. Paul: le ______

Section 4. Conversations

E. Compréhension orale

1. What day is it today?
   a. Tuesday
   b. Wednesday
   c. Friday
2. When is Charlotte's birthday?
   a. in March
   b. in October
   c. in December
3. When is David's birthday?
   a. in January
   b. in August
   c. in September
4. When will David and Charlotte meet again?
   a. tomorrow
   b. tonight
   c. in a week

Section 5. Dictée

F. Écoutez et écrivez.

—C'est quand, ton ____________?

—C'est le deux______. C'est un ____________. Et toi?

—Moi, c'est le ____________ novembre. C'est un ____________.

Nom ______________________________ Discovering FRENCH Nouveau!

Classe ______________________ Date ______________

BLEU

WRITING ACTIVITIES

1. La semaine

Can you fit the seven days of the week into the following French puzzle?

1. S _ _ _ _ _
2. _ E _ _ _
3. M _ _ _ _ _ _ _
4. _ A _ _ _
5. _ I _ _ _ _ _ _
6. _ _ N _ _
7. _ E _ _ _ _ _ _

2. Les mois

Complete the grid with the names of the missing months.

janvier		mars
avril	mai	
		septembre
octobre	novembre	

FLASH culturel

In France, **le quatorze juillet** is a very important date. What do the French do on that day?

❑ They vote. ❑ They celebrate their national holiday.
❑ They pay their taxes. ❑ They honor their war veterans.

→page 49

Nom ______________________________

Classe ______________________ Date ______________

Discovering FRENCH Nouveau!

BLEU

3. Joyeux anniversaire! *(Happy birthday!)*

Ask five friends when their birthdays are. Write out the information in French on the chart below.

	NOM	ANNIVERSAIRE
▶	David	le trois juillet
1.		
2.		
3.		
4.		
5.		

4. Communication: En français!

Answer the following questions in complete sentences.

1. Quel jour est-ce aujourd'hui?

   ____

2. Et demain?

   ____

3. Quelle est la date aujourd'hui?

   ____

4. C'est quand, ton anniversaire?

   ____

FLASH culturel

On July 14, or "Bastille Day" as it is known in the United States, the French celebrate their national holiday. On July 14, 1789, a Parisian mob stormed **la Bastille**, a state prison which had come to symbolize the king's tyranny. This important historical event marked the beginning of the French Revolution and led to the establishment of a republican form of government for the first time in French history.

Vidéo-scène C. Le temps

LISTENING ACTIVITIES

Section 1. Quel temps fait-il?

A. Compréhension orale

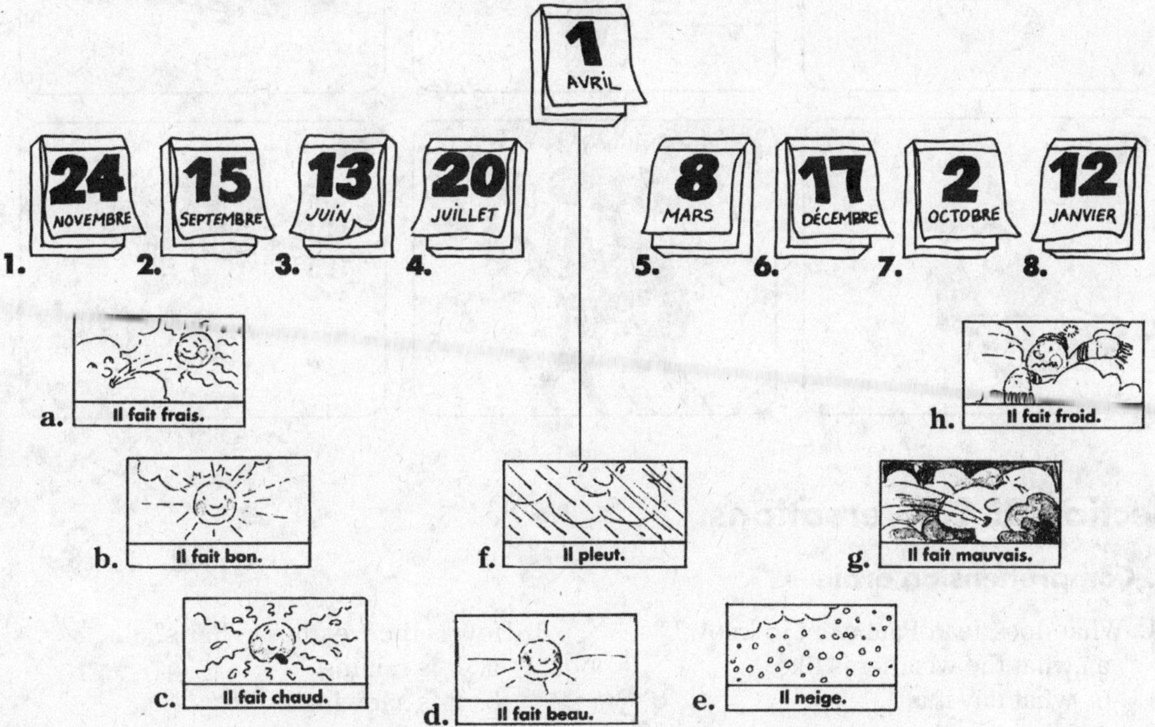

Nom ______________________________

Classe ______________________ Date ______________

B. Questions et réponses

Section 2. Conversations

C. Compréhension orale

1. What does Jean-Paul want to know?
   a. what the weather is like
   b. what day it is
   c. what time it is

2. How is the weather today?
   a. It is nice.
   b. It is cold.
   c. It is warm.

3. How is the weather in Paris?
   a. It is raining.
   b. It is snowing.
   c. It is hot.

4. What is Jean-Paul's favorite season?
   a. spring
   b. summer
   c. fall

Section 3. Dictée

D. Écoutez et écrivez.

—Quel ______ fait-il aujourd'hui?

—Il fait ______.

—Et en ________?

—Il ______.

WRITING ACTIVITIES

1. Les quatre saisons

Write the names of the seasons associated with the following pictures.

___________ ___________ ___________ ___________

2. La météo *(Weather report)*

Look at the map of France and describe the weather in the cities indicated below.

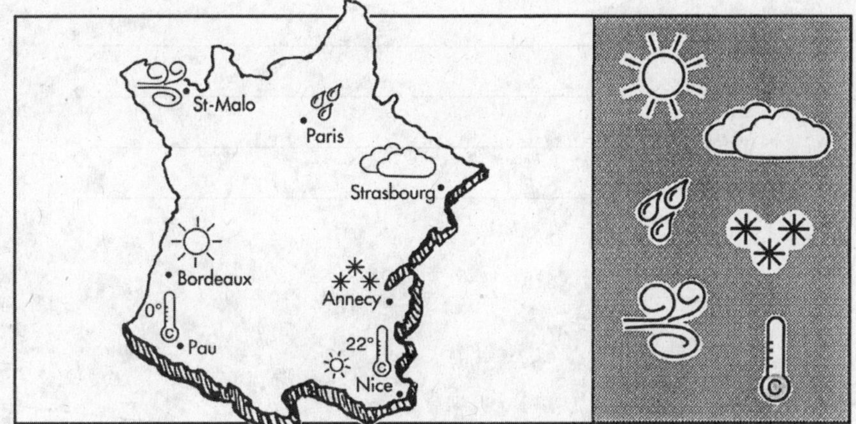

1. À Pau, ___________________.
2. À Nice, ___________________.
3. À Bordeaux, ___________________.
4. À Strasbourg, ___________________.
5. À Annecy, ___________________.
6. À St-Malo, ___________________.
7. À Paris, ___________________.

FLASH culturel

If you went to France for Christmas vacation, what kind of weather should you expect?

❑ rain ❑ snow ❑ cold weather ❑ mild weather

→page 54

Nom ______________________________

Classe ______________________ Date ______________________

3. Communication: Quel temps fait-il?

Describe the weather in the city where you live.

1. Aujourd'hui, ______________________.
2. En été, ______________________.
3. En automne, ______________________.
4. En hiver, ______________________.
5. Au printemps, ______________________.

4. Communication: As-tu faim? As-tu soif?

When we go to a café, what we order often depends on the weather. Read each of the weather descriptions and then indicate what you would like to eat and/or drink.

Le Temps	Au Café
	S'il vous plaît, . . .
▶ Il fait froid.	donnez-moi un croissant et un chocolat.
1. Il fait chaud.	donnez-moi ______________________.
2. Il pleut.	donnez-moi ______________________.
3. Il neige.	donnez-moi ______________________.
4. Il fait frais.	donnez-moi ______________________.

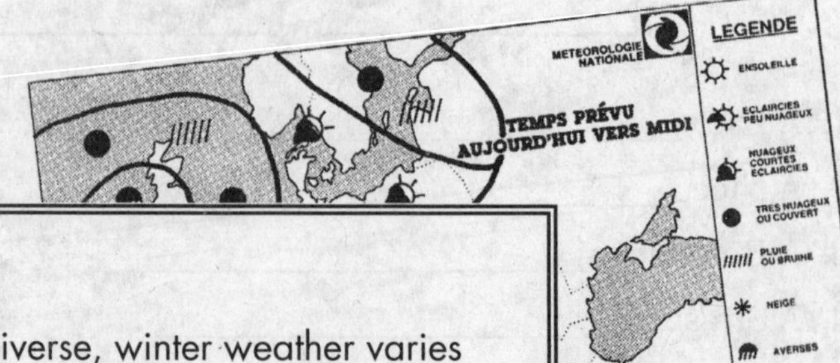

FLASH culturel

Since France is very geographically diverse, winter weather varies from region to region. It may snow and be quite cold in the Alps, the Pyrenees, and the mountains of central France. The weather may be rather mild along the Mediterranean and in southern France. In the rest of the country it may be cool and sometimes rainy.

Nom ______________________________

Classe ____________________ Date ______________

Discovering FRENCH Nouveau!

BLEU

Unité 2 Resources

Workbook Reading and Culture Activities

UNITÉ 2 Reading and Culture Activities

A. À la Terrasse Mailloux

The Terrasse Mailloux is a restaurant in Quebec City. This morning you visited the Citadelle with a classmate, and now you have stopped at the Terrasse Mailloux for lunch.

Together with your classmate, read the menu carefully and select three dishes that you will each have.

- Write down the dishes you have selected.
- Then enter the prices in Canadian dollars for what you have chosen and total up each bill.

MOI		MON COPAIN/MA COPINE	
PLAT	PRIX	PLAT	PRIX
____________	______	____________	______
____________	______	____________	______
____________	______	____________	______
TOTAL	______	TOTAL	______

Terrasse Mailloux

entrées

Frites (French fries)	**0.80**
Frites avec sauce hot chicken (French fries with hot chicken sauce)	**1.00**
Frites avec sauce spaghetti (French fries with spaghetti sauce)	**1.65**
Oignons français (Onion rings)	**1.50**

salades

Au poulet (Chicken)	**3.95**
Au homard (en saison) Lobster (in season)	**9.50**
Salade du chef (Chef's salad)	**1.50**

pizza 9''

Fromage (Cheese)	**3.25**
Pepperoni	**3.75**
Garnie (All dressed)	**4.25**

sandwichs
(servis avec frites et salade de choux)
(served with French fries and cole slaw)

Salade aux oeufs (Egg salad)	**2.00**
Jambon (Ham)	**2.50**
Poulet (Chicken)	**2.25**
Tomates et bacon (Tomato & bacon)	**2.50**
Croque Monsieur	**3.25**

desserts

Salade de fruits (Fruit salad)	**1.25**
Tartes (Pies)	**1.00**
Gâteau moka (Mocha cake)	**1.50**
Gâteau Forêt Noire (Black Forest cake)	**1.75**

Nom _______________________________

Classe ______________________ Date ______________

B. Agenda

Look at the following page from Stéphanie's pocket calendar.

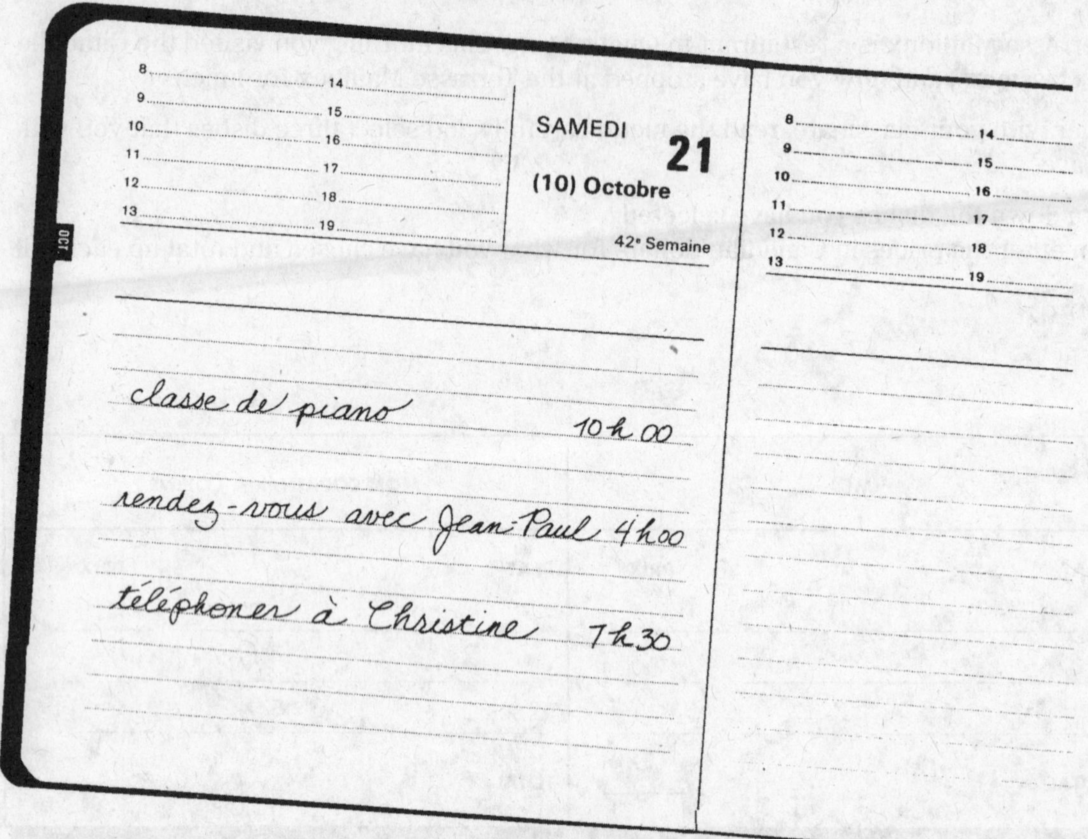

- What does Stéphanie have scheduled for Saturday morning at 10 A.M.?

____

- When is Stéphanie going to meet Jean-Paul?

____

- What is Stéphanie planning to do at 7:30?

____

C. Les boutiques du Palais des Congrès

In this ad, the shops at the Paris Convention Center **(le Palais des Congrès)** are announcing a large sale. Look at the ad carefully.

- What is the French word for *sale*?
  ____
- On what day does the sale begin?
  ____
- On what day does the sale end?
  ____
- Is there parking available? _______________
- For how many cars? _______________

D. « Un bon patriote »

Look at this Paris ticket for "Un bon patriote."

- Where is the performance being held?
  ____
- How much does the ticket cost?
  ____
- What is the date on the ticket?
  ____
- What day of the week is the performance?
  ____
- What time does the performance begin?
  ____

Nom ______________________________

Classe ____________________ Date ____________________

BLEU

E. La météo

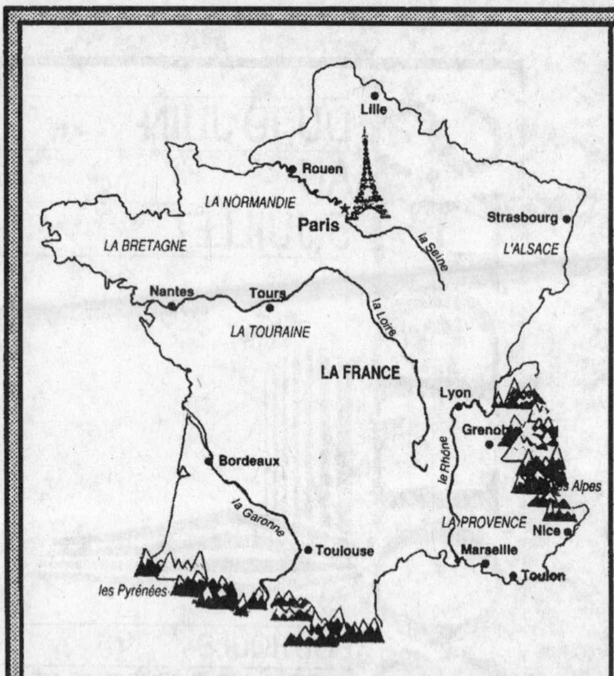

La météo en bref:
23 avril

En Bretagne et en Normandie, il pleut.

Dans la région parisienne, il fait beau.

Dans les Alpes, il fait frais.

Cependant sur la Côte d'Azur, à Nice et à Cannes, il fait du vent.

1. What is the weather like in Brittany and Normandy?
   - ❑ It's sunny.
   - ❑ It's windy.
   - ❑ It's rainy.
   - ❑ It's snowing.
2. What is the weather like in Paris?
   - ❑ It's sunny.
   - ❑ It's windy.
   - ❑ It's rainy.
   - ❑ It's snowing.
3. What is the weather like in Nice?
   - ❑ It's sunny.
   - ❑ It's windy.
   - ❑ It's rainy.
   - ❑ It's snowing.

Nom ______________________________

Classe ______________________ Date ______________________

Unité 3. Qu'est-ce qu'on fait?

LEÇON 5 Le français pratique: Mes activités

LISTENING ACTIVITIES

Section 1. J'aime . . . Je n'aime pas . . .

A. Compréhension orale

M = Marc   C = Caroline

1. ____________

2. ____________

3. ____________

4. ____________

5. ____________

6. ____________

7. ____________

8. ____________

9. ____________

10. ____________

11. ____________

12. ____________

Nom ___________________________________

Classe ___________________________ Date _______________

B. Parlez.

Modèle: J'aime écouter la radio.
(Je n'aime pas écouter la radio.)

▶ 

1. 

2. 

3. 

4. 

5. 

6. 

7. 

Section 2. Invitations

C. Compréhension orale

Est-ce que vous allez aller au cinéma?

1. At a party.	a. ____ accepts	b. ____ declines
2. By the tennis courts.	a. ____ accepts	b. ____ declines
3. At home.	a. ____ accepts	b. ____ declines

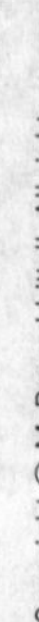

D. Parlez.

Modèle: Est-ce que tu veux jouer au foot avec moi?

▶ 

1. 

2. 

3. 

4. 

5. 

Section 3. Dictée

E. Écoutez et écrivez.

— Dis, Stéphanie, est-ce que tu ______ jouer au tennis ______ moi?

— Je regrette, mais je ne ______ pas.

— Pourquoi? *(Why?)*

— Je ______ étudier.

Nom ______________________________

Classe ______________________ Date ______________________

Discovering FRENCH Nouveau!

BLEU

WRITING ACTIVITIES

A* 1. Qu'est-ce qu'ils aiment faire? *(What do they like to do?)*

The following people are saying what they like to do. Complete the bubbles, as in the model.

2. Et toi?

Say whether or not you like to do the activities suggested by the pictures.

1. ______________________________

2. ______________________________

3. ______________________________

4. ______________________________

5. ______________________________

6. ______________________________

7. ______________________________

8. ______________________________

*NOTE: Beginning with this unit, activities are coded to sections in your textbook (Ex: Leçon 5, Section A) for your reference.

B/C 3. Communication: En français!

1. You are spending your vacation in a French summer camp.

   Ask your friend Patrick . . .

   - *if he likes to swim*

     ____

   - *if he likes to play basketball*

     ____

   - *if he wants to play soccer with you*

     ____

2. Your friend Cécile is phoning to invite you to go to a restaurant. Unfortunately you have an English exam tomorrow.

   Tell Cécile . . .

   - *that you are sorry*

     ____

   - *that you cannot have dinner at the restaurant with her*

     ____

   - *that you have to study*

     ____

3. At the tennis court, you meet your friend Jean-Claude.

   - *Tell him that you would like to play tennis.*

     ____

   - *Ask him if he wants to play with you.*

     ____

Nom ______________________

Classe ______________ Date ______________

Discovering FRENCH Nouveau!

BLEU

LEÇON 6 Une invitation

LISTENING ACTIVITIES

Section 1. Le verbe être

A. Écoutez et parlez.

Modèle: Paris **Vous êtes de Paris.**

1. Québec
2. Lille
3. New York
4. Montréal
5. Los Angeles
6. Manchester
7. Lyon
8. Boston

Section 2. Tu ou vous?

B. Écoutez et parlez.

Modèle: Stéphanie **Tu es française?**
Monsieur Lambert **Vous êtes français?**

Commençons.

1. Philippe
2. Mélanie
3. Madame Dubois
4. Mademoiselle Masson
5. Thomas
6. Monsieur Dorval

Section 3. Où sont-ils?

C. Compréhension orale

Modèle: Pierre au restaurant

1. Charlotte en ville
2. Monsieur Leblanc à la maison
3. Julien et Nicolas au café
4. Le prof en vacances
5. Stéphanie et François au cinéma
6. Monsieur et Madame Arnaud en classe

Nom ______________________________

Classe ____________________ Date ____________________

BLEU

D. Questions et réponses

▶ —Est-ce qu'il est à la maison ou au restaurant?
—Il est au restaurant.

▶

Section 4. Non!

E. Écoutez et parlez.

Modèle: Kevin: français?
Non, il n'est pas français.

1. Stéphanie: canadienne?
2. Jean-Paul: à la maison?
3. Juliette: au cinéma?
4. Thomas: en classe?

Modèle: Éric et Nicolas: en ville?
Non, ils ne sont pas en ville.

5. Anne et Claire: à la maison?
6. Monsieur et Madame Moreau: à Québec?
7. Monsieur et Madame Dupont: en vacances?

Section 5. Dictée

F. Écoutez et écrivez.

—Salut Thomas! Tu ________________ à la maison?

—Non, je ________________ au café.

—Est-ce que ta soeur est avec toi?

—Non, elle ________________ avec moi.

Elle est ________________ avec une copine.

Elles ________________ au cinéma.

Nom ______________________________

Classe ______________________ Date ______________

Discovering FRENCH Nouveau!

BLEU

WRITING ACTIVITIES

A 1. Mots croisés *(Crossword puzzle)*

Complete the crossword puzzle with the forms of **être**. Then write the corresponding subject pronoun in front of each form.

▶ nous — S O M M E S

1. ________ — _ S
2. ________ — S _ _ S
3. ________ — _ _ _ S
4. ________ — S _ _ T
5. ________ — _ S _

2. En vacances

The people in parentheses are on vacation. Say where they are, using the appropriate pronouns: **il, elle, ils,** or **elles**.

▶ (Cécile) Elle est à Québec.

1. (Jean-Marc) ________ à Tours.
2. (Catherine et Sophie) ________ à Nice.
3. (Mademoiselle Simon) ________ à Montréal.
4. (Jérôme et Philippe) ________ en Italie.
5. (Isabelle, Thomas et Anne) ________ au Mexique.
6. (Monsieur et Madame Dupin) ________ au Japon.

3. Où sont-ils?

Complete the following sentences, saying where the people are.

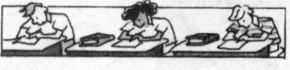

Nous ________________.

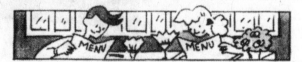

Vous ________________.

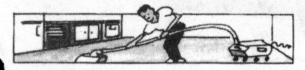

M. Bernard ________________.

Éric et Claire ________________.

Nom ______________________________

Classe ____________________ Date ____________________

Discovering FRENCH Nouveau!

BLEU

B/C 4. Non!

Answer the following questions in the negative, using pronouns in your answers.

1. Est-ce que tu es français (française)?
____
2. Est-ce que ton copain est canadien?
____
3. Est-ce que ta copine est anglaise?
____
4. Est-ce que tu es au cinéma?
____
5. Est-ce que tes (*your*) parents sont en vacances?
____

5. Communication: En français!

1. The phone rings. It is your French friend Caroline who wants to talk to your brother.

   Tell Caroline that he is not home.

   ____

   Tell her that he is downtown with a friend.

   ____

2. You are phoning your friend Marc. His mother answers.

   Ask her if Marc is there.

   ____

   Ask her if you can please speak with Marc.

   ____

Nom ______________________ Discovering FRENCH Nouveau!

Classe ______________ Date ______________

BLEU

LEÇON 7 Une boum

LISTENING ACTIVITIES

Section 1. Je parle français.

A. Questions et réponses

Modèle: Tu parles français.
Oui, je parle français.

B. Regardez et parlez . . .

Modèle: [Pauline} **Elle joue au foot.**

Pauline

1. Thomas

2. Stéphanie

3. Marc

4. Isabelle

5. Frédéric

6. Mélanie

7. M. Rémi

8. Mme Dupin

Section 2. Nous parlons français.

C. Questions et réponses

Modèle: Vous parlez français ?
Oui, nous parlons français.

Nom ______________________________

Classe ______________________ Date ______________

Discovering FRENCH Nouveau!

BLEU

D. Compréhension orale

	Modèle	1	2	3	4	5	6	7	8
A. oui									
B. non	✓								

E. Questions et réponses

▶—Est-ce qu'il travaille?
—Non, il ne travaille pas.

Section 4. Dictée

F. Écoutez et écrivez.

—Est-ce que tu ______________ jouer au basket?

—Oui, je joue ______________ avec ma cousine.

—Est-ce qu'elle joue ______________?

—Non, elle ______________ très bien, mais elle ______________ jouer!

Nom ______________________________

Classe ______________ Date ______________

Discovering FRENCH Nouveau!

BLEU

Unité 3 Leçon 7

Workbook

WRITING ACTIVITIES

A/B 1. Tourisme

The following people are traveling abroad. Complete the sentences with the appropriate forms of **visiter.**

1. Nous __________ Québec.
2. Tu __________ Fort-de-France.
3. Jean et Thomas __________ Paris.
4. Vous __________ Genève.
5. Hélène __________ San Francisco.
6. Je __________ La Nouvelle Orléans.
7. Marc __________ Tokyo.
8. Monsieur et Madame Dupont __________ Mexico.

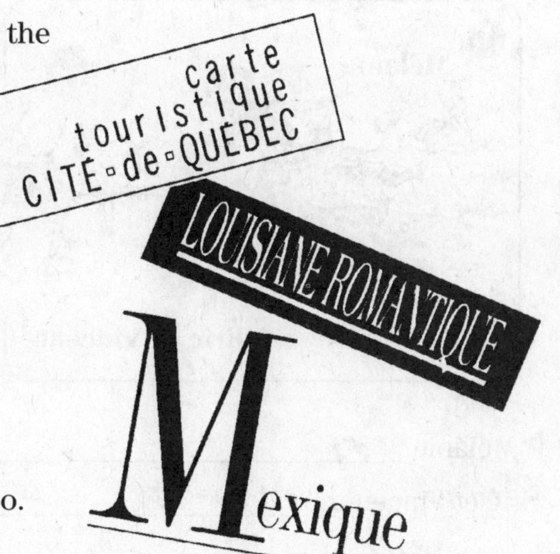

2. Qu'est-ce qu'ils font?

Describe what people are doing by completing the sentences with the appropriate verbs. First write the infinitive in the box, and then fill in the correct form in the sentence. Be logical.

manger	**écouter**	*regarder*	**dîner**
jouer	**organiser**	**parler**	

	Infinitive	Sentence
▶	dîner	Nous dînons au restaurant.
1.		Christine et Claire __________ au tennis.
2.		Vous __________ la télé.
3.		J' __________ la radio.
4.		Tu __________ français avec le professeur.
5.		Jérôme __________ un sandwich.
6.		Nous __________ une boum.

Nom ______________________________

Classe ____________________ Date ____________________

Discovering FRENCH Nouveau!

BLEU

3. Descriptions

Look carefully at the following scenes and describe what the different people are doing.

1

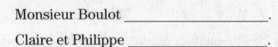

2
Claire et Philippe
M. Boulot

▶ Mélanie nage.

Éric et Vincent jouent au foot.

Monsieur Boulot ____________________.

Claire et Philippe ____________________.

3

4

Le professeur ____________________.

Hélène et Marc ____________________.

Diane ____________________.

Jean-Paul et Bernard ____________________.

C 4. Et toi?

Your French friend Caroline wants to know more about you. Answer her questions, affirmatively or negatively.

1. Tu parles anglais?
   ____
2. Tu parles souvent français?
   ____
3. Tu habites à New York?
   ____
4. Tu étudies l'espagnol?
   ____
5. Tu joues aux jeux vidéo?
   ____
6. Tu dînes souvent au restaurant?
   ____

5. Dimanche

For many people, Sunday is a day of rest. Say that the following people are not doing the activities in parentheses.

▶ (étudier) Tu n'étudies pas ____________.
1. (étudier) Nous ____________.
2. (travailler) Vous ____________.
3. (parler) Mon copain ____________ français.
4. (téléphoner) La secrétaire ____________.
5. (jouer) Paul et Thomas ____________ au foot.
6. (voyager) Tu ____________.

Nom ______________________________

Classe ____________________ Date ____________

BLEU

6. Communication (sample answer)

You have a new French pen pal named Isabelle. Write her a short letter introducing yourself.

Date your letter.

- *Tell Isabelle your name.*
- *Tell her in which city you live.*
- *Tell her at what school you study.*
- *Tell her whether or not you often speak French.*
- *Tell her what sports you play.*
- *Tell her two things you like to do.*
- *Tell her one thing you do not like to do.*

Sign your letter.

Chère Isabelle,

- ______________________
- ______________________
- ______________________
- ______________________
- ______________________
- ______________________
- ______________________

Amitiés,

____

Nom ______________________

Classe ______________ Date ______________

Discovering FRENCH Nouveau!

BLEU

LEÇON 8 Un concert de musique africaine

LISTENING ACTIVITIES

Section 1. Questions

A. Compréhension orale

	A	B	C	D	E	F
	où?	**quand?**	**à quelle heure?**	**comment?**	**à qui?**	**avec qui?**
▶	✔					
1						
2						
3						
4						
5						
6						
7						
8						

B. Questions et réponses

Modèle: . . . à Québec.
J'habite à Québec.

1. . . . à huit heures
2. . . . bien
3. . . . en France
4. . . . en été
5. . . . à une copine
6. . . . avec mon oncle
7. . . . une pizza
8. . . . une promenade

Nom ________________________________

Classe ____________________ Date ____________________

Discovering FRENCH Nouveau!

BLEU

Section 2. La réponse logique

C. Compréhension orale

1. a. À sept heures.
   b. Avec un copain.
   c. À la maison.

2. a. Dimanche.
   b. À huit heures.
   c. Avec ma cousine.

3. a. Oui, bien sûr!
   b. Très bien.
   c. Au club de sport.

4. a. À un copain.
   b. À la maison.
   c. Parce que je veux parler à ma mère.

5. a. Une omelette.
   b. À la cafétéria.
   c. À six heures et demie.

6. a. En France.
   b. Avec mon cousin.
   c. Parce que j'aime voyager.

Section 3. Dictée

D. Écoutez et écrivez.

—Dis, Patrick, qu'est-ce que tu __________ demain?

—Je joue au tennis avec ma cousine. Nous __________ un match. __________?

—__________ je peux jouer avec vous?

—Oui, bien sûr!

WRITING ACTIVITIES

A 1. Dialogue

Complete the following dialogues with the appropriate interrogative expressions.

1. —______________ est-ce que tu habites?
   —J'habite à Dakar.
2. —______________ est-ce que tu dînes?
   —En général, je dîne à huit heures.
3. —______________ est-ce que tu chantes?
   —Je chante assez bien.
4. —______________ est-ce que tu étudies l'italien?
   —Parce que je veux visiter l'Italie.
5. —______________ est-ce que tu voyages?
   —Je voyage en juillet.
6. —______________ est-ce que ta mère travaille?
   —Elle travaille dans *(in)* un hôpital.

B 2. Répétitions

Philippe did not quite hear what Annie told him and he asks her to repeat what she said. Complete his questions.

	ANNIE:	PHILIPPE:
▶	Je joue au tennis avec Vincent.	Avec qui est-ce que tu joues au tennis?
1.	Je téléphone souvent à Olivier.	À ______________?
2.	Je parle rarement à Valérie.	À ______________?
3.	J'étudie avec Jean-Claude.	Avec ______________?
4.	Je travaille pour M. Bertrand.	Pour ______________?
5.	Je parle anglais avec Vanessa.	Avec ______________?
6.	Je parle de Pierre.	De ______________?

Nom ______________________________

Classe ____________________ Date ____________

BLEU

A/B/C 3. Curiosité

You want to know more about what the following people are doing. Write your questions using subject pronouns and the expressions in parentheses.

▶ Jérôme dîne. (avec qui?)
Avec qui est-ce qu'il dîne?

1. Madame Martin travaille. (où?)
   ____
2. Nathalie téléphone. (à qui?)
   ____
3. Antoine organise une boum. (quand?)
   ____
4. Thomas et Patrick étudient beaucoup. (pourquoi?)
   ____
5. Hélène et Sylvie jouent au tennis. (à quelle heure?)
   ____
6. Béatrice étudie. (qu'est-ce que?)
   ____

D 4. Conversations

Complete the following mini-dialogues with the appropriate forms of **faire.**

1. —Qu'est-ce que tu __________ à deux heures?
   —Je __________ un match de tennis.
2. —Qu'est-ce que vous __________ maintenant?
   —Nous __________ une salade de fruits.
3. —Où est ta cousine?
   —Elle __________ un voyage au Sénégal.
4. —Où sont Paul et Marc?
   —Ils sont en ville. Ils __________ une promenade.

Nom ______________________________

Classe ______________________ Date ______________

Discovering FRENCH Nouveau!

BLEU

5. Communication

1. You want to invite your friend Nathalie to your home for dinner.

   Ask her . . .

   - *at what time she has dinner* ______________________
   - *what she likes to eat* ______________________

2. You are interviewing Madame Ricard, a French businesswoman, for your school newspaper. (Do not forget to address her as **vous!**)

   Ask her . . .

   - *where she lives* ______________________
   - *where she works* ______________________
   - *when she travels* ______________________

3. You meet your friend Marc.

   Ask him . . .

   - *what he is doing now* ______________________
   - *what he is doing tomorrow* ______________________
   - *if he wants to play video games* ______________________

Nom ______________________________

Classe ______________________ Date ______________

Discovering FRENCH *Nouveau!*

BLEU

Unité 3 Resources

Workbook Reading and Culture Activities

UNITÉ 3 Reading and Culture Activities

A. En France et en Louisiane

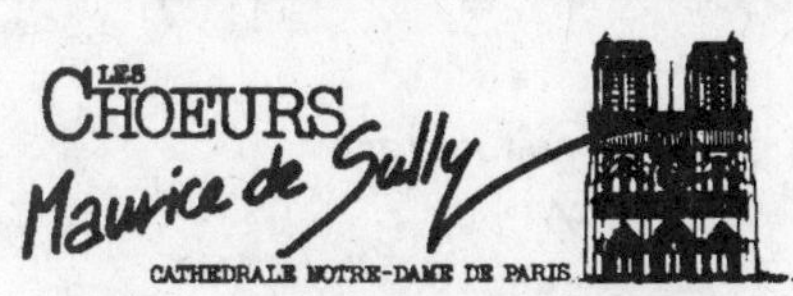

LES CHOEURS
Maurice de Sully
CATHEDRALE NOTRE-DAME DE PARIS

Nous avons besoin de nouvelles voix pour renforcer notre groupe.

CHANTEZ AVEC NOUS...

... J.S. BACH, VIVALDI, MOZART, CHANTS GREGORIENS, REPERTOIRE CONTEMPORAIN.

—INSCRIPTIONS: Père A. Buisslaere—

8, rue Massillon Paris 4ᵉ - Téléphone: 01 43 54 71 53 ou 01 56 33 01 01

1. You would pay attention to this ad if you were interested in . . .
   - ❑ singing
   - ❑ traveling
   - ❑ going to a concert
   - ❑ visiting a church

NOUS SOMMES FIERS

DE PARLER

FRANÇAIS.

2. If you were traveling in Louisiana, you might see this sign in certain shops. What does it mean?
   - ❑ We are French.
   - ❑ French is spoken here.
   - ❑ We sell French products.
   - ❑ We like French people.

3. Here is another sign you might see in Louisiana. What does it mean?
   - ❑ We do not speak French.
   - ❑ We are proud to speak French.
   - ❑ We sell French products.
   - ❑ We love people who speak French.

Nom _______________________________ **Discovering FRENCH** *Nouveau!*

Classe _______________________ Date _______________

BLEU

B. La Maison des Jeunes et de la Culture

Sandrine Moreau has dropped by Les Marquisats to get more information about their activities. She was asked to fill out the following form.

Je souhaite recevoir régulièrement des informations sur les activités culturelles de la Maison des Jeunes et de la Culture "Les Marquisats" d'Annecy.

Je suis plus particulièrement intéressé(e) par :

☐ CINÉMA ☑ DANSES SPÉCIALES ☐ CONFÉRENCES

☑ STAGES DANSE ☐ JAZZ ☐ ROCK ☐ CHANSON

NOM MOREAU, Sandrine

INSTITUTION / PROFESSION Étudiante

ADRESSE 136, rue Descartes

74000 Annecy

TÉL. ______________ (facultatif).

LES MARQUISATS

M. J. C. 52, RUE DES MARQUISATS
74000 ANNECY TEL. 04.50.45.08.80

1. Sandrine is especially interested in . . .
   - ❑ movies
   - ❑ music
   - ❑ dance
   - ❑ lectures
2. Who is Sandrine?
   - ❑ A student.
   - ❑ A homemaker.
   - ❑ A guitarist.
   - ❑ A retired person.

C. Conversation

Carefully read the following phone conversation between Carole and her friend Julien.

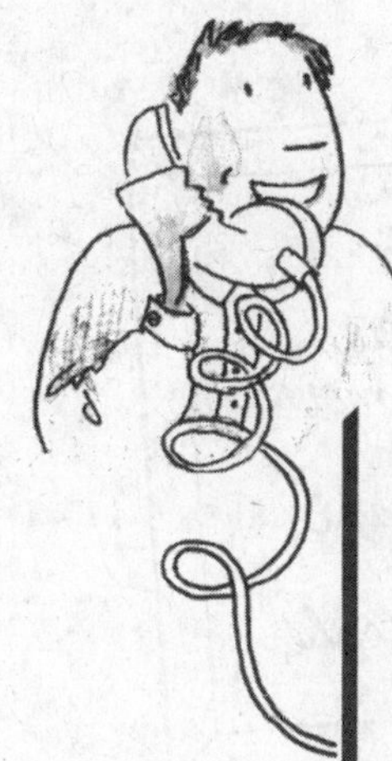

CAROLE: Allô, Julien?
JULIEN: Ah, c'est toi, Carole. Mais où es-tu?
CAROLE: Je suis à Tours.
JULIEN: À Tours? Mais pourquoi es-tu là-bas?
CAROLE: Je fais un voyage avec ma cousine.
JULIEN: Ah bon! Qu'est-ce que vous faites?
CAROLE: Oh là là, nous faisons beaucoup de choses. Nous visitons les châteaux. Nous dînons dans les restaurants. Nous . . .
JULIEN: Quand est-ce que vous rentrez à Paris?
CAROLE: Le quinze août.
JULIEN: Alors, bonnes vacances et bon retour!

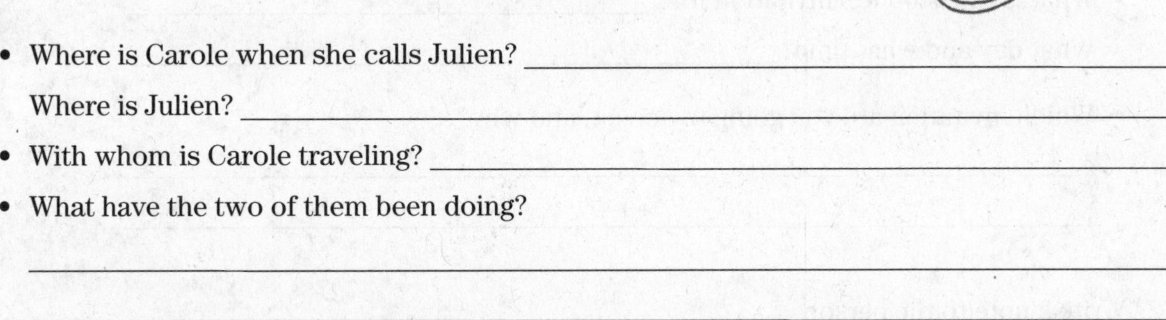

- Where is Carole when she calls Julien? ______________

  Where is Julien? ______________
- With whom is Carole traveling? ______________
- What have the two of them been doing?

  ____

  ____
- When is Carole returning home? ______________

Nom ______________________________

Classe ____________________ Date ____________________

Discovering FRENCH Nouveau!

BLEU

D. Invitations

1. You recently received two invitations. (Note: **venir** means *to come.*)

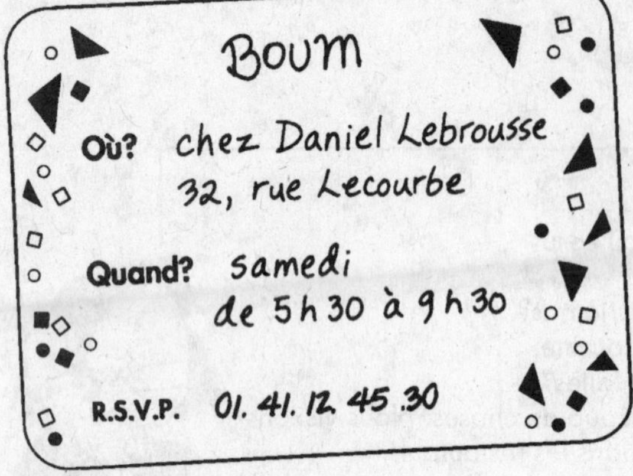

Boum
Où? chez Daniel Lebrousse
32, rue Lecourbe
Quand? samedi
de 5h30 à 9h30
R.S.V.P. 01. 41. 12. 45. 30

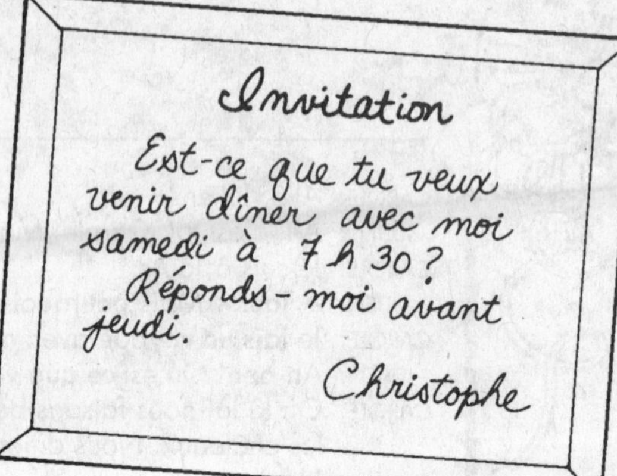

venir dîner avec moi
samedi à 7 h 30?
Réponds-moi avant

- What is Daniel's invitation for? ______________________

  What day and what time? ______________________

- What is Christophe's invitation for? ______________________

  What day and what time? ______________________

- Which invitation are you going to accept, and why?

  ____

  ____

2. Write a note to the person whose invitation you have to turn down.
   - Express your regret.
   - Explain that you have other plans.
   - Sign your note.

Cher ______________,

____

____

____

____

____

Nom ______________________________

Classe ____________________ Date ____________________

Discovering FRENCH Nouveau!

BLEU

Unité 4. Le monde personnel et familier

LEÇON 9 Le français pratique: Les personnes et les objets

LISTENING ACTIVITIES

Section 1. La description des personnes

A. Compréhension orale

Antoine

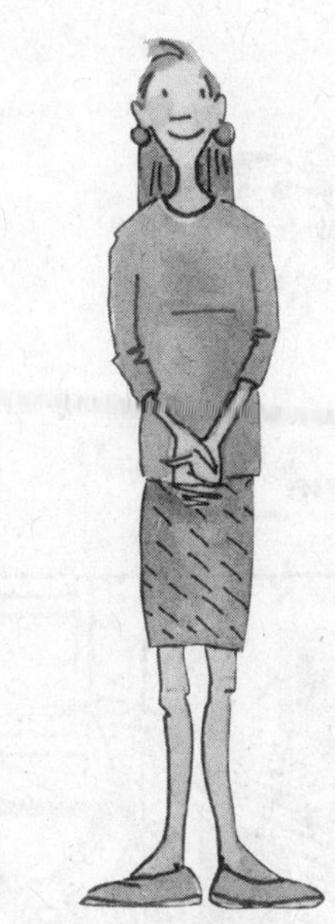

Mélanie

1

Section 2. Les objets

B. Compréhension orale

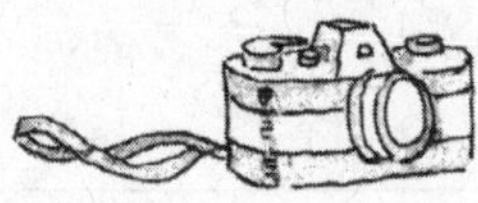

a. ____

b. ____

c. ____

d. ____

e. ____

f. ____

g. ____

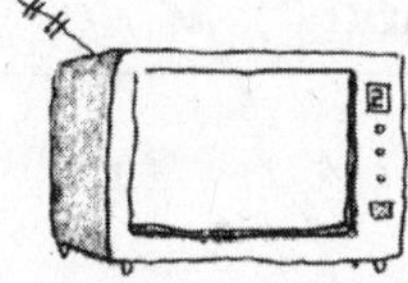

h. 0

Nom ______________________________

Classe ______________________ Date ______________________

Discovering FRENCH Nouveau!

BLEU

C. Questions et réponses

▶ — Qu'est-ce que c'est?
— C'est un appareil-photo.

▶ 

1. 
2. 
3. 
4. 
5. 
6. 
7. 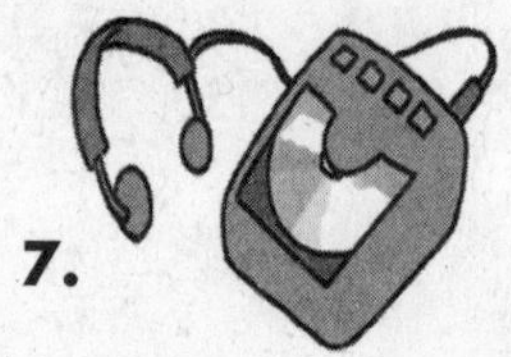

D. Compréhension orale

	Modèle	1	2	3	4	5	6	7	8	9	10
A: oui											
B: non	✔										

Nom ______________________________

Classe ______________________ Date ______________

Discovering FRENCH Nouveau!

BLEU

Section 3. Où est-il?

E. Questions et réponses

▶ — Est-ce que l'appareil-photo est sur la table ou sous la table?
— Il est sur la table.

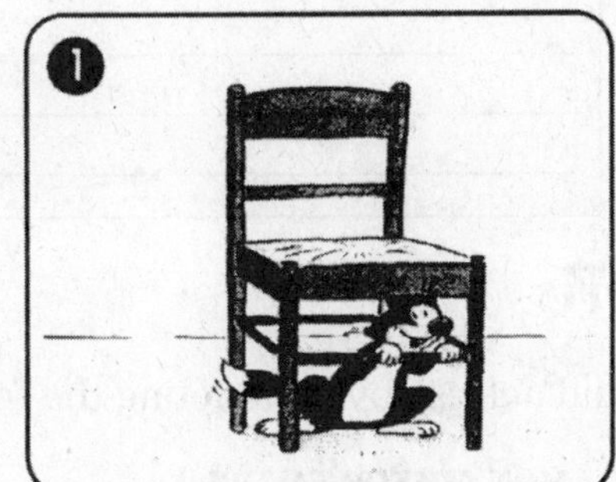

Section 4. Dictée

F. Écoutez et écrivez.

— Dis, Sylvie. Est-ce que tu as une ________________?

— Non, mais j'ai un ________________.

— Est-ce qu'il ________________ bien?

— Mais oui, bien sûr. Tu veux écouter?

Nom ______________________________

Classe ______________________ Date ______________

Discovering FRENCH Nouveau!

BLEU

WRITING ACTIVITIES

A 1. Auto-portrait

Write a short paragraph describing yourself. Give the following information:

- your name
- your age
- two physical traits

____

____

____

2. Mes acteurs favoris

Describe your favorite actor and actress by completing the following chart. Use complete sentences.

- name
- age (approx.)
- physical traits (affirmative or negative)

MON ACTEUR FAVORI	MON ACTRICE FAVORITE
Il ______________	Elle ______________
______________	______________
______________	______________
______________	______________
______________	______________

3. Communication

1. Your French friend Sophie has a new neighbor—a boy—and you want to know more about him.

   Ask Sophie . . .

   - *his name* ______________________________
   - *how old he is* ______________________________
   - *if he is tall or short* ______________________________
   - *if he is good-looking* ______________________________

2. Your friend Christophe has just told you that one of his cousins—a girl—is going to visit him next week.

   Ask Christophe . . .

   - *her name* ______________________________
   - *if she is blond or brunette* ______________________________
   - *if she is pretty* ______________________________

Nom ______________________________

Classe ______________________ Date ______________

Discovering FRENCH Nouveau!

BLEU

Unité 4 Leçon 9

Workbook

B/C 4. L'intrus *(The intruder)*

The following sentences can be completed logically by three of the items A, B, C, and D. One item does not fit. It is the intruder. Cross it out.

	A	B	C	D
1. Dans le garage, il y a . . .	une voiture	un vélo	une chambre	un scooter
2. Dans le sac, il y a . . .	un portable	une porte	un baladeur	un appareil-photo
3. Sur le bureau, il y a . . .	un ordinateur	une calculatrice	un téléphone	une chaise
4. Sur le mur *(wall)*, il y a . . .	une affiche	une montre	une photo	un poster
5. Sur la table, il y a . . .	un crayon	une lampe	un stylo	une mobylette
6. Dans la chambre, il y a . . .	une moto	une table	deux chaises	une chaîne hi-fi
7. Sous le lit, il y a . . .	un scooter	un livre	un cahier	un chat

5. Quatre listes

Complete each list with three items.

What I carry in my school bag:

- ______________________
- ______________________
- ______________________

What I would like to have for my birthday:

- ______________________
- ______________________
- ______________________

What I would take on a trip to Paris:

- ______________________
- ______________________
- ______________________

What I would want to have if I were lost on a desert island:

- ______________________
- ______________________
- ______________________

Nom ______________________________

Classe ______________ Date ______________

6. Leurs possessions *(Their belongings)*

Look at the illustrations and describe four things that each of the following people own. Be sure to use **un** or **une,** as appropriate.

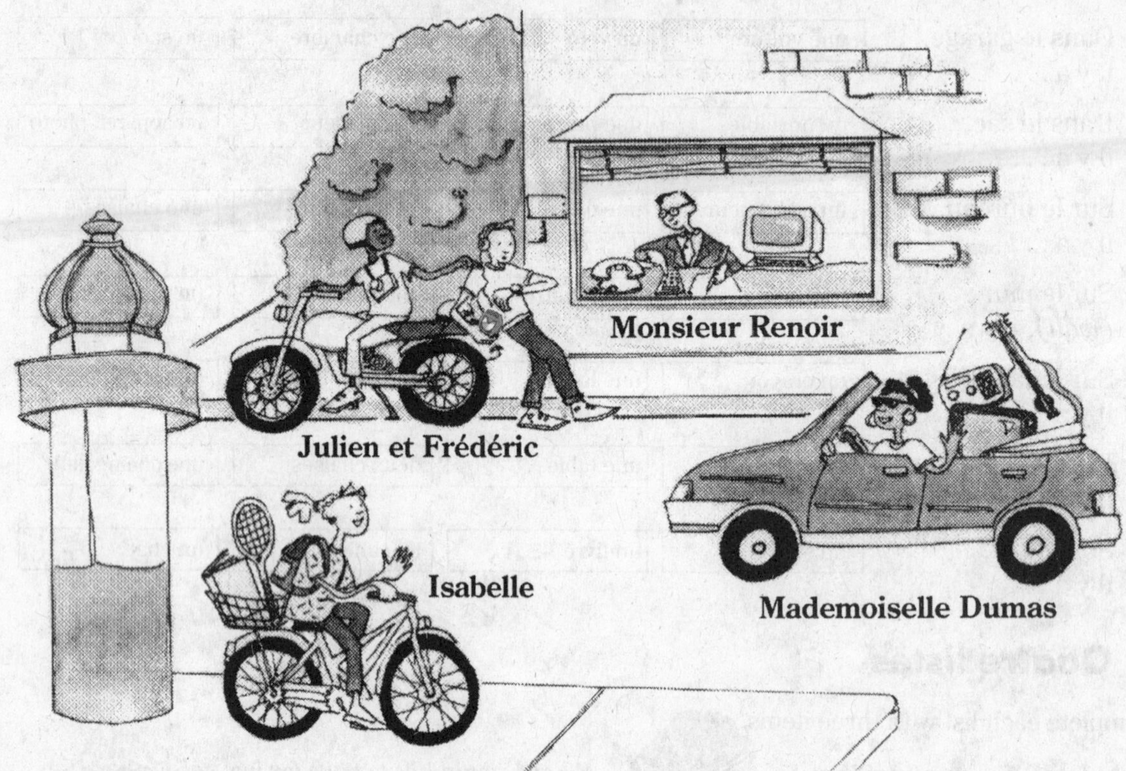

1. Isabelle a *(has)* ______________________________.
2. Mademoiselle Dumas a ______________________________.
3. Julien et Frédéric ont *(have)* ______________________________
______________________________.
4. Monsieur Renoir a ______________________________
______________________________.

Nom ______________________________

Classe ______________________ Date ______________

Discovering FRENCH Nouveau!

B L E U

D 7. Ma chambre

Make a floor plan of your room, indicating the position of the door, the window(s), and the various pieces of furniture. Label everything in French.

Nom ____

Classe ____________________ Date ____________________

8. Où sont-ils?

Describe the cartoon by completing the sentences with the appropriate expressions of location.

1. Le policier est ____________________ la voiture.
2. L'homme est ____________________ la voiture.
3. Le chien est ____________________ la voiture.
4. Le chat est ____________________ la voiture.
5. Le vélo est ____________________ la voiture.

Nom ______________________________

Classe ____________________ Date ____________

Discovering FRENCH Nouveau!

BLEU

LEÇON 10 Vive la différence!

LISTENING ACTIVITIES

Section 1. Les articles

A. Singulier ou pluriel?

	Modèle	1	2	3	4	5	6	7	8
A:									
B:	✔								

B. Parlez!

Modèles: une radio **Où est la radio?**
des livres **Où sont les livres?**

Section 2. Oui ou non?

C. Compréhension orale

1. a. une raquette oui non
2. a. une calculatrice oui non
   b. un ordinateur oui non
3. a. une chaîne hi-fi oui non
   b. un baladeur oui non
   c. des CD oui non
4. a. un stylo oui non
   b. des crayons oui non
   c. des livres oui non
   d. des cahiers oui non

Nom ______________________________

Classe ______________________ Date ______________

D. Questions et réponses

▶ —Est-ce que tu as un vélo?
—Oui, j'ai un vélo.
(Non, je n'ai pas de vélo.) ▶

E. Questions et réponses

Modèle: Est-ce qu'il y a un ordinateur?
Non, il n'y a pas d'ordinateur.

Section 3. Conversations

F. La réponse logique

1. a. Oui, j'ai soif.
   b. Non, je n'ai pas faim.
   c. Non, je n'ai pas soif.
2. a. Il est sur la table.
   b. Elle est là-bas.
   c. Elles sont dans le garage.
3. a. Isabelle et Françoise.
   b. Stéphanie.
   c. Elle s'appelle Mélanie.
4. a. Non, je n'ai pas de vélo.
   b. Si, j'ai un vélo.
   c. Oui, j'ai une moto.
5. a. Oui, ils ont une voiture.
   b. Oui, il a une voiture.
   c. Non, elle n'a pas de voiture.
6. a. Oui, elle aime la musique.
   b. Oui, elle joue au foot et au tennis.
   c. Non, elle n'a pas de vélo.

Section 4. Dictée

G. Écoutez et écrivez

—Tu aimes ________ cinéma?

—Oui, j'aime beaucoup ________ films d'action.

—Est-ce que tu aimes ________ musique?

—Bien sûr. J'ai un baladeur et ________ CD.

—Et une chaîne hi-fi?

—Non, je n'ai pas ________ chaîne hi-fi.

Nom ______________________________

Classe ____________________ Date ____________

Discovering FRENCH Nouveau!
BLEU

WRITING ACTIVITIES

A 1. Au café

A group of friends is at a café. Read what everyone is ordering. Then say if they are hungry or thirsty, using the appropriate forms of **avoir faim** or **avoir soif.**

▶ Hélène commande *(orders)* un jus de tomate. Elle a soif.

1. Nous commandons une pizza. ____________
2. Je commande une limonade. ____________
3. Tu commandes un steak-frites. ____________
4. Patrick commande un sandwich. ____________
5. Vous commandez un jus de raisin. ____________
6. Pauline et Sophie commandent un soda. ____________

B 2. Au choix (Your choice)

Complete the sentences with one of the suggested nouns. Be sure to use **un** or **une,** as appropriate.

▶ Éric mange une pizza (un sandwich). (sandwich? pizza?)

1. Nathalie commande ____________. (glace? soda?)
2. Sophie regarde ____________. (DVD? cassette-vidéo?)
3. J'écris *(write)* avec ____________. (crayon? stylo?)
4. Pour mon anniversaire, je voudrais ____________. (vélo? portable?)

Nom ____

Classe ______________________ Date ______________

Discovering FRENCH Nouveau!

BLEU

C 3. Quel article?

Complete the following sentences with the suggested articles, as appropriate.

(un, une, des)

1. Dans le garage, il y a ____ voiture et ____ bicyclettes.
2. Dans ma chambre, il y a ____ chaises et ____ lit.
3. Thomas a ____ portable et ____ baladeur.
4. Isabelle est ____ copine. Paul et Marc sont ____ copains.

(le, la, l', les)

5. ____élèves et ____ professeur sont dans la classe.
6. ____ ordinateur est sur ____ bureau.
7. ____ stylo est sur ____ table.
8. Où sont ____ cahiers et ____ livres?

Nom ____________________

Classe ____________ Date ____________

Discovering FRENCH *Nouveau!*

BLEU

D 4. Pourquoi pas?

Sometimes we do not do certain things because we do not have what we need. Read about what the following people do not do. Then explain why by saying that they do not have one of the things in the box.

une télé	une voiture	une radio
une raquette	une montre	un portable

▶ Monsieur Dumont ne voyage pas. Il n'a pas de voiture.

1. Claire ne regarde pas le match de foot. ____________
2. Paul ne joue pas au tennis. ____________
3. Henri n'écoute pas le concert. ____________
4. Sophie ne téléphone pas à Céline. ____________
5. Jean n'est pas ponctuel *(punctual)*. ____________

E 5. Qu'est-ce que tu préfères?

Indicate your preferences by choosing one of the items in parentheses. (Note: * = a feminine singular noun; ** = a plural noun)

▶ (soda ou limonade*?) Je préfère la limonade (le soda).

1. (théâtre ou cinéma?) ______________
2. (musique* ou sports**?) ______________
3. (gymnastique* ou foot?) ______________
4. (français ou maths**?) ______________
5. (pizza* ou spaghetti**?) ______________
6. (carottes** ou salade*?) ______________

F 6. Quel jour?

Say on which days of the week you do the following things.

▶ J'ai une classe de maths le mardi et le jeudi.

1. J'ai une classe de français ______________.
2. J'ai une classe de musique ______________.
3. Je dîne au restaurant ______________.
4. Je fais les courses *(go shopping)* ______________.

	LUNDI	MARDI	MERCREDI	JEUDI	VENDREDI	SAMEDI
8h30 à 9h30	Histoire	Allemand		Informatique		Français
9h30 à 10h30	Anglais	Français	Anglais	Physique	Allemand	Français
10h30 à 11h30	Sport	Français	Informatique	Maths	Latin	Latin
11h30 à 12h30	Français	Latin	Maths		Sciences vie et terre	Histoire ou civilisation
13h00 à 14h00				Allemand		
14h00 à 15h00	Sciences vie et terre	Maths		Sport		
15h00 à 16h00	Géographie	Maths				
16h00 à 17h00	Physique	Anglais				

Nom ______________________

Classe ______________ Date ______________

Discovering FRENCH Nouveau!

BLEU

7. Communication: En français!

1. You want to organize a party but you need help with the music. You phone your friend Mélanie.
   - *Tell her that you do not have a stereo.* ______________
   - *Ask her if she has a boom box.* ______________
   - *Ask her if she has CDs.* ______________
2. You have invited Stéphanie to your house.
   - *Ask her if she is thirsty.* ______________
   - *Ask her if she likes orange juice.* ______________
   - *Ask her if she wants to play video games.* ______________

LEÇON 11 Le copain de Mireille

LISTENING ACTIVITIES

Section 1. Les adjectifs

A. Compréhension orale

Modèle: amusante

Modèle		✔
1.		
2.		
3.		
4.		
5.		
6.		
7.		
8.		

B. Parlez!

Modèle: Phillipe est amusant. Et Mélanie?
Elle est amusante.

1. Et Stéphanie?
2. Et Véronique?
3. Et Isabelle?
4. Et Marie?
5. Et Julie?
6. Et Pauline?

Nom ______________________________

Classe ______________________ Date ______________ ______________

BLEU

Section 2. Les nationalités

C. Compréhension orale

▶  (a.) américain b. américaine

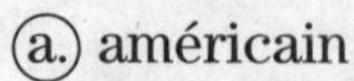

1.  a. anglais b. anglaise

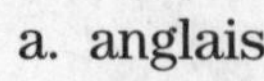

2.  a. canadien b. canadienne

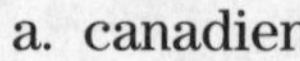

3.  a. chinois b. chinoise

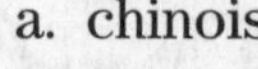

4.  a. japonais b. japonaise

5.  a. italien b. italienne

6.  a. mexicain b. mexicaine

D. Parlez.

Modèle: Mes copines (Italie). **Elles sont italiennes.**

1. Mon cousin (Mexique)
2. Ma tante (Espagne)
3. Mes cousines (Canada)
4. Madame Katagiri (Japon)
5. Monsieur Tang (Chine)
6. Mon oncle (Suisse)

Section 3. Dictée

E. Écoutez et écrivez.

—Qui sont les filles sur la photo?

—Ce sont des copines de Québec.

—Elles sont ________________?

—Non, elles sont ________________.

Elles sont ________________ et très ________________.

—Et les garçons qui jouent au foot?

—Ils sont ________________. Ils sont très ________________.

Nom ______________________

Classe ______________ Date ______________

Discovering FRENCH Nouveau!

B L E U

WRITING ACTIVITIES

A 1. Frères et soeurs

The following brothers and sisters are like each other. Describe the sisters, according to the model.

▶ Alain est blond.	Monique est blonde .
1. Marc est petit.	Yvonne ______ .
2. Philippe est grand.	Françoise ______ .
3. Jean-Claude est timide.	Stéphanie ______ .
4. Pierre est intelligent.	Alice ______ .
5. Paul est sympathique.	Juliette ______ .
6. Jérôme est beau.	Hélène ______ .
7. Julien est mignon.	Céline ______ .
8. Patrick est sportif.	Catherine ______ .

2. Cousin, cousine

Describe two cousins of yours, one male, one female. Write four sentences for each person. (Your sentences may be affirmative or negative.)

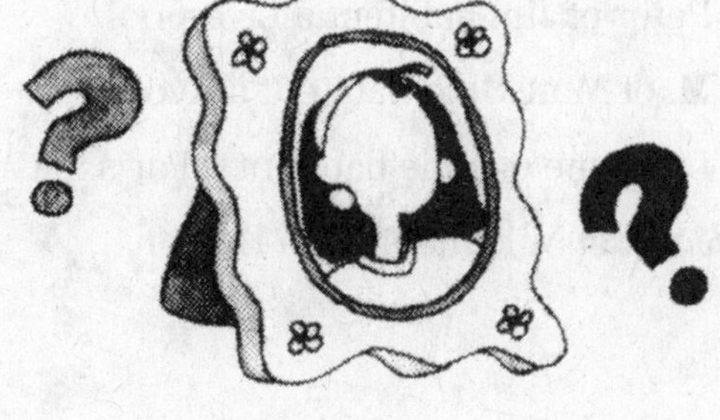

▶ Il n'est pas très grand.	Elle est assez mignonne.
Mon cousin s'appelle ______ .	Ma cousine s'appelle ______ .
1. ______	1. ______
2. ______	2. ______
3. ______	3. ______
4. ______	4. ______

Nom ______________________________

Classe ______________________ Date ______________

Discovering FRENCH *Nouveau!*

B L E U

A/B 3. Descriptions

Complete the following descriptions with **le, la,** or **les** and the appropriate forms of the adjectives in parentheses.

▶ Les livres sont intéressants. (intéressant)

1. _____ poster est ______________. (amusant)
2. _____ chats sont ______________. (mignon)
3. _____ table est ______________. (grand)
4. _____ chambre est ______________. (petit)
5. _____ chiens sont ______________. (gentil)

4. Quelle nationalité?

Read where the people live and give their nationalities. (Be sure to give the appropriate form of the adjective.)

▶ Madame Li habite à Hong Kong. Elle est chinoise.

1. Anne et Marie habitent à Québec. Elles ______________.
2. Madame Suárez habite à Mexico. Elle ______________.
3. Mon cousin habite à Zurich. Il ______________.
4. Silvia et Maria habitent à Rome. Elles ______________.
5. Peter et Jim habitent à Liverpool. Ils ______________.
6. M. et Mme Sato habitent à Kyoto. Ils ______________.
7. Delphine et Julie habitent à Paris. Elles ______________.
8. John et Mike habitent à Boston. Ils ______________.

C 5. Les voisins

Sandrine is talking about her neighbors. Write what she says using the words in parentheses. Follow the model.

▶ (fille / amusant) Catherine est une fille amusante.

1. (garçon / timide) Charles ______________.
2. (amie / gentil) Véronique ______________.
3. (homme / sympathique) M. Dupont ______________.
4. (femme / intelligent) Mme Bérard ______________.

A/B/C 6. Commérages *(Gossip)*

Jean-Paul likes to talk about other people. Write what he says, using the suggested words.

▶ Philippe / avoir / amie / japonais
Philippe a une amie japonaise.

1. Frédéric / inviter / fille / anglais
____
2. Jacques et Olivier / dîner avec / amies / canadien
____
3. Bernard / téléphoner à / copine / mexicain
____
4. Le professeur / avoir / élèves / bête
____
5. Jean-Pierre / avoir / livres / intéressant
____

Tu connais la dame?
Oui, c'est Madame Vallée.

Nom ______________________________

Classe ______________________ Date ______________________

7. Communication

Write a short letter in French in which you describe yourself and two of your best friends.

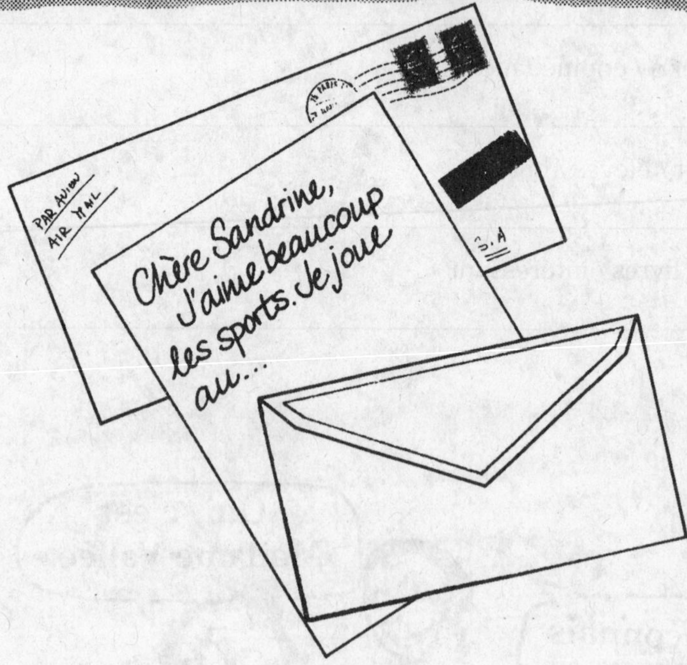

Nom ______________________________

Classe ______________________ Date ______________

Discovering FRENCH Nouveau!

BLEU

LEÇON 12 La voiture de Roger

LISTENING ACTIVITIES

Section 1. Les couleurs

A. Écoutez et répétez.

rouge / rouge
noir / noire
blanc / blanche
marron / marron
rose / rose
bleu / bleue
vert / verte
orange / orange
jaune / jaune
gris /grise

B. Questions et réponses

▶ —Est-ce que tu préfères la voiture rouge ou la voiture grise?
—Je préfère la voiture rouge.
(Je préfère la voiture grise.)

▶ 

1.

2.

3.

4.

jaune
gris

5.

6.

Nom ______________________________________

Classe ______________________ Date ______________ ______________

Section 2. La description

C. Parlez.

Modèle: une lampe / jolie
Voici une lampe.
C'est une jolie lampe.

1. un vélo / beau
2. un cahier / petit
3. une voiture / belle
4. un chien / joli
5. un CD / bon
6. un livre / mauvais
7. une pizza / grande
8. un chat / petit

D. Compréhension orale

1. C'est la voiture de Jean-Claude.	vrai	faux
2. C'est une Renault.	vrai	faux
3. Elle marches très bien.	vrai	faux
4. Elle n'est pas rapide.	vrai	faux
5. Elle fait du 160 à l'heure *(160 kilometers per hour).*	vrai	faux
6. Jean-Claude a son permis *(driver's license).*	vrai	faux

Section 3. Il est ou c'est?

E. Questions et réponses

Modèle: François / un garçon
Oui, c'est un garçon sympathique.

1. Stéphanie / une copine
2. Marc / un garçon
3. Isabelle / une fille
4. Monsieur Dumas / un prof
5. Teresa / une amie
6. Antoine / un copain

Section 4. Dictée

F. Écoutez et écrivez.

—Ta mère a une ________?
—Oui, elle a une ________ voiture.
—________ une voiture ________?
—Non, ________ est rouge et ________.

WRITING ACTIVITIES

A 1. Drapeaux de pays francophones
(Flags of French-speaking countries)

Color the flags according to the instructions.

BLEU	BLANC	ROUGE

France

NOIR	JAUNE	ROUGE

Belgique

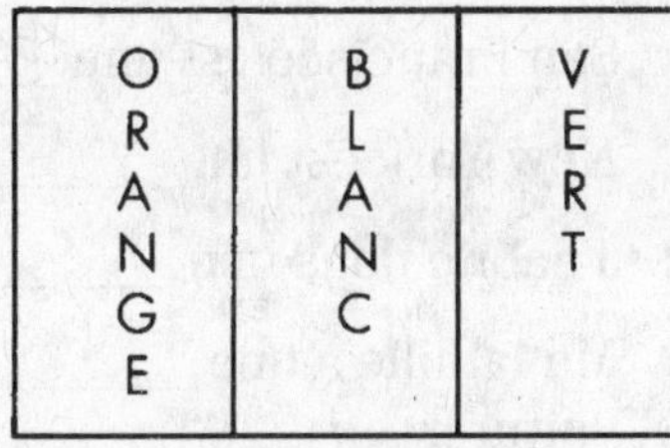

Côte d'Ivoire

2. De quelle couleur?

Describe the colors of the following items. (Use your imagination, if necessary.)

▶ Mon jean est bleu.

1. Mon tee-shirt est ______________________.
2. Mon crayon est ______________________.
3. Ma chambre est ______________________.
4. Ma bicyclette est ______________________.
5. Mon chien est ______________________.
6. La voiture de ma famille est ______________________.

Nom ______________________________

Classe ______________________ Date ______________________

Discovering FRENCH Nouveau!

BLEU

B 3. Descriptions

Complete the following descriptions by writing in the appropriate form of one of the adjectives from the box.

bon	**mauvais**	**grand**	**beau**	**petit**

▶ San Francisco est une belle (grande) ville *(city)*.

1. New York est une ______________ ville.
2. J'habite dans une ______________ ville.
3. Ma famille a une ______________ voiture.
4. J'ai une ______________ chambre.
5. Les Red Sox sont une ______________ équipe *(team)*.
6. Les Cowboys sont une ______________ équipe.
7. Le président est un ______________ président.

4. Le Rallye cycliste

A group of friends is bicycling together. Each one has a different bicycle. Describe the bicycles using the suggested adjectives.

▶ Éric a un vélo anglais. (anglais)

▶ Isabelle a un grand vélo. (grand)

1. Philippe a ______________. (italien)
2. Thomas a ______________. (rouge)
3. Claire a ______________. (petit)
4. Hélène a ______________. (vert)
5. Marc a ______________. (joli)
6. Laure a ______________. (japonais)

Nom ______________________________

Classe ____________________ Date ____________

C 5. Panne sèche *(Out of ink)*

Nathalie had planned to stress certain words by writing them in red ink. She realized—too late—that her red pen had dried up. Complete her assignment by filling in the missing words: **c'est, il est,** or **elle est**.

1. Voici Jean-Pierre.

    ____________ un copain.

    ____________ canadien.

    ____________ un garçon sympathique.

2. Voici Madame Leblanc.

    ____________ une voisine.

    ____________ une personne intéressante.

    ____________ très intelligente.

3. Regarde la voiture là-bas.

    ____________ une voiture française.

    ____________ une Renault.

    ____________ petite et rapide.

4. J'ai un scooter.

    ____________ rouge.

    ____________ italien.

    ____________ un bon scooter.

Nom ______________________________

Classe ______________ Date ______________

Discovering FRENCH Nouveau!
BLEU

D 6. Opinions personnelles

Here is a list of activities. Choose three activities you like and one activity you do not like. Explain why, using adjectives from the box.

Activités:

- danser
- chanter
- nager
- jouer au foot
- jouer au basket
- voyager
- visiter les musées
- organiser des boums
- inviter des copains
- étudier
- parler français
- travailler à la maison

chouette	**pénible**
super	**facile**
génial	**difficile**
drôle	

▶ *J'aime organiser les boums. C'est chouette!*

▶ *Je n'aime pas visiter les musées. C'est pénible.*

1. ______________________________
2. ______________________________
3. ______________________________
4. ______________________________

7. Communication: La voiture familiale *(The family car)*

Write a short description of your family car—or the car of someone you know. You may want to answer the following questions—in French, of course!

- Is it an American car? ______________________________
  (if not, what is it?) ______________________________
- What color is it? ______________________________
- Is it large or small? ______________________________
- Is it a good car? ______________________________

Nom ______________________________________

Classe ______________________ Date ______________

UNITÉ 4 Reading and Culture Activities

A. En France

1. You would go to this place if you had a problem with your . . .
   - ❑ bicycle
   - ❑ watch
   - ❑ car
   - ❑ computer

2. This is an ad for . . .
   - ❑ a book
   - ❑ a CD
   - ❑ a concert
   - ❑ a TV program

3. According to this ad, which of the following items could you buy at this store?
   - ❑ a stereo set
   - ❑ a cell phone
   - ❑ a computer
   - ❑ a movie camera

Nom ______________________________

Classe ____________________ Date ____________________

PARMELAN
★★
Annecy coup de cœur

30 chambres plein centre ville, à 100 m de la gare et du lac
T.V. - Téléphone
Insonorisation

Wir sprechen Deutsch
We speak English

41, av. Romains
74000 ANNECY
Tel. 04 50 57 14 89

4. The following ad was placed by Parmelan, which is the name of . . .
   - ❑ a hotel
   - ❑ a travel agency
   - ❑ a phone company
   - ❑ a TV store

le magazine de l'informatique pour tous

5. You would buy this magazine if you were interested in . . .
   - ❑ music
   - ❑ photography
   - ❑ history
   - ❑ computers

LIBRAIRIE • PAPETERIE

GIBERT JOSEPH

achat vente

4000M² à PARIS

neuf occasion

LIBRAIRIE UNIVERSITAIRE ET GENERALE
LIVRES
26, BOULEVARD Saint-Michel
LIBRAIRIE SCOLAIRE
SERVICE ACHAT OCCASION
5, rue Racine
PAPETERIE
30, BOULEVARD Saint-Michel

M RER ODEON • CLUNY SORBONNE • LUXEMBOURG

6. According to the ad, this would be the place to go if you wanted to buy . . .
   - ❑ used books
   - ❑ secondhand computers
   - ❑ stereo equipment
   - ❑ old clothes

Nom ________________________________

Classe ______________________ Date ______________

Discovering FRENCH Nouveau!

BLEU

B. Articles à vendre

You are in France and have gone to the local supermarket. There, on the board, you see the following announcements for items for sale.

OCCASION EXCEPTIONNELLE
vends
Appareil-photo OLYMPUS AM 100
avec Flash intégré
Prix: 50€
Téléphoner à Sophie Lebihan
01.49.22.61.32

- What is Sophie selling? ______________________

  What price is she asking? ______________________
- How can you reach her? ______________________

À VENDRE
Vélo tout terrain
10 vitesses
Excellente condition
Prix: à débattre
Téléphoner à Didier Muller
entre 16 heures et 19 heures
03. 88. 22. 61. 32

- What is Didier selling? ______________________

  What price is he asking? ______________________
- When can you reach him? ______________________

Nom ______________________________

Classe ____________________ Date ____________

C. Le Club des correspondants

You have been looking at a French youth magazine and noticed the following requests for pen pals.

Le Club des correspondants

Garçon français, 16 ans, brun, yeux bleus, sympathique mais un peu timide, voudrait correspondre avec Américaine ou Anglaise parlant le français. Aime le sport, le ciné et la moto. Joindre photo. Réponse assurée.
Olivier Lambesq
25, place Gambetta
24100 Bergerac

Jeune Française, 15 ans, sportive (tennis, basket, ski) désire correspondre avec étudiants américains ou anglais du même âge pour échanger posters et CD de rock et de rap.
Écrire à:
Dominique Loiseau
32, rue du Dragon
75006 Paris

J'aime la danse, le cinéma et la musique. J'ai 16 ans et je suis française. Je voudrais correspondre avec fille ou garçon de mon âge, de préférence porto-ricain ou mexicain, pour échanger CD de musique latine ou de guitare espagnole.
Carole Gaune
45, boulevard de la Mer
76200 Dieppe, France

Jeune Américain, 16 ans, voudrait correspondre avec jeunes Français du même âge parlant l'anglais. Aime le ciné, la musique classique et la moto. Joindre photo. Réponse assurée.
Patrick Smith
1329 Cole Street
San Francisco, CA 94117

Je m'appelle Julie, et j'ai douze ans. Je voudrais correspondre avec un garçon canadien de 13 à 15 ans, parlant anglais, pour échanger CD. J'aime le jazz, le rock et le rap.
Julie Cartier
25, rue Colbert
63000 Clermont-Ferrand

Mots croisés

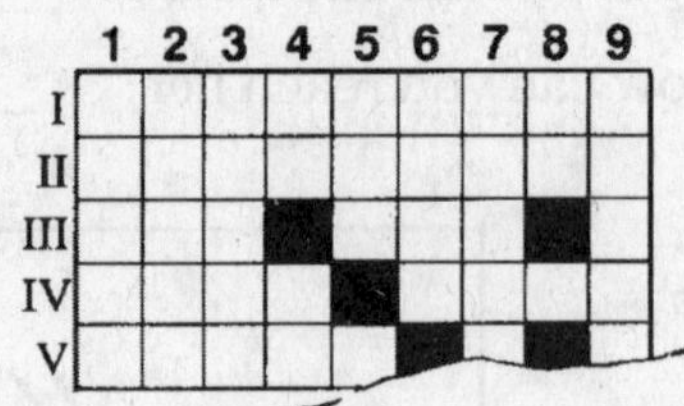

- Which of the young people like music? ______________________________
  Which one does not mention music? ______________________________
- Which ones want to trade things? ______________________________
  What do they want to trade? ______________________________
- Which ones mention sports? ______________________________
- Would you like to correspond with any of these young people?
  Why or why not? ______________________________

Unité 5. En ville

LEÇON 13 Le français pratique: La ville et la maison

LISTENING ACTIVITIES

Section 1. La ville

A. Compréhension orale

▶ Dans ma rue, il y a . . .
- a. ☑ un hôtel
- b. ☑ un magasin
- c. ❑ un café
- d. ☑ un restaurant

1. Dans ma rue, il y a . . .
   - a. ❑ une bibliothèque
   - b. ❑ un cinéma
   - c ❑ un magasin
   - d. ❑ un supermarché

2. Dans mon quartier, il y a . . .
   - a. ❑ une église
   - b. ❑ une école
   - c. ❑ un hôpital
   - d. ❑ un café

3. Dans ma ville, il y a . . .
   - a. ❑ une bibliothèque
   - b. ❑ une église
   - c. ❑ un théâtre
   - d. ❑ un musée

4. Dans ma ville, il y a aussi . . .
   - a. ❑ un supermarché
   - b. ❑ un hôpital
   - c. ❑ un centre commercial
   - d. ❑ une piscine

5. Il y a aussi . . .
   - a. ❑ un stade
   - b. ❑ une plage
   - c. ❑ un parc
   - d. ❑ un musée

Nom ______________________________

Classe ____________________ Date ____________________

Discovering FRENCH *Nouveau!*

B L E U

B. Questions et réponses

▶—Qu'est-ce que c'est?
—**C'est un cinéma.**

Section 2. Les directions

C. Compréhension orale

Now you will hear several people asking how to get to certain places. Listen carefully to the answers. Select the corresponding completions in your Workbook.

1. Le Café de l'Univers?
   a. ❑ C'est tout droit.
   b. ❑ C'est là-bas à droite.
   c. ❑ C'est là-bas à gauche.

2. Le Grand Hôtel?
   a. ❑ C'est loin.
   b. ❑ Ce n'est pas très loin.
   c. ❑ C'est à côté *(next door)*.

3. Un restaurant?
   a. ❑ Là-bas, vous tournez à gauche.
   b. ❑ Là-bas, vous tournez à droite.
   c. ❑ Là-bas, vous allez tout droit.

4. La cathédrale?
   a. ❑ Vous continuez tout droit.
   b. ❑ Vous tournez à droite et vous continuez tout droit.
   c. ❑ Vous tournez à gauche et vous continuez tout droit.

Nom ____

Classe ______________________ Date ______________________

D. Écoutez et répétez.

C'est tout droit.

C'est à droite.

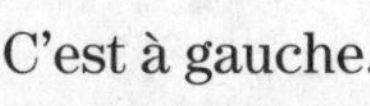

C'est à gauche.

C'est en haut.

C'est en bas.

Section 3. La maison

E. Compréhension orale

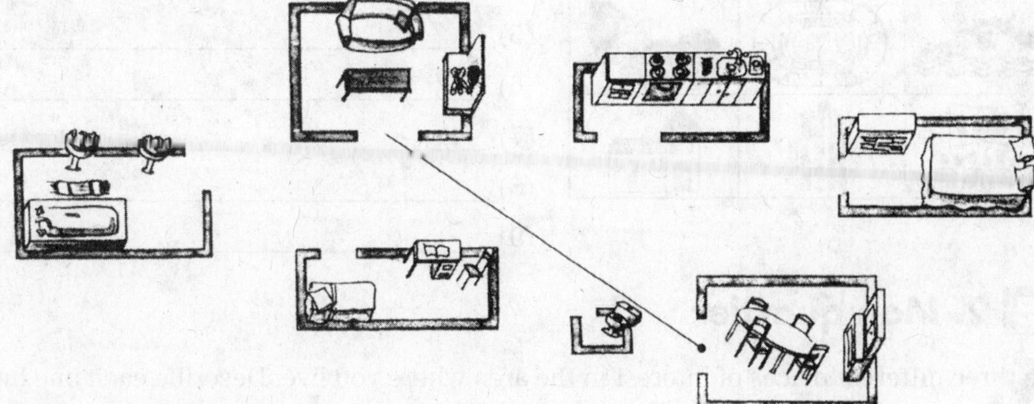

F. Questions et réponses

Modèle: —Où est la cuisine?
—C'est à droite.

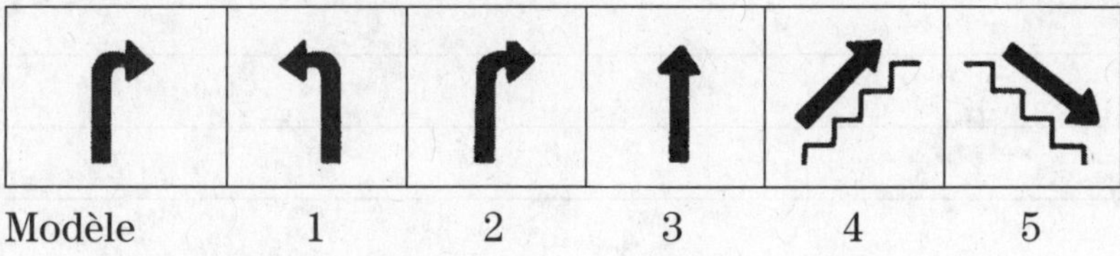

Modèle 1 2 3 4 5

Section 4. Dictée

G. Écoutez et écrivez.

—Pardon, mademoiselle, où est ________ des Anglais?

—Il est dans la ________ de la République.

—C'est ________?

—Non, vous tournez à ________ et vous continuez tout ________.

—Merci.

Nom ______________________________

Classe ______________________ Date ______________

WRITING ACTIVITIES

A/B 1. Bienvenue à Bellerive-du-Lac *(Welcome to Bellerive-du-Lac)*

Imagine that you are spending your vacation in the small French town of Bellerive-du-Lac. The various facilities that the town has to offer are represented on an information panel. List as many of these facilities as you can.

BIENVENUE À
BELLERIVE-DU-LAC
INFORMATION

À Bellerive, il y a . . .

(1) ______________________

(2) ______________________

(3) ______________________

(4) ______________________

(5) ______________________

(6) ______________________

(7) ______________________

(8) ______________________

(9) ______________________

A/B 2. Mon quartier

Name three different places of interest in the area where you live. Describe each one briefly.

▶ *Dans mon quartier, il y a un restaurant français. Il s'appelle Chez Tante Louise. C'est un assez bon restaurant.*

1. ______________________

2. ______________________

3. ______________________

Nom ______________________________

Classe ____________________ Date ______________

Discovering FRENCH Nouveau!

BLEU

C/D 3. Où est-ce?

Imagine that you are living in a French town. Someone is asking you for directions. Help the person out, according to the suggestions.

▶ —Pardon, où est l'hôtel Beau-Rivage?

—C'est tout droit.

1. —S'il vous plaît, où est l'hôpital Velpeau?

—C'est ____________.

2. —Excusez-moi, où est la bibliothèque municipale?

—C'est ____________.

3. —Pardon, où sont les toilettes?

—C'est ____________.

4. — S'il vous plaît, où est le garage?

—C'est ____________.

D 4. Ma maison

Draw a floor plan of your house or apartment. Label each room. (If you prefer, you can draw the floor plan of your dream house.)

Nom ____

Classe ____________________ Date ______________

LEÇON 14 Week-end à Paris

LISTENING ACTIVITIES

Section 1. Je vais à . . .

A. Écoutez et répétez.

1. Je vais en classe.
2. Tu vas au café.
3. Il va au cinéma.
4. Nous allons à une boum.
5. Vous allez à Paris.
6. Ils vont en France.

Section 2. Où vont-ils?

B. Compréhension orale

a. _____ au stade

b. _____ au café

c. 1____ à l'école

d. _____ au musée

e. _____ au centre commercial

f. _____ au restaurant

g. _____ au lycée

h. _____ au supermarché

C. Compréhension orale

a. _____ la bibliothèque

b. _____ l'hôtel

c. _____ la piscine

d. _____ le cinéma

Tu vas au café?
Non, je vais à la plage.

Nom ______________________________________

Classe ______________________ Date ______________

BLEU

D. Questions et réponses

▶ —Est-ce qu'il va au restaurant ou au stade?
—Il va au restaurant.

E. Questions et réponses

Modèle: le cinéma —Où vas-tu?
—Je vais au cinéma.

1. le supermarché
2. la piscine
3. le café
4. la bibliothèque
5. l'école

Nom ______________________________

Classe ______________________ Date ______________

Discovering FRENCH Nouveau!

BLEU

Section 3. Qu'est-ce que vous allez faire?

F. Compréhension orale

a. ____

b. ____

c. ____

d. 1

e. ____

f. ____

g. ____

h. ____

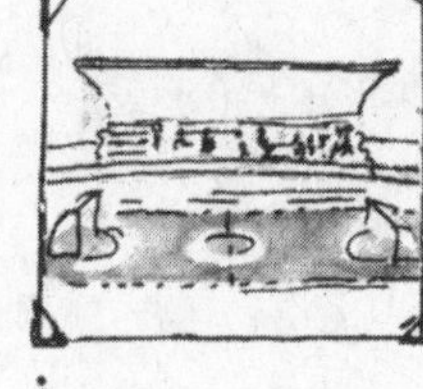
i. ____

G. Questions et réponses

Modèle: dîner —Tu vas au restaurant?
—Oui, je vais dîner.

1. nager
2. étudier
3. jouer au foot
4. faire une promenade
5. danser
6. jouer aux jeux vidéo

Section 4. Conversations

H. La réponse logique

1. a. Oui, j'ai faim.
   b. À sept heures.
   c. Chez un copain.
2. a. En bus.
   b. À huit heures.
   c. Je vais au restaurant.
3. a. À pied.
   b. Oui, je vais nager.
   c. Oui, je fais une promenade.
4. a. Je vais à une boum.
   b. Je fais une omelette.
   c. Oui, d'accord!
5. a. Oui, je vais au concert.
   b. Oui, je vais étudier.
   c. Oui, je vais au cinéma avec un ami.
6. a. Oui, je vais à une soirée.
   b. Oui, je vais regarder la télé.
   c. Oui, je fais une promenade.

Nom ____

Classe ______________________ Date ______________

Discovering FRENCH Nouveau!

BLEU

Section 5. Dictée

I. Écoutez et écrivez.

—Vous ________ à la maison aujourd'hui?

—Non, nous ________ en ville. Moi, je ________ aller au cinéma.

—Et ton frère?

—Il a un ________ avec une copine. Ils ________ faire une promenade ________ dans le parc municipal.

Nom ______________________________

Classe ______________________ Date ______________

WRITING ACTIVITIES

A 1. La tour Eiffel

Fit the six forms of **aller** into the Eiffel Tower. Then fill in the blanks to the left with the corresponding subject pronouns.

1. __________
2. __________
3. __________
4. __________
5. __________
6. __________

A/B 2. Le week-end

On weekends, people go to different places. Read what the following people like to do. Then say where each one is going by choosing an appropriate place from the list. Use the appropriate forms of **aller à.**

piscine	**restaurant**	**cinéma**	**musée**	**stade**
plage	**bibliothèque**	**concert**	**centre commercial**	

▶ Caroline aime nager. *Elle va à la piscine.*

1. Philippe et Jean-Louis aiment jouer au football. ______________
2. Mademoiselle Bellamy aime l'art moderne. ______________
3. Brigitte aime les westerns. ______________
4. Paul et Marc aiment la musique. ______________
5. J'aime regarder les magazines français. ______________
6. Tu aimes dîner en ville. ______________
7. Nous aimons nager. ______________
8. Vous aimez le shopping. ______________

Nom ______________________________

Classe ______________ Date ______________

Discovering FRENCH Nouveau!

BLEU

B 3. Qu'est-ce qu'ils font?

Describe what the following people are doing. Use the suggested words to form complete sentences.

▶ Jacqueline / parler à / le garçon français
Jacqueline parle au garçon français.

1. Marc / parler à / le professeur
____
2. Le professeur / parler à / les élèves
____
3. Le guide / parler à / les touristes
____
4. Nathalie / téléphoner à / le garçon canadien
____
5. Hélène / téléphoner à / l'étudiant français
____
6. Jean-Pierre / être à / le cinéma
____
7. Juliette / étudier à / la bibliothèque
____
8. Le taxi / arriver à / l'aéroport
____

C 4. Les voisins de Mélanie

Mélanie is selling tickets to the school fair and hopes her neighbors will buy some. Indicate that Mélanie is visiting the houses in the illustration. Use the expression **chez.**

▶ Mélanie va chez Bernard ______________________.

1. Elle va ______________________.
2. Elle va ______________________.
3. Elle va ______________________.
4. Elle va ______________________.

Nom ____________________

Classe ____________________ Date ____________________

D 5. Qu'est-ce qu'ils vont faire?

The following people are going out. Describe what each one is going to do, using the construction **aller** + infinitive.

▶ Je vais faire une promenade à vélo.

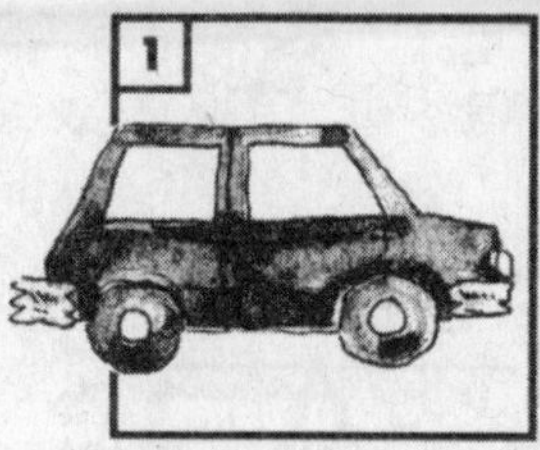

1. Nous ____________________.
2. Vous ____________________.
3. Tu ____________________.
4. Sylvie ____________________.
5. M. et Mme Dumaine ____________________.

6. Communication: Le week-end

Write a short paragraph about your weekend plans. Describe four things that you are going to do and two things you are not going to do.

OUI!

- ____________________
- ____________________
- ____________________
- ____________________

NON!

- ____________________
- ____________________

LEÇON 15 Au Café de l'Univers

LISTENING ACTIVITIES

Section 1. Je viens de . . .

A. Écoutez et répétez.

1. Je viens du café.
2. Tu viens du cinéma.
3. Elle vient de la plage.
4. Nous venons de la piscine.
5. Vous venez du supermarché.
6. Elles viennent du musée.

B. Questions et réponses

Modèle: —Tu vas au café?
—Non, je viens du café.

Section 2. Les sports et la musique

C. Compréhension orale

D. Questions et réponses

▶—Est-ce que Paul joue au tennis ou au ping-pong?
—Il joue au ping-pong.

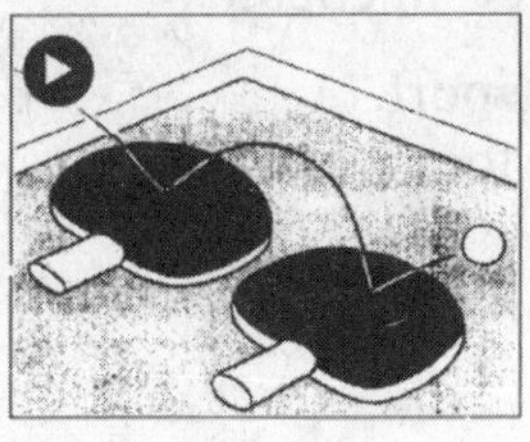

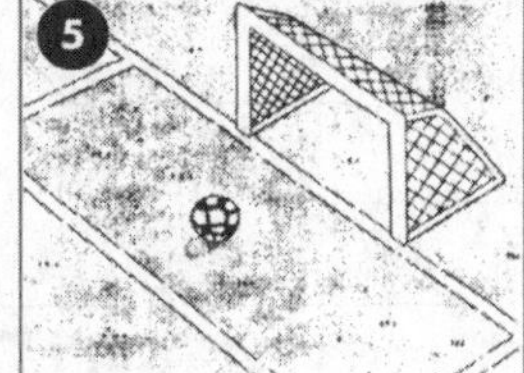

Nom ______________________________

Classe ______________________ Date ______________

Discovering FRENCH Nouveau!

BLEU

Section 3. Les pronoms accentués

E. Écoutez et répétez.

Moi, je suis chez moi. Nous, nous dînons chez nous.

Toi, tu restes chez toi. Vous, vous mangez chez vous.

Lui, il étudie chez lui. Eux, ils regardent la télé chez eux.

Elle, elle travaille chez elle. Elles, elles mangent une pizza chez elles.

F. Parlez.

Modèle: Toi **Tu vas chez toi.**
Jean-Paul **Jean-Paul va chez lui.**

1. Stéphanie
2. Nicolas
3. Vous
4. Nous
5. Alice et Véronique
6. Pierre et François
7. Moi
8. Mon cousin

Section 4. Conversations

G. La réponse logique

1. a. À pied.
   b. Au café.
   c. Du cinéma.
2. a. En ville.
   b. Du musée.
   c. À la bibliothèque.
3. a. J'ai une voiture de sport.
   b. Je joue aux cartes.
   c. C'est le foot.
4. a. Oui, j'aime la musique.
   b. Oui, je joue de la clarinette.
   c. Oui, je joue au baseball.
5. a. Non, mais je joue aux échecs.
   b. Oui, je joue du piano.
   c. Non, je n'aime pas la musique.
6. a. Oui, il est chez lui.
   b. Oui, il est chez moi.
   c. Oui, il est chez elle.
7. a. Oui, je vais chez moi.
   b. Oui, je suis chez moi.
   c. Oui, je vais chez un copain.
8. a. Oui, il aime le sport.
   b. Oui, il joue au foot.
   c. Oui, il a une Jaguar.

Section 5. Dictée

H. Écoutez et écrivez.

—Est-ce que ton copain est chez __________?

—Non, il __________ __________ cinéma avec son frère.

—À quelle heure est-ce qu'ils __________ __________ cinéma?

—À six heures.

—Et qu'est-ce qu'ils vont __________ après *(afterwards)*?

—Ils rentrent *(are going back)* dîner chez __________.

Nom ______________________

Classe ______________ Date ______________

Discovering FRENCH *Nouveau!*

BLEU

WRITING ACTIVITIES

A 1. La boum de Catherine

Catherine is organizing a party. Say who is coming and who is not, using the appropriate forms of **venir.**

▶ Claire a un examen demain. — Elle ne vient pas.

1. Philippe et Antoine aiment les boums. ______________
2. Je dois étudier. ______________
3. Nous aimons danser. ______________
4. Tu acceptes l'invitation. ______________
5. Vous n'êtes pas invités. ______________
6. Thomas est malade *(sick)*. ______________

A/B 2. D'où viennent-ils?

It is dinner time and everyone is going home. Say which places each person is coming from.

▶ Éric vient du cinéma.

1.

2.

3.

4.

5.

1. Nathalie ______________.
2. Les élèves ______________.
3. Nous ______________.
4. Monsieur Loiseau ______________.
5. Vous ______________.

Nom ______________________

Classe ______________ Date ______________

B 3. À la Maison des Jeunes

La Maison des Jeunes is a place where young people go for all kinds of different activities. Say what the following people are doing, using **jouer à** or **jouer de,** plus the illustrated activity.

▶ Nous jouons au ping-pong.

1. Diane ______________________.
2. Stéphanie et Claire ______________________.
3. Vous ______________________.
4. Tu ______________________.
5. Marc et Antoine ______________________.
6. Ma cousine ______________________.

C 4. Conversations

Complete the following mini-dialogues, using stress pronouns to replace the underlined nouns.

▶ —Tu dînes avec Jean-Michel?
—Oui, je dîne avec lui.

1. —Tu étudies avec ta copine?
—Oui, ______________________.
2. —Tu travailles pour Monsieur Moreau?
—Oui, ______________________.
3. —Tu vas chez Vincent et Thomas?
—Oui, ______________________.
4. —Tu voyages avec Hélène et Alice?
—Oui, ______________________.

Nom ______________________________

Classe ______________________ Date ______________

Discovering FRENCH Nouveau!

BLEU

5. L'orage (The storm)

Because of the storm, everyone is staying home today. Express this by completing the sentences below with **chez** and the appropriate stress pronoun.

▶ Nous étudions chez nous.

1. Monsieur Beaumont reste ______________.
2. Madame Vasseur travaille ______________.
3. Je regarde un DVD ______________.
4. Tu joues aux jeux vidéo ______________.
5. Vous dînez ______________.
6. Vincent et Philippe jouent aux échecs ______________.
7. Cécile et Sophie étudient ______________.
8. Jean-Paul regarde la télé ______________.

D 6. Qu'est-ce que c'est?

Identify the following objects more specifically.

▶ C'est une raquette de tennis.

1. C'est une raquette ______________.
2. C'est un ballon ______________.
3. C'est une batte ______________.
4. C'est un album ______________.
5. C'est un livre ______________.
6. C'est un CD ______________.

Nom _______________

Classe _______________ Date _______________

7. Communication

1. Et vous?
   Describe your leisure activities.
   Say . . .
   - *which sports you play* _______________.
   - *which games you play* _______________.
   - *which instrument(s) you play* _______________.

2. Lettre à Jérôme
   Your friend Jérôme is going to spend Saturday with you.
   Ask him . . .
   - *at what time he is coming*
   - *if he plays tennis*
   - *if he has a tennis racket*
   - *if he likes to play chess*

   Tell him that you are going to have dinner at your cousins'.

   Ask him . . .
   - *if he wants to go to their place too*
   - *what time he has to go home*

Nom ______________________________

Classe ______________________ Date ______________

Discovering FRENCH Nouveau!

BLEU

LEÇON 16 Mes voisins

LISTENING ACTIVITIES

Section 1. La famille

A. Écoutez et répétez.

la famille		
les grands-parents	le grand-père	la grand-mère
les parents	le père	la mère
	le mari	la femme
les enfants	un enfant	une enfant
	le frère	la soeur
	le fils	la fille
des parents	l'oncle	la tante
	le cousin	la cousine

B. Compréhension orale

a. _______ la grand-mère d'Olivier

b. _______ la mère d'Olivier

c. _______ la tante Alice

d. _______ le mari de tante Alice

e. _______ l'oncle Édouard

f. _______ le père d'Olivier

g. _______ les cousins d'Olivier

h. _______ Olivier

1.

2.

3.

4.

Nom ______________________________

Classe ______________________ Date ______________

C. Questions et réponses

▶ —Qui est Éric Vidal?
—C'est le cousin de Frédéric.

Section 2. Les adjectifs possessifs

D. Écoutez et répétez.

mon copain, ma copine, mes amis

ton père, ta soeur, tes parents

son baladeur, sa chaîne hi-fi, ses CD

notre maison, nos voisins

votre école, vos profs

leur tante, leurs cousins

E. Écoutez et parlez.

Modèle: une guitare **C'est ma guitare.**

un baladeur
une chaîne hi-fi
des livres
un portable
des CD

Modèle: une maison **C'est notre maison.**

une voiture
un ordinateur
des photos

Nom ____________________

Classe ____________________ Date ____________________

Discovering FRENCH Nouveau!

BLEU

F. Parlez.

Modèle: C'est la voiture de Marc? **Oui, c'est sa voiture.**

Modèle: C'est la maison de tes voisins? **Oui, c'est leur maison.**

G. Compréhension orale

	Modèles		1	2	3	4	5	6	7	8	9	10
A:	✔											
B:		✔										

Section 3. Dictée

H. Écoutez et écrivez.

Modèle: Eh bien, voilà. C'est ma maison.

1. Et ça, c'est la maison des voisins. C'est ______ maison.
2. Ça, c'est ______ voiture. Et ça c'est leur voiture.
3. Voici ______ mobylette.
4. Et voilà la mobylette de mon frère. C'est ______ mobylette.
5. Voici ______ cuisine.
6. Voici ______ chambre.
7. Et voici la chambre de mes parents. C'est ______ chambre.
8. Voici la chambre de ma soeur. C'est ______ chambre.
9. Ah, mais ça, ce n'est pas son baladeur! C'est ______ baladeur.

Nom ______________________________

Classe ____________________ Date ____________________

BLEU

WRITING ACTIVITIES

A 1. La consigne *(The check room)*

The following objects have been left at the check room, tagged with their owner's names. Identify each item.

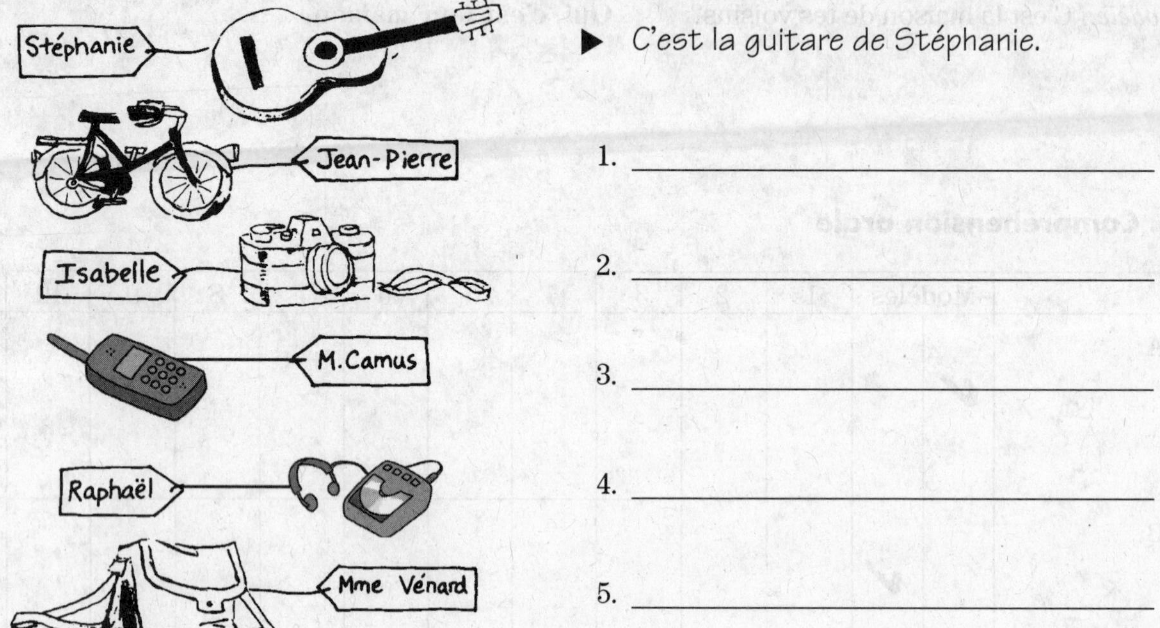

▶ *C'est la guitare de Stéphanie.*

1. ______________________________
2. ______________________________
3. ______________________________
4. ______________________________
5. ______________________________

2. En famille

Look at the family tree and explain the relationships between the following people.

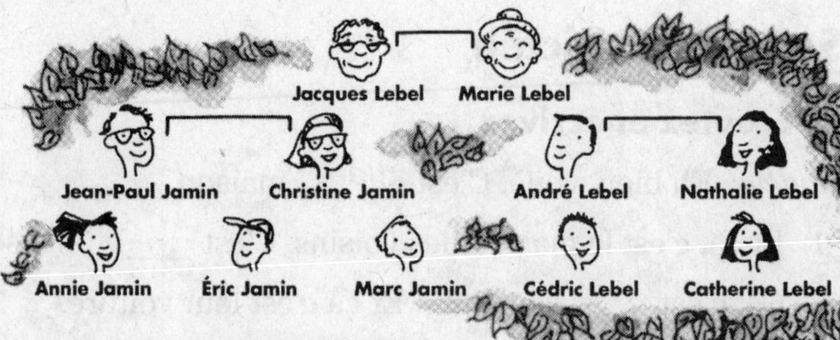

▶ Jean-Paul Jamin est *le mari* de Christine Jamin.

1. Nathalie Lebel est ______________ d'André Lebel.
2. Jacques et Marie Lebel sont ______________ de Cédric.
3. Marie Lebel est ______________ de Christine Jamin.
4. Éric et Marc sont ______________ de Christine Jamin.
5. Cédric est ______________ d'Éric.
6. Catherine est ______________ de Marc.
7. Catherine est ______________ d'André et Nathalie Lebel.
8. Jean-Paul Jamin est ______________ de Cédric et de Catherine.
9. Nathalie Lebel est ______________ d'Annie Jamin.

Nom ______________________________

Classe ______________________ Date ______________

Discovering FRENCH Nouveau!

BLEU

Unité 5 Leçon 16

Workbook

B 3. En vacances

The following people are spending their vacations with friends or family. Complete the sentences below with **son, sa,** or **ses,** as appropriate.

1. Guillaume voyage avec ______ soeur et ______ parents.
2. Juliette visite Paris avec ______ frère et ______ cousines.
3. Paul va chez ______ ami Alain.
4. Sandrine est chez ______ amie Sophie.
5. En juillet, Jean-Paul va chez ______ grands-parents.
   En août, il va chez ______ tante Marthe. En septembre,
   il va chez ______ amis anglais.
6. Hélène va chez ______ grand-père. Après (*afterwards*), elle
   va chez ______ oncle François.

B/C 4. Pourquoi pas?

The following people are not engaged in certain activities because they do not have certain things. Complete the sentences with **son, sa, ses, leur,** or **leurs** and an appropriate object from the box. Be logical.

radio	**voiture**	*ordinateur*	**mobylette**
stylos	**raquettes**	**livres**	portable

▶ Isabelle et Cécile n'étudient pas. Elles n'ont pas leurs livres.

1. Pierre et Julien ne jouent pas au tennis. Ils n'ont pas ______________________.
2. Philippe ne va pas en ville. Il n'a pas ______________________.
3. Alice et Claire n'écoutent pas le concert. Elles n'ont pas ______________________.
4. Madame Imbert ne travaille pas. Elle n'a pas ______________________.
5. Mes parents ne voyagent pas. Ils n'ont pas ______________________.
6. Les élèves n'écrivent pas (*are not writing*). Ils n'ont pas ______________________.
7. Élodie ne téléphone pas. Elle n'a pas ______________________.

Nom ______________________________ Discovering FRENCH Nouveau!

Classe ______________ Date ______________

BLEU

5. Le week-end

On weekends we like to do things with our friends and relatives. Complete the sentences below with the appropriate possessive adjectives.

▶ Nous faisons une promenade en voiture avec nos parents.

1. Isabelle et Francine vont au cinéma avec ______ cousins.
2. Je joue au tennis avec ______ copains.
3. Tu dînes chez ______ oncle.
4. Philippe et Marc vont au restaurant avec ______ copines.
5. Hélène fait une promenade à vélo avec ______ frère.
6. Nous téléphonons à ______ grand-mère.
7. Vous allez au musée avec ______ oncle.
8. Nous jouons aux cartes avec ______ amis.
9. Vous visitez un musée avec ______ soeur.

D 6. La course cycliste

Say how the following people finished the bicycle race.

▶ Nicolas est sixième.

1. Philippe ______________________.
2. Claire ______________________.
3. Marc ______________________.
4. Hélène ______________________.
5. Jean-Paul ______________________.
6. Thomas ______________________.
7. Stéphanie ______________________.

7. Communication: La famille de mes amis

Think of two of your friends. For each one, write four sentences describing his/her family. (If you wish, you can describe the families of imaginary friends.)

▶ Mon copain s'appelle Tom.

Sa soeur s'appelle Wendy.

Son père travaille dans un magasin.

Sa mère travaille dans un hôpital.

Ses cousins habitent à Cincinnati.

- Mon copain s'appelle ______.

____

____

____

____

- Ma copine s'appelle ______.

____

____

____

____

UNITÉ 5 Reading and Culture Activities

A. En voyage

1. This ad is for . . .
   - ❑ a vacation condo for sale
   - ❑ a house for sale
   - ❑ a house for rent
   - ❑ a small hotel

Auberge pasta PIERRE

Cette belle d'autrefois
au coeur du village de Rawdon!
Salle à manger de 132 places
22 chambres, piscine extérieure
Bar, discothèque, terrasse
Grand salon avec foyer
Forfaits 4 saisons

3663, rue Queen, Rawdon
J0K 1S0, (514) 834-5417

2. This concert is going to be held . . .
   - ❑ in a subway station
   - ❑ in a school
   - ❑ in a concert hall
   - ❑ in a church

EGLISE de la MADELEINE
Place et métro Madeleine

Jeudi 29 novembre à 20h 30

MOZART
Concerto pour Clarinette en La M.
REQUIEM

Monique POURADIER DUTEIL, soprano
Sylvie OUSSENKO, mezzo-soprano
Francis BARDOT, ténor
Thierry de GROMARD, basse
Marie-Cécile COURCIER, clarinette

Chœurs de Montmorency
(chef des chœurs : **Philippe BRANDEIS**)

SINFONIETTA de PARIS
direction : Dominique FANAL

Nom ______________________________________

Classe ______________________ Date ______________

3. An attraction of this hotel is that it is located
   - ❑ downtown
   - ❑ near a beach
   - ❑ near an airport
   - ❑ near an amusement park

4. You would go to this place …
   - ❑ to buy CDs
   - ❑ to read books
   - ❑ to listen to music
   - ❑ to consult bus schedules

5. This map shows you how to get …
   - ❑ to the downtown area
   - ❑ to a large shopping mall
   - ❑ to a hockey rink
   - ❑ to a racetrack

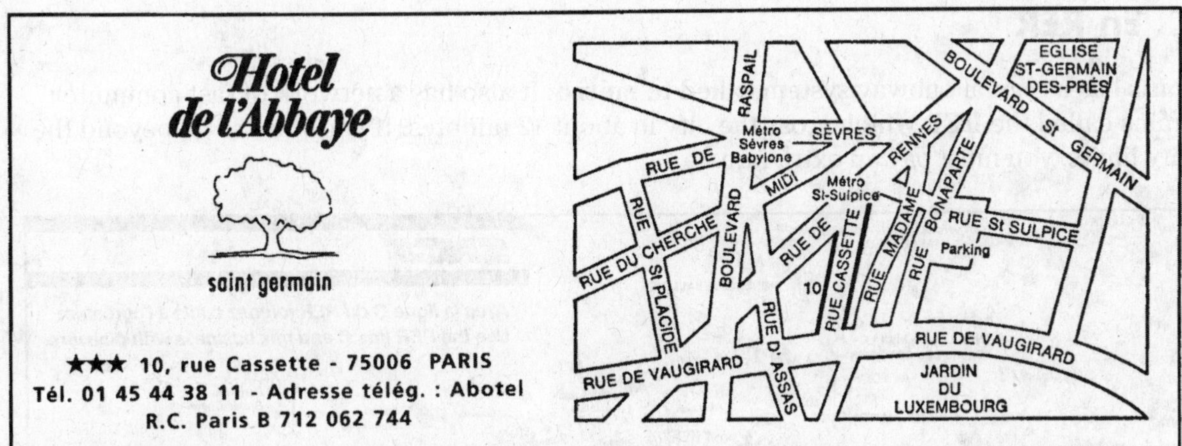

B. À l'hôtel de l'Abbaye

1. You are visiting France with your family and are looking for a hotel.
   - What is the name of the hotel shown on the card? ____________________
   - In which city is it located? ____________________
   - On which street? ____________________
   - If you wanted to make a reservation, which number would you call? ____________________
2. You have just made your reservation.
   - Check the address of the hotel and find its location on the map. Mark the location with an "X."
   - You and your family are planning to rent a car while in France. On the map, find and circle the nearest parking garage.
   - Paris has a convenient subway system: **le métro.**

     How many subway stations are shown on the map? ____________________

     What is the name of the subway station closest to the hotel? ____________________
   - The map shows one of the oldest churches in Paris. (It was built in the 12th century.) Find this church and draw a circle around it.

     What is its name? ____________________

     On which street is it located? ____________________
   - The map also shows a large public garden where many people go jogging.

     What is the name of the garden? ____________________

     On which street is it located? ____________________

Nom ______________________________________

Classe ____________________________ Date ______________

C. En RER

Paris has a regular subway system called **le métro.** It also has a network of fast commuter trains called the **RER** which cross the city in about 12 minutes. If you want to go beyond the city limits, you must pay an extra fare.

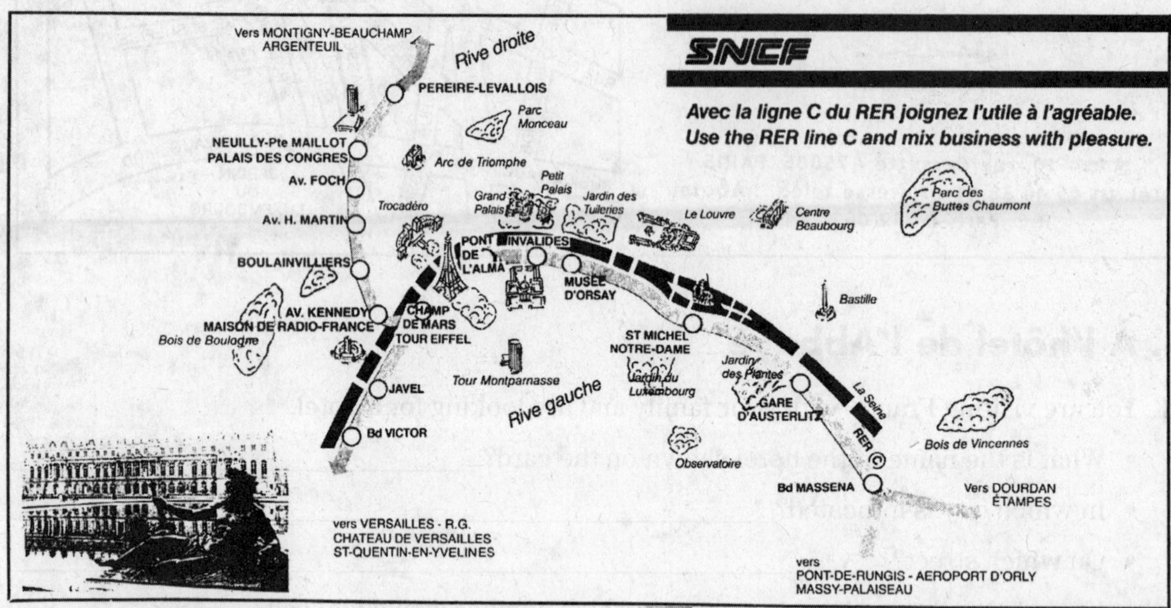

This map shows the C-line of the RER. Many famous monuments and places of interest are located along this line.

1. Look at the map and find at which stop you would get off to visit each of the following places.

   La Tour Eiffel ______________________________

   La Cathédrale Notre-Dame ______________________________

   Le Grand Palais (un musée) ______________________________

   Le Jardin des Tuileries ______________________________

   Le Musée d'Orsay ______________________________

   Le Palais des Congrès ______________________________

   Le Louvre ______________________________

2. You can also use the C-line to get to places outside of Paris.

   Which airport can you reach with this train? ______________________________

   Which famous historical château can you visit? ______________________________

Nom ____

Classe ______________________ Date ______________

Discovering FRENCH Nouveau!

BLEU

Unité 6. Le shopping

LEÇON 17 Le français pratique: L'achat des vêtements

LISTENING ACTIVITIES

Section 1. Les vêtements et les accessoires

A. Écoutez et répétez.

B. Compréhension orale

a. ____

b. ____

c. ____

d. ____

e. ____

f. ____

g. ____

h. 1

i. ____

j. ____

k. ____

l. ____

m. ____

n. ____

o. ____

p. ____

Nom ______________________________

Classe ______________________ Date ______________________

C. Questions et réponses

▶ Vous désirez?
Je cherche un tee-shirt. ▶

D. Compréhension orale

Section 2. Les nombres de 100 à 1000

E. Écoutez et répétez.

100	200	500	800
101	300	600	900
102	400	700	1000

F. Questions et réponses

▶—Combien coûte la veste?
—Elle coûte 100 euros.

▶ 100€

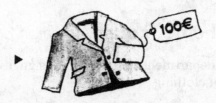

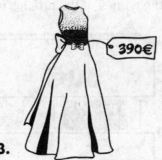

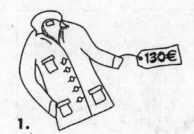

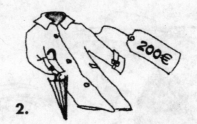

1. 130€

2. 200€

3. 390€

Section 3. Conversations

G. La réponse logique

1. a. J'ai une veste bleue.
   b. Je porte des bottes.
   c. Je cherche un imperméable.
2. a. Un blouson.
   b. Une boutique.
   c. Un grand magasin.
3. a. Un imper.
   b. Des bottes.
   c. Mon maillot de bain.
4. a. Il est trop grand.
   b. Il est démodé.
   c. 160 euros.
5. a. Oui, il est marron.
   b. Oui, il est très joli.
   c. Non, il est grand.
6. a. Non, elle est bon marché.
   b. Non, il est démodé.
   c. Non, il est trop petit.

Section 4. Dictée

H. Écoutez et écrivez.

—Qu'est-ce que tu penses du __________ rouge ?

—Il est __________.

—Combien est-ce qu'il __________?

—__________ euros.

—Oh là là ! Il n'est pas __________!

Nom ______________________________

Classe ____________________ Date ____________________

WRITING ACTIVITIES

A/B 1. Une affiche de mode *(A fashion poster)*

You are working in the ad department of a fashion designer. Complete the poster below with the names of the articles of clothing.

30€

45€

60€

25€

60€

75€

85€

Nom ______________________________

Classe ____________________ Date ____________

Discovering FRENCH Nouveau!

BLEU

Unité 6 Leçon 17

Workbook

2. Qu'est-ce que vous portez?

Describe in detail what you are wearing. Give the colors of each item of clothing. Then select two other people (one male and one female) and describe their clothes in the same manner.

▶ Aujourd'hui, je porte une chemise verte et jaune, un pantalon noir, . . .

1. Aujourd'hui, je porte ______________________________
____
2. ____________ porte ______________________________
____
3. ____________ porte ______________________________
____

Nom ____

Classe ______________________ Date ______________________

3. Les valises *(Suitcases)*

Imagine you are planning for four trips. Make a list of at least four items of clothing that you will pack in each of the following suitcases.

1. un week-end à la plage

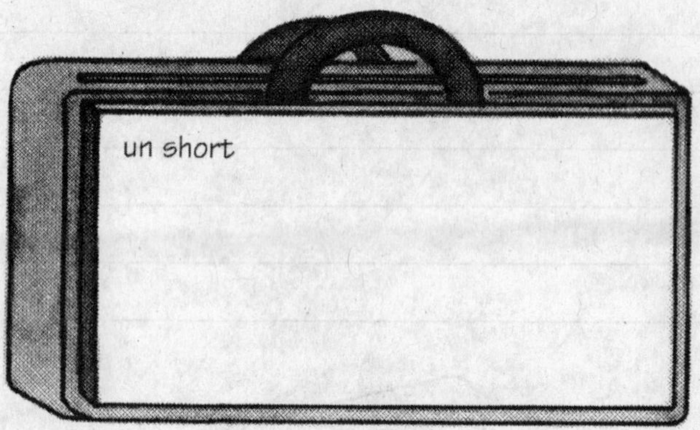

2. un week-end de ski

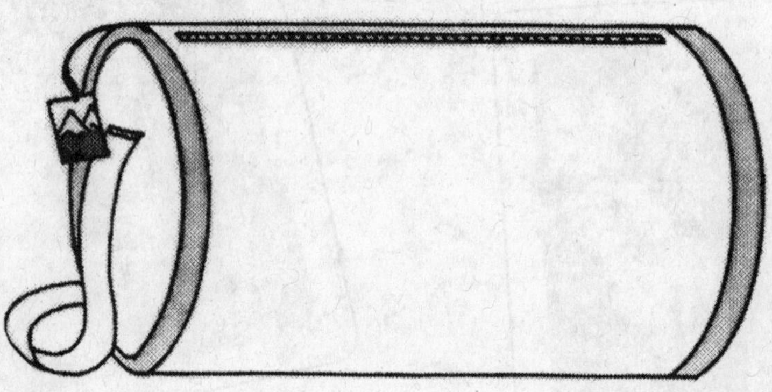

3. un mariage élégant

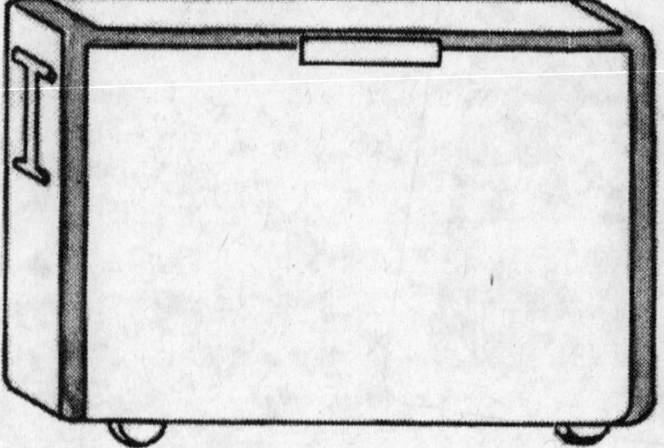

4. une semaine à Québec

Nom ______________________________

Classe ______________________ Date ______________

Discovering FRENCH Nouveau!

BLEU

4. Conversations : Dans un magasin

Complete the dialogues on the basis of the illustrations. Use expressions from page 262 of your student text.

1. 

—Vous ______________________ monsieur ?

—Je ______________________.

2. 

—Pardon, mademoiselle.

Combien ______________________?

—______________________euros.

3. 

—S'il vous plaît, madame, ______________________

______________________?

—______________________.

4. 

—Est-ce que le manteau est ______________________?

Oh là là, non. Il est très ______________________.

Il coûte ______________________euros.

5. 

—Qu'est-ce que tu penses de ma ______________________?

—Elle est trop ______________________.

6. 

—Comment ______________________

______________________?

—Il est trop ______________________.

LEÇON 18 Rien n'est parfait!

LISTENING ACTIVITIES

Section 1. Acheter et préférer

A. Écoutez et répétez.

J'achète une veste. #
Tu achètes une cravate. #
Il achète un imper. #
Nous achetons un jean. #
Vous achetez un chemisier. #
Elles achètent un pull. #

Je préfère la veste bleue. #
Tu préfères la cravate jaune. #
Il préfère l'imper gris. #
Nous préférons le jean noir. #
Vous préférez le chemisier blanc. #
Elles préfèrent le pull rouge. #

Section 2. Ce et quel

B. Écoutez et répétez.

le blouson

la veste

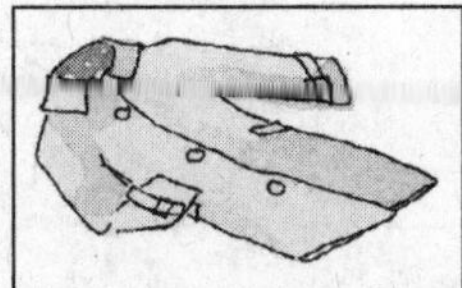
l'imper

les chaussures

les affiches

C. Écoutez et parlez.

Modèle: une casquette
Regarde cette casquette.

1. un pull
2. une guitare
3. des vestes
4. un vélo
5. des tee-shirts
6. des lunettes
7. un ordinateur
8. des appareils-photo

Nom ____________________

Classe ____________________ Date ____________________

D. Écoutez et parlez.

Modèle: Je vais acheter une veste.
Quelle veste?

Section 3. Conversations

E. La réponse logique

1. a. Oui, il est génial.
   b. Oui, j'ai un tee-shirt.
   c. Oui, je porte une chemise.

2. a. Oui, c'est vrai.
   b. Un jean et un polo.
   c. J'ai une classe de français.

3. a. Ma guitare.
   b. Des CD.
   c. Mon copain Nicolas.

4. a. Des sandwichs.
   b. Ma cousine.
   c. Un survêtement.

5. a. Je n'étudie pas.
   b. Je voudrais aller à la piscine.
   c. Oui, je fais une promenade.

Section 4. Dictée

F. Écoutez et écrivez.

— __________ vêtements est-ce que tu vas __________ pour le pique-nique?

— __________ jean et __________ chemise bleue.

— Et __________ chaussures est-ce que tu vas porter?

— __________ tennis.

Nom ____

Classe ______________________ Date ______________

Discovering FRENCH Nouveau!

B L E U

WRITING ACTIVITIES

A 1. Au centre commercial

Friends are shopping. Say what everyone is buying by completing the sentences with the appropriate forms of **acheter.**

1. Nous ____________________ des vêtements.
2. Claire ____________________ une ceinture.
3. Vous ____________________ une casquette.
4. Virginie et Christine ____________________ des CD.
5. Tu ____________________ une veste.
6. Marc ____________________ un survêtement.
7. J'____________________ un sweat.
8. Mes copains ____________________ des chaussures.

2. Une boum

Christine has invited her friends to a party. Some of them are bringing other friends. Others are bringing things for the party. Complete the sentences below with the appropriate forms of **amener** or **apporter.**

1. François ____________________des sandwichs.
2. Stéphanie ____________________un copain.
3. Nous ____________________des CD.
4. Vous ____________________vos cousins.
5. Tu ____________________ta guitare.
6. Nous ____________________des copines.
7. Vous ____________________un DVD.
8. Marc et Roger ____________________leur soeur.

Nom ______________________________

Classe ____________________ Date ____________

BLEU

B 3. Dans la rue

Olivier and Béatrice are walking in town. Olivier is pointing out various people and commenting on various things he sees. Complete his questions, as in the model.

▶ Tu connais ces filles ?

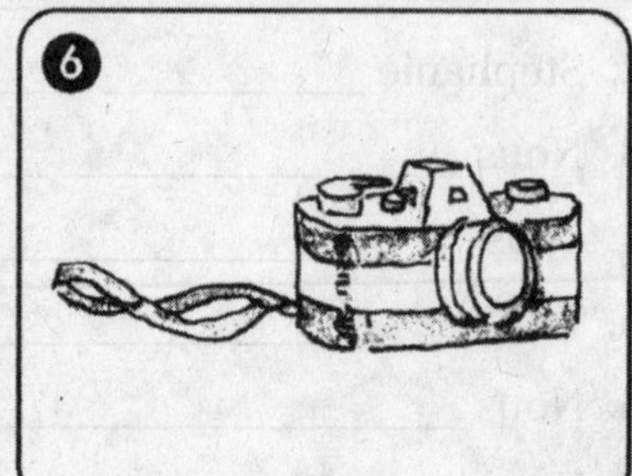

1. Qui sont ____________________?
2. Regarde ____________________!
3. Veux-tu aller dans ____________________?
4. Regarde ____________________!
5. Comment trouves-tu ____________________?
6. Combien coûte ____________________?

B/C 4. Conversations

Complete the following mini-dialogues.

▶ —Quelle ______ cravate préfères-tu?

—Je préfère cette cravate ______ jaune.

1. —______ imperméable vas-tu acheter?

   —Je vais acheter ______ beige.

2. —______ bottes vas-tu mettre?

   —Je vais mettre ______ noires.

3. —______ blousons préfères-tu?

   —Je préfère ______ bleus.

4. —______ veste vas-tu porter pour la boum?

   —______ verte.

D 5. Qu'est-ce qu'ils mettent?

Read what the following people are doing or are going to do. Then complete the second sentence with the verb **mettre** and one of the items in the box. Be logical!

la table	**la télé**	**un maillot de bain**
la radio	**un survêtement**	**des vêtements élégants**

1. Julien va nager. Il ______.
2. Vous allez dîner. Vous ______.
3. Nous allons écouter le concert. Nous ______.
4. Tu vas regarder le match de foot. Tu ______.
5. Je vais faire du jogging. Je ______.
6. Mes cousins vont à un mariage. Ils ______.

Nom ______________________________

Classe ____________________ Date ____________________

6. Communication

Some French friends have invited you to a picnic.

Write a short paragraph saying . . .

- *what clothes you are going to wear to the picnic*
- *what items you are going to bring to the picnic*
- *whom you are going to bring along*

LEÇON 19 Un choix difficile

LISTENING ACTIVITIES

Section 1. Les verbes en *-ir*

A. Écoutez et répétez.

Je choisis une casquette.
Tu choisis un blouson.
Il choisit une chaîne hi-fi.
Nous choisissons des CD.
Vous choisissez des vêtements.
Ils choisissent une voiture.

Section 2. Les comparaisons

B. Répétez.

plus grand que	Pierre est plus grand que Marc.
moins grand que	Pierre est moins grand que Jacques.
aussi grand que	Pierre est aussi grand que Nicolas.

C. Compréhension orale

Modèle: Sophie [–] Mélanie
Sophie est moins grande que Mélanie.

1. la veste [ ] le blouson
2. les tennis [ ] les baskets
3. la casquette [ ] le chapeau
4. Isabelle [ ] Stéphanie
5. mon chien [ ] mon chat
6. mes copains [ ] que moi

Nom ______________________________

Classe ____________________ Date ____________

Discovering FRENCH Nouveau!

BLEU

D. Questions et réponses

Modèle: [–]
Est-ce que la chemise est plus chère ou moins chère que le polo?
Elle est moins chère.

1. [+]
2. [=]
3. [–]
4. [+]
5. [=]
6. [–]

Section 3. Conversations

E. La réponse logique

1. a. Mardi.
   b. À dix heures.
   c. Elle ne finit pas.
2. a. Oui, elle est trop longue.
   b. Non, je préfère la veste jaune.
   c. Oui, je porte une veste bleue.
3. a. J'étudie le français.
   b. Je n'étudie pas.
   c. Je veux réussir à l'examen.
4. a. Je veux maigrir.
   b. Je veux grossir.
   c. Je mange une pizza.

Section 4. Dictée

F. Écoutez et écrivez.

—Qu'est-ce que tu ________? Le hamburger ou la salade?

—Je ________ la salade.

—Pourquoi?

—Parce que je veux ________.

—J'espère que tu vas ________.

Nom ______________________

Classe ______________ Date ______________

Discovering FRENCH Nouveau!

BLEU

Unité 6 Leçon 19

Workbook

WRITING ACTIVITIES

A 1. Au Bon Marché

The people below are shopping at Le Bon Marché. Say what each one is choosing, using the appropriate form of **choisir.**

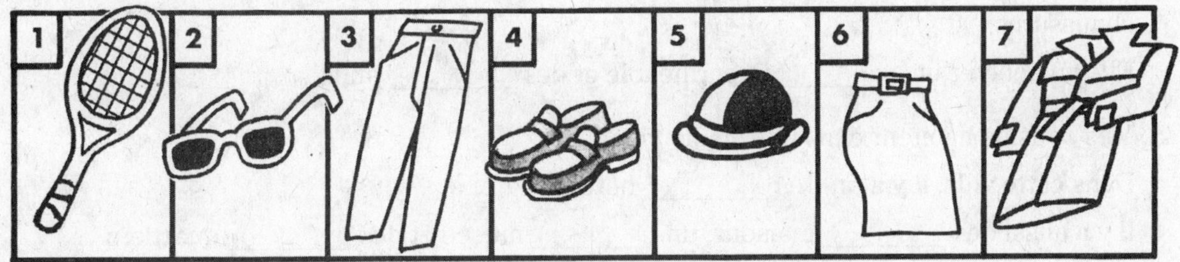

1. Tu ______________________.
2. Vous ______________________.
3. Je ______________________.
4. Nous ______________________.
5. M. Voisin ______________________.
6. Mme Lamy ______________________.
7. Isabelle et Marthe ______________________.

2. Oui ou non?

Read about the following people. Then describe a LOGICAL conclusion by completing the second sentence with the *affirmative* or *negative* form of the verb in parentheses.

▶ Alice fait beaucoup de jogging. Elle ne grossit pas. (grossir?)

1. Nous étudions. ______________ à l'examen. (réussir?)
2. Vous êtes riches. ______________ des vêtements chers. (choisir?)
3. Marc regarde la télé. ______________ la leçon. (finir?)
4. Mes cousins mangent beaucoup. ______________. (maigrir?)
5. Vous faites beaucoup de sport. ______________. (grossir?)
6. Les élèves n'écoutent pas le prof. ______________ à l'examen. (réussir?)

Nom ______________________________

Classe ____________________ Date ____________

B 3. Descriptions

Roger is describing certain people and things. Complete each description with the appropriate forms of the underlined adjectives.

1. Isabelle a beaucoup de <u>beaux</u> vêtements.
   Aujourd'hui elle porte une ________ jupe, un ________ chemisier et des ________ chaussures.
   Elle va acheter un ________ imperméable et des ________ pulls.
2. Mes cousins habitent dans une <u>vieille</u> ville.
   Dans cette ville, il y a un très ________ hôtel.
   Il y a aussi des ________ maisons, un ________ musée et des ________ quartiers.
3. Cet été, je vais acheter une <u>nouvelle</u> veste.
   Je vais aussi acheter un ________ maillot de bain, des ________ pantalons et des ________ chemises.
   Si j'ai beaucoup d'argent *(money)*, je vais aussi acheter un ________ appareil-photo.

C 4. Fifi et Nestor

Look at the scene and complete the comparisons, using the adjectives in parentheses.

(grand) ▶ Fifi est moins grand que ________ Nestor.

(sympathique) 1. Fifi ________________ Nestor.

(méchant) 2. Fifi ________________ Nestor.

(grande) 3. Mme Paquin ________________ Catherine.

(jeune) 4. Mme Paquin ________________ Catherine.

5. Opinions

Compare the following by using the suggested adjectives. Express your personal opinions.

▶ un imper / cher / un manteau
Un imper est moins (aussi, plus) cher qu'un manteau.

1. une chemise / chère / une veste

2. une moto / rapide / une voiture

3. un chat / intelligent / un chien

4. le Texas / grand / l'Alaska

5. la Californie / jolie / la Floride

6. les filles / sportives / les garçons

7. la cuisine italienne / bonne / la cuisine américaine

8. les Royals / bons / les Yankees

Nom ______________________________

Classe ____________________ Date ____________________

6. Communication: En français !

Make four to six comparisons of your own involving familiar people, places, or things.

- Ma soeur est plus jeune que mon frère. Elle est aussi intelligente que lui.
- Notre maison est moins grande que la maison des voisins.

LEÇON 20 Alice a un job

LISTENING ACTIVITIES

Section 1. Le pronom *on*

A. Compréhension orale

a. ____

b. ____

c. 1

d. ____

e. ____

f. ____

g. ____

B. Questions et réponses

Qu'est-ce qu'on vend ici?

On vend des ordinateurs.

1.

2.

3.

Nom ______________________________

Classe ____________________ Date ____________________

Discovering FRENCH Nouveau!

BLEU

C. Questions et réponses

Modèle: —Vous parlez anglais?
—Bien sûr, on parle anglais.

Section 2. L'impératif

D. Compréhension orale

	Modèle	1	2	3	4	5	6	7	8
A: statement	✓								
B: suggestion									

E. Parlez.

Modèle: Tu dois écouter le professeur
Écoute le professeur.

Modèle: Nous aimons jouer au foot.
Jouons au foot.

Section 3. Conversations

F. La réponse logique

1. a. Un copain.
   b. Ma tante Victoire.
   c. Le musée Picasso.
2. a. À mon oncle.
   b. Notre Dame.
   c. La France.
3. a. Oui, je suis riche.
   b. Oui, j'ai 20 euros.
   c. Oui, prête-moi 10 euros, s'il te plaît.
4. a. Oui, j'ai faim.
   b. Oui, je mange une pizza.
   c. Non, je suis au restaurant.
5. a. L'école.
   b. Ma montre.
   c. Le bus.
6. a. J'ai besoin d'argent.
   b. Je vais faire une promenade.
   c. Je vais en ville.

Section 4. Dictée

G. Écoutez et écrivez.

You will hear a short dialogue spoken twice. First listen carefully to what the people are saying. The second time you hear the dialogue, fill in the missing words.

Écoutez.

—Qu'est-ce qu' __________ fait?

—J'ai __________ d'aller au cinéma, mais je n'ai pas d' __________.

—De __________ est-ce que tu as __________?

—De dix euros.

—Tiens, voilà dix euros.

Nom ______________________________________

Classe ____________________ Date ____________________

Discovering FRENCH Nouveau!

BLEU

WRITING ACTIVITIES

A 1. Où?

Say where one usually does the activities suggested in parentheses. Choose one of the places from the box. Be logical!

- au Mexique
- en France
- au stade
- à la piscine
- à l'école
- au restaurant
- dans les grands magasins

▶ (étudier) On étudie à l'école.

1. (nager) ______________________
2. (dîner) ______________________
3. (jouer au foot) ______________________
4. (acheter des vêtements) ______________________
5. (parler français) ______________________
6. (parler espagnol) ______________________

B 2. Jobs d'été

The following students have jobs as salespeople this summer. Say what each one is selling.

▶ Caroline vend des maillots de bain.

1. Nous ______________________.
2. Vous ______________________.
3. Éric et Pierre ______________________.
4. Tu ______________________.
5. Je ______________________.
6. Corinne ______________________.

3. Pourquoi?

Explain why people do certain things by completing the sentences with the appropriate form of the verbs in the box. Be logical!

• **attendre**	• **répondre**
• **entendre**	• **vendre**
• **perdre**	• **rendre**

1. Olivier ________________ son vélo parce qu'il a besoin d'argent.
2. Nous ________________ le match parce que nous ne jouons pas bien.
3. Vous ________________ correctement aux questions du prof parce que vous êtes de bons élèves.
4. Tu n'________________ pas parce que tu n'écoutes pas.
5. Je ________________ souvent visite à mes voisins parce qu'ils sont sympathiques.
6. Martine et Julie ________________ leurs copains parce qu'elles ont un rendez-vous avec eux.

C 4. Oui ou non?

Tell a French friend to do or not to do the following things according to the situation. Be logical.

▶ (téléphoner) Ne téléphone pas à Sophie. Elle n'est pas chez elle.
▶ (inviter) Invite Jean-Paul. Il est très sympathique.
1. (acheter) ________________ cette veste. Elle est trop longue.
2. (choisir) ________________ ce tee-shirt. Il est joli et bon marché.
3. (attendre) ________________ tes copains. Ils vont venir dans cinq minutes.
4. (mettre) ________________ ce pantalon. Il est moche et démodé.
5. (aller) ________________ au cinéma. Il y a un très bon film.
6. (venir) ________________ chez moi. J'organise une boum.
7. (apporter) ________________ tes CD. Nous allons danser.
8. (manger) ________________ la pizza. Tu vas grossir.

Nom ______________________

Classe ______________ Date ______________

Discovering FRENCH Nouveau!

BLEU

5. Au choix *(Your choice)*

Your friends have asked your advice. Tell them what to do, choosing one of the suggested options. If you wish, you may explain your choice.

▶ aller au théâtre ou au cinéma?

Allez au cinéma. C'est plus amusant (moins cher)!

(Allez au théâtre. C'est plus intéressant!)

1. regarder le film ou le match de baseball?

____

2. dîner à la maison ou au restaurant?

____

3. organiser une boum ou un pique-nique?

____

4. étudier le français ou l'espagnol?

____

6. Suggestions

It is Saturday. You and your friends are wondering what to do. Suggest that you do the following things together.

▶ Jouons au basket.

1. ______________ 4. ______________

2. ______________ 5. ______________

3. ______________ 6. ______________

7. Communication

Describe three things that you would like to do or buy, and say how much money you need to do so.

▶ *J'ai envie d'acheter un baladeur.*

J'ai besoin de cinquante dollars.

1. ______________________________

____

2. ______________________________

____

3. ______________________________

____

Le Club 20 Ans
à la mode américaine

Nom ______________________________

Classe ______________________ Date ______________

Discovering FRENCH Nouveau!

BLEU

UNITÉ 6 Reading and Culture Activities

A. Six boutiques

1.

PRIX SPECIAUX
JANVIER
Des exemples:
COSTUME pure laine 165€
VESTE pure laine 130€
BLAZER pure laine 125€
PULLOVER laine d'agneau
«Fabriqué en Ecosse» 40€
ASTER
hommes

2.

Les fameuses CHEMISES Arrow

toutes tailles
toutes longueurs
Dépositaire

JOCKEY-CLUB

240 bis, bd Saint-Germain. M° Bac
167, rue de la Pompe
Près avenue Bugeaud

3.

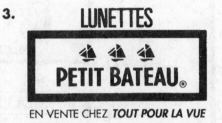

LUNETTES

PETIT BATEAU®

EN VENTE CHEZ *TOUT POUR LA VUE*

4.

les cravates

JEAN PATOU

sont en vente à

MADELIOS

PLACE DE LA MADELEINE - PARIS

5.

Chaussures

RALLYE

VILLE - SPORT - MONTAGNE

ARCUS - TECNICA

14, rue Royale, Annecy Tél. 04.50.45.09.88

6.

ouvre sa boutique

Maillots de bain, danse, jogging, ski

HOMMES FEMMES ENFANTS

4, rue de Sèvres PARIS 6e

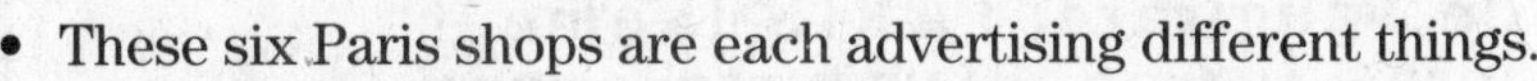

- These six Paris shops are each advertising different things.
- Note that the ads have been numbered 1, 2, 3, 4, 5, and 6.
- Indicate where one would go to buy the following items by circling the number of the corresponding shop.

	BOUTIQUES					
a dress shirt	1	2	3	4	5	6
a jacket	1	2	3	4	5	6
a swimsuit	1	2	3	4	5	6
an elegant tie	1	2	3	4	5	6
a man's suit	1	2	3	4	5	6
a pair of new glasses	1	2	3	4	5	6
a ballet leotard	1	2	3	4	5	6
a pair of walking shoes	1	2	3	4	5	6

Nom _______________________________

Classe ____________________ Date ____________________

BLEU

B. Les soldes

COLLECTION AUTOMNE - HIVER

-30% à -50%

BOUTIQUE HOMME	BOUTIQUE FEMME	BOUTIQUE SPORTSWEAR
CHEMISES à 20€	PULLS à 25€	JEANS à 25€
PULLS à 30€	PANTALONS à 30€	SWEAT SHIRTS à 20€
VESTES "NEW LOOK" à 69€	JUPES LAINAGE à 35€	PANTALONS NEWMAN à 30€
PANTALONS LAINAGES à 35€	ENSEMBLES à 45€	BLOUSONS à 45€
PANTALONS (forme large) à 40€		CHEMISES à 30€

353, Rue de Vaugirard, PARIS 15 ème
OUVERT DE 9 H 30 à 19 H 30 - SANS INTERRUPTION

1. As you were walking down the Boulevard Saint-Michel in Paris, you were handed this flyer announcing a special sale. Read it carefully and answer the following questions.

- Comment s'appelle la boutique? _______________
- Quelle est l'adresse de la boutique? _______________
- À quelle heure est-ce que la boutique ouvre *(open)?* _______________
- Combien coûtent les jeans? _______________

  Est-ce qu'ils sont chers ou bon marché? _______________

Nom ____

Classe ______________________________ Date ______________________

2. You have decided to go shop at the Coroner. Imagine you have saved 100 euros to buy clothes. Make a list of what you are planning to buy and add up the total cost of your intended purchases.

Article	*Prix*
Prix total:	

3. You have tried on the items and they all fit well. You will buy all the things on your list. Write out a check for the total amount.

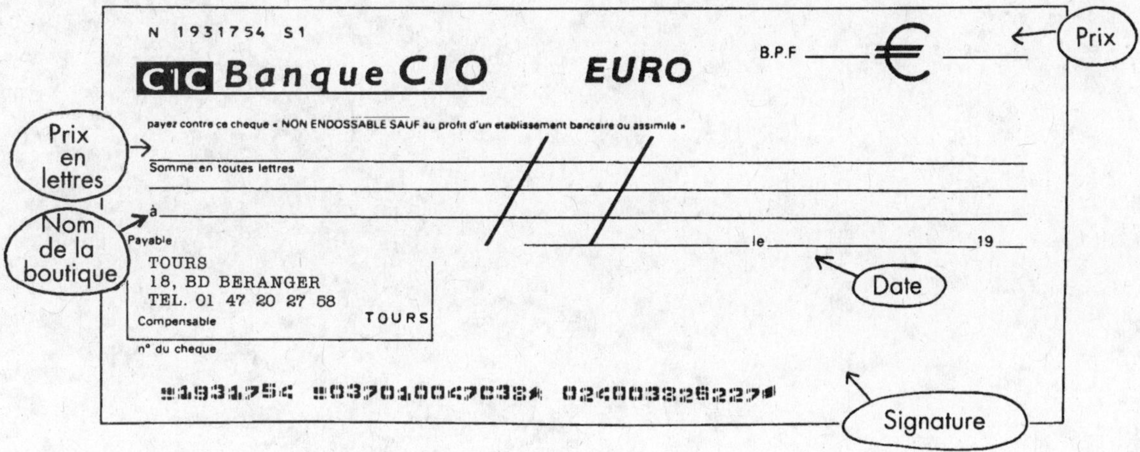
N 1931754 S1
CIC Banque CIO EURO
B.P.F €
payez contre ce cheque « NON ENDOSSABLE SAUF au profit d'un etablissement bancaire ou assimile »
Somme en toutes lettres
à
Payable
TOURS
18, BD BERANGER
TEL. 01 47 20 27 58
Compensable TOURS
n° du cheque
le 19

Nom ______________________________

Classe ____________________ Date ____________

Discovering FRENCH *Nouveau!*

BLEU

Unite 7. Le temps libre

LEÇON 21 Le français pratique: Le week-end et les vacances

LISTENING ACTIVITIES

Section 1. Que faites-vous le week-end?

A. Compréhension orale

	Modèle	1	2	3	4	5	6	7	8
A:									
B:	✓								

B. Questions et réponses

—Est-ce que tu vas ranger ta chambre samedi?
—Oui, je vais ranger ma chambre.
(Non, je ne vais pas ranger ma chambre.)

Nom ____

Classe ______________________ Date ______________

Section 2. Les vacances

C. Compréhension orale

	Modèle	1	2	3	4	5	6	7	8
A:									
B:	✓								

D. Questions et réponses

Modèle: Que fait Thomas?
Il fait du vélo.

Nom ______________________________ Discovering FRENCH Nouveau!

Classe ______________________ Date ______________

BLEU

Section 3. Conversations

E. La réponse logique

1. a. au café
   b. au cinéma
   c. au centre commercial

2. a. J'organise une boum ce week-end.
   b. Je répare mon vélo.
   c. Je vends mes CD.

3. a. Je vais à la campagne.
   b. Je dois aider mes parents.
   c. Je vais faire un pique-nique.

4. a. Oui, j'aime nager.
   b. Oui, je fais du skate.
   c. Non, je n'ai pas faim.

5. a. mes devoirs
   b. de l'escalade
   c. des achats

6. a. du skate
   b. de la planche à voile
   c. du VTT

Nom ____

Classe ____________________ Date ____________________

Discovering FRENCH *Nouveau!*

BLEU

Section 4. Dictée

F. Écoutez et écrivez.

—Qu'est-ce que tu vas faire le week-end prochain?

—Je vais faire des __________ au __________ commercial avec ma cousine.

—Et __________?

—Nous allons __________ un film.

Nom ______________________________________

Classe ____________________ Date ____________

Discovering FRENCH *Nouveau!*

BLEU

WRITING ACTIVITIES

A/B 1. L'intrus *(The intruder)*

Each of the following sentences can be logically completed by three of the four suggested options. The option that does not fit is the intruder. Cross it out.

1. Je ne peux pas aller au cinéma avec toi. Je dois nettoyer . . .
   - ma chambre
   - la cuisine
   - les devoirs
   - le garage
2. Ce soir, je vais . . . mes copains.
   - inviter
   - téléphoner à
   - rencontrer
   - laver
3. Philippe est à la maison. Il . . . ses parents.
   - assiste à
   - parle avec
   - aide
   - prépare le dîner pour
4. Madame Halimi est dans le garage. Elle . . . sa voiture.
   - lave
   - répare
   - nettoie
   - rencontre
5. Frédéric est à la bibliothèque. Il . . .
   - étudie
   - choisit un livre
   - fait des achats
   - fait ses devoirs
6. Alice n'est pas chez elle. Elle assiste à . . .
   - une boutique
   - un concert
   - un récital
   - un match de foot
7. Nous allons à la campagne pour faire . . .
   - un pique-nique
   - les devoirs
   - une promenade à pied
   - une promenade à vélo
8. Marc va en ville. Il va . . .
   - faire de la voile
   - rencontrer des copains
   - voir un film
   - acheter des vêtements
9. On peut aller de Dallas à San Francisco . . .
   - en autocar
   - en voiture
   - en bateau
   - en avion
10. À la mer, on peut faire . . .
    - de l'escalade
    - de la voile
    - du ski nautique
    - de la planche à voile
11. À la montagne, on peut faire . . .
    - du ski
    - du ski nautique
    - de l'escalade
    - des promenades à pied
12. Cet été, je vais . . . un mois en France.
    - rester
    - passer
    - dépenser
    - voyager

Nom ______________________

Classe ______________ Date ______________

Discovering FRENCH Nouveau!

BLEU

2. Les loisirs *(Leisure-time activities)*

What do you think the following people are going to do during their leisure time? Complete the sentences logically.

▶ Béatrice va au centre commercial. Elle va faire des achats (acheter une robe . . .).

1. Philippe va au café. ______________
2. Valérie va au stade. ______________
3. Thomas et Christine vont au cinéma. ______________
4. Martin rentre chez lui. ______________
5. Cet été, Catherine va à la mer. ______________
6. Ce week-end, Isabelle va à la campagne. ______________
7. Pendant les vacances d'hiver, Jean-François va dans le Colorado. ______________
8. Pendant les grandes vacances, Daniel va à la montagne. ______________

3. Communication

In her last letter, your French pen pal Christine asked you several questions. Answer them.

- En général, qu'est-ce que tu fais le week-end?
- Qu'est-ce que tu fais quand tu es chez toi le samedi?
- Qu'est-ce que tu vas faire le week-end prochain?
- Où est-ce que tu vas aller pendant les grandes vacances?

  Combien de temps est-ce que tu vas passer là-bas?

  Comment vas-tu voyager?

  Qu'est-ce que tu vas faire?

LEÇON 22 Vive le week-end!

LISTENING ACTIVITIES

Section 1. Le passé composé

A. Écoutez et répétez.

J'ai travaillé.	Je n'ai pas travaillé.
Tu as étudié.	Tu n'as pas étudié.
Il a joué au foot.	Il n'a pas joué au foot.
Elle a regardé la télé.	Elle n'a pas regardé la télé.
Nous avons nagé.	Nous n'avons pas nagé.
Vous avez mangé.	Vous n'avez pas mangé.
Ils ont visité Québec.	Ils n'ont pas visité Québec.
Elles ont parlé français.	Elles n'ont pas parlé français.

B. Compréhension orale

	Modèle	1	2	3	4	5	6	7	8	9	10
A: aujourd'hui (présent)											
B: ce week-end (passé composé)	✔										

C. Compréhension orale

		Jean-Claude	Nathalie
1	Qui a passé l'après-midi dans les magasins?		
2	Qui a étudié tout l'après-midi?		
3	Qui a regardé les vêtements?		
4	Qui a acheté un CD?		
5	Qui a mangé un sandwich dans un café?		
6	Qui a étudié après le dîner?		
7	Qui a téléphoné à une copine?		
8	Qui a regardé un film à la télé?		

Nom ___________________________

Classe ___________________ Date ___________________

D. Questions et réponses

▶ —Est-ce que tu as joué au tennis?
—Oui, j'ai joué au tennis. (Non, je n'ai pas joué au tennis.)

E. Écoutez et parlez.

Modèle: [Stéphanie] **Elle a joué au foot.**

1.

2.

3.

4.

5.

6.

7.

Nom ______________________________

Classe ______________________ Date ______________

Discovering FRENCH Nouveau!
BLEU

Section 2. Dictée

F. Écoutez et écrivez.

—Tu ___________ chez toi hier?

—Non, je ___________ chez moi.

J'___________ dans un restaurant italien avec ma copine.

—Qu'est-ce que vous ___________?

—Nous ___________ des pizzas.

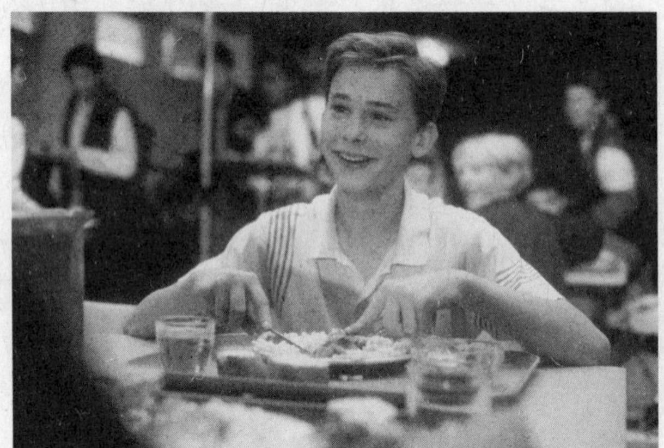

Nom ____

Classe ______________________________ Date ________________

Discovering FRENCH Nouveau!

BLEU

WRITING ACTIVITIES

A 1. Pourquoi?

Read what the following people are doing and then explain why, using **avoir** and one of the expressions in the box.

▶ Alice mange une pizza. Elle a faim.

1. Je mets mon pull. ____________
2. Nous allons à la cafétéria. ____________
3. Tu ouvres *(open)* la fenêtre. ____________
4. Vous achetez des sodas. ____________
5. Robert fait un sandwich. ____________
6. Alice et Juliette vont au café. ____________

faim
soif
chaud
froid

B 2. Vive la différence!

People like to do similar things, but they do them differently. Explain this by completing the sentences below with the appropriate **passé composé** forms of the verbs in parentheses.

1. (visiter)

   À Paris, tu ____________ Notre-Dame. Nous ____________ le musée d'Orsay. Ces touristes ____________ le Centre Pompidou.

2. (manger)

   Au restaurant, j' ____________ des spaghetti. Tu ____________ une pizza. Mes cousins ____________ un steak-frites.

3. (travailler)

   L'été dernier, vous ____________ dans un restaurant.
   J' ____________ dans un hôpital. Alain et Jérôme ____________ dans une station-service.

4. (acheter)

   Au centre commercial, Marie-Christine ____________ une veste. Tu ____________ une casquette. Nous ____________ des lunettes de soleil.

Nom ____

Classe ______________________ Date ______________________

Discovering FRENCH Nouveau!

BLEU

3. Qu'est-ce qu'ils ont fait?

Last Saturday different people did different things. Explain what each one did by completing the sentences with the appropriate **passé composé** forms of the verbs in the box. Be logical.

acheter
assister
ranger
laver
nettoyer
rencontrer
travailler
visiter

1. Ma cousine ____________________ sa chambre.
2. Nous ____________________ à un match de foot.
3. Les touristes ____________________ le musée d'Art Moderne.
4. Pierre et Sébastien ____________________ leur voiture.
5. J' ____________________ mes copains au café.
6. Tu ____________________ ta chambre.
7. Vous ____________________ dans le jardin.
8. Catherine ____________________ des vêtements au centre commercial.

B/C 4. Et toi?

Say whether or not you did the following things last weekend.

1. ____
____

2. ____
____

3. ____
____

4. ____
____

5. ____
____

6. ____
____

C 5. On ne peut pas tout faire. *(One cannot do everything.)*

Say that the people below did the first thing in parentheses but not the second one.

▶ (regarder / étudier)

Hier soir, Jean-Marc a regardé la télé.

Il n'a pas étudié.

1. (travailler / voyager)

   L'été dernier, nous ______________.

   Nous ______________.

2. (rencontrer / assister)

   Samedi, tu ______________ tes copains en ville.

   Tu ______________ au match de foot.

3. (nager / jouer)

   À la plage, vous ______________.

   Vous ______________ au volley.

4. (laver / ranger)

   J' ______________ la voiture de ma mère.

   Je ______________ ma chambre.

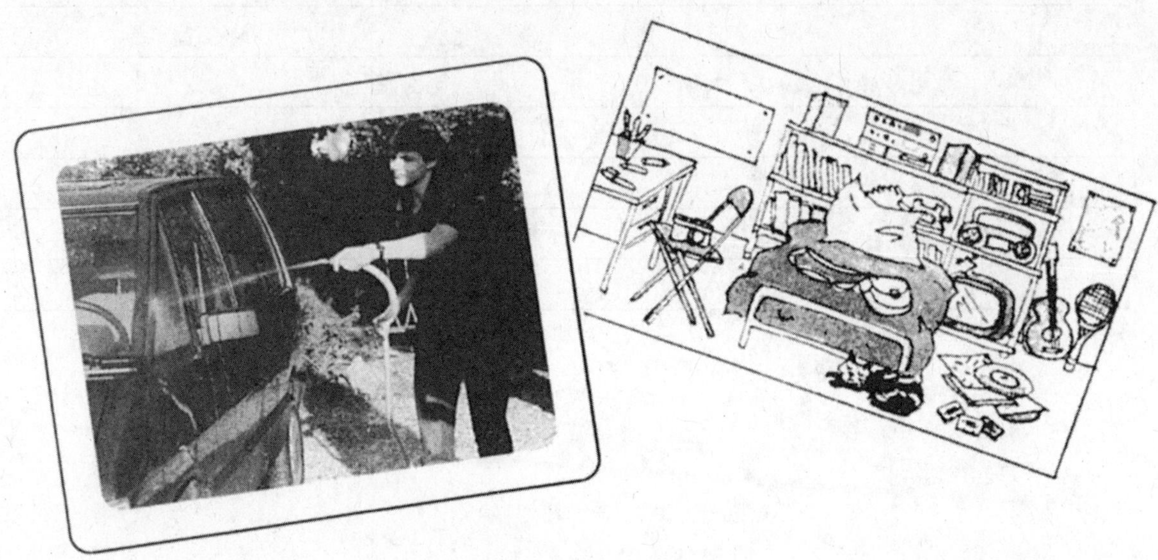

Nom ______________________________

Classe ____________________ Date ____________________

Discovering FRENCH *Nouveau!*

B L E U

D 6. Conversations

Complete each of the following mini-dialogues by writing in the question that was asked.

▶ (où / vous) —*Où est-ce que vous avez dîné* samedi soir?

—Nous avons dîné dans un restaurant vietnamien.

1. (à qui / tu) —______________________________

—J'ai téléphoné à ma cousine.

2. (avec qui / Marc) —______________________________ à la boum?

—Il a dansé avec Caroline.

3. (quand / vous) —______________________________

—Nous avons visité Paris l'été dernier.

4. (où / Alice) —______________________________

—Elle a rencontré Jean-Claude au Café de l'Univers.

7. Communication: Journal personnel *(Personal diary)*

Write a short paragraph in the **passé composé** saying what you did or did not do last weekend. You way want to use the expressions in the box as a guide.

étudier?	**travailler?**	**jouer: à quel sport?**	**téléphoner: à qui?**
inviter: qui?	**dîner: où?**	**regarder: quels programmes?**	**rencontrer: qui?**

____

____

____

____

____

____

____

____

LEÇON 23 L'alibi

LISTENING ACTIVITIES

Section 1. Le passé composé

A. Écoutez et répétez.

choisir → j'ai choisi
finir → j'ai fini

vendre → j'ai vendu
attendre → j'ai attendu

être → j'ai été
avoir → j'ai eu
faire → j'ai fait
mettre → j'ai mis
voir → j'ai vu

B. Compréhension orale

a. ____

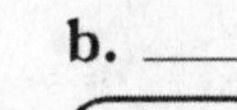

b. ____

c. ____

d. ____

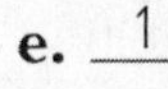

e. __1__

f. ____

g. ____

Nom ______________________________

Classe ____________________ Date ____________________

Discovering FRENCH Nouveau!
BLEU

C. Questions et réponses

▶ —Est-ce qu'ils ont perdu ou est-ce qu'ils ont gagné le match?
—Ils ont gagné le match.

D. Compréhension orale

1. Hier Philippe a eu de la chance.	vrai	faux
2. Philippe n'a pas fait ses devoirs.	vrai	faux
3. Philippe a perdu son sac de classe dans l'autobus.	vrai	faux
4. Philippe a fait un match de tennis.	vrai	faux
5. Philippe a gagné son match.	vrai	faux
6. Philippe a fait une promenade à vélo.	vrai	faux
7. Philippe a eu un accident de vélo.	vrai	faux
8. Ce soir, Philippe va aller au concert.	vrai	faux

Nom ____

Classe ______________________ Date ______________

Discovering FRENCH Nouveau!

BLEU

E. Questions et réponses

Modèle: Tu as acheté des CD?
—Oui, j'ai acheté des CD.
(—Non, je n'ai pas acheté de CD.)

1. ____
2. ____
3. ____
4. ____
5. ____
6. ____
7. ____
8. ____
9. ____

Section 2. Dictée

F. Écoutez et écrivez.

—Qu'est-ce que tu __________ le week-end dernier?

—J' ____________ à mes cousins.

—Qu'est-ce que vous __________?

—On __________ au basket et après on __________ un film à le télé.

Nom ____

Classe ___________________________ Date ___________________

Discovering FRENCH Nouveau!

BLEU

WRITING ACTIVITIES

A 1. Panorama

A group of friends in Normandy has gone on a bicycle ride along the cliffs. They have stopped at a turnout to rest and look at the view. Say what each one sees, using the appropriate forms of **voir**.

1. Alice ______________ un petit village.
2. Nous ______________ des bateaux.
3. Julien et Martin ______________ la mer.
4. Tu ______________une belle maison.
5. Je ______________ un car de touristes.
6. Vous ______________ des campeurs.

B 2. Oui ou non?

Read about the following people and say what they did or did not do, using the **passé composé** of the verbs in parentheses, in the affirmative or negative form.

▶ Nous avons bien joué. Nous n'avons pas perdu le match. (perdre)

1. Marc n'est pas patient. Il ______________ ses amis. (attendre)
2. Les élèves ont étudié. Ils ______________ à l'examen. (réussir)
3. J'ai regardé la télé. Je ______________ mes devoirs. (finir)
4. Éric n'écoute pas. Il ______________ la question. (entendre)
5. Anne n'a pas bien joué. Elle ______________ le match. (perdre)
6. Vous êtes végétariens. Vous ______________ le steak-frites. (choisir)
7. Nous faisons beaucoup d'exercices. Nous ______________. (maigrir)
8. Philippe est un bon élève. Il ______________ à la question du prof. (répondre)

C 3. Et toi?

Say whether or not you did the following things yesterday evening.

▶ faire les devoirs? J'ai fait les devoirs. (Je n'ai pas fait les devoirs.)

1. mettre la table? ______________
2. voir un film à la télé? ______________
3. faire une promenade en ville? ______________
4. être au cinéma? ______________
5. avoir un rendez-vous? ______________

Nom ___________________________________

Classe ____________________ Date ____________________

B/C 4. Pauvre Jérôme

Jérôme is not lucky. Describe what happened to him, by completing the following statements with the passé composé of the verbs in parentheses.

1. (vendre) Jérôme ____________ sa moto.
2. (acheter) Il ____________ une voiture.
3. (faire) Il ____________ une promenade à la campagne.
4. (ne pas mettre) Il ____________ sa ceinture de sécurité *(seatbelt)*.
5. (ne pas voir) Il ____________ l'arbre *(tree)*.
6. (avoir) Il ____________ un accident.
7. (être) Il ____________ à l'hôpital.
8. (passer) Il ____________ trois jours là-bas.
9. (vendre) Finalement, il ____________ sa nouvelle voiture.

5. Communication

On a separate sheet of paper, describe several things that you did in the past month or so. You may use the following questions as a guide.

- As-tu vu un bon film? (Quel film? Où? Quand?)
- As-tu vu un match intéressant? (Quel match? Où? Avec qui?)
- As-tu eu un rendez-vous? (Avec qui? Où?)
- As-tu fait un voyage? (Où? Quand?)
- As-tu fait une promenade en voiture? (Où? Quand?)

LEÇON 24 Qui a de la chance?

LISTENING ACTIVITIES

Section 1. Le passé composé avec être

A. Écoutez et répétez.

Je suis allé au cinéma.

Tu es allé en ville.

Il est allé au café.

Elle est allée à l'église.

Nous sommes allés en France.

Vous êtes allés à Paris.

Ils sont allés au centre commercial.

Elles sont allées à la piscine

B. Écoutez et parlez.

arriver → Je suis arrivé à dix heures.

rentrer → Je suis rentré chez moi.

rester → Je suis resté dans ma chambre.

venir → Je suis venu avec mon cousin.

Nom ______________________________

Classe ______________________ Date ______________________

C. Compréhension orale

a. ____ b. ____ c. ____ d. ____ e. ____

f. ____ g. ____ h. __1__ i. ____ j. ____

Nom ______________________________

Classe ____________________ Date ____________

Discovering FRENCH Nouveau!

BLEU

D. Questions et réponses

▶ —Où est-ce qu'ils sont allés hier? au club de gymnastique ou au restaurant?
—Ils sont allés au restaurant.

Nom ______________________________

Classe ______________________ Date ______________________

E. Compréhension orale

1. Véronique a passé un bon week-end. vrai faux
2. Véronique est allée dans les magasins. vrai faux
3. Véronique est allée au théâtre. vrai faux
4. Véronique a rencontré son cousin Simon. vrai faux
5. Véronique est rentrée chez elle à minuit. vrai faux
6. Alice est restée chez elle. vrai faux
7. Alice est restée seule (*by herself*). vrai faux
8. Christophe est venu chez Alice. vrai faux

F. Écoutez et parlez.

Modèle: Émilie a acheté des vêtements.
Elle est allée dans une boutique.

au restaurant	**à Paris**
au cinéma	
à la plage	**dans une boutique**
à la piscine	**à la montagne**

Section 2. Dictée

G. Écoutez et écrivez.

—Tu ______________ chez toi samedi?

—Non, je ______________ en ville avec un copain.

—Qu'est-ce que vous ______________?

—Nous ______________ des achats et après nous ______________ dans une pizzeria.

Nom ______________________________

Classe ______________________ Date ______________

Discovering FRENCH Nouveau!

BLEU

WRITING ACTIVITIES

A 1. Où es-tu allé(e)?

Say whether or not you went to the following places in the past ten days. Use complete sentences.

1. au cinéma? ______________________
2. à la bibliothèque? ______________________
3. chez un copain ou une copine? ______________________
4. dans un restaurant mexicain? ______________________

2. Où sont-ils allés?

Read what the following people did last week and then say where they went, choosing a place from the box. Be logical.

à une boum	à la campagne	au cinéma
dans un restaurant italien	à la mer	dans un magasin

1. Pauline a vu un film. ______________________
2. Alain et Thomas ont fait de la voile. ______________________
3. Marc a acheté une veste. ______________________
4. Stéphanie a dansé. ______________________
5. Mes cousins ont fait une promenade à pied. ______________________
6. Mélanie et sa soeur ont mangé une pizza. ______________________

Nom ______________________________

Classe ______________________ Date ______________________

3. Voyages

The following people spent a month in France. Describe the things they did during their trip by using the **passé composé** of the verbs in parentheses. Be careful! Some of the verbs are conjugated with **être** and others with **avoir.**

1. Nicolas (arriver / visiter / aller)

   Il ______________________ en France le 2 juillet.

   Il ______________________ Paris.

   Après, il ______________________ à Bordeaux.

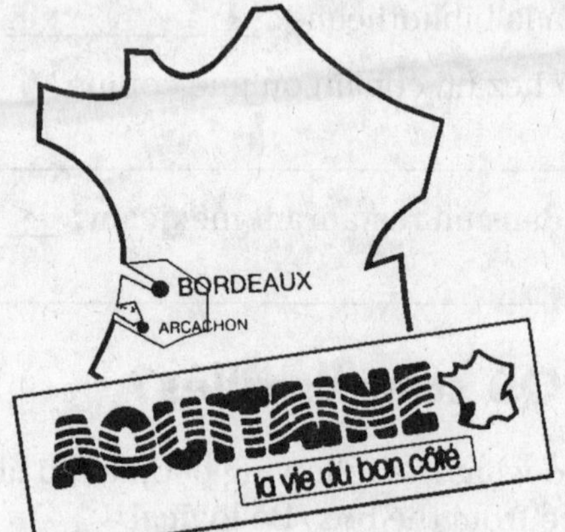

2. Juliette (aller / rester / faire)

   Elle ______________________ à Annecy en juin.

   Elle ______________________ quatre semaines là-bas.

   Elle ______________________ des promenades à la montagne.

3. Philippe et Thomas (aller / rendre visite / rentrer)

   Ils ______________________ à Nice.

   Ils ______________________ à leurs cousins.

   Ils ______________________ chez eux le 15 août.

4. Hélène et Béatrice (venir / rencontrer / voyager)

   Elles ______________________ en France en juillet.

   Elles ______________________ des copains.

   Elles ______________________ avec eux.

Nom _______________________________ **Discovering FRENCH** *Nouveau!*

Classe _______________________ Date _______________

BLEU

B 4. Vive les vacances!

Say that the people below never do the things mentioned in parentheses during their vacations.

▶ (travailler) Monsieur Martin ne travaille jamais pendant les vacances.

1. (travailler) Mes amis _______________.
2. (téléphoner à ses clients) Le docteur Thibault _______________ _______________.
3. (aller à la bibliothèque) Nous _______________.
4. (étudier) Les élèves _______________.
5. (faire les devoirs) Vous _______________.

C 5. Tant pis! *(Too bad!)*

Answer the following questions in the negative.

1. Philippe n'a pas faim. Est-ce qu'il mange quelque chose?
   Non, il _______________.
2. Julien n'est pas très généreux. Est-ce qu'il invite quelqu'un au restaurant?
   Non, il _______________.
3. Christine est fatiguée *(tired)*. Est-ce qu'elle fait quelque chose?
   Non, elle _______________.
4. Olivier est fauché *(broke)*. Est-ce qu'il achète quelque chose?
   Non, il _______________.
5. Alice est très entêtée *(stubborn)*. Est-ce qu'elle écoute quelqu'un?
   Non, elle _______________.

Nom ____________________________________

Classe ______________________ Date ______________

Discovering FRENCH *Nouveau!*

B L E U

6. Communication: Une page de journal *(A diary page)*

Write six sentences describing a recent trip . . . real or imaginary. You may want to answer the following questions—in French, of course!

- Where did you go?
- When did you arrive?
- How long did you stay?
- What/whom did you see?
- What did you visit?
- When did you come home?

Nom ______________________________

Classe ____________________ Date ____________________

Discovering FRENCH Nouveau!

BLEU

UNITÉ 7 Reading and Culture Activities

A. En vacances

1. On peut pratiquer les sports décrits dans cette annonce . . .
   - ❑ à la mer
   - ❑ à la montagne
   - ❑ dans une piscine
   - ❑ dans un stade

SPORTS

CERCLE NAUTIQUE MARTINIQUE

Ski nautique– Planche à voile–
parachute ascentionnel– Voiliers–
Locations Bateaux moteur avec ou sans permis

Tous les jours de 8h à 17h30 – Avant 8h sur R.V
Plage Hôtel Casino BATELIERE
Tél: 05 61 66 03 pour réservation

2. Les gens qui répondent à cette annonce vont . . .
   - ❑ faire une promenade à pied
   - ❑ aller à la campagne
   - ❑ rester dans un hôtel de luxe
   - ❑ faire une visite guidée en autocar

Visiter Montréal dans un autocar de luxe muni d'un toit vitré.

Découvrir Montréal, sa "Joie de vivre" et ses charmes par le service de tours guidés de Gray Line.

Tour de ville : 3 hres ; Adulte : 17$; Enfant : 8,50 $

INFORMATION • RÉSERVATION

(514) 934-1222

3. On peut pratiquer les activités décrites dans cette annonce . . .
   - ❑ à la mer
   - ❑ à la montagne
   - ❑ à la campagne
   - ❑ en ville

Sports

ALPINISME – ESCALADE
RANDONNEES
COMPAGNIE DES GUIDES
DE ST GERVAIS – VAL MONTJOIE

Promenade du Mont Blanc 04 50 78 35 37
Du 15/6 au 30/6 de 15h30 à 19h.
Du 1/07 au 31/08:
de 10h à 12h et de 15h30 à 19h30.
Du 1/09 au 30/09 de 15h30 à 19h30.
Dimanches jours fériés de 16h à 19h30.
Ecole d'escalade de glace – Sorties Collectives – Stages – Randonnées en moyenne montagne.

Nom ______________________________

Classe ____________________ Date ____________________

4. Les touristes intéressés par cette annonce vont . . .
   - ❑ visiter Paris
   - ❑ visiter Rome
   - ❑ voyager en train
   - ❑ faire du camping

45 Rome par avion

Voyage Individuel d'avril à octobre
399 €
Hôtel standard

Départ de Paris le jour de votre choix. Retour à Paris le jour de votre choix (mais pas avant le dimanche suivant le départ).

Prix pour 2 jours à Rome (1 nuit): 399€. comprenant le voyage aérien en classe "vacances" (vols désignés), le logement en chambre double avec bains ou douche, le petit déjeuner.

Suppléments:
Chambre individuelle: 13€ par nuit.
Nuit supplémentaire: 39€ par nuit et par personne en chambre double avec petit déjeuner.
Vol "visite": 50€.

5. Pendant le voyage décrit dans cette annonce, qu'est-ce que les touristes *ne* vont *pas* faire?
   - ❑ Faire une promenade en bateau.
   - ❑ Voir des tulipes.
   - ❑ Visiter Rotterdam.
   - ❑ Voyager en avion.

28 Tulipe Express

Départ vendredi 2 mai
300 €
tout compris sauf boissons

Vendredi 2 mai: Départ de Paris gare du Nord vers 23 h en places assises de 2e classe.
Samedi 3 mai: Arrivée à Rotterdam tôt le matin. Visite du port en bateau. Petit déjeuner à bord. Visite de Rotterdam et promenade à pied dans le centre commerical. Visite de Delft (ville et faïencerie). Déjeuner à La Haye, découverte de la ville. Visite de Madurodam. Dîner à Amsterdam. Logement.
Dimanche 4 mai: Petit déjeuner. Visite d'Amsterdam et promenade en vedette sur les canaux. Déjeuner. Visite des champs de fleurs et de l'exposition florale du Keukenhof. Départ par train en places assises de 2e classe. Dîner libre. Arrivée à Paris-Nord vers 23 h.

Supplément chambre individuelle: 20€.
Supplément couchette à l'aller: se renseigner.

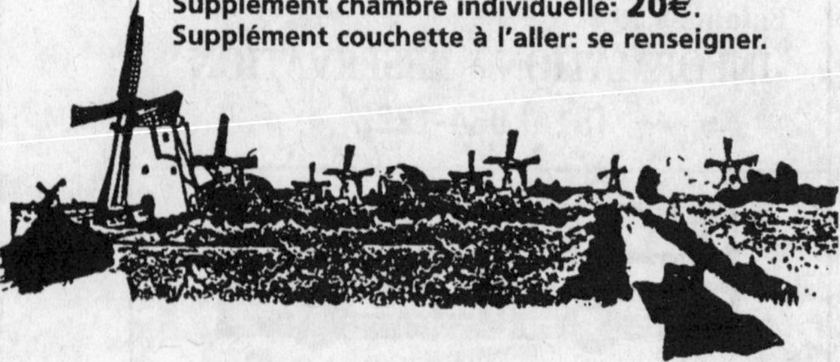

Nom ______________________________

Classe ______________ Date ______________

Discovering FRENCH Nouveau!

BLEU

B. À la télé ce soir

1. En France

20.40

CINÉMA OU TÉLÉVISION : TOUS LES SOIRS, UN FILM

CONAN LE BARBARE ★★★

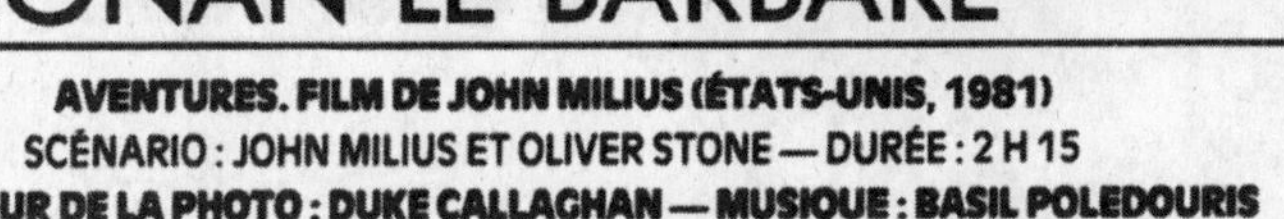
AVENTURES. FILM DE JOHN MILIUS (ÉTATS-UNIS, 1981)
SCÉNARIO : JOHN MILIUS ET OLIVER STONE — DURÉE : 2 H 15
DIRECTEUR DE LA PHOTO : DUKE CALLAGHAN — MUSIQUE : BASIL POLEDOURIS

Fou de ciné

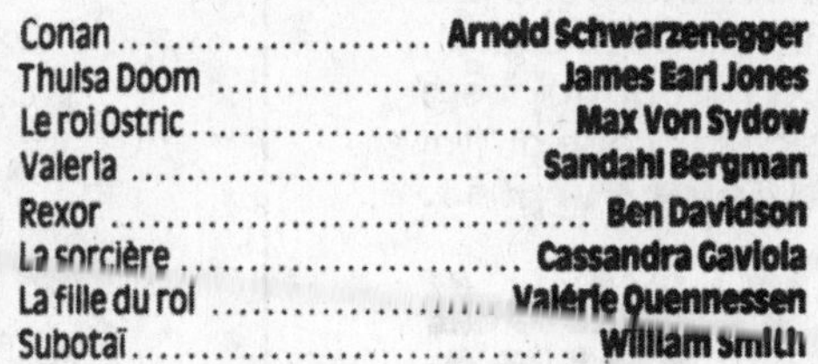
Conan .... **Arnold Schwarzenegger**
Thulsa Doom .... **James Earl Jones**
Le roi Ostric .... **Max Von Sydow**
Valeria .... **Sandahl Bergman**
Rexor .... **Ben Davidson**
La sorcière .... **Cassandra Gaviola**
La fille du roi .... **Valérie Quennessen**
Subotaï .... **William Smith**

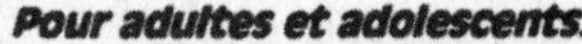
Pour adultes et adolescents.

Conan (Arnold Schwarzenegger) et sa fameuse épée.

- Qu'est-ce qu'on peut voir à la télé ce soir? ______________
- Comment s'appelle le film? ______________
- Qui est l'acteur principal? ______________
- Est-ce que c'est un film américain ou français?
  ____
- À quelle heure est le film? ______________
- Regardez le texte sous la photo. Que veut dire «épée»? ______________

Nom ______________________________

Classe ____________________ Date ____________________

2. Au Canada

- Comment s'appelle ce film en français? ______________________
- Quel est son titre anglais? ______________________
- Qui est l'actrice principale? ______________________
- Quel jour est-ce qu'on peut voir ce film? ______________________
- À quelle heure est le film? ______________________
- Regardez le petit texte.

  Le mot «cheminement» veut dire *path.* Peux-tu deviner *(guess)* l'équivalent anglais des mots suivants?

  l'escalavage= ______________

  la conquête= ______________

  la dignité= ______________

  une vedette= ______________

Nom ______________________________

Classe ______________________ Date ______________

Discovering FRENCH Nouveau!

BLEU

Unité 8. Les repas

LEÇON 25 Le français pratique: Les repas et la nourriture

LISTENING ACTIVITIES

Section 1. La nourriture

A. Compréhension orale

A	B
1. les frites	les spaghetti
2. le jus d'orange	le jus de pomme
3. le fromage	le yaourt
4. le gâteau	la glace

B. Compréhension orale

A

1 

2 

3 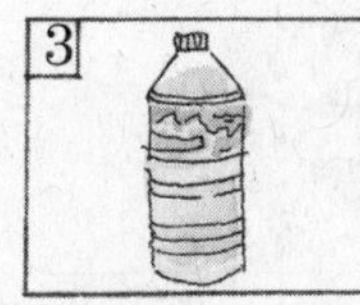

4 

5 

6 

7 

8 

9 

Nom ______________________________

Classe ______________ Date ______________

Discovering FRENCH Nouveau!
BLEU

C. Compréhension orale

	Modèle	1	2	3	4	5	6	7	8
A: viande	✓								
B: lait									

D. Questions et réponses

Modèle: —Qu'est-ce que vous préférez? la soupe ou la salade?
—Je préfère la soupe.
(Je préfère la salade.)

Nom ______________________________

Classe ____________________ Date ______________

Discovering FRENCH Nouveau!

BLEU

Section 2. Les fruits et les légumes

E. Compréhension orale

	Modèle	1	2	3	4	5	6	7	8
A: fruits	✓								
B: légumes									

Section 3. Conversations

F. La réponse logique

1. a. À midi.
   b. À quatre heures.
   c. À sept heures et demie.
2. a. Pour la salade.
   b. Pour le jus d'orange.
   c. Pour le sucre.
3. a. Pour la viande.
   b. Pour le yaourt.
   c. Pour l'eau minérale.
4. a. Oui, j'aime le thon.
   b. Non, je n'aime pas les légumes.
   c. Non, je suis végétarien.
5. a. Non, je préfère la glace.
   b. Oui, j'aime le dessert.
   c. Non, je n'aime pas la glace.
6. a. Oui, donnez-moi des cerises.
   b. Oui, je voudrais des pommes de terre.
   c. Non, je n'aime pas les pommes.

Nom ____

Classe ______________________ Date ______________

BLEU

Secion 4. Dictée

G. Écoutez et écrivez.

—Tu as fait ____________ ce matin?

—Oui, je suis allée au ____________.

—Qu'est-ce que tu as acheté?

—Des ____________ et un ____________.

—Est-ce que tu as acheté des fruits?

—Oui, des ____________ et des ____________.

Nom ____

Classe ______________________ Date ______________________

WRITING ACTIVITIES

A/B/C 1. L'intrus *(The intruder)*

For each of the boxes, the item that does not fit the category is the intruder. Find it and cross it out.

FRUITS
- poire
- fromage
- cerise
- pamplemousse

LÉGUMES
- fraises
- carottes
- haricots verts
- pommes de terre

VIANDE
- veau
- rosbif
- poulet
- frites

DESSERTS
- glace
- gâteau
- jambon
- tarte

BOISSONS
- lait
- confiture
- eau minérale
- thé glacé

PRODUITS LAITIERS *(dairy products)*
- yaourt
- fromage
- lait
- poire

PETIT DÉJEUNER
- pain
- thon
- beurre
- confiture

UN REPAS VÉGÉTARIEN
- riz
- légumes
- salade
- saucisson

DANS LE RÉFRIGÉRATEUR
- serviette
- oeufs
- thé glacé
- beurre

REPAS
- dîner
- nourriture
- petit déjeuner
- déjeuner

Nom ______________________________

Classe ______________ Date ______________

2. Tes préférences

List the foods you like for each of the following courses.

1. Comme hors-d'oeuvre, j'aime ______________________________.
2. Comme viande, j'aime ______________________________.
3. Comme légumes, j'aime ______________________________.
4. Comme fruits, j'aime ______________________________.
5. Comme dessert, j'aime ______________________________.

3. Au menu

Imagine you are working for a French restaurant. Prepare a different menu for each of the following meals.

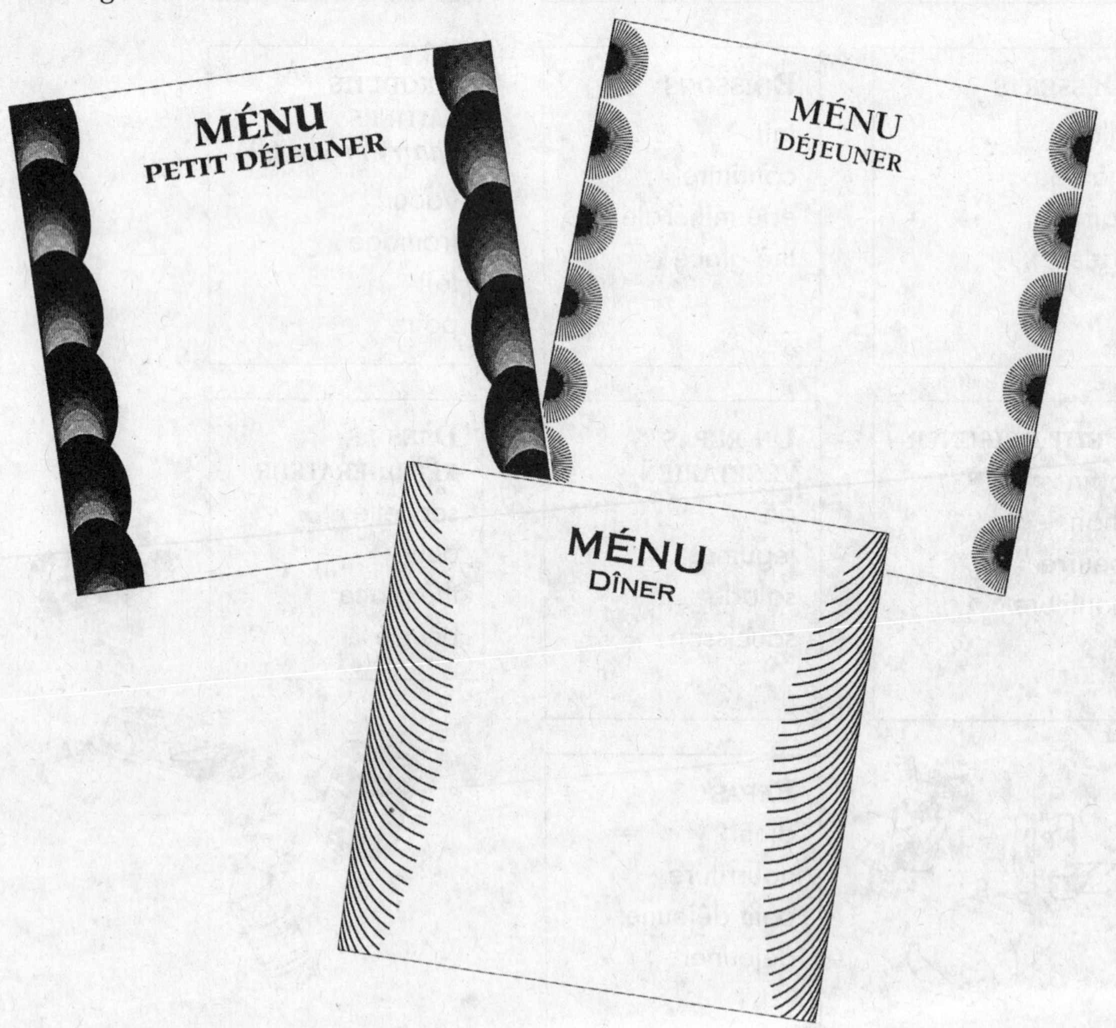

4. Le pique-nique

You have decided to organize a picnic for your French friends. Prepare a shopping list.

Nom ______________________________

Classe ____________________ Date ______________

Discovering FRENCH Nouveau!

BLEU

5. Le mot juste

Complete each of the following sentences with a word from the box. Be logical!

légumes	**livre**	**verre**	**couteau**
courses	**viande**	**cuisine**	**petit déjeuner**

1. Demain, je vais prendre le ________________ à huit heures et quart.
2. J'ai besoin d'un ____________ pour couper *(to cut)* mon steak.
3. Ma soeur a passé l'été au Mexique. Maintenant elle adore la ____________mexicaine.
4. Alice est végétarienne. Elle ne mange jamais de ____________.
5. Voici un ____________ d'eau minérale.
6. Au supermarché j'ai acheté des fruits et des ____________.
7. Nous avons besoin de nourriture. Je vais faire les ____________.
8. S'il vous plaît, donnez-moi une ____________ de cerises.

Nom ______________________________

Classe ____________________ Date ____________________

Discovering FRENCH Nouveau!

BLEU

LEÇON 26 À la cantine

LISTENING ACTIVITIES

Section 1. Vouloir et prendre

A. Écoutez et répétez.

VOULOIR	PRENDRE
Je **veux** un sandwich.	Je **prends** mon livre.
Tu **veux** une pizza.	Tu **prends** ton portable.
Il **veut** une glace.	Il **prend** son baladeur.
Nous **voulons** dîner.	Nous **prenons** le gâteau.
Vous **voulez** déjeuner.	Vous **prenez** vos CD.
Ils **veulent** aller au café.	Ils **prennent** des photos.

Section 2. L'article partitif

B. Écoutez et répétez.

du pain	du beurre	du rosbif
de la salade	de la moutarde	de la glace
de l'eau	de l'eau minérale	

C. Parlez.

Modèle: [le pain] **Je voudrais du pain.**

Nom ______________________________________

Classe ______________________ Date ______________________

Discovering FRENCH Nouveau!

BLEU

D. Compréhension orale

	Modèle	1	2	3	4	5	6	7	8
A:									
B:	✓								

E. Compréhension orale

1. Monsieur Martin et son fils achètent du pain. vrai faux
2. Ils achètent du beurre. vrai faux
3. Ils achètent du yaourt. vrai faux
4. Ils achètent du jambon et du saucisson. vrai faux
5. Ils achètent du poulet. vrai faux
6. Ils prennent du ketchup. vrai faux
7. Ils prennent de l'eau minérale. vrai faux
8. Ils prennent du jus de pomme. vrai faux

F. Compréhension orale

	A	B	C	D
	Mme Aubin	**M. Aubin**	**Nathalie**	**Caroline**
1. du café				
2. du café au lait				
3. du chocolate				
4. du thé nature				
5. du pain				
6. du beurre				
7. de la confiture				
8. du yaourt				
9. des céréales avec du lait				

G. Questions et réponses

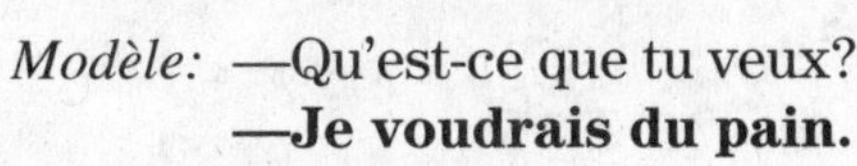

Modèle: —Qu'est-ce que tu veux?
—Je voudrais du pain.

Section 3. L'article partitif au négatif

H. Écoutez et répétez.

Je mange du pain. #	Tu ne manges pas de pain. #
Je veux de la glace. #	Tu ne veux pas de glace. #
Il y a du poulet. #	Il n'y a pas de poulet. #

Nom ____

Classe ______________________________ Date ________________

Discovering FRENCH Nouveau!

BLEU

I. Questions et réponses

Modèle: —Est-ce qu'il y a du pain?

—Non, il n'y a pas de pain.

Section 4. Dictée

J. Écoutez et écrivez.

—Qu'est-ce que vous __________ manger?

—Moi, je vais __________ __________ rosbif et __________ salade. Et toi?

—Moi, je __________ un hamburger avec __________ moutarde et __________ ketchup.

WRITING ACTIVITIES

A 1. Quand on veut . . .

Read about the following people. Then decide whether or not they want to do certain things. Complete the sentences with the appropriate affirmative or negative forms of **vouloir.**

▶ Nous sommes en vacances. Nous ne voulons pas étudier.

1. J'ai envie de voir un film. Je ______________ aller au cinéma.
2. Tu es timide. Tu ______________ parler en public.
3. Mes cousines ont envie de voyager cet été. Elles ______________ aller au Pérou.
4. Olivier est fatigué. Il ______________ aller au concert avec nous.
5. Nous avons faim. Nous ______________ déjeuner.
6. Stéphanie a besoin d'argent. Elle ______________ vendre son vélo.
7. Vous êtes très impatients. Vous ______________ attendre vos copains.
8. Mes petits cousins regardent un film. Ils ______________ aller au lit.

B 2. Quel objet?

In order to do certain activities, people must take along certain things. Write complete sentences to say what people are taking, using the appropriate form of **prendre** and one of the objects in the box. Be logical.

argent **appareil-photo** **livres** **raquette**
maillot de bain **vélo** **calculatrices**

▶ Paul va jouer au tennis. Il prend sa raquette.

1. Caroline va nager. ______________
2. Les élèves vont en classe. ______________
3. Je vais faire des achats. ______________
4. Tu veux prendre des photos. ______________
5. Vous faites une promenade à la campagne. ______________
6. Nous faisons des devoirs de maths. ______________

Nom ______________________

Classe ______________ Date ______________

Discovering FRENCH Nouveau!

B L E U

C 3. «À la bonne auberge»

You are working as a waiter/waitress in a French restaurant named "À la bonne auberge." Explain the menu to your customers. Fill in the blanks with the appropriate partitive articles.

1. Comme hors-d'oeuvre, il y a __________ jambon et __________ soupe.
2. Comme viande, il y a __________ poulet et __________ rosbif.
3. Comme poisson, il y a __________ sole et __________ thon.
4. Après, il y a __________ salade et __________ fromage.
5. Comme dessert, il y a __________ glace et __________ tarte aux fraises.

4. À votre tour

Now it is your turn to be the client. The waiter is offering you the following choices. Tell him what you would like.

▶ soupe ou saucisson? *Je voudrais du saucisson (de la soupe).*

1. poisson ou viande? __________
2. veau ou poulet? __________
3. ketchup ou mayonnaise? __________
4. yaourt ou fromage? __________
5. gâteau ou tarte? __________
6. thé ou café? __________
7. eau minérale ou jus d'orange? __________

5. Les courses

Your brother is going shopping and is making a list. Tell him what to buy.

▶ *Achète du pain.*

1. __________ 5. __________
2. __________ 6. __________
3. __________ 7. __________
4. __________ 8. __________

Nom ______________________

Classe ______________ Date ______________

Discovering FRENCH Nouveau!

BLEU

D 6. Un végétarien

You are under doctor's orders not to eat meat. Imagine you are having lunch at a French restaurant. What will you answer when the waiter offers you the following foods?

▶ (la salade) Oui, je veux bien de la salade.

▶ (le rosbif) Non, merci. Je ne veux pas de rosbif.

1. (la soupe) ______________________
2. (le melon) ______________________
3. (le poulet) ______________________
4. (le jambon) ______________________
5. (le veau) ______________________
6. (la glace) ______________________

7. À la cantine

Look at the various items on Michel's cafeteria tray and answer the questions accordingly.

▶ Est-ce que Michel a pris de la soupe? Non, il n'a pas pris de soupe.

1. Est-ce que Michel a mangé du fromage? ______________________
2. Est-ce qu'il a mangé de la salade? ______________________
3. Est-ce qu'il a mangé de la viande? ______________________
4. Est-ce qu'il a pris de l'eau minérale? ______________________
5. Est-ce qu'il a pris du jambon? ______________________
6. Est-ce qu'il a mangé du pain? ______________________

Nom ____

Classe ______________________ Date ______________________

Discovering FRENCH Nouveau!

B L E U

E 8. À la boum

Say what the guests are drinking at the party. Complete the sentences with the appropriate forms of **boire.**

1. Alain ____________ du thé glacé.
2. Bruno et Guillaume ____________ du soda.
3. Je ____________ du soda, aussi.
4. Tu ____________ de l'eau minérale.
5. Nous ____________ de la limonade.
6. Vous ____________ du jus de fruit.

9. Communication

A. Un repas

In a short paragraph, write about a recent meal (real or imaginary). Use words you know to describe . . .

- where you ate
- what you had for each course
- what you drank

▶ Samedi dernier, j'ai dîné dans un restaurant français.
Comme hors-d'oeuvre, j'ai pris du melon.

B. Le réfrigérateur

Check the contents of your refrigerator. List the names of the items that you know in French. Also list some of the things that are not in your refrigerator.

Dans mon réfrigérateur, il y a ...	Il n'y a pas ...
• du lait	• de jus de raisin
•	•
•	•
•	•
•	•
•	

Nom ______________________________

Classe ____________________ Date ______________

Discovering FRENCH Nouveau!

BLEU

LEÇON 27 Un client difficile

LISTENING ACTIVITIES

Section 1. Les services

A. Compréhension orale

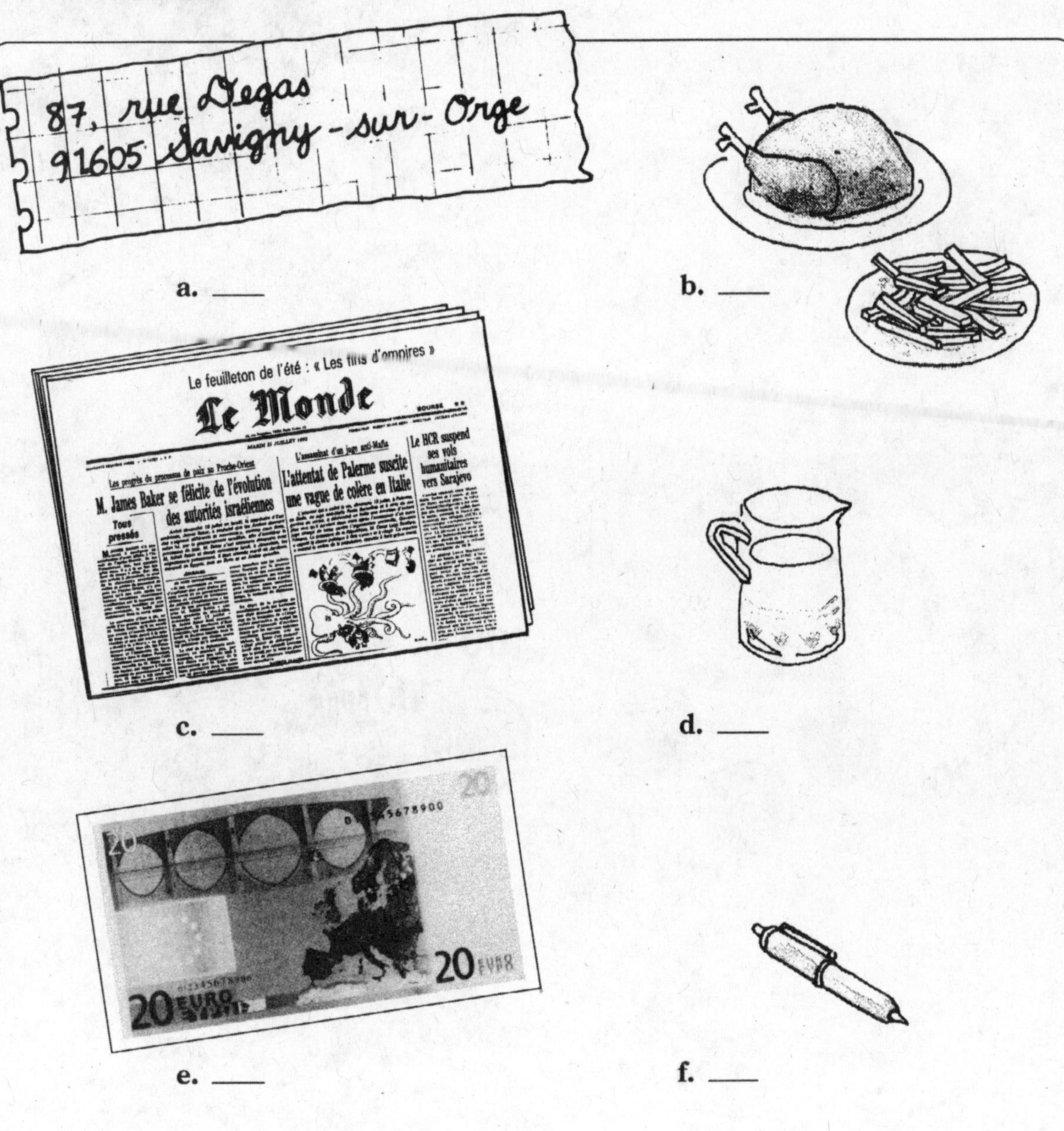

Nom ______________________________

Classe ____________________ Date ____________________

B. Écoutez et parlez.

Modèle: —Tu veux jouer au tennis?
—Oui, prête-moi ta raquette, s'il te plaît.

ton vélo	**ta raquette**	**ton portable**	**ton appareil-photo**
ton baladeur	**cinq euros**	**dix euros**	

Nom ______________________________

Classe ____________________ Date ____________

Discovering FRENCH Nouveau!

BLEU

Section 2. Pouvoir et devoir

C. Écoutez et répétez.

POUVOIR	DEVOIR
Je **peux** venir avec toi.	Je **dois** rentrer avant midi.
Tu **peux** travailler.	Tu **dois** gagner de l'argent.
On **peut** voyager cet été.	On **doit** visiter Genève.
Nous **pouvons** dîner ici.	Nous **devons** regarder le menu.
Vous **pouvez** rester à la maison.	Vous **devez** finir vos devoirs.
Les enfants **peuvent** aider.	Ils **doivent** mettre la table.
Mon père **a pu** maigrir.	Il **a dû** manger moins.

Nom ____

Classe ____________________ Date ____________________

BLEU

Section 3. Dictée

D. Écoutez et écrivez.

—Dis, Stéphanie, j'ai ____________ d'un petit service.

—Qu'est-ce que je ____________ faire pour toi?

—____________ ton scooter, s'il te plaît.

—Je regrette, mais ____________.

Je ____________ aller en ville avec ma copine.

Nous ____________ aller à la bibliothèque.

Nom ______________________

Discovering FRENCH Nouveau!

Classe ______________ Date ______________

BLEU

WRITING ACTIVITIES

A 1. D'accord ou pas d'accord?

Complete the mini-dialogues by answering the questions, using appropriate pronouns. Answer questions 1–3 affirmatively; answer questions 4 and 5 negatively.

1. —Tu m'invites chez toi?

   —D'accord, ______________________.

2. —Tu nous attends après la classe?

   —D'accord, ______________________.

3. —Tu me téléphones ce soir?

   —D'accord, ______________________ après le dîner.

4. —Tu m'attends?

   —Non, ______________________. Je n'ai pas le temps.

5. —Tu nous invites au cinéma?

   —Non, ______________________. Je n'ai pas d'argent.

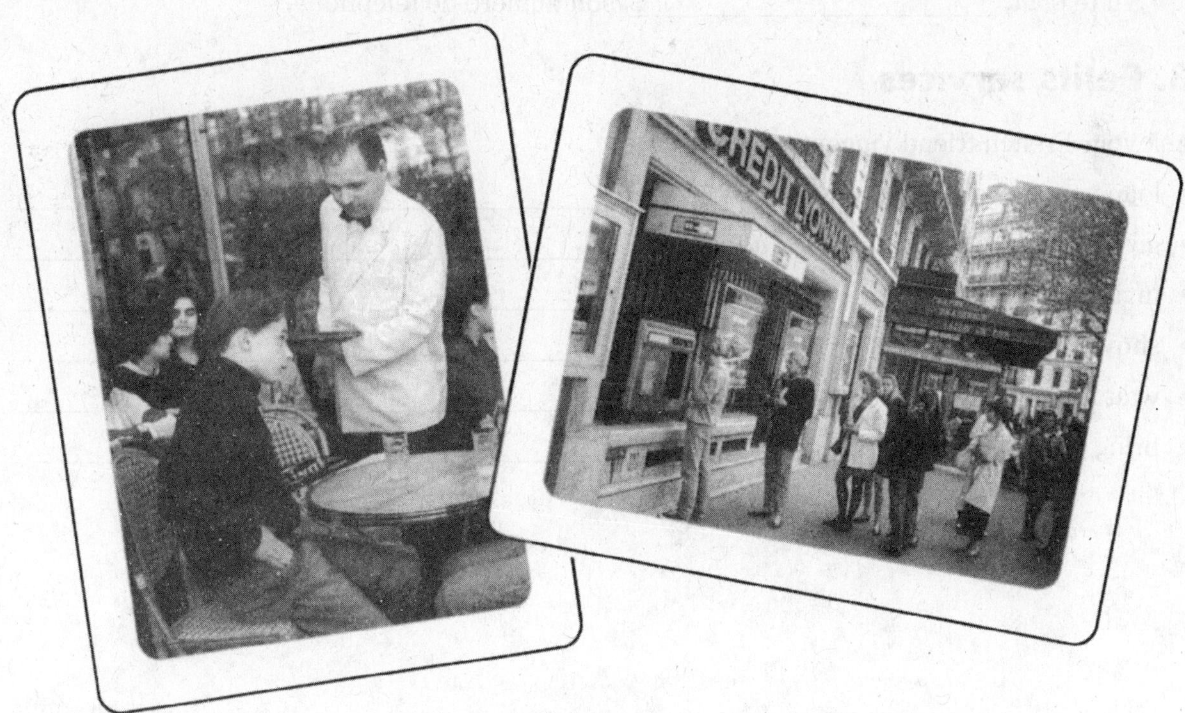

Nom ______________________________

Classe ____________________ Date ____________

Discovering FRENCH Nouveau!

B L E U

B 2. S'il te plaît!

Ask your friends to do certain things for you, using the verbs in parentheses.

▶ J'ai besoin d'argent. (prêter)
S'il te plaît, prête-moi dix euros.

1. Je voudrais réparer mon vélo. (aider)
   S'il te plaît, ____________________.
2. J'ai faim. (donner)
   S'il te plaît, ____________________ un sandwich.
3. Oh là là, j'ai très soif. (apporter)
   S'il te plaît, ____________________ un verre d'eau.
4. Je voudrais prendre des photos. (prêter)
   S'il te plaît, ____________________ ton appareil-photo.
5. Je voudrais téléphoner à ton copain. (donner)
   S'il te plaît, ____________________ son numéro de téléphone.

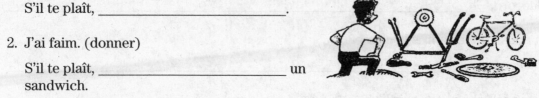

3. Petits services

Ask your French friend Vincent to . . .

- loan you his cell phone ____________________
- give you his cousin's address *(l'adresse)* ____________________
- invite you to his party ____________________
- show you his photos ____________________
- wait for you after the class ____________________
- bring you a sandwich ____________________

C 4. C'est impossible!

The following people cannot do certain things because they have to do other things. Express this by using the appropriate forms of **pouvoir** and **devoir,** as well as your imagination.

▶ Olivier ne peut pas ______________ aller au cinéma.
Il doit étudier (aider sa mère, . . .)

1. Nous ne pouvons pas jouer au basket avec vous.
   Nous ______________________________________.
2. Je ______________ dîner chez toi.
   Je ______________________________________.
3. Véronique et Françoise ______________ venir à la boum.
   Elles ______________________________________.
4. Vous ______________ aller au concert.
   Vous ______________________________________.

5. Jean-Marc ______________ rester avec nous.
   Il ______________________________________.
6. Tu ______________ rencontrer tes copains.
   Tu ______________________________________.

Nom ______________________________

Classe ______________________ Date ______________________

5. Communication: Un bon conseiller *(A good adviser)*

Imagine that you are a newspaper columnist and your readers write you for advice. Here are some of their problems. Write out your advice for each one, using the appropriate present-tense forms of **devoir** or **pouvoir**—and your imagination!

▶ «Je veux voyager cet été, mais je n'ai pas beaucoup d'argent. Qu'est-ce que je peux faire?»
Vous pouvez aller chez des amis à la mer.
Vous pouvez travailler pour gagner de l'argent et pour payer le voyage.

1. «Je n'ai pas de bonnes notes en français. Qu'est-ce que je dois faire?»

____

____

2. «Mon ami et moi, nous voulons faire une surprise à un copain pour son anniversaire. Qu'est-ce que nous pouvons faire?»

____

____

3. «Mes cousins vont en France pendant les vacances. Qu'est-ce qu'ils peuvent faire pendant leur voyage?»

____

____

4. «Avec une copine, nous voulons organiser une boum pour nos amis français. Qu'est-ce que nous devons faire?»

____

____

5. «En ce moment, j'ai des problèmes avec mon copain (ma copine). Qu'est-ce que je dois faire?»

____

____

LEÇON 28 Pique-nique

LISTENING ACTIVITIES

Section 1. Les pronoms le, la, les

A. Compréhension orale

	Modèle	1	2	3	4	5	6	7	8
A. **le**									
B. **la**	✓								
C. **les**									

B. Questions et réponses

Now you will hear a series of questions. Answer each one affirmatively, using the pronouns **le**, **la**, or **les**, as appropriate.

Modèles: —Tu connais Mélanie?
—Oui, je la connais.
—Tu regardes cette photo?
—Oui, je la regarde.

Section 2. Les pronoms lui et leur

C. Compréhension orale

	Modèle	1	2	3	4	5	6
A. **lui**							
B. **leur**	✓						

Nom ____

Classe ______________________ Date ______________________

D. Compréhension orale

1. Jean-Paul et Philippe sont à Deauville.	vrai	faux
2. À la plage, ils voient une fille.	vrai	faux
3. Jean-Paul ne la connaît pas.	vrai	faux
4. Jean-Paul va lui demander quelle heure il est.	vrai	faux
5. Jean-Paul va lui demander si elle est en vacances.	vrai	faux
6. Jean-Paul va l'inviter à aller au cinéma.	vrai	faux
7. Jean-Paul ne lui parle pas.	vrai	faux
8. C'est un nouveau garçon qui parle à la fille.	vrai	faux

E. Questions et réponses

Modèles: —Tu connais tes voisins?
—Oui, je les connais.
—(Non, je ne les connais pas.)
—Tu téléphones à ta cousine?
—Oui, je lui téléphone.
(Non, je ne lui téléphone pas.)

Section 3. Dictée

F. Écoutez et écrivez.

—Qu'est-ce que tu fais?

—J' ____________ à ma cousine.

—Qu'est-ce que tu ____________?

—Je ____________ à la boum samedi prochain.

—Et les voisins, tu ____________ invites aussi?

—Oui, je vais ____________ téléphoner.

WRITING ACTIVITIES

A 1. Connaissances

Complete the sentences below with the appropriate forms of **connaître.** Your answers could be affirmative or negative.

1. Je ______________________ San Francisco.
2. Mes copains ______________________ ma famille.
3. Ma copine ______________________ mes cousins.
4. Ma famille et moi, nous ______________________ bien nos voisins.

B 2. Les photos d'Isabelle

While showing pictures of her friends, Isabelle makes comments about them. Complete her sentences with the appropriate direct object pronouns.

1. Voici Julien.
   Je ____________ connais très bien. Je ____________ rencontre souvent au café. Je ____________ aide avec ses devoirs.

2. Voici Pauline.
   Je ____________ trouve très intelligente. Je ____________ aime beaucoup. Je ____________ vois souvent le week-end.

3. Voici mes cousins.
   Je ____________ vois pendant les vacances. Je ____________ trouve un peu snobs.

4. Voici mes copines.
   Je ____________ trouve très sympathiques. Je ____________ invite souvent chez moi.

Nom ______________________

Classe ______________ Date ______________

3. Correspondance

Jean-François, your French pen pal, has written you a letter asking about your activities. Answer his questions affirmatively or negatively, using direct object pronouns.

▶ Tu regardes la télé? Oui, je la regarde. (Non, je ne la regarde pas.)

1. Tu regardes les matchs de foot? ______________
2. Tu écoutes la radio? ______________
3. Tu écoutes souvent tes CD? ______________
4. Tu prêtes ton portable? ______________
5. Tu prends le bus pour aller à l école? ______________
6. Tu invites souvent tes amis à la maison? ______________
7. Tu aides ta mère? ______________
8. Tu fais les courses? ______________
9. Tu vois tes cousins? ______________
10. Tu connais bien ton professeur de français? ______________

C 4. En colonie de vacances *(At camp)*

You are at a French summer camp. Your roommate is asking whether he/she can do the following things. Answer affirmatively or negatively, according to the way you feel.

▶ Je prends ta raquette? Oui, prends-la.
(Non, ne la prends pas.)

1. Je prends ton appareil-photo? ______________
2. Je mets la radio? ______________
3. Je mets le CD de rap? ______________
4. Je nettoie la chambre? ______________
5. Je fais le lit? ______________
6. Je regarde les photos? ______________

D 5. Les cadeaux *(Presents)*

Imagine that you have bought the following presents. Decide which one you are giving to each of the following people and then write out your choices. If you wish, you may decide on other presents that are not illustrated.

▶ (à mon père) *Je lui donne une cravate* (un livre, etc.).

1. (à ma mère) ______________________
2. (à mes grands-parents) ______________________
3. (à mes cousins) ______________________
4. (au professeur de français) ______________________
5. (à mon meilleur ami) ______________________
6. (à ma meilleure amie) ______________________

6. Les copains d'Hélène

Raphaël wants to know more about Hélène's friends. Complete Hélène's answers with the appropriate pronouns, direct **(le, la, l', les)** or indirect **(lui, leur).**

Raphaël	Hélène
▶ Tu téléphones souvent à Éric?	Oui, je *lui* téléphone assez souvent.
1. Tu connais bien Marthe?	Oui, je ________ connais assez bien.
2. Tu vois Éric et Olivier ce week-end?	Oui, je ________ vois samedi matin.
3. Tu téléphones à Catherine ce soir?	Oui, je ________ téléphone après le dîner.
4. Tu invites Cédric à ta boum?	Bien sûr, je ________ invite. C'est un très bon copain.
5. Tu rends souvent visite à tes copains canadiens?	Oui, je ________ rends visite assez souvent.
6. Tu parles souvent à tes cousins?	Bien sûr, je ________ parle tous les jours *(every day)*.
7. Tu aides ton frère?	Bien sûr. Je ________ aide quand il a un problème.
8. Tu prêtes tes CD à Robert?	En général, oui, je ________ prête mes CD.

Nom ____

Classe ____________________ Date ____________________

Discovering FRENCH Nouveau!

BLEU

E 7. Lettres de vacances

In the summer we like to write to people we know and let them know what we are doing. Complete the following sentences with the appropriate forms of **écrire** and **dire.**

▶ Francis écrit à sa copine.
Il lui dit qu'il veut lui rendre visite.

1. Nous ____________ à nos copains.
   Nous leur ____________ que nous passons des vacances géniales.
2. Caroline ____________ à sa cousine.
   Elle lui ____________ qu'elle a rencontré un garçon très sympathique.
3. Tu ____________ à tes grands-parents.
   Tu leur ____________ qu'il fait beau et que tu apprends à faire de la voile.
4. Vous ____________ au professeur.
   Vous lui ____________ que vous êtes en France.
5. J' ____________ à ma mère.
   Je lui ____________ que j'ai besoin d'argent.
6. Cécile et Mélanie ____________ à leurs parents.
   Elles leur ____________ qu'elles sont très contentes de leurs vacances.

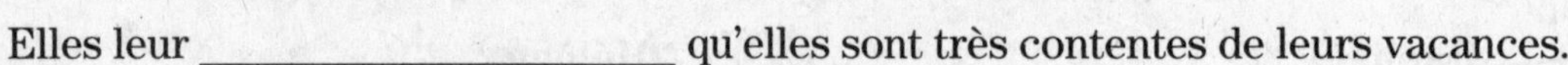

Nom ______________________________

Classe ______________________ Date ______________

Discovering FRENCH Nouveau!

BLEU

8. Communication: Êtes-vous serviable? *(Are you helpful?)*

Are you helpful? Of course you are! Write two things you would do for the following people in the circumstances mentioned below. Be sure to use the appropriate *direct* or *indirect* object pronouns. You may want to select some of the verbs in the box.

acheter	**aider**	*donner*	**écrire**	inviter
parler	**prêter**	*rendre visite*	**téléphoner**	

▶ Ma meilleure amie a un problème avec sa famille.
Je lui téléphone. Je l'aide. (Je lui parle. Je l'invite chez moi.)

1. Mes grands-parents sont malades.
____
2. Ma cousine est à l'hôpital.
____
3. Mes amis ont des problèmes avec la classe de français.
____
4. Mon meilleur copain a besoin d'argent.
____
5. Le professeur est malade.
____
6. Une amie organise une boum et a besoin d'aide.
____

UNITÉ 8 Reading and Culture Activities

A. Dîner en ville

1. Quel plat est-ce qu'on *ne* peut *pas* trouver dans ce restaurant?
   - ❑ Salade de tomates.
   - ❑ Omelette au jambon.
   - ❑ Glace à la vanille.
   - ❑ Yaourt.

2. Qu'est-ce qu'on peut faire dans ce restaurant?
   - ❑ Manger des spaghetti.
   - ❑ Manger de la nourriture chinoise.
   - ❑ Parler japonais.
   - ❑ Écouter de la musique.

3. Quelles sont les spécialités de ce restaurant?
   - ❑ La viande.
   - ❑ Le poisson.
   - ❑ Les fromages.
   - ❑ Les desserts.

4. Qu'est-ce qu'on peut manger dans ce restaurant?
   - ❑ De la cuisine mexicaine.
   - ❑ Des spécialités de la Martinique.
   - ❑ Un bon steak.
   - ❑ Des pizzas.

Spécialités des Iles

LA CREOLE

Le célèbre et renommé restaurant antillais

122, bd du Montparnasse 14e. Rés. 01.43.20.62.12 (Ouvert T.L.J.)

Nom _______________________________

Classe ____________________ Date ____________________

BLEU

B. Vinaigrette

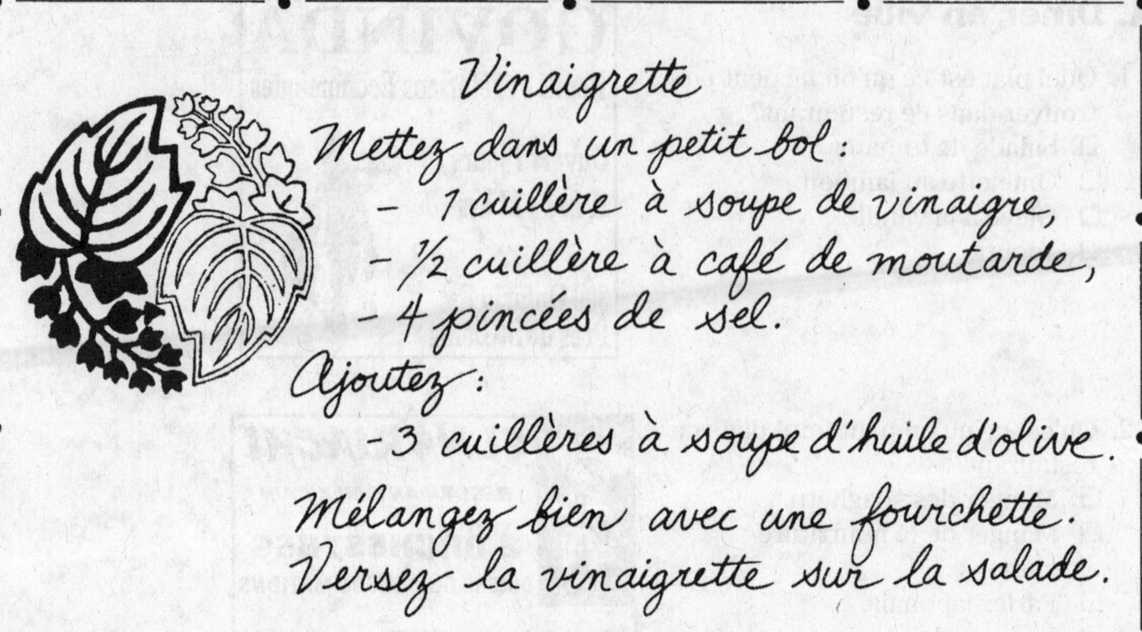

Vinaigrette
Mettez dans un petit bol :
- 1 cuillère à soupe de vinaigre,
- ½ cuillère à café de moutarde,
- 4 pincées de sel.
Ajoutez :
- 3 cuillères à soupe d'huile d'olive.
Mélangez bien avec une fourchette.
Versez la vinaigrette sur la salade.

1. Ce texte est . . .
   - ❑ une recette *(recipe)*
   - ❑ un menu
   - ❑ une liste de courses
   - ❑ la description d'un repas
2. Qu'est-ce que c'est «vinaigrette»?
   - ❑ Un hors-d'oeuvre.
   - ❑ Le nom d'un restaurant.
   - ❑ Une sauce pour la salade.
   - ❑ Le nom d'un magasin.

Nom ______________________ Discovering FRENCH Nouveau!

Classe ______________ Date ______________

BLEU

C. Petit déjeuner dans l'avion

Imaginez que vous allez passer une semaine de vacances en France avec votre famille. Maintenant vous êtes dans l'avion et c'est le moment du petit déjeuner.

Le Petit Déjeuner
sera servi avant l'atterrissage

Choix de Jus de Fruits Frais

Assiette de Fruits Frais de Saison

Choix de Yaourts
Sélection de Céréales

Assortiment de Pains
Danoise aux Graines de Pavot Gâteau aux Pommes
Croissants

Qu'est-ce que vous allez choisir?

- Est-ce que vous prenez un jus de fruits? ______

  Si oui, quel jus de fruits préférez-vous? ______

  Qu'est-ce que vous dites à l'hôtesse?

  ______

- Est-ce que vous voudriez *(would like)* des fruits? ______

  Si oui, quels fruits aimez-vous? ______

  Qu'est-ce que vous dites à l'hôtesse?

  ______

- Est-ce que vous allez prendre un yaourt? ______

  Si oui, quel parfum *(flavor)*? ______

  Qu'est-ce que vous dites à l'hôtesse?

  ______

- Est-ce que vous allez manger des céréales? ______

  Qu'est-ce que vous dites à l'hôtesse?

  ______

- Est-ce que vous allez choisir un pain? ______

  Si oui, quel pain? (Notez: « graines de pavot » = *poppy seeds*)

  ______

  Qu'est-ce que vous dites à l'hôtesse?

  ______

Nom ______________________________

Classe ______________________ Date ______________

Discovering FRENCH Nouveau!

BLEU

D. Les courses

Imaginez que vous êtes en France avec vos parents. Vous venez de faire les courses à La Grande Épicerie de Paris.

Maintenant votre mère, qui ne comprend pas le français, a des questions.

- How much did you spend for the following things?

meat? ______
bread? ______
butter? ______
cheese? ______
fruits and vegetables? ______ + ______ + ______ + ______ = ______

Total = ______

- Is the store open . . .

Monday at 9 A.M.?	yes	no
Tuesday at 9:30 P.M.?	yes	no
Wednesday noon?	yes	no
Thursday at 8 A.M.?	yes	no
Friday at 9:45 P.M.?	yes	no
Saturday morning?	yes	no
Sunday afternoon?	yes	no

* LA GRANDE EPICERIE DE PARIS *
OUVERT DU LUNDI AU SAMEDI

POULET	4,25
PAINS POILANE	2,25
FROMAGE COUPE	3,70
FRUITS ET LEGUMES	1,75
BEURRE CHARENTE/P.	2,50
FRAISE 1L	4,25
FRUITS ET LEGUMES	3,00
CONCOMBRE	50

****

TOT 22,20€
ESPECES 22,20€

26/06/04 11:03 4680 07 0124 138
DE 8H30 A 21H-LUNDI ET VENDREDI 22H
MERCI DE VOTRE VISITE A BIENTOT

E. Aux Deux Magots

Cet été vous avez visité le musée d'Orsay le matin. À midi et demi vous avez déjeuné aux Deux Magots. Regardez bien le menu.

- Regardez le choix de jus de fruits.

  Quel jus de fruit est-ce que vous avez choisi? ______________________

  Combien coûte-t-il? ______________________

- Regardez le choix de sandwichs.

  Quel sandwich avez-vous choisi? ______________________

  Combien est-ce qu'il coûte? ______________________

- Choisissez un dessert: une glace ou un sorbet ou une pâtisserie.

  Qu'est-ce que vous avez choisi? ______________________

  Combien coûte ce dessert? ______________________

- Maintenant faites le total.

  Quel est le prix de votre déjeuner en euros? ______________________

  Combien coûte-t-il en dollars? (Notez: 1 euro = approximativement $.90.)

  ____

DEPUIS 1885
LES DEUX MAGOTS
Café Littéraire
6 PLACE • SAINT GERMAIN DES PRES 75006 PARIS TEL 01. 45 48 5

BOISSONS

Limonade	3,50
Jus de fruit : Ananas, Abricot, Pamplemousse, Orange, Raisin et Jus de tomate	3,50
Eaux minérales (le 1/4) : Evian, Perrier, Vichy, Vittel, Badoit	3,50
Oranges ou citrons pressés	4,25
Lait aromatisé	3,25

LES SANDWICHS

Jambon de Paris	4,00
Jambon de Bayonne	5,00
Saucisson beurre	4,00
Mixte : jambon, Comté	5,00
Fromage Comté ou camembert normand	4,00
Le Croque Monsieur	5,00
La quiche Lorraine	4,75
La salade Deux Magots (salade verte, jambon, poulet, gruyère, tomate, oeuf dur)	7,25
Salade verte	4,25

LES PATISSERIES

Gâteau au chocolat	5,00
Tarte Tatin chaude	5,50
Avec crème fraîche supplément	1,00
Pâtisserie au choix	4,25
Cake	1,50

GLACES ET SORBETS
deux parfums au choix

Café, Vanille, Noisette, Pistache, Rhum raisin, Chocolat	5,00
Cassis, Citron, Fraise, Framboise, Fruits de la passion, Spécial tropic	5,50
Coupe des Deux Magots (glace Vanille, Sorbet et Sirop cassis)	6,00

Contents

Introduction

The twelve trials described in this book read almost like fiction: Socrates was forced to drink poison after he was sentenced to death for his philosophical ideas; Joan of Arc was burned at the stake for her religious beliefs; dozens of bewildered Salem citizens, accused of being witches were hung. With the exceptions of the Lizzie Borden and Nuremberg trials, it is doubtful that any of the defendants described in *Great Trials in History* would be prosecuted today. If any of them *were* brought to trial, new law enforcement technology and enlightened thinking would probably result in totally different verdicts.

Six of the trials described in this book took place in Europe, six in the United States. No two were remotely alike. No matter what the actual charge, it is obvious that some of the defendants were brought to trial for purely political or religious reasons. A few were based on evidence that would be laughed out of court today. But all the trials share a common bond of high drama, and all illustrate the beliefs and opinions, right or wrong, that were strongly held in their day.

For this reason, a sense of history will be gained from reading about the twelve court cases and completing the exercises that follow each one. However, for you to fully enjoy and comprehend these legendary trials, it is important that the vocabulary in each one is studied and mastered in advance. Difficult words have been underlined and should be looked up in the vocabulary section (beginning on page 65) and thoroughly discussed before any script is read for the first time. It is recommended that vocabulary words be used in an oral discussion so that pronunciation and meaning become clear.

There are many other fascinating trials in history. Some of them occurred in the United States during the 20th century—for example, the Lindbergh kidnapping, the Patti Hearst abduction, the Ethel and Julius Rosenberg spy case, the Angela Davis fugitive from justice trial. It is suggested that you visit your school or local library to explore these cases; you may be surprised at some of the turns and twists of our legal system.

The best way to learn about the judicial process is to observe a trial. This can generally be arranged by contacting the Clerk of the Municipal or Superior Court of the county. This person will be able to provide information on times, places, and if local policy permits the public to attend trials in that county.

The Trial of Socrates

Courtesy: San Francisco Public Library

The year was: 399 B.C.

The place was: Athens, Greece

The charge was: Introducing new gods; not worshiping the old gods; corrupting the youth of Athens

The defendant was: Socrates

Background

Socrates is now thought of as one of the greatest of the Greek philosophers. He studied with some of the wisest men of the times before he felt ready to teach his own ideas. He was especially interested in how people's minds worked. His guiding rule was, "Know thyself." He believed that goodness is based on knowledge, and evil is based on ignorance. Socrates felt strongly that no man is really bad. Many young men gathered round him to learn from his wisdom. At that time Athens was a democracy. Its citizens worshipped many gods.

Socrates was born in Athens. His father was a sculptor. He received little education in his youth. For a time he was a sculptor, too. It is thought that he may have worked on some of the finest temples in Athens. Some of these may still be standing today. Later he became a soldier. He fought in a number of important battles and was famous for his fighting skill, courage, and endurance.

As Socrates grew older, he became more and more bold about putting forth his own ideas. These were not always favorable to the government. For this reason many prominent men were worried about his strong influence on the young men of Athens. It was only a question of time until they were able to find a reason to have him arrested. Finally, one day three men came forward and accused Socrates of three things that would not be regarded as crimes today: introducing new gods; not worshiping the old gods; corrupting the youth of Athens.

The Trial

The Athenian courts of justice were very different from courtrooms as we know them today. There were no judges, no prosecutors, no defense lawyers. There was a

jury but it consisted of 501 (or some other large uneven number of men) rather than the 12 jurors used in our present-day legal system. The jurors were paid about nine cents a day. There were other differences, too. Any citizen of Athens could bring an accusation against any other citizen. The accused man would then be tried in a court of law. In the charge, the accuser could name the penalty he wished given to the accused. But if found guilty, the accused was allowed to propose an alternate punishment. If the accuser lost the case, he had to pay all the court costs. And there was one more big difference—all cases had to be completed in one day!

Socrates was now 70 years old. He spoke in his own defense at the trial. To this day the words he spoke are famous. His speech is known as the "Apology of Socrates." In it he tried to explain his views and his humble way of life.

The Verdict

The testimony of the three men convinced the jury that Socrates was a danger to the democratic state of Athens. They found him guilty by a majority of 60 votes. The three men who accused Socrates had asked for the death penalty. Now everyone expected that Socrates would use the rule of asking for an alternate punishment. They felt sure he would ask to be exiled rather than to be put to death. But for Socrates exile would be a disgrace he knew he did not deserve. And life away from his beloved Athens did not seem worthwhile. He preferred death.

Aftermath

The custom in Athenian law was that execution would take place within 24 hours of the guilty verdict. There is an interesting reason why this did not happen with Socrates. Each year a ship was sent to the shrine of the god Apollo at Delos. Until this ship returned, no executions could take place. This year winds caused the ship's delay so Socrates spent a month in prison. Here he was allowed to see friends and admirers. He spent some of his time writing poetry.

At last the ship returned from Delos. On the final day his children and the women of his household came to say goodbye to Socrates and hear his last instructions. When they had gone, Socrates returned to his friends. They all sat quietly, saying very little. The jailer had taken off his chains, which seemed to give Socrates much comfort and pleasure.

A servant standing nearby was sent to get the cup of poisonous hemlock. When he returned with it, Socrates asked for instructions. He was told to walk around after drinking the hemlock until his legs felt heavy, then to lie down and let the poison take effect. After a prayer to the gods, Socrates emptied the cup. His friends broke into tears. Socrates did his best to comfort them. Then he began his last walk around his cell. Soon he felt the heaviness coming on and lay down. From time to time the man who had given him the poison pressed hard on his legs. Socrates said he could not feel anything. Higher and higher the numbness rose until it reached his waist.

His last words were to ask his friend Crito to make an offering to the gods. Crito replied, "It will be done, Socrates. But have you nothing else to say?" There was no answer, for the poison had reached his heart. Socrates was dead.

On a separate sheet of paper list all the underlined words in the story of the trial of Socrates. Find them in the vocabulary section beginning on page 65. Review their meaning and pronunciation. Choose any five and write a sentence for each one.

The Trial of Socrates
FILL IN THE BLANKS

LESSON NO. 1

Circle the word that best completes the sentence.

1. Socrates was a ____________.
   a. musician b. doctor
   c. philosopher d. general

2. Athens was a ____________.
   a. dictatorship b. democracy
   c. republic d. kingdom

3. As a sculptor, Socrates worked on ____________.
   a. temples b. city halls
   c. prisons d. museums

4. As a soldier, Socrates was famous for his ____________.
   a. uniform b. maps
   c. courage d. marksmanship

5. Socrates was very critical of the ____________.
   a. government b. roads
   c. weather d. army

6. In Athens the courts had many ____________.
   a. judges b. prosecutors
   c. jurors d. witnesses

7. In Athens after a guilty verdict, execution had to take place ____________.
   a. in 6 months b. within 24 hours
   c. at once d. in 4 weeks

8. Socrates was accused by ____________.
   a. 4 women b. his wife
   c. his children d. 3 men

9. The jury voted guilty because they believed Socrates was ____________.
   a. insane b. dangerous
   c. lying d. mentally ill

10. His friends hoped Socrates would ask for ____________.
    a. exile b. a new trial
    c. freedom d. a short prison sentence

11. The ship's return from Delos was delayed by ____________.
    a. a mutiny b. strong winds
    c. pirates d. a broken mast

12. During his last days in prison, Socrates wrote ____________.
    a. a novel b. a sermon
    c. poetry d. a short story

13. Socrates was put to death by ____________.
    a. hanging b. drowning
    c. poison d. beheading

The Trial of Socrates
ACTIVITIES

LESSON NO. 2

In Class

1. Socrates said, "Know thyself." What do you think he meant by this? Do you "know yourself"? Write a 75-100 word paragraph on this topic.

   ____

   ____

   ____

   ____

   ____

2. How many adjectives can you think of that might describe Socrates? Try to list at least 10. Select one class member to write all the adjectives on the chalkboard to see which one is listed most often.

   ______________ ______________

   ______________ ______________

   ______________ ______________

   ______________ ______________

   ______________ ______________

At Home

Write 2 paragraphs contrasting trials in the time of Socrates with trials today, including punishment.

OR

Write 2 paragraphs contrasting prisons in the time of Socrates with prisons today, including visiting privileges.

At the Library

1. Find the names of 3 other famous Greek philosophers.
2. We know that Socrates left no written words. Try to find out how we know what he said in the famous "Apology of Socrates."

The Trial of Joan of Arc

The year was: 1431

The place was: Rouen, France

The charge was: Heresy

The defendant was: Joan of Arc

Courtesy: French Government

Background

Joan of Arc (Jeanne d'Arc was her French name) was born in a small French town in 1412. Her brothers and sisters were sent into the fields to work. Joan was kept by her mother's side to help with the household chores. The family was deeply religious. Joan, most of all, was known and loved by people in the village for her kindness, her gentleness, and her holiness.

As she grew older, Joan saw and heard what she believed were visions from heaven. She called the visions her "voices." One of these visions told her to leave home and travel to the court of Charles of France. Although Charles was the king of France, he had not yet been crowned. This was mostly because France and England were at war. The English had won most of the recent battles.

History does not tell us what Charles must have thought when the seventeen-year-old girl insisted that she could lead the French troops to victory. Could he have thought, "Why not? I've nothing more to lose." Whatever his reasons, he gave Joan a full set of armor, a sword, a banner, and a horse, and sent her into battle at the head of the French army. Why did the rough soldiers and officers follow her? Perhaps they, too, felt they had little to lose. Perhaps her courage and enthusiasm impressed and inspired them. At any rate, led by Joan, the French soundly defeated the English, first at the Battle of Orleans and shortly thereafter in four other battles.

These victories meant that Charles VII could finally be crowned king of France. This noteworthy event took place in the Cathedral of Reims in July of 1429. By invitation Joan of Arc stood by the side of Charles VII during his coronation. After the ceremony, she asked to return home, but Charles would not permit it.

At this point Joan's luck seemed to turn. First she was badly wounded. Then she was captured during an attack on Paris. This time the enemy was the Burgundian

army. Although French, the Burgundians at that time had been allies of the English. They were most happy to sell Joan to the English even though a law at that time forbade the sale of prisoners of war.

The English knew exactly what they wanted to do: Get rid of this troublesome girl. Burn her at the stake! They also knew that a trial was necessary if she were to be sentenced to death. A church trial would be the best way to silence critics. While trial plans were underway, Joan was transferred from prison to prison. She finally ended up in a cell at a castle at Rouen. Here she was brutally treated by the guards. Her one consolation was that she still heard her "voices." This was a source of great comfort to her during these painful, difficult days.

The Trial

The English chose an important church official to take charge of trial preparations. His name was Bishop Pierre Cauchon. Cauchon was a greedy, power-hungry man. He was eager to please the English. A number of men of integrity refused to serve at the trial. But there remained plenty of evil, ambitious men willing to follow the wishes of Cauchon. In the end, 117 judges and lawyers were stacked against the lonely young girl. Despite fever and fatigue, Joan was forced to sit on a high, backless stool during the trial.

The questioning lasted more than three weeks. The questions came at her from all directions. There were often several questions at once. Joan answered them all honestly, including questions about her visions. Cauchon then decided that people were beginning to sympathize with Joan in the public trial. So he moved the questioning to her prison cell.

Cauchon had great difficulty getting the guilty verdict he wanted. Meanwhile Joan became seriously ill. This worried the English, who were determined that she die by burning. They were unable to obtain a clear verdict of heresy by honest means, so they finally used a series of tricks. For example, when Joan believed she was signing a paper listing the true facts, they substituted another paper full of untruths which she unwittingly signed. Only by such methods were they able to make it appear that Joan was indeed guilty.

The Verdict

Once she was judged to be guilty, little time was lost. At nine o'clock in the morning Joan was put in a prison cart and taken to the marketplace in Rouen. The square was crowded with soldiers, church officials, and nobles. Joan fell to her knees and prayed. She asked forgiveness for anything she might have done to offend. As she was dragged and tied to the stake, she begged for a crucifix so that she might keep looking at it until the end. Now the executioners lighted the wood in several places. As the first flame touched her, she cried out in terror. Quickly the flames and smoke completely surrounded her. She looked up into the sky and screamed her last word,

"Jesus!" An English soldier claimed he saw a white dove rise from the flames. Some time later that day her ashes were thrown into the River Seine.

Aftermath

In terms of war, it is possible that Joan of Arc did not die in vain. The Burgundians, who may have felt guilty at their part in her death, joined the French. From that point on the English were defeated at almost every turn. Many years later King Charles VII ordered an investigation into Joan's trial and death. The result: It was judged that her trial had been illegal on all counts.

In 1455, after permission had been granted by the Pope, four separate investigations were held. Men who were held in great respect at French universities led these investigations. The results of all four were the same. Joan had been innocent of heresy.

Hundreds of years later on May 9, 1920, Pope Benedict XV declared that Joan of Arc was a saint. The cottage in which she was born still stands in honor of her memory. The spot where the stake stood in the Rouen marketplace is marked by a statue. Paintings, books, plays, all have kept alive the true story of this remarkable young woman whose cause was just but whose death was not.

On a separate sheet of paper list all of the underlined words in the story of the trial of Joan of Arc. Find them in the vocabulary section beginning on page 65. Review their meaning and pronunciation. Choose any five and write a sentence for each one.

The Trial of Joan of Arc

COMPLETE THE SENTENCE

(or use these topics for a class discussion)

LESSON NO. 1

1. Joan of Arc's outstanding qualities were (list at least 3):

   ____

   ____

2. The English were eager to get rid of Joan because:

   ____

   ____

3. The Church officials were eager to get rid of Joan because:

   ____

   ____

4. Joan of Arc did not die in vain because:

   ____

   ____

5. If a seventeen-year-old girl said she could lead American troops into battle in this century, people would:

   ____

   ____

6. (Answer a or b)

   a. If I were on trial, I would prefer the verdict to be reached by a judge because:

   ____

   ____

   b. If I were on trial, I would prefer the verdict to be reached by a jury because:

   ____

   ____

7. People are no longer tried for heresy in the United States because:

   ____

   ____

8. The phrase "innocent until proven guilty" means:

   ____

   ____

The Trial of Joan of Arc
ACTIVITIES

LESSON NO. 2

In Class

1. Pretend that you are one of the prosecutors in Joan of Arc's trial. You are sure that she is guilty of heresy. It is your job to convince the jury (your classmates) of this. Write a short speech explaining why you feel this person is dangerous and should be found guilty and burned at the stake. Read your speech to the class.

   ____

   ____

   ____

   ____

   OR

   Pretend that you are a defense attorney in Joan of Arc's trial. You are sure that she is really innocent. It is your job to convince the jury (your classmates) of this. Write a short speech explaining why you feel Joan is not dangerous and should be set free. Read your speech to the class.

   ____

   ____

   ____

   ____

At Home

Write a 75-100 word paragraph about what might have happened to Joan if Charles VII had allowed her to go home after her victories. Do you think she might have led a normal life, perhaps married and had children? Might she have entered the church as a nun? Let your imagination soar!

At the Library

1. Look up Charles VII of France. Find out how long he was king and any other interesting facts about this man.
2. See if you can find pictures of the kind of armor Joan and her armies wore.

The Trial of Galileo

The year was: 1632

The place was: Rome, Italy

The charge was: Heresy

The defendant was: Galileo Galilei

Courtesy: San Francisco Public Library

Background

Galileo was born in 1564. This was a time when the Church was the most powerful force in Italy. This fact would eventually cause Galileo's death.

Galileo has been called the founder of modern experimental science. His father was a cloth merchant, an educated man of many abilities. He was especially talented in music. He taught his son to play the flute and the organ. As a child, Galileo sketched and painted well. He also liked to design and build toys.

His first teachers were monks. As a result of their teaching, Galileo was deeply religious all of his life. His father saw how easily and quickly his son learned. He decided Galileo should study medicine. At the University of Pisa, Galileo studied the works of Aristotle, who had lived many centuries earlier. Aristotle was the recognized authority on many sciences. At this time Church officials accepted his views on all scientific matters. However, Galileo began to point out errors in Aristotle's works. Because people distrusted anyone who did not believe the word of Aristotle, Galileo was forced to leave the university.

The next year he accepted a teaching post at the University of Padua. He was still a young man, but he had already become famous as an experimental physicist. In the early years at Padua, he began making a reputation in astronomy, too. Many people think Galileo invented the telescope. He did not. But he was the first to improve and make practical use of it.

As he studied the heavens, Galileo became more and more interested in the theories of Nicolaus Copernicus. Copernicus was a Polish scientist. He believed that the earth revolved around the sun. This was a revolutionary idea. At that time churchmen and other followers of Aristotle believed that the earth was the center of the universe. They were convinced that the sun revolved around the earth. Copernicus had been a quiet,

cautious man. He knew the dangers of opposing the Church. His theories were not published until after his death. Galileo, on the other hand, was reckless. He tried to convince the Church that he and Copernicus were right. As time went on, high Church officials grew angrier and angrier.

During one of his first summers at Padua, Galileo and two other young men spent a few days at the country home of a friend. This man had dug a tunnel from a nearby cavern to his house. It was designed to serve as a primitive air conditioner. One hot day the three guests took a nap by the door of the tunnel. When they awoke they were racked with pain and fever. One died. Galileo got better but suffered from arthritis for the rest of his life.

It was about this time that Galileo made one of his most important discoveries: the planet Jupiter had four moons. (We now know that Jupiter has twelve moons, but Galileo's telescope was not strong enough to see them all.) This discovery made Galileo even more famous. It also brought him extreme abuse from the Church. In an effort to help, the Grand Duke of Tuscany became Galileo's protector. He invited Galileo to become his personal mathematician and philosopher at Florence, Italy. Galileo was happy to accept the royal invitation.

The next year he visited Rome. Here he was given an audience by Pope Paul V. Even though this visit seemed to be a success, Galileo's work and his books were again attacked. Eventually, he was summoned before the Inquisition. It is important to understand that the Roman Inquisition was a kind of court. It was made up of men who were important Church officials. It was their duty to find and try heretics. Even to be called before the Inquisition meant one had already been found guilty of heresy. The minimum penalty was disgrace; the maximum penalty was death.

The Trial

It was the rule of the Inquisition that defendants be kept in solitary confinement during their trials. Because of his age and illness, Galileo was not put in a dungeon but was given several comfortable rooms. Friends sent cakes, cold meats, fruit, and wine.

The Inquisition moved slowly. Galileo was questioned day after day for weeks, then months. Gradually he became more tired, more ill. At first he held fast to the ideas he had set forth in his writings. But gradually the old man began to weaken. Finally he was forced to announce that his findings in astronomy were false. How difficult this must have been for the man who has been called the father of experimental science!

The Verdict

Galileo was found guilty and sentenced to an indefinite term in prison. Perhaps because of his age and ill health, he was not put in prison. Instead he was confined to his home in Florence for the rest of his life.

Aftermath

Galileo dedicated his later years to writing on the laws of force and motion. His last book in 1636 gave Isaac Newton his basis for the three laws of motion almost fifty years later.

Galileo was blind during the final years of his life. Yet he was still constantly watched by guards from the Inquisition in his own home. He died in 1642. His trial conducted by the Roman Inquisition seems unfair to us. Yet it was fair by the standards of the times. It is interesting to note that the verdict of guilty remained on the records until 1885 when it was quietly reversed.

On a separate sheet of paper list all of the underlined words in the story of the trial of Galileo. Find them in the vocabulary section beginning on page 65. Review their meaning and pronunciation. Choose any five and write a sentence for each one.

The Trial of Galileo
FACT OR OPINION

LESSON NO. 1

A fact is very different from an opinion but sometimes we confuse the two. A fact is something that really happened, that is true, that can be proved.

Example: Washington, D.C. is the capital of our country.

An opinion is a belief or feeling that is not necessarily based on truth or proof.

Example: Dogs make better pets than cats.

Some of the statements below are facts and some are opinions. Write an F in front of the facts. Write an O in front of the opinions. You may refer back to the script on Galileo's trial if you wish.

1. ______ Monks were very good teachers.
2. ______ Galileo made several improvements to the telescope.
3. ______ Copernicus was a Polish scientist.
4. ______ Arthritis can be caused by sleeping in a draft.
5. ______ Physics is a difficult subject for everyone.
6. ______ Galileo's life proved that a scientist can also be religious.
7. ______ Pope Paul V gave an audience to Galileo.
8. ______ The Inquisition was made up of Church officials.
9. ______ Aristotle was wiser than Galileo.
10. ______ The earth revolves around the sun.
11. ______ Someone who is good in mathematics is always good in music.
12. ______ Isaac Newton developed the three laws of motion.

The Trial of Galileo
ACTIVITIES

LESSON NO. 2

In Class

1. Pretend that you are a television commentator. You are going to have to describe the trial of Galileo to the TV audience on the evening news. Be sure to include some important background information on Galileo's life.

____
____
____
____
____
____

2. When we use the word "trial," we generally think of a court of law. But the word has several other meanings. Find at least two other definitions in the dictionary. Write them down and then create a sentence using each one correctly.

____
____
____
____
____
____

At Home

Galileo was both an astronomer and a physicist. Describe the differences between the two. Which would you rather be? Why? Is there another science that interests you more? Which one? Why?

At the Library

1. Learn all you can about Jupiter, its 12 moons, and other characteristics, including how far it is from Earth.
2. Try to find out who actually invented the telescope that Galileo improved.

The Salem Witchcraft Trials

The year was: 1692

The place was: Salem, Massachusetts

The charge was: Witchcraft

The defendants were: Tituba, Sarah Good, Sarah Osborn, and approximately 200 other Massachusetts men and women

Courtesy: San Francisco Public Library

Background

It seems hard to believe that there was ever a time in our country when people believed in witchcraft. A time when they were so terrified that men and women accused of witchcraft were jailed or put to death.

In 1692 Salem was a gloomy town. The Puritans who lived there were deeply religious. They had fled persecution and suffering in England and other countries of Europe. Yet life was not always better in the new land. Their town was surrounded by a dark forest. Heavy taxation kept them poor. Pirates still raided coastal towns and villages. They had no luxuries and little fun. Their church was the center of their lives. And they strongly believed in the Devil. It was the Devil, they felt, who caused all the sin and mischief in the world.

It all began quite innocently in the Salem household of Sam Parris. Parris had a West Indian servant named Tituba. Tituba had brought many superstitions from her native land. When a group of Salem teenagers learned of this, they begged Tituba to teach them to tell fortunes, to read palms, and to work other forms of magic. After a while the group grew to ten girls: Elizabeth Parris and Abigail Williams (daughter and niece of Sam Parris), Ann Putnam, Mary Walcott, Mercy Lewis, Elizabeth Hubbard, Elizabeth Booth, Susannah Sheldon, Mary Warren, and Sarah Churchill. The youngest was eleven years old; the oldest was twenty.

At first it was just fun, a kind of entertainment for a group of girls who had little pleasure in their daily lives. But gradually the game grew more serious. The girls began to show off before others in the town. They threw themselves on the ground and moaned and groaned. They pretended to faint, to be possessed by the Devil. They screamed as if they were being tortured. Soon all of Salem was aware of their strange behavior. The village doctor was called. Dr. Grigg's medical knowledge was sadly limited. His diagnosis: The ten girls were bewitched!

Alarm spread throughout Salem. The more attention paid the girls, the worse they

got. They upset church services. They pretended to see "a yellow bird sitting on the minister's hat." Even the minister agreed that the Devil was the cause of the girls' strange behavior.

It is important to understand that at that time the Puritans believed that the Devil could not work directly on his victims but had to do so through witches. The girls were then pressured to name these agents of the Devil. At first they were reluctant to do so. Finally one after another named three Salem women: Tituba, the Parris servant; Sarah Good, a desperately poor woman who, with her children, was often homeless; and Sarah Osborn, who was not well thought of in Salem because she did not attend church regularly. All three of these women were unprotected and vulnerable. On February 29, 1692, warrants were issued for their arrest.

The Trial

In terms of the laws of our land as we now know them, the trials were a mockery of justice. None of the defendants had a defense attorney. The accused women were questioned day after day by well-known Massachusetts men. Among these was Cotton Mather, a highly respected minister from Boston. Sometimes the poor confused women even accused one another. This further complicated the situation. Now and then, if an accused began to sound innocent, one or more of the girls would put on their usual act. They would scream loudly in the courtroom and then pretend that the woman was still tormenting them.

The following is a short portion of the examination of Sarah Good by magistrates John Hathorne and Jonathan Corwin:

> *Sarah Good, what evil spirit are you familiar with?*
> *None.*
> *Have you made contracts with the Devil?*
> *No.*
> *Why do you hurt these girls?*
> *I do not hurt them. I scorn it.*
> *Then what creature do you employ to do it?*
> *I employ nobody.*
> *Sarah Good, do you not see now what you have done? Why do you not tell the truth? Why do you torment these poor girls?*
> *I do not torment them. I do not.*

The Verdicts

All three women were found guilty. And this was just the beginning of the madness. By the end of the year, 20 persons, including Sarah Good, would be tried, found guilty, and hanged for the crime of witchcraft. It is interesting to note that those who admitted they had been witches but had repented for their pact with the Devil were never hanged. (Tituba was one of these.) It was those poor victims who insisted

that they were innocent who received the death penalty. Also, by this time, a number of men had been accused of being wizards, found guilty, and suffered the same fate as the women.

Aftermath

By late September, 1692, a change was beginning to take place in the New England colonies. Prominent men of good reputation, including many ministers, were beginning to doubt that the ten girls were telling the truth. On September 22, 1692, the final executions took place when six women and two men were hanged. Within weeks the Governor of Massachusetts dismissed the special court that had been convened for the witchcraft trials.

It was the custom in those days to require prisoners to pay their own costs for food and other services. Those jailed for witchcraft who could pay were released. The rest had to remain in jail indefinitely.

To complete the witchcraft trials of people who had been accused but not yet tried, a travelling court was formed. It heard 52 cases in January of 1693. All 52 were eventually set free. Never again was a witch condemned to death in this country.

And so at a time when the American colonies did not yet have a Constitution stating that "all men are innocent until proven guilty," when trial by jury was not yet the law of the land, the Salem witchcraft trials finally ended. They will always stand as a prime example of rule by mob and how unfounded charges fueled by mass hysteria, gossip, fear, and hatred can result in terrible injustice.

On a separate sheet of paper list all of the underlined words in the story of the Salem witchcraft trials. Find them in the vocabulary section beginning on page 65. Review their meaning and pronunciation. Choose any five and write a sentence for each one.

The Salem Witchcraft Trials
PUT FACTS IN ORDER

LESSON NO. 1

The following is a list of events that took place during the Salem witchcraft trials but they are out of order. Number the events so that they are in the correct order.

______ Tituba, Sarah Good, and Sarah Osborn are found guilty.

______ A group of Salem teenagers ask the servant Tituba to teach them to tell fortunes and other kinds of magic.

______ Sarah Good is hanged.

______ The Salem teenagers use Tituba's magic as fun and entertainment.

______ The minister Cotton Mather takes part in the trial of the three Salem women.

______ The Salem teenagers begin to act as if they are possessed by the Devil.

______ People begin to doubt that the girls are telling the truth.

______ Dr. Griggs states that the girls are bewitched.

______ Tituba says she is sorry and is set free.

______ The last 52 people accused of witchcraft all go free.

______ The Governor of Massachusetts dismisses the special court.

______ Tituba, Sarah Good, and Sarah Osborn are arrested as witches.

The Salem Witchcraft Trials
ACTIVITIES

LESSON NO. 2

In Class

1. Pretend that you are the parent of one of the Salem teenagers who is acting as if she is bewitched. At first you believed her but now you are beginning to think she may be faking. List 3 things you might do to find out the truth.

   ____
   ____
   ____

2. Pretend that you are one of the Salem teenagers who had been acting as if you were bewitched. Now that Tituba and the others have been arrested, you think the game has gone too far. Write a note to your parents confessing your part in the witchhunt and asking their advice about how to stop it.

   ____
   ____
   ____
   ____
   ____

At Home

Pretend that you are a good friend of one of the men or women in prison awaiting trial for witchcraft. You are sure they need someone to take care of their children, feed their animals, bring in their harvest, etc. Write him or her a letter asking what you can do to help.

At the Library

1. Find a book on superstitions. Try to list at least six. Example: A black cat crossing your path means bad luck.
2. Look up present-day Salem. Describe what kind of town or city it is now, including size of population, industries, etc.

The Trial of Peter Zenger

The year was: 1735

The place was: New York City

The charge was: Libel

The defendant was: Peter Zenger

Background

Courtesy: San Francisco Public Library

Peter Zenger's parents were German refugees who came to this country in 1710. Peter was quickly apprenticed to a New York printer, William Bradford. At that time apprentices were bound by a legal agreement. The agreement provided that Peter had to work in Bradford's print shop for eight years. He received no pay but he did learn the printing trade.

The eight years passed slowly but Zenger learned a lot. He was twenty when he completed the long apprenticeship. He moved to Maryland, married, and opened his own print shop. After his wife died, he returned to New York with his young son. There he went back to work for William Bradford. He was first a journeyman printer, later a partner. Soon after his return to New York, Zenger married again. His wife, Anna Zenger, was an unusually intelligent woman. She not only kept house but helped in the print shop as well.

A year later Zenger left Bradford to set up his own print shop. At this time many of the New York colonists were violently opposed to the governor. Governor Cosby had been appointed by the English king. Even though at that time the people were still loyal to the king, they were not happy with the man he had sent to govern the colony. He was a greedy, dishonest man who inspired little loyalty from the citizens of New York. A group of men felt it was time to let everyone know about the governor's corrupt practices. They asked Peter Zenger to start a newspaper. Shortly afterwards the *New York Weekly Journal* was born. The agreement was that the New Yorkers would write the articles if Zenger would print and distribute them. Needless to say, the *New York Weekly Journal* with its many essays, poems, and cartoons that criticized and made fun of Governor Cosby was not popular with the governor and his followers.

Zenger was not the author of the articles that were printed in his newspaper. But he was the editor, so he was held responsible for them. The angry governor started a

rival newspaper, *The Gazette*. It did him no good. Everyone continued to read the *New York Weekly Journal*. It became more and more popular, mostly because the people agreed with the articles in it. After about a year, the governor could stand it no longer. Zenger was charged with libel and thrown into jail. At first he was not allowed to see his wife, friends, or lawyers. He complained bitterly. Finally he was permitted to talk with visitors through a small opening in his cell door. During these unhappy days his wife and son continued publishing the *Journal*. Friends wrote the articles for it.

The Trial

Days were long, and time passed slowly. It was almost nine months later that Peter Zenger was finally brought to trial. Everyone was sure he would lose. Through legal trickery his lawyers were prevented from representing him in court. Things looked dark indeed. The case was coming to an end when Alexander Hamilton stood up in the courtroom and offered to defend Zenger. Hamilton was the most outstanding lawyer in all the Colonies. He was known and respected by everyone.

Now the case changed. Hamilton put forth a new and interesting defense. He freely admitted that Zenger had printed certain things in his newspaper. But, Hamilton said, if these facts were true, they could not be called libel. Only when *false* statements were printed could they be called libel. Therefore, Hamilton said that it was up to the prosecution to prove that the facts printed in the *New York Weekly Journal* were false. The prosecuting attorney refused to do so. From a simple case of libel, Alexander Hamilton changed the trial of Peter Zenger into a defense of the rights of free men everywhere.

The Verdict

The jury left the courtroom and returned only ten minutes later. It must have been a long ten minutes for Peter Zenger, his family, and his friends. Finally the foreman announced the verdict: "Not guilty."

Aftermath

In this period of our history, prisoners still had to pay for their food and other expenses. They were even charged a set amount for each day and each night they were kept in prison. Peter Zenger had been in custody eight and a half months, so he owed a lot of money. Although he was technically free, he had to remain in his cell until the next day. Then his friends arrived. They had been able to collect enough money to pay his bill at the prison.

Zenger returned to his shop and continued to print criticism of Governor Cosby's dishonest administration. Eventually Cosby died and was replaced by a more liberal governor. This came as a great relief to the colonists. Zenger was made public printer

of New York and later for New Jersey as well. After his death his wife and then his son carried on the business.

Alexander Hamilton's defense of Peter Zenger became known throughout the American colonies. It has remained a landmark in American history. From that day on, no governor of any colony tried to suppress the contents of a newspaper. Peter Zenger has come to be known as the founder of freedom of the press, one of the most important features of our American democracy. Today all of us in the United States who enjoy freedom in the media owe a great debt to Alexander Hamilton and to Peter Zenger.

On a separate sheet of paper list all of the underlined words in the story of the trial of Peter Zenger. Find them in the vocabulary section beginning on page 65. Review their meaning and pronunciation. Choose any five and write a sentence for each one.

The Trial of Peter Zenger
IN OTHER WORDS

LESSON NO. 1

Here are 12 words that appear in *The Trial of Peter Zenger.* The object of the assignment is to find words of 1, 2, 3, 4, or more letters by using letters from each clue word IN THE SAME ORDER IN WHICH THEY APPEAR IN THE WORD.

Example: apprentice = ape (This goes in the 5 point column.)
apprentice = rent (This goes in the 10 point column.)
apprentice = tie (This goes in the 15 point column.)

A perfect score is 360. Remember! You cannot change the order of the letters in the clue word.

Clue Word	5 Points	10 Points	15 Points
apprentice	ape	rent	tie
journeyman			
representing			
prosecution			
custody			
administration			
landmark			
corrupt			
technically			
refugees			
intelligent			
distribute			
Total Points			

GRAND TOTAL ________________

The Trial of Peter Zenger

ACTIVITIES

LESSON NO. 2

In Class

1. Many people confuse the two words **libel** and **slander**. They do not mean the same thing. Find their definitions in the dictionary. Then try to compare them using both words in a sentence.

   ____
   ____
   ____
   ____

2. Write a letter to the King of England. You are angry about Governor Cosby. Ask that he be replaced. Also, tell the king that Peter Zenger is innocent and should be set free at once.

   ____
   ____
   ____
   ____
   ____

At Home

Pretend that Anna Zenger has asked you to write an account of Peter's trial for the *New York Weekly Journal*, the newspaper that Anna is trying to keep publishing while Peter is in jail. See if you can give just the highlights in 75/100 words.

At the Library

1. There are many interesting facts about the statesman Alexander Hamilton in addition to his defense of Peter Zenger. List at least four things for which he is well known, including the manner in which he died.
2. Johann Gutenberg (1397-1468) changed the world of printing. What did he do? Answer in 50 words or less.

The Impeachment Trial of Andrew Johnson

The year was: 1868

The place was: Washington, D.C.

The charge was: High crimes and misdemeanors in office

The defendant was: Andrew Johnson

Courtesy: San Francisco Public Library

Background

Vice President Andrew Johnson became President of the United States when Abraham Lincoln was assassinated. He had to deal with some of the most difficult problems ever faced by an American President. Although the Civil War was over, a huge question remained: How to bring the Southern states that had seceded back into the Union.

Andrew Johnson was born at Raleigh, North Carolina. The Johnson family was so poor, his parents could not afford to send Andrew to school. When he was 14, he was apprenticed to a tailor. Apprentices were supposed to serve six years. In those days the life of an apprentice was usually very hard. Long hours, little or no pay, poor food, a hard cot on which to sleep. Legend has it that the shop foreman taught Andrew to read while the boy was an apprentice. After two years he ran away. Several years later he opened his own tailor shop in Tennessee. He married Eliza McCardle, an intelligent, educated woman. It was she who taught Andrew to write and do simple arithmetic. She also encouraged him to read and study.

Johnson's first political office in Tennessee was alderman of the town of Greenville. Next he became mayor and then a member of the Tennessee House of Representatives. During these years his reputation as a powerful speaker grew. In 1843 he was elected to the United States House of Representatives. Ten years later he became governor of Tennessee. In 1857 he was back in Washington as a United States Senator. He was the only member of Congress who refused to secede with his southern state. This may have been one reason Lincoln, a Republican, chose Johnson, a Democrat, to run with him in 1864. It was only six weeks after the inauguration that Lincoln was assassinated, and Johnson took office as President.

His troubles with Congress began almost immediately. Many Congressmen felt that the South should be punished. Southern states should be allowed back into the

Union only on harsh terms dictated by Congress. Johnson did not agree. Congress pushed through a whole series of bills which Johnson vetoed. One of these was the 14th Amendment to the Constitution. (This Amendment is often considered a cornerstone of our country's liberty.) Although the 14th Amendment was designed to protect the civil rights of the black people, it contained other provisions that Johnson felt interferred with the rights of the states. Although he opposed it, the 14th Amendment was ratified by the required number of states and went into effect July 28, 1868.

Probably the final battle lines between Congress and the President were drawn when Congress passed the Tenure of Office Act. This law said that the President could not fire any official whose appointment had been confirmed by the Senate. Of course, the President vetoed the bill but it was passed over his veto. When Johnson attempted to fire Secretary of War Stanton, Congress rejoiced. The President was clearly breaking the Tenure of Office law.

The Trial

On February 25, 1868, the House of Representatives passed a resolution impeaching the President. The impeachment trial opened before the Senate less than two weeks later. There were eleven charges. The most important were the first (charging Johnson had broken the Tenure of Office Act) and the eleventh (charging that Johnson had commited various offenses in his attacks on Congress).

Presiding at the trial was the Chief Justice of the Supreme Court. Johnson wisely decided not to appear at the impeachment trial. He was well defended by a distinguished New York lawyer. At times the shrill words of his accusers seemed almost ridiculous to the rest of the country. The people began to get impatient as the trial wore on and on. However, on the closing day of the trial, the headline of the *New York Times* read, "CONVICTION ALMOST A CERTAINTY."

The Verdict

Finally the 54 Senators voted on the eleventh charge. Votes from two-thirds (or 36 votes) were necessary to convict. Thirty-five Senators voted to convict Johnson, and nineteen to acquit him. The President was saved by one vote! Two days later a vote was taken on two other impeachment charges. The results were the same 35-19. Johnson's enemies in Congress realized they had lost. No further votes on any charges were taken. The office of the Presidency as it had been created by the Constitution, was safe. Johnson could finish his term as President.

Aftermath

As Johnson's term as President drew to a close, he won more and more respect for the honorable way he had faced Congress. His last official receptions were attended by large crowds. Even men who had been his political enemies came. His final important official act came on Christmas Day. It was a proclamation that pardoned everyone who had been involved in the secession of the states.

The Impeachment Trial of Andrew Johnson

ACTIVITIES

LESSON NO. 2

In Class

1. Do you feel the President of the United States is doing a good job protecting the environment? A poor job? Write him a letter telling him how you feel about his stand on environmental issues. The address is: President ________________ , 1600 Pennsylvania Avenue, N.W., Washington, D.C. 20500

   ____
   ____
   ____
   ____
   ____

2. The United States is a democracy run by a system of local, state, and federal laws. Write a paragraph about what might happen in this country if suddenly there were no laws.

   ____
   ____
   ____
   ____
   ____

At Home

In 75/100 words write what you would do if you were President of the United States for one day.

At the Library

1. How many U.S. Presidents have been assassinated? List their names and the names of the vice presidents who then became President.
2. Look up the 14th Amendment. After you have read it, see if you understand why President Johnson vetoed it. Do you agree with him?

The Trial of Lizzie Borden

Courtesy: New York Public Library

The year was: 1893

The place was: Fall River, Massachusetts

The charge was: Murder

The defendant was: Lizzie Borden

Background

The Borden household at 92 Second Street in Fall River, Massachusetts, consisted of Andrew J. Borden, a wealthy banker; Abby Borden, his second wife; Emma and Lizzie Borden, his daughters; Bridget Sullivan, a maid. At the time of the crimes, John Morse, the brother of the first Mrs. Borden, was visiting the family. Emma, the elder of the two daughters, was out of town visiting friends.

August 4, 1892, began at 6:15 for Bridget Sullivan. First she started the fire in the kitchen stove. Then she served breakfast to Mr. and Mrs. Borden and John Morse between 7:00 and 7:30. Lizzie did not join them for breakfast. Shortly after John Morse left the house at 8:45, Lizzie Borden came downstairs and ate a light meal. Her father left for the bank about 9:00. His wife went upstairs to tidy up the guest room. Just about the time Mr. Borden was walking into his bank, his wife was brutally beaten with an axe in the guest room. She died instantly.

A neighbor saw Mr. Borden arrive back home in the middle of the morning. He had some trouble unlocking the front door. Bridget had just come inside after washing windows. She let him in. She heard Lizzie tell him that Mrs. Borden had received a note saying that someone was ill and had then gone out.

Mr. Borden went into the sitting room and lay down on the couch. According to the story she told later, Lizzie walked outside to the barn. Then she climbed the stairs to its loft where she searched for sinkers. Bridget had gone up to her room in the attic to rest.

A few minutes after 11:00 Bridget heard Lizzie scream and rushed to the head of the stairs. "What's the matter?" she called.

"Come down quick. Father's dead. Someone came in and killed him," Lizzie answered.

Bridget rushed down the stairs and started to go into the sitting room. Lizzie stopped her and sent her for a doctor. Dr. Bowen, who lived across the street, was not at home. Lizzie then asked a neighbor, Adelaide Churchill, for help. Mrs. Churchill ran

to Hall's stable and asked a man there to go for a doctor. Someone at the stable heard her and phoned the police. Within a few minutes the Borden house began to fill with police and neighbors. Dr. Bowen had finally been located. He got there quickly, too.

It was at this point that Lizzie mentioned Mrs. Borden. "I don't know but she is killed, too, for I thought I heard her come in," Lizzie said.

Mrs. Borden's body was immediately found in the upstairs guest room. Both she and her husband had died from multiple wounds to the head and body.

After a long investigation and an inquest, the grand jury indicted Lizzie for murder on December 2nd. She remained in jail until the trial began on June 5th.

The Trial

The prosecution set out to prove Lizzie Borden guilty based on a number of facts.

1. There had been a controversy between Lizzie and her stepmother over some property.
2. The day before the murders Lizzie had tried to buy some poison but the druggest would not sell it to her without a prescription.
3. There was no note from a sick friend. Lizzie had plenty of time to kill her stepmother while Bridget was washing windows.
4. Lizzie had not gone to the barn but had killed her father while Bridget was resting upstairs.
5. Lizzie had burned the clothes she had been wearing the day of the murders because they were covered with bloodstains.
6. An axe which had been found without a handle was probably the murder weapon. Lizzie had burned the handle in the kitchen stove.
7. There was no sign of a robbery and no sign of a struggle. This indicated that the victims probably knew the killer.

The defense attorney tried to counteract these facts as follows:

1. The lock on the front door was faulty, so anyone might have entered the house.
2. The killer might have hidden in a closet and not have been seen by anyone.
3. Bridget had never seen Lizzie and Mr. or Mrs. Borden quarrel.
4. Mrs. Churchill testified that Bridget had told her, "Mrs. Borden had a note to see someone who was sick."
5. Emma testified that the dress Lizzie burned was an old one that had paint on it.
6. Lizzie had no motive for the crime. No weapon was ever found.
7. On the day of the murders several people had seen a stranger in the neighborhood who was acting in an odd manner.

The Verdict

In exactly one hour and ten minutes the jury returned with a verdict of not guilty. The trial had lasted only thirteen days.

Aftermath

Mr. Borden's money and property was divided equally between Emma and Lizzie. They lived for only a short time in the Second Street house. Then they sold it and moved to a fashionable section of Fall River. They were hounded by newspaper reporters for years. In 1905 they quarreled, and Emma moved out. Lizzie died at the age of 66 after a serious operation. She had lived 34 years after the murders.

Was she really innocent? The jury thought so. The local newspapers thought so. The people of Fall River thought so. But through the years a debate has raged. One scholar feels strongly that Bridget Sullivan might have been the killer although once again there seems to be no motive.

Guilty or innocent, the trial of Lizzie Borden has come down to us in song, legend, rumor, and gossip as one of the most fascinating in the world's history of crime. And, strangely enough, despite the not guilty verdict, most people today are convinced that Lizzie did indeed "get away with murder."

On a separate sheet of paper list all of the underlined words in the story of the trial of Lizzie Borden. Find them in the vocabulary section beginning on page 65. Review their meaning and pronunciation. Choose any five and write a sentence for each one.

The Trial of Lizzie Borden

SYNONYMS, ANTONYMS, AND HOMONYMS

LESSON NO. 1

A. Write a synonym for the underlined words.

1. Bridget Sullivan was a maid in the Borden home.

   ____

2. Mrs. Borden received a note saying someone was ill.

   ________________ ________________

3. Lizzie remained in jail until the trial began.

   ________________ ________________ ________________

4. Bridget heard Lizzie scream.

   ____

5. In 1905 Lizzie and Emma quarreled.

   ____

B. Write an antonym for the underlined words.

1. Andrew J. Borden was a wealthy banker.

   ____

2. Bridget had just come inside after washing windows.

   ________________ ________________

3. "Come down quick. Father's dead," Lizzie answered.

   ________________ ________________

4. The day before the murders, Lizzie had tried to buy some poison.

   ________________ ________________ ________________

5. They lived for only a short time in the Second Street home.

   ____

C. Each of the words given below has a homonym in the story of the trial of Lizzie Borden. Find it and write it in the space provided. The first one has been done for you.

1.	close	clothes	6.	knot	________________
2.	by	________________	7.	stares	________________
3.	dyed	________________	8.	cent	________________
4.	made	________________	9.	their	________________
5.	too	________________	10.	new	________________

The Trial of Lizzie Borden
ACTIVITIES

LESSON NO. 2

In Class

1. Do you think Lizzie was guilty? Not guilty? Give your verdict but you must back it up with at least 4 reasons.

   ____

   ____

   ____

   ____

2. Name 2 or 3 methods police can use today to catch and convict a murderer that were not in use in 1892.

   ____

   ____

   ____

At Home

Pretend that you are Bridget Sullivan. The police have asked you to write down everything you did and saw and heard on the morning of August 4, 1892. Begin when you woke up, got dressed, and went downstairs to fix breakfast. End when Lizzie called and told you her father was dead.

At the Library

1. Find a floor plan of the Borden house, first and second floors, and copy it.
2. The year was 1892. Try to find a Farmer's Almanac for that year and see what kind of weather was predicted for August 4th.

The Trials of Alfred Dreyfus

Cinq Centimes

L'AURORE

Littéraire, Artistique, Sociale

J'Accuse...!

LETTRE AU PRÉSIDENT DE LA RÉPUBLIQUE

Par ÉMILE ZOLA

Courtesy: San Francisco Public Library

The year was: 1895 and 1899

The place was: Paris and Rennes, France

The charge was: High Treason

The defendant was: Alfred Dreyfus

Background

Alfred Dreyfus held the rank of captain in the French army. Dreyfus was a Jew at a time when prejudice against Jews ran high in France, especially in the military. Dreyfus received a low standing when he graduated from the army training school in spite of the fact that his marks had been high. This was a direct result of the anti-Semitism that existed in France. The newspaper *The Free Word* daily printed anti-Semitic articles. It had a huge circulation, and Dreyfus often saw his fellow officers reading it. He paid little attention. He was a shy, quiet man who was interested only in his family and his work.

One of his fellow officers in the French army was a man named Esterhazy. Esterhazy needed money and offered to sell French military secrets to the Germans. A note that he wrote was intercepted by a French spy. It caused a lot of worry because it meant there was a traitor in the army. Who could it be? Another piece of intercepted mail mentioned "Scoundrel D." Could this be a clue? French officers ran to their files and started examining men whose name began with a D. At last they came to Dreyfus. There they stopped. Drefus was a Jew. That was enough. They had their man.

Now it was necessary to prove that Dreyfus had written the intercepted note. Samples of his handwriting were taken from his personal file and compared to the note. Some experts said the same person wrote both pieces of handwriting. Others strongly disagreed. There were other factors that pointed to Dreyfus' innocence. His home was searched. His wife was questioned. She was not allowed to see him.

Trial No. 1 (1895)

The trial lasted several weeks. Witness after witness took the stand. When it was necessary to prove the case against Dreyfus, they lied. Dreyfus never had a chance.

The Verdict

Dreyfus was found guilty. He was sentenced to be expelled from the army and to deportation for the rest of his life.

Aftermath of Trial No. 1

Two weeks later Dreyfus was stripped of his military insignia in a public ceremony. His former comrades insulted him and spat upon him. "I am innocent," he shouted. "Long live France!" A few days later he was put on a prison ship bound for Devil's Island in Dutch Guiana. Here he lived in a dirty, dark stone hut. He fixed his own meals, using tin cans for dishes. He was constantly watched although his guards had orders never to speak to him. Often he was ill from the heat, poor food, and insect bites. All in all, it was a miserable, depressing life to which there seemed to be no end.

Back in France a number of people were still convinced that Dreyfus was innocent. The story was given attention in newspapers all over the world, especially when it was finally proved that Esterhazy had written the famous note. Although it is hard to believe, Esterhazy was actually tried for treason and acquitted. By this time many people were demanding the release of Dreyfus. Finally the case attracted the attention of Emile Zola, a famous French writer. Zola wrote a letter to the President of the French Republic. This letter became famous all over the world. It was called *J'Accuse (I accuse).* Eventually the High Court of Appeals decided that Dreyfus should have a new trial.

Trial No. 2 (1899)

Dreyfus was brought back from Devil's Island. After four years in that awful place, he had become an old man even though he was only thirty-eight. His friends and family barely recognized him. Unfortunately, feeling in the French army against Jews was still bitter. The second trial was no fairer to Dreyfus than the first. Any testimony that was favorable to him was banned.

The Verdict

Dreyfus was once again found guilty. His prison sentence was reduced from life to ten years.

Aftermath of Trial No. 2

This time the entire world protested. Mass meetings were held in major cities. People were urged to boycott everything in an effort to hurt France economically. Dreyfus received thousands of letters and telegrams of support. Finally, to appease world opinion, Dreyfus was pardoned.

It should be understood that there is a vast difference between being pardoned and being found innocent. A pardon implies that one is guilty but has been forgiven. Although Dreyfus was relieved at being out of prison, a pardon was clearly not enough

for him. Why should a man be pardoned for a crime he had not committed? Many others felt the same way. They continued to work to clear Dreyfus' name.

Finally, in 1906, eleven years after the first trial, the case was reviewed by the highest court in France. Dreyfus, who had gradually recovered his health, was declared innocent. He was taken back into the French army and given the rank of major. Later, in a public ceremony, Dreyfus was made a Knight of the Legion of Honor. This is one of the highest honors that France can bestow. "Long live Dreyfus! Long live justice!" shouted the crowd. After twelve long years, the Dreyfus affair was finally over.

When World War I broke out between Germany and France, Alfred Dreyfus went on active duty. He commanded one of the forts defending Paris. Dreyfus survived the war and lived until 1935.

At its height the Dreyfus affair inflamed anti-Semitism. But as events gradually took place, it ultimately did much to discredit anti-Semitism.

On a separate sheet of paper list all of the underlined words in the story of the trials of Alfred Dreyfus. Find them in the vocabulary section beginning on page 65. Review their meaning and pronunciation. Choose any five and write a sentence for each one.

The Trials of Alfred Dreyfus
CONFIGURATIONS

LESSON NO. 1

Draw a line from the word to the pattern (configuration) that matches it. Then print the word in the space. The first one has been done for you.

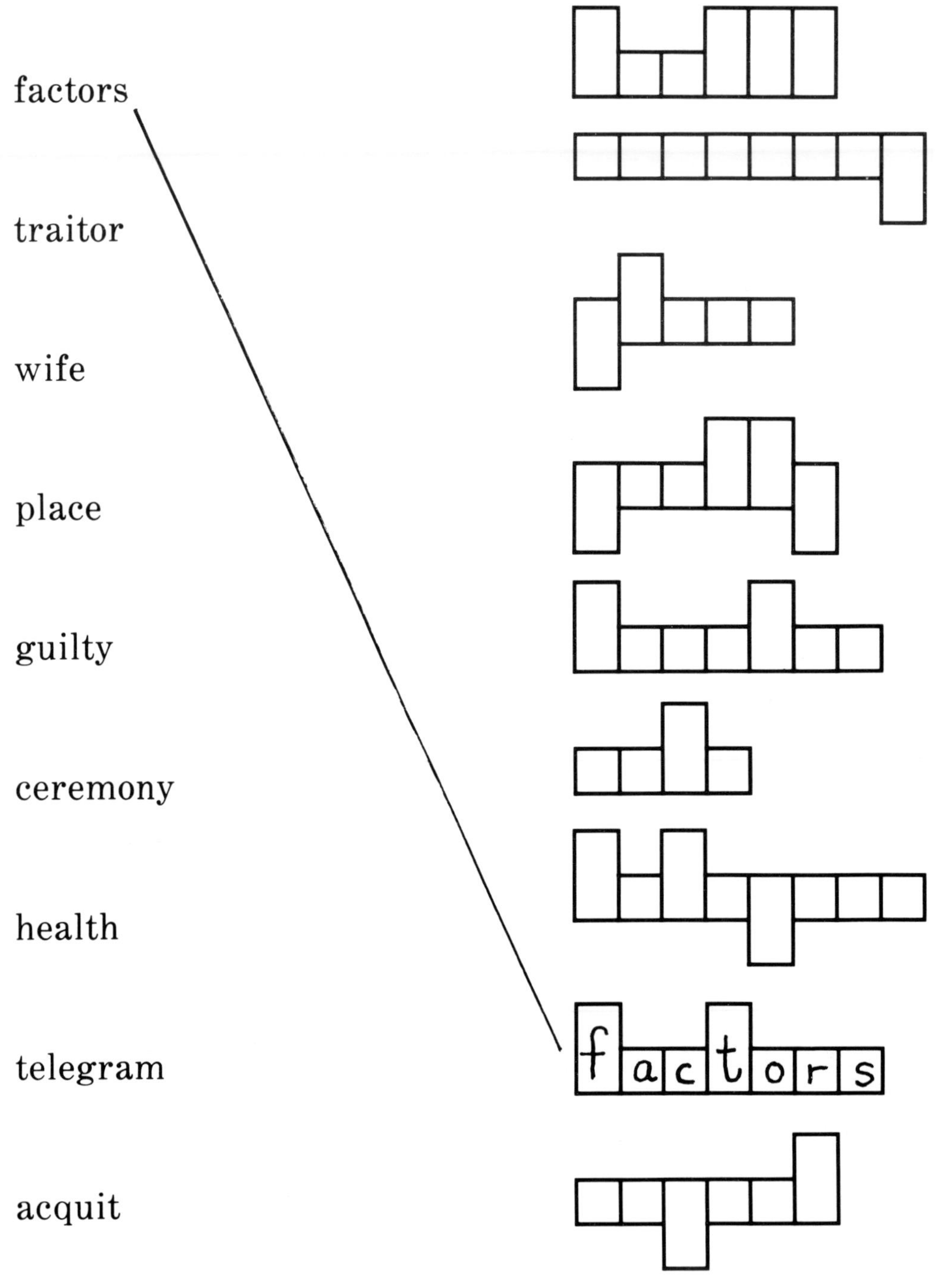

The Trials of Alfred Dreyfus
ACTIVITIES

LESSON NO. 2

In Class

1. When Dreyfus was sent to Devil's Island for life, he probably believed he would never return to France. In such a case, most men would draw up a will. This legal document declares how a person wishes his possessions to be disposed of after his death. Make a will of your own. Include, for example, who should receive your clothes, bike, stereo, records, and any other prized possessions.

   ____

   ____

   ____

   ____

   ____

2. The tragic story of Dreyfus was made into a movie about 50 years ago. If another movie were to be made, who should play the role of Dreyfus? Of his wife? Of Esterhazy? Of Zola?

   ______________ ______________

   ______________ ______________

At Home

Pretend that it is the year 1895 and Dreyfus has just been convicted for the first time. Write a letter of protest to the French government stating the reasons that you believe Dreyfus is innocent and should be given a new trial.

At the Library

1. The conditions at the prison on Devil's Island were among the world's worst. Find out everything you can about Devil's Island and describe it in a paragraph of 75/100 words.
2. Look up Emile Zola and see what happened to him after he tried to defend Dreyfus.

The Trial of Edith Cavell

The year was: 1915

The place was: Brussels, Belgium

The charge was: Treason

The defendant was: Edith Cavell

Background

Courtesy: San Francisco Public Library

Edith Cavell was born in England. She chose nursing as a career early in her life. After she had finished her training and had some experience, she moved to Brussels. There she became head of a hospital. World War I broke out in August of 1914. Nurse Cavell decided not to return to England but to remain at her job. It was not long before Brussels was captured by the advancing German army.

One of the first moves the Germans made was to put up an important order in a central spot in Brussels where everyone could see it. The order said that all French and English soldiers must be turned over to the Germans at once. The penalty for helping them would be death. For the most part, no one paid any attention to this order. Instead a system was set up to provide false identification papers and passports for French and English soldiers who were hiding from the German authorities. With such papers it became possible for them to escape across the border. In this way they could rejoin their military units and fight against Germany once more. Nurse Cavell took an active part in setting up this system. In fact, her hospital was probably headquarters for most of the men and women who were working in the escape movement. She knew it was dangerous work but she also knew she had to try to save lives.

It has never been learned who tipped off the German authorities. But someone did! On August 15, 1915, the hospital was raided. A letter from the American consul in Brussels was found at the hospital. The Germans felt this was sufficient evidence to arrest Edith Cavell and her assistant, Miss Wilkins. Both were taken to military headquarters and questioned for hours. Miss Wilkins was then released. Nurse Cavell was taken to prison. She was held for several weeks in a cell. It was rumored that she had made a full confession. What is not known is whether she confessed of her own free will or confessed under extreme pressure or even torture.

The Trial

Edith Cavell was only one of 35 defendants accused by the Germans of various illegal activities, including treason. Thirty-one were Belgian, and three were French. Nurse Cavell was the only English prisoner.

The German military court had five judges: a lieutenant colonel, two captains, and two officers of lower rank. Five Belgian lawyers acted for the defense. But in the case of Edith Cavell, there could be little defense. Her confession admitted her guilt in clear terms. In it she gave details of how she had helped not only French and English soldiers but also civilians fleeing from the Germans. The prosecution was able to find a number of witnesses who were more than willing to testify against an English woman. Some of their testimony was probably true but there were also people who would do or say anything to find favor with the German authorities.

The lawyers for Edith Cavell made a last-minute plea. They pointed out that as a nurse, she was dedicated to helping others. She had been sure that the French and British soldiers would be killed if caught by the Germans. Therefore, her only thought was to save their lives. Her lawyers reminded the court that during her career she had also nursed many German soldiers. And to sum it all up, they said there was no proof that any of the men she had helped had ever again fought against Germany. It was a good defense. It was the best the lawyers could do under the circumstances. Everything they said was true. But was it enough to overcome her confession?

The court then asked Nurse Cavell if she had anything to say. She was silent for a moment and then she answered, "Nothing."

The Verdict

Court was then adjourned. Edith Cavell and the other prisoners must have spent a long weekend waiting for the verdict. On Monday they were returned to the courtroom and the names of those sentenced to death were read. Edith Cavell was among these. Eight people were acquitted. The rest were given prison sentences of up to 15 years. That night the American ambassador did everything he could to get the Germans to postpone the death sentence—or to show mercy for this English citizen. His pleas were ignored. Even Cavell's fellow prisoners begged her to ask for mercy. She refused. The very next morning she and another prisoner were taken from their cells and executed by a firing squad.

Aftermath

When news of her execution reached England, anger against the Germans climbed to a new high all over the world. Many men enlisted in the army eager to fight against the evil forces that had killed this brave woman. The Bishop of London called her death "the greatest crime in history." It was widely described and discussed in American

newspapers and may even have influenced the entry of the United States into World War I. It was one of the most talked about events of the first World War.

Following the end of the war, Edith Cavell's body was brought back to London. She was given the burial of a war hero. A statue of her can be found near Trafalgar Square in London. There she stands, a tall majestic woman with long flowing robes. Above her head is chiseled one word: "Humanity." Below her name the words read:

Brussels, Dawn, October 12, 1915
"Patriotism is not enough. I must
have no hatred or bitterness for anyone."

On a separate sheet of paper list all of the underlined words in the story of the trial of Edith Cavell. Find them in the vocabulary section beginning on page 65. Review their meaning and pronunciation. Choose any five and write a sentence for each one.

The Trials of Edith Cavell

CHOOSE THE RIGHT WORD

LESSON NO. 1

authorities	sufficient	chisel
confession	experience	plea
dedicated	adjourned	postpone
influence	identification	assistant
hospital		

Fill in the blanks in each sentence by choosing one or two of the words listed above. Some of the words are used more than once. The first one has been done for you.

1. The *authorities* would not *postpone* the execution.
2. She was a ________________ nurse.
3. After the court heard her ________________, it ________________ for the weekend.
4. His ________________ was asked to show some ________________.
5. She had a lot of ________________ running a ________________.
6. Show some mercy and hear my ________________.
7. Please use your ________________ to get me that job.
8. My funds are not ________________ to last me through the year.
9. I am going to ________________ hiring a new ________________.
10. The ________________ needed some new nurses with ________________.
11. Are you sure he was telling the truth in his ________________?
12. My ________________ was not ________________ to get me into the guarded building.

One word in the above list was not used in the sentences. Write it here. ________________

The Trial of Edith Cavell

ACTIVITIES

LESSON NO. 2

In Class

1. List 3 reasons why you would like to become a nurse.

____

____

____

OR List 3 reasons why you would not like to become a nurse.

____

____

____

2. List 3 reasons why you would like to become a spy.

____

____

____

OR List 3 reasons why you would not like to become a spy.

____

____

____

At Home

You are the editor of an English newspaper in 1915. You are extremely angry at what was done to Edith Cavell by the Germans. Write a strong editorial describing how you and the entire world feels and what might be done to make the Germans pay for the death of this brave woman.

At the Library

1. Florence Nightingale was another English nurse who became famous for her courage during a war. Compare her life with that of Edith Cavell. In which war did she serve? What was her nickname?
2. Mata Hari was the most famous spy of World War I. On whose side was she on? What finally happened to her?

The Trials of Sacco and Vanzetti

The year was: 1921

The place was: Plymouth and Dedham, Massachusetts

The charge was: Attempted murder and robbery (1st trial) murder (2nd trial)

The defendants were: Nicola Sacco and Bartolomeo Vanzetti

Courtesy: San Francisco Public Library

Background

Beginning in 1919, the fear of Communists ("Reds") was nationwide. A number of bombings had taken place. All foreigners were under suspicion. Massachusetts shared in this mass hysteria. Hundreds of aliens were rounded up and taken to jail. Their rooms were searched. Their private possessions were seized unlawfully. Then two incidents stirred up the people even more. The first took place on December 24, 1919, in Bridgewater, Massachusetts. An attempt was made to steal the payroll of the L.Q. White Shoe Company. It was unsuccessful. No one was hurt. The robbers were not caught. This minor incident was the beginning of what was to develop into one of the most famous trials of the 20th century—a trial that would cause protests and riots all over the world, a trial that was still the topic of argument and debate many years later.

The second incident was successful—and tragic. On April 15, 1920, the payroll for the Slater and Morrill factory in South Braintree, Massachusetts, was robbed. This time the robbers got away with the payroll. Two Slater and Morrill employees were killed. Somehow the two crimes became linked, mostly because eye witnesses testified that in both crimes the bandits were foreigners, probably Italians.

State and local police and private detectives launched a massive search for the killers. During a trap laid for two other suspects, Nicola Sacco and Bartolomeo Vanzetti were seized. They were Italian. They were aliens. Even more important, both were known to have advocated the overthrow of the U.S. government. Under questioning they both told a number of lies. Many people believed they lied because no one told them why they had been arrested. Both men believed they were being held as radicals. They lied to protect themselves and their friends from deportation. Sacco produced an unshakable alibi for the Bridgewater robbery, so only Vanzetti was tried for this crime.

Trial No. 1

To prove Vanzetti guilty, the prosecution relied chiefly on eyewitness identification and circumstantial evidence. Both were flawed. Vanzetti was not placed in a lineup with other people. Instead he was paraded alone before eyewitnesses who were then asked if this was the man they had seen. Also, a shotgun shell found on the street near Bridgewater and one taken from Vanzetti were similar. These were used as evidence even though they could not be positively identified. Vanzetti's defense relied on alibi witnesses to prove that he was with them on the morning of the Bridgewater robbery. Vanzetti never took the witness stand in his own defense. This may have raised doubt in the minds of the jury.

The Verdict

Vanzetti was found guilty of assault with intent to rob and assault with intent to murder. He received a prison sentence of 12 to 15 years.

Trial No. 2

The prosecution's case rested on several points:

1. Eyewitnesses claimed to have seen Sacco in South Braintree on the morning before the crime, at the scene of the crime, and leaving it.
2. At least one shell taken from the body of one of the murdered employees was said by ballistics experts to have been fired from a gun owned by Sacco.
3. Sacco's absence from work on the day of the crime.
4. The resemblance between the car belonging to Sacco's friends, which he occasionally borrowed, and the murder car, found abandoned in the woods near the scene of the crime.
5. The behavior of the defendants at the time of their arrest and interrogation.

The defense was based on a number of factors:

1. Contradictory information by eyewitnesses at various times during the investigation of the crime; also, their identification which took place in a prison without a lineup.
2. Testimony from people who had seen Vanzetti at various times of the day on April 15th, far from the scene of the murders.
3. Testimony from many people who had seen Sacco in Boston at the time of the crime.
4. Explanation of the behavior of the defendants in terms of their fear of deportation.
5. The denials on the witness stand by the defendants themselves.

This time both Sacco and Vanzetti testified in their own defense but it did no good.

The Verdict

Guilty! The sentence: Death!

Aftermath

For six years defense attorneys fought to free the two men from what they felt was a tragic miscarriage of justice. They were not the only ones who were convinced that justice, fear, dishonesty, misunderstanding, bad police methods, and a rigid court system all played a part. Labor leaders, poets, novelists, artists, members of the intellectual community all over the world, members of the most respected families in Massachusetts, professors of law—all took up the fight for Sacco and Vanzetti. But it did not help. One appeal for a new trial after another was unsuccessful. In the last months of the long period of appeals, there were general strikes for Sacco and Vanzetti in South America, demonstrations in Europe, and mass meetings in Asia and Africa. United States embassies were stoned. American prestige fell to a new low.

In the end, it was not Sacco and Vanzetti who were on trial. It was American justice and particularly justice as practiced in Massachusetts. No matter that evidence of their innocence continued to pile up. Sacco and Vanzetti were executed on August 23, 1927.

This controversial trial still stands as a demonstration of how a judicial system, if allowed to become inflexible, may lose sight of the goal of justice.

On a separate sheet of paper list all of the underlined words in the story of the trials of Sacco and Vanzetti. Find them in the vocabulary section beginning on page 65. Review their meaning and pronunciation. Choose any five and write a sentence for each one.

The Trials of Sacco and Vanzetti

BREAK THE CODE

LESSON NO. 1

The following questions are in code. Break the code by changing each letter to the one that precedes it in the alphabet. Then write your one-word answer in the same code. The first one has been done for you.

1. XIBU XBT UIF GJSTU OBNF PG TBDDP?
   WHAT WAS THE FIRST NAME OF SACCO?
   OJDPMB (NICOLA)

2. XIBU XBT UIF GJSTU OBNF PG WBOZFUUJ?
   ____
   ____

3. XIBU DPVOUSZ EJE UIF UXP EFGFOEBOUT DPNF GSPN?
   ____
   ____

4. XIFSF EJE UIF GJSTU SPCCFSZ UBLF QMBDF?
   ____
   ____

5. JO XIBU NPOUI EJE UIF TFDPOE SPCCFSZ UBLF QMBDF?
   ____
   ____

6. XIBU XBT UIF WFSEJDU JO UIF TFDPOE USJBM?
   ____
   ____

7. XIBU XBT UIF TFOUFODF JO UIF TFDPOE USJBM?
   ____
   ____

8. XIBU LJOE PG TIFMM XBT VTFE BT FWJEFODF?
   ____
   ____

The Trials of Sacco and Vanzetti
ACTIVITIES

LESSON NO. 2

In Class

1. Hundreds of thousands of immigrants like Nicola Sacco and Bartolomeo Vanzetti came to the United States from Europe at the turn of the century (late 1800's, 1900's). Explain why you feel they left their native countries to try life in a strange land.

   ____

   ____

   ____

2. Today many thousands of immigrants are coming to the United States from Southeast Asia and Central America. What do you think they hope to find here?

   ____

   ____

   ____

3. Describe the many benefits which immigrants from all over the world have brought to the United States.

   ____

   ____

   ____

At Home

1. You have probably watched many courtroom scenes on television or in a movie. Draw a floorplan of a courtroom. Be sure to include a place for: the judge, jury, witness box, prosecutors, defense attorneys, and spectators.
2. A custom in the prisons of this country is to let a person who is about to be executed have anything he or she wants to eat for his last meal. If you were in this situation, what would you order for your final meal?

At the Library

Check out a book about the Sacco-Vanzetti case or look it up in an encyclopedia. After you have read about these two men and their trials, write your verdict (guilty or innocent) and give at least 4 reasons for your opinion.

The Trial of John Scopes

SCOPES GUILTY, FINED $100, SCORES LAW; BENEDICTION ENDS TRIAL, APPEAL STARTS; DARROW ANSWERS NINE BRYAN QUESTIONS

Both Sides Speed Procedure for Scopes Appeal; Defense Cost $25,000, With Lawyers Serving Free

Special to The New York Times.

KNOXVILLE, Tenn., July 21.—With the conviction of John Thomas Scopes, attorneys for the defense at Dayton began at once to formulate their plans for the appeal. The case will come before the Supreme Court when that tribunal sits in Knoxville in September. Attorneys for both sides today agreed to expedite the appeal procedure in order to assure a hearing of the issues at that session.

Clarence Darrow, chief of the defense staff, is expected to argue the case before the Supreme Court here. Frank Spurlock, prominent attorney of Chattanooga, assisting the defense, will also plead for Mr. Scopes, being well versed in the peculiarities of Tennessee law. John R. Neal of Knoxville also is expected to take an important part in the appeal proceedings.

For the State, Attorney General Stewart and Ben G. McKenzie doubtless will carry the burden.

The defense's appeal will consist of two main points: First, that the Anti-Evolution law is unconstitutional; second, that even though the law were valid, Mr. Scopes did not violate it, and that the defense was prohibited from proving this at the Dayton trial.

DAYTON, Tenn., July 21 (AP).—A misdemeanor case carrying as a penalty to the guilty offender a fine of $100 and costs of the trial brought an expenditure to the defenders of John Thomas Scopes of about $25,000.

The actual court costs are estimated at well over $300, or more than treble the fine assessed.

The greatest expense of the trial was the cost of bringing expert witnesses, who were not allowed to testify. Defense counsel estimated that cost to be $20,000 to $25,000.

Attorneys on both sides bore their own expenses and served without fees.

In addition several hundred dollars was paid out by the county in preparing the Court House for the trial.

FINAL SCENES DRAMATIC

Defense Suddenly Decides to Make No Plea and Accept Conviction.

BRYAN IS DISAPPOINTED

Loses Chance to Examine Darrow and His Long-Prepared Speech Is Undelivered.

HIS EVIDENCE IS EXPUNGED

Differences Forgotten in the End as All Concerned Exchange Felicitations.

Special to The New York Times.

DAYTON, Tenn., July 21.—The trial of John Thomas Scopes for teaching evolution in Tennessee, which Clarence Darrow characterized today as "the first case of its kind since we stopped

Courtesy: New York Times

The year was: 1925

The place was: Dayton, Tennessee

The charge was: Breaking a state law (the Butler Act which forbade teaching the theory of evolution in a public school)

The defendant was: John Scopes

Background

After World War I laws were proposed in several states that made it illegal to teach Darwin's theory of evolution. What was this theory that drew so much attention and about which people felt so strongly? It was this: Darwin claimed that Man is not descended from Adam and Eve. This contradicts the theory of Divine Creation set forth in the Bible. Darwin believed that Man has gradually evolved over thousands of centuries from a low order of animal (some kind of monkey).

In Tennessee a bill (the Butler Act) was passed by the lower branch of the state legislature. This bill forbade teachers to teach evolution in the schools. Everyone expected the bill to be defeated in the state senate. However, the senate passed it, expecting the governor to veto it. The governor did not wish to offend the voters, so he signed the bill. Suddenly, to everyone's surprise, the Butler Act had become law. No one expected it to be enforced.

The ACLU (American Civil Liberties Union) wanted to test the Butler Act in the courts. They hoped to prove that the new law was unconstitutional and that teachers should be free to teach Darwin's theory of evolution. The name of John Scopes was mentioned. Whether or not he was even aware of the new law is uncertain. But the ACLU knew that he had been teaching evolution in his biology class. They asked him to allow himself to be arrested and tried in a test case of the Butler Act.

The people who believed in Adam and Eve and in the theory of Divine Creation were led, for the most part, by members of the World Fundamentalist Association. They were called Fundamentalists. The trial began to grow in importance when the Fundamentalists asked Williams Jennings Bryan to prosecute the case. Bryan was nationally known because he had run unsuccessfully for President three times. He had

also served as Secretary of State under Woodrow Wilson. He was known as a powerful speaker who thundered against sinners in churches all over America.

Bryan's entrance into the case was a challenge that could not be ignored. Clarence Darrow, America's most famous criminal lawyer, offered his services to the defense without charge. Darrow was an opponent not only of the Fundamentalists but of all organized religion.

Overnight Dayton turned into a carnival town. Reporters and curious people came from all over the nation. The streets were jammed with strangers. Popcorn and hot dog venders were on every corner. The weather was uncomfortably hot.

The Trial

The jury was chosen. The attorneys gave their opening statements, and the trial began in earnest. There was only one issue, said the prosecution: Did John Scopes break the law or didn't he? To prove that he did, the prosecution brought in some of his students to testify. The youngsters were reluctant. They liked Scopes and didn't want to harm him in any way. But he assured them that it was all right to tell the truth. And so they described what their teacher had said in class about evolution. This quickly and clearly proved the case against Scopes.

The defense refused to limit the case to this single accusation. Darrow felt much larger issues were at stake. He wanted to bring in scientists to prove that Darwin's theory of evolution was valid. But the prosecution blocked this tactic. Finally, in desperation, the defense put the prosecuting attorney, William Jennings Bryan on the witness stand. Bryan's performance was embarrassing. Darrow showed no mercy in his examination of Bryan, who was supposed to be an expert on the Bible. Time and time again he showed his ignorance of it.

The Verdict

The verdict of guilty was just what Darrow and the ACLU wanted. This meant that the case could be appealed and would eventually be tried before the United States Supreme Court. First, however, the matter had to go to the state court of appeals. This is the court that has the authority to hear and decide appeals from decisions of a lower court. In other words, if a defense attorney does not feel his client has received a fair verdict, he can appeal the decision in a higher court.

The Scopes case was neither won nor lost in the Tennessee court of appeals. Instead, the justices of the court of appeals decided that the judge had made a technical mistake during the trial. They threw out the guilty verdict.

This meant that Scopes was innocent, which frustrated Clarence Darrow and the ACLU. The appeals court ruled there were no grounds for a new trial, so this meant that the constitutionality of the Butler Act would never be tested.

John Scopes prospered after the famous trial. He was given a scholarship by the University of Illinois so that he could continue his education. He enjoyed a successful

career as a geologist in Louisiana and in South America. Later on he wrote a book about the trial.

The events at Dayton probably could never be repeated in the United States today. However, there are still people who do not believe in Darwin's theory of evolution. They have the freedom in our country to make their opinions known. In some cases, they have been able to convince book publishers to give equal treatment to Darwin's theory of evolution and the biblical Divine Creation theory. The debate will probably continue as long as both sides hold to their strong viewpoints.

On a separate sheet of paper list all of the underlined words in the story of the trial of John Scopes. Find them in the vocabulary section beginning on page 65. Review their meaning and pronunciation. Choose any five and write a sentence for each one.

The Trials of John Scopes
SYLLABLES

LESSON NO. 1

Pronounce each word slowly. On the line in front of each word, write the number of syllables you heard. Remember: Each syllable must have one vowel sound.

_______ theory
_______ attention
_______ people
_______ claimed
_______ gradually
_______ evolution
_______ offend
_______ aware
_______ biology
_______ grounds
_______ agree
_______ authority
_______ prosecution
_______ blocked
_______ president

_______ fundamental
_______ thundered
_______ jammed
_______ reluctant
_______ established
_______ scientist
_______ prosecution
_______ valid
_______ examination
_______ geologist
_______ freedom
_______ ruled
_______ descended
_______ tactic
_______ witness

_______ mercy
_______ embarrassing
_______ deliberation
_______ innocent
_______ constitutional
_______ trial
_______ scholarship
verdict
_______ viewpoints
_______ however
_______ uncertain
_______ association
_______ unsuccessful
_______ popcorn
_______ performance

How many words did you find with 1 syllable? _________
with 2 syllables? _________
with 3 syllables? _________
with 4 syllables? _________
with 5 syllables? _________

The Trial of John Scopes
ACTIVITIES

LESSON NO. 2

In Class

1. Write a letter to your State Department of Education. Ask:
   a. Is Darwin's theory of evolution taught in your state?
   b. Is the biblical Divine Creation taught in your state?
   c. Are both theories taught in your state?
   d. Is there a textbook committee in your state that decides what must be taught in science?

   ____
   ____
   ____
   ____
   ____

2. Write a letter to the Chamber of Commerce of Dayton, Tennessee (ZIP: 37321) and ask them to send you information on their town. It will be interesting to see if any material from Dayton mentions the famous Scopes trial.

   ____
   ____
   ____
   ____
   ____

At Home

The story of Adam and Eve is written in the Book of Genesis in the Bible. You have probably heard at least one version of it. Write a description of Adam and Eve and the events in the Garden of Eden.

At the Library

Choose either Darwin's theory of evolution or the biblical Divine Creation theory and learn all you can about it. Then write 75/100 words on why you do or do not agree with this theory.

The Nuremberg Trials

"All the News That's Fit to Print"

The New York Times.

VOL. XCVI...No. 32,393. NEW YORK, WEDNESDAY, OCTOBER 2, 1946. THREE CENTS

12 NAZI WAR LEADERS SENTENCED TO BE HANGED; GOERING HEADS LIST OF THOSE TO DIE BY OCT. 16; HESS GETS LIFE, SIX OTHERS ORDERED TO PRISON

Courtesy: New York Times

The year was: 1945

The place was: Nuremberg, Germany

The charges were:
1. Conspiracy to seize power
2. Crimes against peace (starting a war)
3. Violation of the international laws of war
4. Crimes against humanity (torture, killing, imprisonment of innocent people)

The defendants were: 21 men who had held high positions in the government of Nazi Germany

Background

The Nuremberg trial was called the First International Military Tribunal. It was planned by 21 nations as soon as World War II ended. These nations felt that all the world should know about the crimes of the German Nazi party that took place before and during World War II.

Nuremberg was chosen as the place to hold the trial. It seemed right to select the city where important events of the Nazi party had once been held. The city had been bombed regularly during the war. It was now in almost total ruins. People lived in shacks built from rubble. No street cars or buses were running. There was no electricity or running water. Little to buy could be found in the few tumbledown stores.

To get ready for the trial, much rebuilding had to be done quickly. Two large hotels had to be put in shape. They were needed to house the hundreds of men and women involved in the trial. The trial would be held in the city's courthouse. It, too, had been badly damaged and needed major repairs. The work was done by soldiers, civilians, and German prisoners-of-war. Most of the building materials had to be flown in from the United States. The repairs took six months.

The Trial

There were four judges—one from the United States, and one each from France, England, and Russia. There were also four alternate judges. In addition, there were 52

prosecutors, 49 defense attorneys, dozens of staff people, court reporters, interpreters, newspaper reporters, etc. The trial attracted world-wide attention. It lasted 216 days. All of the 21 defendants pleaded "not guilty."

The prosecution called very few witnesses. Instead it relied on 3,000 tons of evidence. This included Nazi government documents, private diaries, conference reports, letters, records of telephone conversations and secret meetings. Most condemning of all were the stacks of photographs that shows the horrible persecution of the Jews and other innocent peoples.

This was a trial of Germans by Germany's conquerors and held in Germany. The strongest safety measures were taken. Everyone entering the courthouse had to show a blue pass with his photo on it. All handbags and parcels were carefully inspected. The nearby area was heavily guarded with tanks and machine guns.

The prosecution set the stage. It set out to prove that once Hitler and his Nazi party came to power in Germany in the 1930's, the country was set on its brutal, destructive path. Jews were hauled off to concentration camps where millions died of starvation or were murdered. Christian leaders who criticized the Nazi actions were thrown into prison without trials. Unions were wiped out. Books that did not agree with the Nazis were burned.

Hitler was ambitious and determined to make Germany the most powerful country on earth. To this end, without warning or excuse, he invaded Austria, Czechoslovakia, Poland, Norway, Denmark, France, and finally Russia. Nazi treatment of the peoples of these countries was savage and vicious. Cities were destroyed for no good reason. Treasures, raw materials, and food were plundered. Prisoners-of-war were beaten, tortured, and killed. Men, women, and children who had committed no crimes were shot, drowned, or marched until they dropped of cold and hunger. Day after day the prosecution built up its massive case against each defendant.

All 21 defendants used the same absurd defense. They knew nothing, had seen nothing, had done nothing but follow orders. Some claimed they had merely done their duties as soldiers. Most said they had never heard of the concentration camps and tried to place the blame on others. In other words, the defendants lied.

The Verdicts

Eleven defendants were found guilty and sentenced to death by hanging. Three were sentenced to life in prison. Four were sentenced to terms of 10 to 20 years. Three were acquitted on the grounds that there was reasonable doubt as to their guilt.

Ten men were executed by hanging on October 16th. The eleventh committed suicide by swallowing a capsule of cyanide the night before the executions were scheduled.

Aftermath

This was just the first of the Nuremberg trials. In December, 1945, the Allied Control Council established military tribunals in each of the four zones into which

Germany had been divided. Between 1947 and 1949 the United States tribunal conducted 12 more trials in which 183 Nazi criminals were indicted. Twenty four of these were sentenced to hang. Many more went to prison.

The most important thing about the Nuremberg trials is the fact that they were held. They discouraged future generations from starting wars. They collected a body of true information about the rise and the crimes of Nazism. No one can ever say that these things did not happen. It is all there on the record for anyone to read.

On a separate sheet of paper list all of the underlined words in the story of the Nuremberg trials. Find them in the vocabulary section beginning on page 65. Review their meaning and pronunciation. Choose any five and write a sentence for each one.

The Nuremberg Trials

WORD MATCHING

LESSON NO. 1

All of the words in the left-hand columns come from the script of the Nuremberg trials.

1. Draw a line to the word that means the same or almost the same. The first one has been done for you.

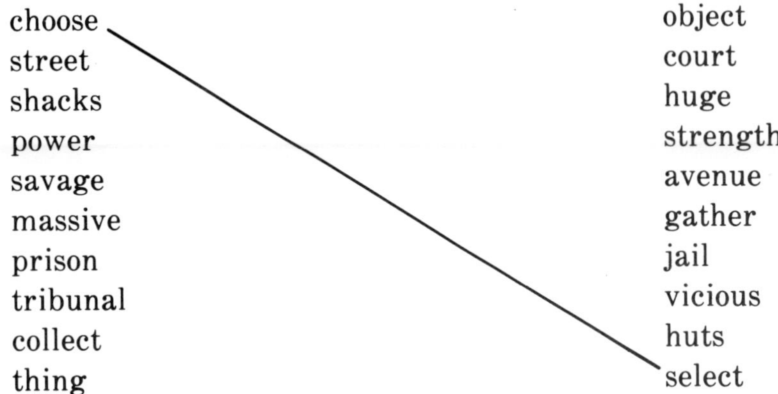

choose	object
street	court
shacks	huge
power	strength
savage	avenue
massive	gather
prison	jail
tribunal	vicious
collect	huts
thing	select

2. Draw a line to the word that means the opposite. The first one has been done for you.

found	public
few	peace
quickly	minor
major	lost
addition	small
days	nights
war	slowly
little	many
large	subtraction
private	big

3. Draw a line to the word that has the same sound but a different meaning (homonym). The first one has been done for you.

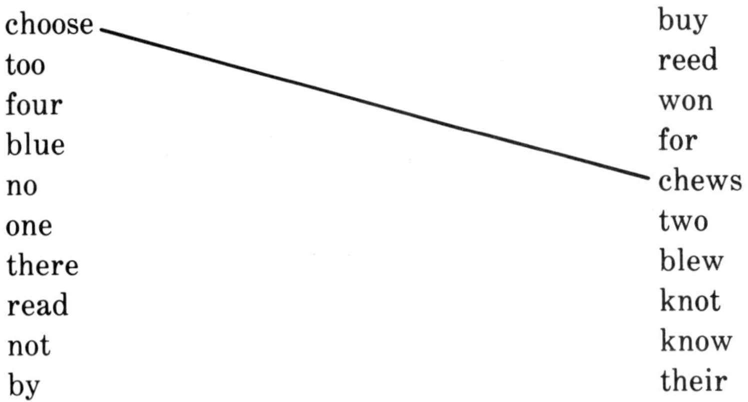

choose	buy
too	reed
four	won
blue	for
no	chews
one	two
there	blew
read	knot
not	know
by	their

The Nuremberg Trials
ACTIVITIES

LESSON NO. 2

In Class

1. Pretend you are a judge. What character strengths would you need to do a good job?

   ____

   ____

2. Pretend you are a member of a jury. What qualities would you need to do a good job?

   ____

   ____

3. Which would you rather be—a judge or a member of a jury? Why?

   ____

   ____

4. How are judges and jury members alike? How are they different?

   ____

   ____

At Home

Pretend that you lived in Europe during the war. Your city has been bombed night after night by enemy aircraft. Your house has been damaged and is almost unlivable. There is little food. You have no heat or electricity. Describe how you might exist under such circumstances.

At the Library

1. Check out a copy of *The Diary of Anne Frank* from the library and read it.
2. Write a book review of *The Diary of Anne Frank.*

Vocabulary

ab-surd (ăb-zûrd′)	ridiculous; unsound; not believable *The idea is absurd.*
ac-cu-sa-tion (ə-kyōō-zā′-shən)	to charge with a crime or offense *The army brought an accusation of desertion against him.*
ac-quit (ə-kwĭt′)	to pronounce not guilty; to clear of a charge *He was acquitted of the crime.*
ad-journ (ə-jûrn′)	to stop until a later time *Let's adjourn the meeting until tomorrow.*
ad-min-is-tra-tion (ăd-mĭn-ĭs-trā′-shən)	the executive functions or management of a government *The president worked hard during his administration.*
ad-vo-cate (ăd′-və-kāt)	to speak in favor of; recommend; to argue for a cause or a person *I advocate changing the time school starts from 8:30 to 10:00.*
af-ter-math (ăf′-tər-măth)	result; that which follows an event *The aftermath of the earthquake was worse than the earthquake itself.*
al-der-man (əl′-dər-mən)	a member of a town or city government ranking below a mayor *He served as an alderman in Youngstown for seven years.*
al-i-bi (ăl′-ə-bĭ)	a form of defense in which a defendant tries to prove he was somewhere else when a crime was committed; an excuse *He had no alibi for the night of the robbery.*
a-li-en (ā′-lē-ən)	not being a citizen of the country one is living in *Many aliens in the United States have plans to become citizens.*

al-ter-nate (ôl′-tər-nĭt)	substitute *We will need to have an alternate plan in case it rains.*
am-bas-sa-dor (ăm-băs′-ə-dôr)	a high ranking official sent to represent his country before the government of a foreign country *He became our ambassador to China.*
an-ti - Sem-i-tism (ăn-tē - Sem′-ĭ-tĭz-ŭm)	hostility or discrimination against the Jews *It is hoped that one day there will be no anti-Semitism in the world.*
ap-peal (ə-pēl′)	the transfer of a case from a lower to a higher court for a new hearing *The defense attorney decided to appeal the guilty verdict.*
ap-pease (ə-pēz′)	to make quiet; to calm down *No one was able to appease her until her father arrived.*
ap-pren-tice (ə-prĕn′-tĭs)	one who is learning a trade under a skilled craftsman; a beginner *The blacksmith agreed to take him on as an apprentice.*
as-tron-o-my (ə-strŏn′-ə-mē)	the scientific study of the universe beyond the earth *I want to learn about stars so I am going to study astronomy.*
au-di-ence (ô′-dē-əns)	an opportunity to be heard; also, a group of spectators or listeners *He asked for an audience before the king.*
au-thor-i-ty (ə-thôr′-ə-tē)	person who has the right and the power to enforce laws and obedience *The town authorities passed some new traffic laws.*
bal-lis-tics (bə-lĭs′-tĭks)	the examination of bullets and guns to determine the source of a bullet *He hoped the ballistics report would clear him.*
boy-cott (boi′-kŏt)	to refuse to buy or use the services of *The union asked the public to boycott lettuce while the workers were on strike.*
bru-tal-ly (bro͝ot′-l-lē)	cruelly; harshly; savagely *He was treated brutally by the guards.*

ca-the-dral
(kə-thē′-drəl)
a large important church usually headed by a bishop
The wedding of the king took place in a cathedral.

chis-el
(chĭz′-əl)
to cut into stone using a sharp tool
They will chisel the date of the groundbreaking on the cornerstone of the building.

cir-cu-la-tion
(sûr-kyo͞o-lā-shən)
the number of copies of a newspaper or magazine that are sold or distributed
In the first year the new magazine's circulation climbed to half a million.

cir-cum-stan-tial ev-i-dence
(sûr-kəm-stăn′-shəl ĕv′-ə-dəns)
indirect evidence which lawyers will use to try to prove a case; not direct proof
They could not convict him because they had only circumstantial evidence.

con-fes-sion
(kən-fĕsh′-ən)
an act of admitting something one has done that is wrong
He felt better after he had made a full confession of his crime.

con-fined
(kən-fīnd′)
restricted; imprisoned
After the accident he was confined to a wheelchair.

con-so-la-tion
(kŏn′-sə-lā-shən)
the act of bringing comfort
She offered me consolation when I lost my job.

con-spir-a-cy
(kən-spîr′-ə-sē)
a plot, usually secret, to plan a wrongful act
There was a conspiracy to kidnap the rich man.

con-sul
(kŏn′-səl)
someone appointed by a government to represent it in in a foreign city
China sent a consul to San Francisco.

con-tra-dic-to-ry
(kŏn-trə-dĭk′-tə-rē)
the opposite view of a statement
The statements of the two eyewitnesses were contradictory.

con-tro-ver-sial
(kŏn-trə-vûr′-shəl)
a disputed question; not agreed upon
It seemed as if every subject we tried to talk about was controversial.

con-tro-ver-sy
(kŏn-trə-vûr′-sē)
argument or disagreement on a matter of opinion
The two countries had a serious controversy over their borders.

con-vene
(kən-vēn′)

to call together
The chairman wants to convene the committee.

cor-o-na-tion
(kōr-ə-nā′-shən)

the ceremony of crowning a king, queen, pope, etc.
I attended Queen Elizabeth's coronation.

cor-rupt
(kə-rŭpt′)

dishonest; sometimes influenced by bribery
The corrupt official was sent to prison.

cor-rup-ting
(kə-rŭp′-tĭng)

exerting an evil influence
The dictator's speeches were corrupting the citizens.

coun-ter-act
(koun-tər-ăkt′)

to soften the effects by taking a contrary action
I will try to counteract her bad temper by not paying attention to it.

crit-ics
(krĭt′-ĭks)

one who judges something; one who finds fault
I liked that movie but the critics hated it.

cru-ci-fix
(krōō′-sə-fĭks)

an image of Christ on the cross
There was a crucifix on the church altar.

cus-to-dy
(kŭs′-tə-dē)

to guard, protect, or take care of someone
He was kept in custody until the trial began.

ded-i-ca-ted
(dĕd′-ə-kā-tĕd)

to commit oneself to a special cause or thought or action
Before his trip, he dedicated himself to learning how to speak French.

de-fen-dant
(dĭ-fĕn′-dənt)

a person against whom a legal action is brought in a court of law
She was the defendant in the murder case.

de-lib-er-a-tion
(dĭ-lĭb-ə-rā′-shən)

careful consideration before a decision is made
The jury gave the matter its full deliberation.

de-por-ta-tion
(dē-pōr-tā-shən)

the act of expelling someone from a country
The court ordered the deportation of the criminal.

des-per-a-tion
(dĕs-pə-rā′-shən)

giving up hope leading to a disregard of danger; recklessness
In desperation he jumped from the fourth floor to escape the flames.

de-struc-tive
(dĭ-strŭk′-tĭv)

causing something to be destroyed
The storm was terribly destructive.

di-ag-no-sis
(dī-ăg-nō′-sĭs)

to identify a disease by examination
After the examination, the doctor made his diagnosis.

dis-tin-guished
(dĭs-tĭng′-gwĭsht)

famous; special; having superior qualities
The distinguished gentleman from New York will now lead us in the Pledge of Allegiance.

ec-o-nom-ic
(ĕk-ə-nŏm′-ĭk)

pertaining to the wealth of a country
Inflation threatens the economic health of our country.

en-dur-ance
(ĕn-do͞or′-əns)

the power to put up with hardship or stress
She showed a great deal of endurance during the meet.

en-force
(ĕn-fôrs′)

to compel or impose upon by force
It is up to the police to enforce the laws.

ev-o-lu-tion
(ĕv-ə-lo͞o′-shən)

a gradual process in which something changes into a more complex form; a process by which organisms change over time so that descendents are different from their ancestors
Not everyone agrees with Darwin's theory of evolution.

e-volve
(ĭ-vŏlv′)

to develop very slowly or gradually
The plan to start a revolution evolved over several years.

ex-e-cu-tion
(ĕk-sĭ-kyo͞o′-shən)

the act of being put to death, sometimes as legal punishment
No one was allowed to watch the execution.

ex-ile
(ĕg′-zīl)

forced removal from one's own country
The government decided to exile the spy.

ex-pel
(ĕk-spĕl′)

to force or drive out
The boy was expelled from school for cutting classes.

fac-tor
(făk′-tər)

something that contributes to a result or process
There were many factors that went into his decision to quit his job.

fash-ion-a-ble
(făsh′-ən-ə-bəl)

elegant; in style
All of her new clothes were fashionable.

fault-y
(fôlt′-ē)

having defects; not working properly
The carburetor in the secondhand car was faulty.

flawed
(flôd)

imperfect; defective
The diamond was flawed.

for-eign-er
(fôr′-ə-nər)

a person born in or a citizen of a foreign country; an alien
Many foreigners want to go to college in the United States.

foun-der
(found′-ər)

one who establishes something new; an originator
He was the founder of the company.

hem-lock
(hĕm′-lŏk)

a poisonous plant
Hemlock is a fast-acting poison.

her-e-sy
(hĕr′-ə-sē)

a belief opposed to the accepted religion
People are no longer burned at the stake for heresy.

hu-man-i-ty
(hyo͞o-măn′-ə-tē)

kindness; mercy; the quality of being human (can also mean all of mankind; people)
She let her humanity shine through.

hum-ble
(hŭm′-bəl)

not proud; meek; respectful
The humble peasants bowed to the queen.

hys-te-ri-a
(hĭ-ster′-ē-ə)

an emotional outbreak; uncontrollable emotion
Mass hysteria often occurs after a major disaster.

im-peach
(ĭm-pēch′)

to accuse (usually a public official) of wrongdoing
The legislators voted to impeach him.

in-au-gu-ra-tion
(ĭn-ô-gyə-rā′-shən)

the ceremony by which an official (for example, the President of the United States) begins his term of office
He was pleased to be asked to play in the band at the inauguration.

in-ci-dent
(ĭn′-sə-dənt)

a minor event or occurrence
At the time the incident seemed unimportant.

in-dict
(ĭn-dīt′)

to accuse of or charge with a crime
The grand jury is expected to indict him.

in-flame
(ĭn-flām′)

to set on fire; to rouse strong emotion
His powerful speech inflamed the mob.

in-flex-i-ble (ĭn-flĕk′-sə-bəl)	rigid; incapable of changing *She was inflexible about the rules of her classroom.*
in-flu-ence (ĭn′-flo͞o-əns)	the power to affect or change persons or events *He had great influence with the city council.*
in-quest (ĭn′-kwĕst)	legal investigation, usually before a formal trial *Everyone felt there should be an inquest.*
in-sig-ni-a (ĭn-sĭg′-nē-ə)	a badge of office or military rank; an emblem *He was pleased with the way his uniform looked after he had put on the new insignia.*
in-teg-ri-ty (ĭn-tĕg′-rə-tē)	honesty; high moral principles *Lincoln was a man of great integrity.*
in-tel-lec-tu-al (ĭn-tə-lĕk′-cho͞o-əl)	having superior intelligence and knowledge; highly creative *He pretended to be an intellectual but he really wasn't.*
in-ter-cept (ĭn-tər-sĕpt′)	to stop or interrupt the progress of *The message to headquarters was intercepted by the spy.*
in-ter-pret-er (ĭn-tûr′-prə-tər)	one who translates what is said in a foreign language *They needed an interpreter to translate French into English.*
is-sue (ĭsh′-o͞o)	an idea that requires discussion or decision *Many important issues were discussed in the debate.*
jour-ney-man (jûr′-nē′-mən)	a skilled workman who has served his apprenticeship *There were two apprentices but he was the only journeyman in the print shop.*
ju-di-cial (jo͞o-dĭsh′-əl)	something that relates to a court of law or the administration of justice *The judicial process can sometimes be very long and boring.*
land-mark (lănd′-märk)	a historically significant event; a turning point *Winning a college scholarship was a landmark in his life.*
launch (lônch)	to set in motion; to put into action *We will launch our fundraising project next week.*
leg-end (lĕj′-ənd)	a popular story handed down from the past *Have you ever read "The Legend of Sleepy Hollow"?*

li-bel
(lī′-bəl)

a written or printed statement that unjustly damages a person's reputation
He sued the magazine for libel.

lib-er-al
(lĭb′-ər-əl)

tolerant; open-minded
His views were extremely liberal.

mag-is-trate
(măj′-ĭs-trāt)

a low-ranking judge
The magistrate listened to his case and fined him $10.

ma-jes-tic
(mə-jĕs′-tĭk)

splendid, dignified
The Queen Elizabeth was a majestic ship.

ma-jor-i-ty
(mə-jôr′-ĭ-tē)

the greater part of a number
He received the majority of the votes.

mas-sive
(măs′-ĭv)

large; bulky; solid
Some of the rocks in the landslide were massive.

mis-car-riage
(mĭs-kăr′-ĭj)

failure; lack of success in bringing about a fair and desired result in court
His sentence to life in prison was a great miscarriage of justice.

mis-de-mean-or
(mĭs-dĭ-mē′-nər)

a minor offense that is not so serious as a felony
The police officer charges him with a misdemeanor.

mock-er-y
(mŏk′-ər-ē)

something false that pretends to be genuine
The outbreak of war made a mockery of the peace treaty.

mo-tive
(mō′-tĭv)

the reason for doing something
He said that his motive for robbing the store was that he needed money.

mul-ti-ple
(mŭl′-tə-pəl)

more than one; several
The test had some multiple choice questions.

note-wor-thy
(nōt′-wûr-thē)

remarkable; worth of notice
Our trip to Europe was noteworthy in every way.

of-fi-cial
(ə-fĭsh′-əl)

someone who holds a position of authority
He was an official in the government.

op-po-nent
(ə-pō′-nənt)

one who takes the opposite side in a battle, game, argument, etc.
His opponent had a lot of experience in debate.

op-pose (ə-pōz′)	to be against; to be in conflict with *I am opposed to any form of censorship.*
pact (păkt)	an agreement: a treaty *They made a pact always to remain friends.*
par-ty (pär′-tē)	a political group that promotes its own ideals and candidates *When I am 18, I plan to join a political party.*
pen-al-ty (pĕn-əl-tē)	a punishment for a crime or other offense *He received a heavy penalty for driving while drunk.*
per-se-cu-tion (pûr-sə-kyōō′-shən)	cruel punishment because of a difference in beliefs, often religious or political *The Nazis persecuted the people in the countries they conquered.*
phi-los-o-pher (fĭ-lŏs′-ə-fər)	one who is calm, wise, and lives by certain ideals and principles *Many philosophers lived in ancient Greece.*
phys-i-cist (fĭz′-ə-sĭst)	a scientist who studies matter, motion, and energy *In college he planned to study to become a physicist.*
plea (plē)	a strong request *They did not listen to his plea for mercy.*
plun-der (plŭn′-dər)	to rob of goods by force; to loot *The enemy plundered the city.*
post-pone (pōst-pōn′)	to put off; to delay until a later time *If it rains, we will postpone the ceremony.*
pre-scrip-tion (prĭ-skrĭp′-shən)	a doctor's written instructions for medicine *She took the prescription to the drugstore.*
prim-i-tive (prĭm′-ə-tĭv)	crude; simple, early stages of development *The tools used by the cave men were primitive.*
proc-la-ma-tion (prŏk-lə-mā′-shən)	a public announcement *The vice president read the proclamation to the audience.*

pros-e-cu-tion (prŏs-ə-kyo͞o′-shən)	to conduct legal action against someone, usually in court *In the trial the prosecution came first, then the defense.*
pros-e-cu-tor (prŏs′-ə-kyo͞o-tər)	the defense attorney who conducts a legal case against a defendant *The prosecutor asked very tough questions.*
pros-per (prŏs′-pər)	to be successful *He was sure that his new business would prosper.*
pro-vi-sion (prə-vĭzh′-ən)	measures or steps taken beforehand *The new law had many complicated provisions.*
rad-i-cal (răd′-ĭ-kəl)	extreme; one who seeks political and social revolution *The speaker at the demonstration was known to be a radical.*
ra-ti-fy (răt′-ə-fī)	to confirm; to approve *So far six states have ratified the amendment to the Constitution.*
rea-son-a-ble (rē′-zən-ə-bəl)	sound judgment; moderate *They reached a reasonable decision.*
re-cep-tion (rĭ-sĕp′-shən	a formal social function *She was invited to their wedding reception.*
rec-og-nized (rĕk-əg-nīzd)	accepted; known *She was the recognized leader of the group.*
re-luc-tant (rĭ-lŭk′-tənt)	unwilling to do or try something *She was reluctant to move to a new city.*
re-pent-ed (rĭ-pĕn′-tĭd)	to feel sorry about a past action *When he grew old, he repented of all his mistakes.*
rep-re-sent (rĕp-rĭ-zĕnt′)	to serve as the agent for someone *I like the way Senator Smith has been representing me in Congress.*
rep-u-ta-tion (rĕp-yū-tā′-shən)	how one is thought of by other people *He has a very good reputation.*

res-o-lu-tion
(rĕz-ə-lo͞o′-shən)

a formal statement of a decision that has been reached, usually by a group
The committee passed a resolution to hold a fundraising project every year.

rev-o-lu-tion-ar-y
(rĕv-ə-lo͞o′-shə-nĕr-ē)

drastic change or upheaval in thought or action
The idea that the world was round was revolutionary in the 15th century.

rub-ble
(rŭb′-əl)

pieces of stone or brick left after severe destruction
After the bombing all that was left of the city was rubble.

schol-ar
(skŏl-ər)

a learned person, pupil, or student
The author of that history book was a great scholar.

scoun-drel
(skoun′drəl)

a rascal; a worthless person
The place for that scoundrel is jail!

se-cede
(sĭ-cēd′)

to withdraw, especially from a government organization
South Carolina was the first state to secede from the Union.

shrine
(shrīn)

a place or object that is thought to be sacred or holy
They built a shrine to Joan of Arc.

sink-er
(sĭng′-kər)

a weight on a fish line
She tied a new sinker on her fishing line.

sol-i-tar-y
(sŏl′-ə-tĕr-ē)

alone; the only one in a place
The hermit lived a solitary life.

suf-fi-cient
(sə-fĭsh′-ənt)

enough; as much as is needed
The water supply was sufficient for the needs of the town.

su-per-sti-tion
(so͞o-pər-stĭsh′-ən)

a belief not based on fact; faith in magic or chance
Superstition is interesting but never scientific.

sup-press
(sə-prĕs′)

to overpower and crush
The government troops suppressed the riot.

sym-pa-thize
(sĭm′-pə-thīz)

to understand or agree with another's feelings or ideas
I sympathize with your grief over losing your dog.

ten-ure
(tĕn′-yər)

the terms under which a public position is held, often making the position permanent
They could not fire her because she had tenure.

tes-ti-fy
(tĕs′-tə-fī)

to make a statement under oath
He was asked to testify at the trial.

tes-ti-mo-ny
(tĕs′-tə-mō-nē)

a statement made under oath
He swore that his testimony would be the truth and nothing but the truth.

the-o-ry
(thē′-ə-rē)

an idea based on observed facts; assumption; speculation; organized knowledge
He had a theory about what caused the accident.

trea-son
(trē′-zən)

disloyalty to one's country; the illegal act of giving aid to the enemies of one's country
The spy was convicted of treason and sent to prison for life.

tri-bu-nal
(trī-byo͞o′-nəl)

a court of justice
The military tribunal found him guilty.

ul-ti-mate-ly
(ŭl′-tə-mĭt-lē)

the final result
He ultimately reached his goal of sailing around the world.

un-con-sti-tu-tion-al
(ŭn-kŏn-stə-to͞o′-shən-əl)

not in accord with the basic laws of a constitution of a country
It is unconstitutional to tell a person what candidate he must vote for.

un-found-ed
(ŭn-foun′-dĭd)

not confirmed; not based on fact
That rumor is totally unfounded.

un-ion
(yo͞on′-yən)

an organization of workers with common needs and goals
When he started to work at the steel mill, he decided to join the union.

u-ni-verse
(yo͞o′-nə-vûrs)

all that exists, including the earth and everything in space
There is still much to explore in the universe.

un-wit-ting-ly
(ŭn-wĭt′-tĭng-lē)

not knowing; not understanding; not aware
She unwittingly bought a fake diamond ring.

val-id
(văl′-ĭd)

strong; supported by fact; having legal strength
Every single one of his arguments was valid.

ven-dor
(vĕn′-dər)

a peddlar; someone who sells goods from a cart on the street
The ice cream vendor pushed his cart up and down the street.

ver-dict
(vûr′-dĭkt)

decision reached by a jury at the end of a trial
Everyone felt the verdict was fair.

ve-to
(vē′-tō)

the power of the President to reject a bill passed by Congress
We all hoped he would not veto the highway improvement bill.

vul-ner-a-ble
(vŭl′-nər-ə-bl)

easily hurt or wounded; unprotected from danger
The coast of Florida is vulnerable to hurricanes.

war-rant
(wôr′-ənt)

an order to search or to arrest
The police officer handed him a warrant.

Introduction

Calidoscopio gathers together pieces about current and historical events, popular fashions and traditions, humorous and serious topics, scientific data and folk wisdom. These pieces are presented in such a way as to be not only readily accessible to both the beginning and advanced students, but to be informative and entertaining as well. The items have been collected from throughout the Spanish-speaking world over a period of several years. Taken together they form a source supplement to be used in conjunction with *Nuestros amigos* or any other basic student text from the beginning level upward. But above all, the book should be fun to read and to browse through.

As the title implies, *Calidoscopio* makes available a richly diverse collection of information—from realia to photographs to both literary and non-literary reading materials—that reflects both what is changing and what is constant in Hispanic life. While the subjects of the pieces are as diverse and rich as Hispanic culture itself, the collection attempts to capture, amidst all the changing pictures, something of the distinctiveness and flavor that make Hispanic culture unique. While the list of the top ten songs of a certain week in Santo Domingo may not have changed the course of history, it may reveal something of the people who once made them popular—if only for a week. A poem that has stood the test of time might well tell today's students about something that has endured in a particular Spanish-speaking culture for generation after generation.

Throughout the text, careful consideration has been given to the use of cognates that, although new in their Spanish-speaking context, are readily understandable to the native English speaker. Much of the original source material has been taken from areas where Spanish and English are heard side by side, where bilingualism is a simple fact of life. Such passages will be appropriate for both the beginning student, who can read even a complex passage guided by the accompanying translation, and for the advanced student, who can learn from the two passages by comparing one text with the other. For both beginning and advanced student alike, *Calidoscopio* can be used as the source basis for innumerable student projects both inside and outside the classroom. The book hopes to be entertaining, informative, and stimulating.

So, read on and have some fun. And now and then stop to think about what you are reading, and what it is saying to you. Then talk about it.

Contents

Español/Inglés

How much Spanish do you already know?

Take a look at the following words. Do they look familiar?

ARMADA	**GRATIS**	**PLAZA**	**SOMBRERO**
CONQUISTADOR	**MOSQUITO**	**SIESTA**	

They're Spanish words. They're also English words. Many more words are used in both Spanish and English.

ADMIRABLE	**FAMILIAR**	**MATERIAL**	**SALIVA**
CEREAL	**GAS**	**METAL**	**SIMILAR**
CHOCOLATE	**GOLF**	**MINERAL**	**SIMPLE**
COLOR	**HOTEL**	**PIANO**	**TAXI**
DOCTOR	**IDEAL**	**POPULAR**	**TOTAL**
EXTRA	**MANGO**	**RADIO**	

The list could go on and on. These words are called "cognates." They are reCOGNizable despite the language context. Of course, when they are pronounced, their differences in pronunciation can throw you off, but in reading they help you move along and make sense out of sentences although "you've never seen them before."

There is an even longer list of Spanish words that should give you very little trouble. Take a look at some of these words.

AEROPUERTO	**ESPECIAL**	**NACIÓN**	**ROSA**
AUTOBÚS	**GARAJE**	**OCÉANO**	**TELÉFONO**
AUTOMÓVIL	**GORILA**	**PENÍNSULA**	**TELEGRAMA**
DENTISTA	**LEÓN**	**PROVINCIA**	**TELEVISIÓN**
DIRECCIÓN	**MUSEO**	**RADIACIÓN**	**TIGRE**

These words have a little different spelling, but what they mean is pretty clear to anyone who knows the words in English. (Of course, there are some tricky ones that look like they mean one thing, and make no sense at all as cognates, but they're outnumbered by the helpful ones.)

Don't be afraid of new words. Many times you'll know what they mean. Other times you'll have to look them up. Pretty soon you'll feel comfortable dealing with all of them—and the sooner you start, the sooner you'll get there.

Look through a dictionary that gives word origin—most full-size dictionaries do—and find a few English words that were derived from Spanish.

---

inglés *English*

¿Dónde se habla español?

---

se habla *is spoken* **suroeste** *southwest;* **Marruecos** *Morocco*

¿En qué países hablan español?
¿Qué países de las Américas hablan español?
¿Y de Europa? ¿Y de África? ¿Y de Asia?
¿Cómo se llaman los países?

Índico *Indian*

Letreros en español y en inglés

Signs are very useful. In a few words they communicate important information. The signs on this page are from San Juan, Puerto Rico; Santo Domingo, Dominican Republic; and Miami, Florida. These three cities have large Spanish- and English-speaking populations, so the message is in both languages.

CASA DE HUÉSPEDES GUESTHOUSE

OFICINA DE CRÉDITO
CREDIT MANAGER

GENTLEMEN
CABALLEROS

RESTAURANT TROPICANA
OPEN FOR DINNER
ABIERTO PARA CENA

LADIES
DAMAS

WATER FOUNTAIN
FUENTE DE AGUA

PERSONAS AUTORIZADAS SOLAMENTE
AUTHORIZED PERSONNEL ONLY

NO SMOKING
NO FUME

NO ADMITTANCE
NO ENTRE

NO SE PERMITEN RADIOS—TOCACINTAS EN EL ÁREA DE PISCINA
RADIOS—CASSETTE PLAYERS ARE NOT ALLOWED IN POOL AREA

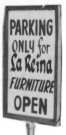

PARQUEO SÓLO Para La Reina MUEBLERÍA ABIERTO

PARKING ONLY for La Reina FURNITURE OPEN

CAJEROS
CASHIERS

Look for signs around the classroom and in your school. See if you can make the same signs in Spanish, with the help of your teacher.

MAFALDA

letreros *signs;* **escuela** *school*

Nombres

¿Cómo se llama él?

Nombres de chicos hispanos

ALBERTO BASILIO CARLOS CHUCHO* DAVID

ERNESTO FEDERICO GUILLERMO HÉCTOR

IGNACIO JACINTO KIKO* LEONARDO LL¿?

MIGUEL NICOLÁS ÑAÑO* OSCAR

PANCHO* QUIQUE* RICARDO SALVADOR TIMOTEO

ULISES VALENTÍN WILFREDO XAVIER

YOYI* ZACARÍAS

¿Cómo se llama ella?

Nombres de chicas hispanas

AURORA BERTA* CELIA CHARO* DELIA

ENRIQUETA FELICIDAD GLORIA HORTENSIA

IRMA JULIA KIKI* LUISA LL¿?

MÓNICA NILDA ÑAÑA* OLGA

PATRICIA QUINTINA ROCÍO SARA TEODORA

ÚRSULA VIOLETA WILFREDA XOCHITL

YOLANDA ZAIDA

Some of the names above have ready English equivalents, others do not. The names followed by stars are nicknames. Kiko *and* Pancho *are both used for* Francisco. Berta *is a name of its own, but it is also used to refer to* Roberta. Yoyi *is a Spanish version of Georgie.* Ñaño *and* Ñaña *are popularly used in Ecuador to refer to older brothers and sisters Many nicknames are the result of baby-talk mispronunciation of the names of older brothers and sisters.* Xochitl *is popular in Mexico—it is a Nahuatl Indian word meaning "flower."*

Nombres, nombres y más nombres

Everything has a name. How else would we know what to call someone or something?

Ferretería
Marisol
*Artículos de Ferretería en General
*Materiales de Construcción
*Varillas *Cemento
*Tuberías *Plywood
TEL. 687-8642
Manuela Diez No. 55
Esq. Ramón Matías Mella, Sto. Dgo.

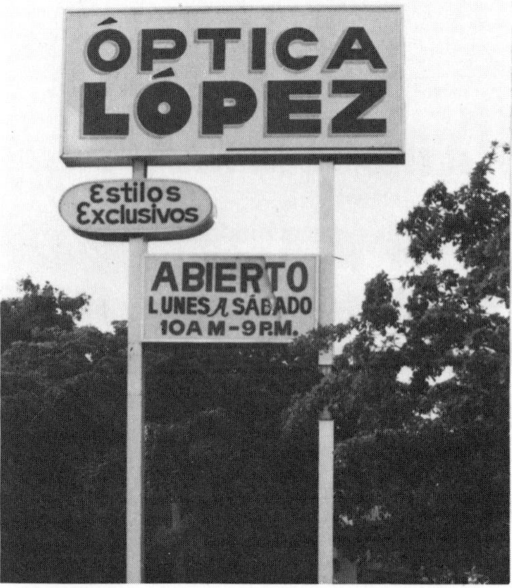

ÓPTICA
LÓPEZ
Estilos
Exclusivos
ABIERTO
LUNES A SÁBADO
10A M-9P.M.

FERRETERÍA
VICTORIA, C. POR A
FERRETERÍA Y QUINCALLERÍA EN GENERAL.
SERVICIO A DOMICILIO
VENTAS AL POR MAYOR
ALMACÉN Y OFICINA:
689-1464/689-1854
DELMONTE Y TEJADA No. 9
689-2344
JUAN ISIDRO PÉREZ No. 205, S.D.

Many names are more than just names. Marisol *is a girl's name made up of* **mar** *(sea) and* **sol** *(sun).* Aurorita *is a nickname for* Aurora *(dawn).* Adelita *is a nickname for* Adela. San Cristóbal *is St. Christopher and* Santiago *is St. James.* **Don** *is a title of respect used with a man's first name.* **Doña** *is its feminine form.* Pedro Calderón de la Barca *was a Spanish playwright who lived from 1600 until 1681 and wrote many comedies and dramas. His best-known play is probably* **La vida es sueño** *(Life Is a Dream).*

---

más *more* **ferretería** *hardware (store)* **calle** *street* **óptica** *optician;* **lunes** *Monday;* **sábado** *Saturday* **quincallería** *housewares;* **servicio a domicilio** *home delivery;* **ventas al por mayor** *wholesale;* **almacén** *store* **cerramos** *we close;* **aceptamos** *we accept;* **tarjetas de crédito** *credit cards*

FERRETERÍA SANTOS, C. por A.

MATERIALES DE CONSTRUCCIÓN

SUCURSAL
565•4324

JUAN ERAZO No. 27,
ESQ. PROF. AMIAMA GÓMEZ S. D.

Adelita's

RESTAURANTE MEXICANO

LA MÁS AUTÉNTICA Y VARIADA
COMIDA MEXICANA EN PUERTO RICO.
ABIERTO TODOS LOS DÍAS DE 11:00 AM. A 10:00 PM.
ESTACIONAMIENTO GRATIS

141 Calle O'Neill, Hato Rey, P. R.
(detrás de Costa Brava)

753-6010

Hotel Don Diego

UN HOTEL NACIONAL
CON EL CONFORT INTERNACIONAL

AV. ESTRELLA SAHDALA, SANTIAGO

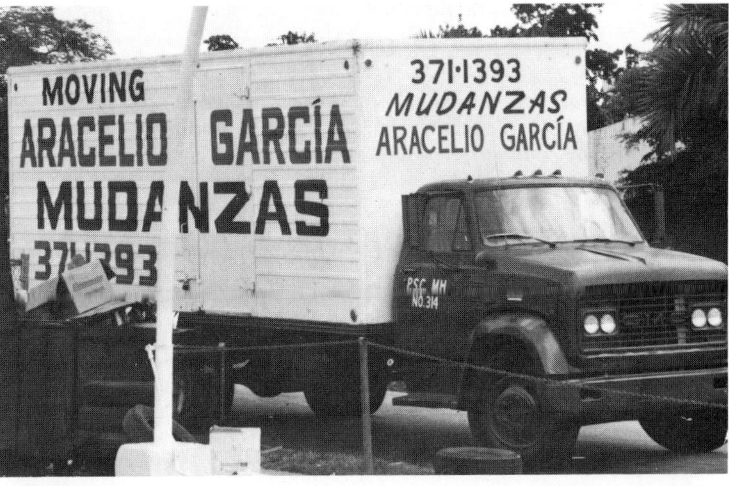

¿Cómo se llaman tres ferreterías en Santo Domingo?
¿Cómo se llama un restaurante mexicano abierto todos los días?
¿Cómo se llama un hotel nacional con el confort internacional?

Apellidos hispanos

ÁLVAREZ	BERMÚDEZ	COLÓN	CHÁVEZ	DELGADO	ESTRADA	FERNÁNDEZ
GONZÁLEZ	HERNÁNDEZ	IGLESIAS	JIMÉNEZ	KERKADÓ	LÓPEZ	LLANOS
MARTÍNEZ	NÚÑEZ	ÑECO	ORTEGA	PÉREZ	QUINTANA	RODRÍGUEZ
SUÁREZ	TORRES	UBIÑAS	VARGAS	W ¿ ?	X ¿ ?	YÁÑEZ	ZAPATA

Go through your local telephone directory and list other Spanish surnames. (Hint: many Spanish last names end in -ez.)

---

la más *the most;* **comida** *food;* **todos los días** *every day;* **estacionamiento** *parking;* **detrás de** *behind* **sucursal** *branch office;* **esq. (esquina)** *(on) the corner (of)* **con** *with* **mudanzas** *movers* **apellidos** *surnames*

Ana Lucero García Allende	Enriquito Luis García Allende	Guille Alberto García Allende	Marisol Ada García Allende
MADRE Estrella Ada Allende González		PADRE Guillermo Luis García Guerra	
ABUELA María del Carmen González Prado	ABUELO Enrique Manuel Allende Estrada	ABUELA María Dolores Guerra Sánchez	ABUELO Arnaldo Eusebio García Rey
BISABUELA Rosa Victoria Estrada Pérez	BISABUELO Manuel Octavio Allende Vélez	BISABUELA América Luisa Rey de la Peña	BISABUELO Mario Luis García Núñez
TATARABUELA Luz Mariana Castro Vélez	TATARABUELO Juan Anselmo Allende Guerra	TATARABUELA Aurora Blanca Núñez Herrera	TATARABUELO Francisco Ernesto García Martínez

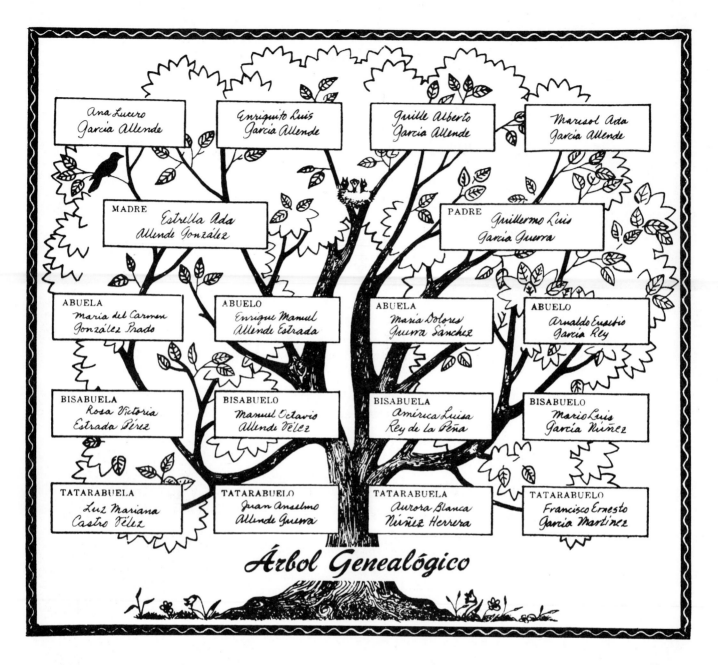

Árbol Genealógico

MAFALDA

Look at the family tree above. Do you understand the Spanish way of passing on surnames from generation to generation? Everyone has two last names. The father's first last name and the mother's first last name make up the child's full last name. Now make your own family tree using all the maiden names you can find out about.

---

bisabuela, bisabuelo *great-grandmother, great-grandfather;* **tatarabuela, tatarabuelo** *great-great-grandmother, great-great-grandfather*

Por el mundo hispano

Una chica rubia y otra chica morena—las dos hispanas de Nueva York.

Dos hermanos en Santo Domingo, la capital de la República Dominicana.

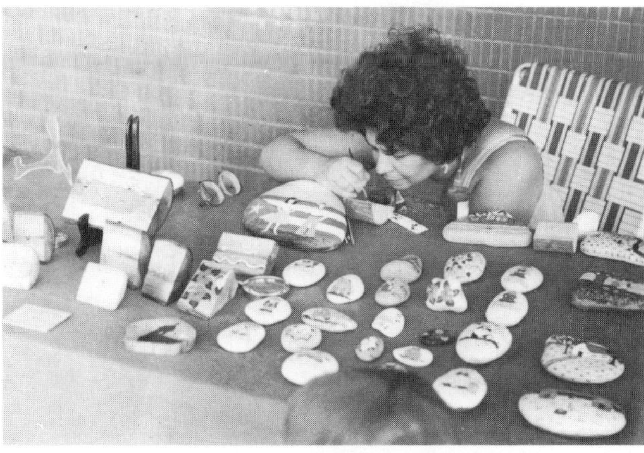

En San Juan, Puerto Rico, una señora pinta° piedras° con escenas típicas.

Ella usa° uniforme cuando° ella trabaja°. Ella trabaja en Puerto Rico.

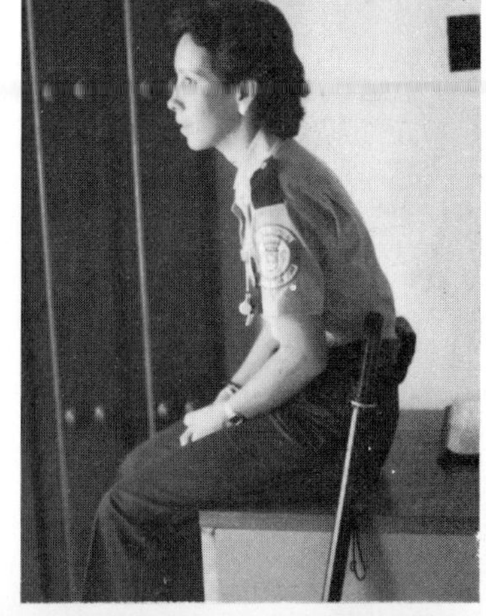

Un turista de Filadelfia en San Juan, la capital de Puerto Rico.

Describe las fotos.

1. ¿Cómo son las dos chicas hispanas de Nueva York?
2. ¿Qué son los chicos de Santo Domingo?
3. ¿De qué país es Santo Domingo la capital?
4. ¿Qué pinta la señora de San Juan?
5. ¿Qué usa ella cuando ella trabaja?
6. ¿En qué capital está° el turista de Filadelfia?

---

mundo *world* **pinta** *paints;* **piedras** *stones;* **usa** *wears;* **cuando** *when;* **trabaja** *works* **está** *is*

En la Feria Mundial Hispana de Nueva York

Every August, a Hispanic World's Fair is held in New York City. Merchants, manufacturers, entertainers, and artists all join to celebrate EL MUNDO HISPANO.

feria mundial *world's fair* **coliseo** *coliseum;* **viernes** *Friday;* **domingo** *Sunday;* **mediodía** *noon;* **hasta** *until;* **cerveza** *beer;* **helados** *ice cream;* **sorteos** *raffles;* **regalos** *gifts;* **entradas** *entrance fees;* **niños** *children;* **llame** *call;* **venga** *come;* **su** *your*

El Coliseo de Nueva York es muy grande.

Un grupo de músicos° sudamericanos°. Su música es muy bonita y muy animada°.

Otros° tocan° música puertorriqueña y dominicana—salsa° y merengue°, la música del Caribe.

El café es fuerte . . . y muy sabroso°.

---

músicos *musicians;* **sudamericanos** *South American;* **animada** *lively;* **otros** *others;* **tocan** *play;* **salsa, merengue** *Caribbean dance music;* **sabroso** *delicious*

Los trajes° son bonitos y la música es alegre°. Las chicas cantan° y bailan° muy bien°, y todas° las personas en la feria preguntan°, ¿quiénes son ellas? ¡Qué° guapas!

El payaso° es muy alto y ve° todo. Todos preguntan, ¿quién es el payaso?

Él es pequeño°. ¡Pero él quiere° ver° también!

---

trajes *costumes;* **alegre** *happy;* **cantan** *sing;* **bailan** *dance;* **bien** *well;* **todo (-a, -os, -as)** *all;* **preguntan** *ask;* **qué** *how;* **payaso** *clown;* **ve** *sees;* **pequeño** *small;* **quiere** *wants;* **ver** *to see*

La belleza hispana

Una chica chilena usa un vestido tradicional de Chile.

¿De dónde es ella?

Una chica cubana habla con un admirador.

Todas las representantes de los países hispanos son bonitas y están° alegres . . . pero ¿qué pasa° ahora°?

Take a group of your own photographs taken at some family or school event. Lay them out on a piece of paper and write your own set of captions describing the photos and what was happening when they were taken—in Spanish.

MAFALDA

---

 belleza *beauty* **están** *are;* **qué pasa** *what's happening;* **ahora** *now*

Educación

Education is carried out on many different levels throughout the Spanish-speaking world. There are many posters and ads that promote the importance of learning—from learning to read to the specialized levels offered by the universities.

Obra° de Jaime Villa, pintor ecuatoriano, para el Programa Nacional de Alfabetización° de Ecuador.

Estudiantes en una escuela pequeña de San Pedro de Macorís, en la República Dominicana. Ellos estudian inglés. ¡Todos aprendemos!°

UNIVERSIDAD
SIMÓN BOLÍVAR
LA UNIVERSIDAD DEL FUTURO
COLEGIO DE PROFESORES DE VENEZUELA
Curso de Actualización
Académica
LA GEOGRAFÍA Y SU ENSEÑANZA
UNIVERSIDAD NACIONAL EXPERIMENTAL SIMÓN RODRÍGUEZ
REPÚBLICA DE VENEZUELA

In Spanish, many printers and sign-makers leave accents off capital letters. This is too bad, because the written accent mark tells us exactly how to pronounce a word we have never seen before—and is often the only difference between two completely different words. (We'll put them in wherever they are needed to make the meaning clear.)

---

obra *work;* **alfabetización** *literacy;* **¡Todos aprendemos!** *We all learn!* **enseñanza** *teaching*

El alfabeto

The Spanish alphabet has twenty-eight letters—including CH, LL, *and* Ñ. *It does not have a* W; *but* W's *are called* "doble ve" *or* "doble u" *depending on the country. (Spanish words with the letter* W *are of foreign origin.) Can you think of any other Spanish words that you can illustrate?*

a
A ARCA
El arca de Noé°.

be
B BUEY
El buey es fuerte.

ce
C CASTILLO
El castillo está en Castilla°.

che
CH CHINELA°
Una chinela de China.

de
D DIENTES°
Los dientes de la dentadura°.

e
E ESPEJO°
¿Qué ves° en el espejo?

efe
F FLECHA°
¿Dónde está la flecha?

ge
G GALLO
El gallo canta° temprano°.

hache
H HOMBRE
El hombre hierve° huevos°.

i
I INDIO
Un indio americano.

jota
J JARRA
La jarra es para agua.

ka
K KIOSKO
¿Para qué es un kiosko?

Noé *Noah;* **Castilla** *Castile, a region of Spain;* **chinela** *slipper;* **dientes** *teeth;* **dentadura** *denture;* **espejo** *mirror;* **ves** *do you see;* **flecha** *arrow;* **canta** *crows, sings;* **temprano** *early;* **hierve** *boils;* **huevos** *eggs*

 **ele** **L LEÓN** El león vive° en la selva°.	 **ere, erre** **R RATÓN** El ratón corre° rápido.
 **elle** **LL LLAMA°** La llama de la vela°.	 **ese** **S SABLE°** Un sable es una espada°.
 **eme** **M MUJER** Una mujer elegante.	 **te** **T TINTERO°** La tinta° está en el tintero.
 **ene** **N NIDO°** Las aves° nacen° en nidos.	 **u** **U URNA** Una urna griega°.
 **eñe** **Ñ NIÑO** El niño viene° mañana°.	 **ve** **V VACA** Las vacas dan° leche°.
 **o** **O OJO** Ojos oscuros° y misteriosos.	 **equis** **X XILÓFONO** Un xilófono es una marimba.
 **pe** **P PUERCO** Los puercos no comen° perlas.	 **i griega** **Y YUNQUE°** Un yunque de hierro°.
 **cu** **Q QUIJOTE** Don Quijote y Rocinante°.	 **zeta** **Z ZEBRA** Pero, ¿son zebras o cebras?

---

vive *lives;* **selva** *jungle;* **llama** *flame;* **vela** *candle;* **nido** *nest;* **aves** *birds;* **nacen** *are born;* **viene** *comes;* **mañana** *tomorrow;* **oscuros** *dark;* **comen** *eat;* **Rocinante** *Don Quijote's horse;* **corre** *runs;* **sable** *saber;* **espada** *sword;* **tintero** *inkwell;* **tinta** *ink;* **griega** *Greek;* **dan** *give;* **leche** *milk;* **yunque** *anvil;* **hierro** *iron*

El boletín

There is something universal about the look of a report card. This one is from Maracaibo, Venezuela. The grading system is a little different—but not really!

COLEGIO
"SAN VICENTE DE PAÚL"
TELÉFONOS: 72327 Y 82781
MARACAIBO

Resumen de la Actuación del Alumno

BOLETÍN

ESCALAS UTILIZADAS PARA LA EVALUACIÓN

Cuantitativa (numérica)

del 19 al 20 - Sobresaliente
del 16 al 18 - Distinguido
del 13 al 15 - Bueno
del 10 al 12 - Regular
del 5 al 9 - Deficiente
del 1 al 4 - Muy deficiente

Cualtitativa

A : Sobresaliente
B : Distinguido
C : Bueno
D : Regular
E : Deficiente
F : Muy Deficiente

actuación *performance;* **utilizadas** *used;* **sobresaliente** *outstanding*

RENDIMIENTO ESCOLAR

ASIGNATURAS	1er. Lapso		2o. Lapso		3er. Lapso		PREVIA	FINAL
	Califi-cación	Ina-sis-ten.	Califi-cación	Ina-sis-ten.	Califi-cación	Ina-sis-ten.		
Castellano y Literatura	13	1	12	3	15		13	13
Matemáticas	14	2	16	2	12	3	14	15
Ciencias Biológicas	17	2	14	2	13		15	16
Química								
Física								
Geografía e Historia	16	1	11	4	13		13	15
Formación Social, Moral y Cívica	12		12		12	1	12	14
Inglés	12	2	13	1	13	1	13	13
Educación Artística	13		14		12		13	15
Manualidades	A		B	2	A	3	B/A	A
Religión								
Educación Física	10		16		16		14	14

Promedio: 14,4

OTROS RASGOS DE LA ACTUACIÓN ESCOLAR	1er. Lapso	2do. Lapso	3er. Lapso		
Responsabilidad	C	D	D		
Hábitos de trabajo y de salud	C	C	C		
Presentación Personal y Cortesía	C	C	B		
Creatividad e Iniciativa	B	B	B		
Ajuste Social	B	B	B		
Confianza en sí mismo	C	B	B		

¿En qué asignaturas es el alumno sobresaliente? ¿Y distinguido? ¿Y bueno? ¿Y regular? ¿Y . . . ? ¿Cómo es el alumno? ¿Cuál es su promedio?

Make your own report card in Spanish (for all your school subjects). Remember to be fair when you grade yourself.

---

rendimiento escolar *scholastic performance;* **asignaturas** *subjects;* **lapso** *marking period;* **calificacción** *grade, mark;* **inasisten, (inasistencia)** *days absent;* **castellano** *Spanish, Castilian;* **e**=**y** *and;* **manualidades** *arts and crafts* **promedio** *average;* **rasgos** *traits, characteristics;* **trabajo** *work;* **salud** *health;* **confianza** *confidence;* **sí mismo** *oneself*

LETRA CURSIVA°

The following letters appeared as models for penmanship in a primer from the beginning of the century. Why don't you try your own hand?

A B C CH D E F G H I J K L LL M N Ñ O P
Q R S T U V X Y Z

a b c ch d e f g h i j k l ll m n ñ o p q r s t u v x y z. --- 1 2 3 4 5 6 7 8 9 0

MAFALDA

 cursiva *in script* **así** *like that;* **entiendes** *do you understand*

Publicaciones en español

There are hundreds, perhaps thousands, of newspapers in Spanish that are published daily. Turn the page for a few of them.

PRENSA LIBRE
POR UN PERIODISMO INDEPENDIENTE HONRADO Y DIGNO

ÍNDICE DE SECCIONES

índice

Índice Clasificado	Classified Index
100 EMPLEOS	100 EMPLOYMENT
150 CURSOS Y CARRERAS	150 COURSES & CAREERS
200 ALQUILERES	200 RENTALS
300 BIENES RAÍCES	300 REAL ESTATE
400 MERCADERÍA	400 MERCHANDISE
500 OPORTUNIDADES COMERCIALES	500 BUSINESS OPPORTUNITIES
600 SERVICIOS PROFESIONALES	600 PROFESSIONAL SERVICES
700 SERVICIOS COMERCIALES	700 COMMERCIAL SERVICES
750 SERVICIOS PERSONALES	750 PERSONAL SERVICES
800 AVISOS PERSONALES	800 ANNOUNCEMENTS
900 AUTOMÓVILES	900 AUTOMOBILES

---

prensa *press;* **periodismo** *journalism;* **honrado** *honest;* **digno** *dignified;* **anuncio clasificado, clasificados** *classified ads;* **tiras cómicas** *comic strips* **deportes** *sports;* **espectáculos** *shows;* **feminidades** *women's page;* **variedades** *variety shows, entertainments*

EL TIEMPO

EDICIÓN DE 36 PÁGINAS
TRES SECCIONES

EL UNIVERSAL

Fundado en 1909 · ANDRES MATA + Fundador
AFILIADO AL "BLOQUE DE PRENSA VENEZOLANO"

38 PÁGINAS
3 SECCIONES

TELÉFONOS:
CENTRAL DIURNA:
7511 - 561.73.55
12 de la noche
561.34.18
1.263

EL NACIONAL

Depósito Legal pp 76-0536/Lunes a viernes Bs. 1.50/Sábado y domingo Bs. 2.50/Circulación ABC /Transporte al exterior por VIASA

EL PERIÓDICO

Campeón de los hispanos
el Diario
La Prensa

EL VOCERO
DE PUERTO RICO
SAN JUAN, P.R.

EL ESPECTADOR
Bogotá, martes, junio 29
AÑO XCV N.° 26.636

Un periódico de todos
y para todos

Año C

1. ¿Cuántas páginas tiene el periódico más grande?
2. ¿Cómo se llama el periódico de Guayaquil, Ecuador?
3. ¿De dónde es "El Vocero"?
4. ¿De qué país es "El Colombiano"? ¿Dónde está Medellín?
5. ¿Cómo se llama un periódico de la capital de Uruguay?

---

tiempo *time* **páginas** *pages* **periódico** *newspaper* **campeón** *champion;* **diario** *daily (newspaper)*
vocero *spokesman* **espectador** *spectator*

DIARIO
EL UNIVERSO
EL MAYOR DIARIO NACIONAL
AÑO 61 — N° 285 — Guayaquil — Ecuador — Domingo 27 de Junio
5 Secciones
60 Páginas
DE MAYOR CIRCULACIÓN
Esta edición consta de tres secciones
EL COLOMBIANO
AÑO LXXI NUMERO 23.269
VIA AVIANCA y ACES
Tarifa Postal Reducida N° 77 de la Administración Postal Nacional
Medellín, Miércoles 30 de Junio
EDICIÓN DE 84 PÁGINAS
LA NACIÓN
San José, Costa Rica, lunes 28 de junio
EL COMERCIO
DIARIO INDEPENDIENTE
Quito - Ecuador, domingo 27 de junio
144
PÁGINAS
Cuatro Cuerpos
PRENSA LIBRE
POR UN PERIODISMO INDEPENDIENTE HONRADO Y DIGNO
EL PERIÓDICO DE MAYOR CIRCULACIÓN
GUATEMALA
22 PÁGINAS EN 2 SECCIONES
Incluido Supl. Deportivo $ 6.000.
Núm. 33.501
LOS ANDES
Publicación adherida al Instituto Verificador de Circulaciones
MENDOZA — Lunes 12 de
CON SUPLEMENTO CULTURAL
EL DÍA
Fundado por DON JOSÉ BATLLE Y ORDONEZ el 16 de junio de 1886
Siempre al Servicio de la Libertad
MONTEVIDEO, DOMINGO 27 DE JUNIO

---

el mayor *the largest* **consta de** *is composed of* **comercio** *business* **cuerpos** *parts* **incluido supl. deportivo** *sports supplement included* **fundado por** *founded by*

Escudos de las repúblicas de Hispanoamérica

Argentina, Bolivia, Chile, Colombia, Costa Rica, Cuba, Ecuador, El Salvador, Guatemala, Honduras, México, Nicaragua, Panamá, Paraguay, Perú, República Dominicana, Uruguay, Venezuela

¿Cuántos países están representados por los escudos en esta página y no en los periódicos en las páginas 22 y 23?

Choose one of the countries represented above and do a little research in the library about its history, geography, customs. What is it known for internationally? If you wanted to visit that country, how would you get there? Maybe you can find some people that you know, who have visited or lived in that country.

MAFALDA

 escudos *shields, coats of arms* **gestión** *measure, step, action;* **para lograr el desarme** *to achieve disarmament*

Teléfonos

It took Columbus over two months to sail from Spain to the New World. It still takes hours—even by jet—to go from one country to another. But pick up a telephone in New York City and within minutes you can speak to a friend in Buenos Aires, Argentina. Many international calls can be dialed directly, using a series of code numbers for the countries and cities.

Argentina	54	Honduras	504
Bolivia	591	Nicaragua	505
Colombia	57	Panamá	507
Costa Rica	506	Paraguay	595
Chile	56	Perú	51
Ecuador	593	El Salvador	503
España	34	Venezuela	58
Guatemala	502		

Puerto Rico has an area code and seven-digit phone numbers, just like most American telephone lines. The area code for Puerto Rico is 809.

While many telephone operators in Spanish-speaking countries speak some English, it doesn't hurt to be prepared and know what to say in Spanish.

¿Operadora? Larga distancia, por favor.

Quiero° llamar un número en Nueva York.

El número es área (212) 666-0493.

Persona a persona a Juan Pérez, por favor.

Mi número es área (809) 754-3303.

Gracias.

¿La línea está ocupada?

Bueno°, entonces llamo más tarde°, gracias.

¡Líneas disponibles en esta colonia!
¡Solicite su teléfono!

quiero *I want;* **bueno** *fine;* **más tarde** *later* **disponibles** *available;* **esta** *this;* **colonia** *housing development;* **solicite** *apply for;* **TM (Teléfonos de México)** *Mexican telephone company*

En San Juan, Puerto Rico, la guía telefónica tiene una página con muchos teléfonos importantes en caso de emergencia.

GUÍA INFORMATIVA

ÁREA METROPOLITANA

TELÉFONOS DE EMERGENCIA

POLICÍA EMERGENCIAS	343-2020
BOMBEROS	343-2330
EMERGENCIA MÉDICA	343-2550
SERVICIO EMERGENCIA DE HOSPITALES	VÉASE PÁGINA 28
MÉDICO	Oficina ______ Residencia ______
CENTRO MÉDICO DE P.R.	754-3535
SERVICIO SECRETO FEDERAL	753-4539
DEFENSA CIVIL	724-0124
GUARDACOSTAS	722-2943
NEGOCIADO FEDERAL DE INVESTIGACIÓN (F.B.I.)	754-6000
CENTRO DE TRATAMIENTO POR ENVENENAMIENTO	754-3515

 guía *guide, directory;* **véase** *see;* **envenenamiento** *poison*

Llamadas internacionales

Llamadas internacionales, como° todas llamadas de larga distancia, son más económicas si llamamos durante° las horas cuando no llaman muchas personas —de noche°, por ejemplo°. Una página de la guía telefónica de Santo Domingo, República Dominicana, tiene diferentes tarifas° que dependen en la hora y el día cuando uno llama.

Período inicial de 3 minutos.

Para tarifas a países no indicados favor de llamar al O

	ESTACIÓN A ESTACIÓN		PERSONA A PERSONA	
	LUNES A SÁBADO	LUNES A SÁBADO Y DOMINGO	LUNES A SÁBADO	LUNES A SÁBADO Y DOMINGO
CURAZAO	4.50	3.30 7:p.m. - 7:a.m.	6.00	4.50 7:p.m. - 7:a.m.
E. FLORIDA	4.00	3.00 5:p.m. - 4:a.m.	6.00	4.50 5:p.m. - 4:a.m.
E. NEW JERSEY	6.00	5.00 5:p.m. - 4:a.m.	9.00	7.50 5:p.m. - 4:a.m.
U. NEW YORK	6.00	5.00 5:p.m. - 4:a.m.	9.00	7.50 5:p.m. - 4:a.m.
U. WASHINGTON, D. C.	5.00	4.00 5:p.m. - 4:a.m.	7.50	6.00 5:p.m. - 4:a.m.
PUERTO RICO	3.00	2.50 5:p.m. - 7:a.m.	4.50	3.75 5:p.m. - 7:a.m.
VENEZUELA	4.50	3.30 5:p.m. - 5:a.m.	6.00	4.50 5:p.m. - 7:a.m.
	LUNES A SÁBADO	LUNES A SÁBADO 8P.M. - 8A.M. Y DOMINGO	LUNES A SÁBADO	LUNES A SÁBADO 8P.M. - 8A.M. Y DOMINGO
ESPAÑA	9.00	7.50	12.00	10.00
	LUNES A SÁBADO	DOMINGO		TODA LA SEMANA
COLOMBIA	9.00	7.50	ALEMANIA	15.00
INGLATERRA	15.60	7.80		9.00 Estación a Estación
JAMAICA	7.50	6.00	FRANCIA	12.00 Persona a Persona
MÉXICO	10.50	8.25	ITALIA	15.00

Valores indicados más el impuesto

como *like;* **durante** *during;* **de noche** *at night;* **por ejemplo** *for example;* **tarifas** *rates* **favor de** *please* **Inglaterra** *England;* **Alemania** *Germany;* **toda la semana** *all week long;* **más el impuesto** *plus tax*

This repairman's calling card was in use in Spanish-speaking areas of New York City. The wording of the Spanish and English texts is not exactly the same. In Spanish, a more polite tone is kept, avoiding "must" and using "please." Yet the English text is perfectly cordial and to the point.

Un mensaje de su compañía de Teléfono

*SENTIMOS MUCHO NO HABERLO VISTO PARA REPARAR SU TELÉFONO

Por favor llame al teléfono indicado cuando sea conveniente para darle una nueva cita.

*CONFIAMOS QUE USTED ENCUENTRE SU SERVICIO COMPLETADO SATISFACTORIAMENTE.

Pero si usted encuentra algo en el trabajo realizado que quiera discutir por favor llame a la Oficina de servicio de reparar el teléfono.

entre 9:00 A.M. y 9:00 P.M. Refiérase al # de teléfono.

**Servicio gratis*

SU HOMBRE REPARADOR

IMPORTANT

A word about your Telephone Service

*WE'RE SORRY WE MISSED YOU WHEN WE CALLED TO REPAIR YOUR TELEPHONE SERVICE.

YOU MUST CALL THE NUMBER BELOW AS SOON AS YOU CAN FOR A NEW APPOINTMENT

*WE TRUST THAT YOU WILL FIND YOUR SERVICE COMPLETELY SATISFACTORY.

But if there is anything about this repair you'd like to discuss, please call your REPAIR SERVICE OFFICE DIRECT.

between 9:00 A.M. & 9:00 P.M. and refer to your telephone number.

**no charge for this call*

YOUR REPAIRMAN

Using the telephone dial, translate a Spanish word into numbers. For example, DOMINGO *would be* 3664646. *Then ask a classmate to guess the word.*
(Remember not to mix up O *— the letter — and* 0 *—* Operadora *— or it just won't work.)*

Make your own telephone directory in Spanish.

MI DIRECTORIO	
NOMBRE Y DIRECCIÓN	TELÉFONO
DOCTOR	
DENTISTA	
MAMI (oficina)	
PAPI (oficina)	

In Spanish, memorize a few of your most-often called telephone numbers. (Start with your own.)

MAFALDA

 dirección *address* **veo** *I see;* **cosa** *thing*

Comidas

The appeal of food is universal. Discovering new dishes, restaurants, cuisines, and foods is an exciting way to learn about a new culture. Even familiar foods may seem different.

La paella es el plato español de más popularidad° internacional. Su origin es la costa de España en el Mediterráneo. La ciudad de Valencia es famosa por su paella valenciana.

popularidad *popularity*

The language of restaurant menus is always full of surprises. Menu entries have to compete with each other to attract the attention of the diner; and the fancier the restaurant, the more difficult it is to figure out exactly what you are going to get when the food arrives. Anything breaded is suddenly "Milanese," spinach makes it "Florentine," and at the drop of a fork the entire menu becomes French, Hawaiian, or of whatever nationality the cuisine of the restaurant favors. Sometimes ¡Buena suerte! *seems appropriate before saying* ¡Buen apetito! *Look at the following menus and pick your favorite dishes.*

che's RESTAURANT & DELICATESSEN
ARGENTINIAN FOOD & DELICACIES

CAOBA 36, PUNTA LAS MARÍAS — SAN JUAN, PUERTO RICO — 726-7202

soups / sopas

Sopa de cebolla Gratin Onion soup Gratinée	2.50
Crema de espárragos Cream of Asparagus	2.00
Sopa de vegetales Vegetable soup	2.00

pastas

Fettucinis Verdes (Green):
Vermichelli:
Fusilli:

Salsas:	
Tomates Tomatoes	4.95
Mantequilla Butter	4.80
Pulpos y calamares Octopus and squid	6.25
Bolognesa Meat	5.45

Canelones de carne o espinaca y seso Canelloni with beef, or spinach and brains	6.25
Lasaña Lasagna	6.25
Ravioles de carne o espinaca Ravioli, Beef or Spinach	5.95

aperitivos / appetizers

Antipasto (2 personas) Assorted cold cuts (for two)	5.80
Jamón Prosciutto con melón Prosciutto and melon	3.95
Matambre con ensalada rusa Cold rolled meat with potato salad	3.95
Torta pascualina Spinach pie	2.80
Palmitos con salsa golf Hearts of palms with golf sauce	3.85
Empanada de carne o queso Meat or cheese filled pie	1.50
Bróculi a la parmesana Broccoli with Parmesan cheese	3.95
Lengua a la vinagreta Pickled tongue	3.35
Empanada de Jueyes Crabmeat Pie	1.75
Tomate relleno con pollo o Atún Tomato stuffed with chicken or tuna	3.50
Espárragos a la parmesana Asparagus with Parmesan cheese	3.95
Chorizos parrilleros (2) Barbecued Argentinian sausages (2)	3.50
Cóctel de camarones Shrimp cocktail	4.95
1/2 Aguacate (de estación con camarones y salsa golf) Half avocado with shrimp and golf sauce	4.95

parrilla / grill

Bife de chorizo 10 oz. New York sirloin	12.55
Bife de cuadril 10 oz. Top Sirloin 10 oz.	11.50
Bife de vacio 10 oz. Flank steak 10 oz.	8.95
Bife de lomo 10 oz. Mignon steak 10 oz.	12.95
Churrasco Skirt steak	7.95
Asado de tira Beef short ribs	6.95
Salchicha criolla Pork sausages	5.95
Riñones Kidneys	4.95
Bife "Che's" 10 oz. Che's Beef (Rib Eye)	12.35
Mollejas Sweet Breads	8.95
Chorizos parrilleros (2) Barbecued Argentinian sausages (2)	4.75
Carne al Pincho Beef brochettes	9.75
Carne al pincho con camarones Beef and shrimp brochettes	10.95
Parrillada argentina (para 2 personas) Argentinian grill (for two)	17.80
Pollo al limón Grilled chicken dressed with lemon juice	6.25

Acompañado con papas fritas o tostones o arroz y habichuelas o ensalada.
Served with French fries, or plantains or rice and beans or salad.

Hamburger	3.70
Cheeseburger	3.95

entradas / entrees

Milanesa argentina Breaded veal cutlet	5.95
Milanesa a caballo Breaded veal cutlet with two fried eggs	6.95
Milanesa a la napolitana (salsa de tomate, queso y jamón) Breaded veal cutlet with tomato sauce, cheese and ham	7.95
Sesos a la romana Breaded calf brains	6.50
Camarones empanados Breaded Shrimp	5.90

Acompañado con papas fritas o tostones o arroz y habichuelas o ensalada.

salads / ensaladas

Rusa (Papas, arvejas, remolachas y huevo duro) Potato salad with beets, petit pois and hard boiled eggs	1.80
Habichuelas tiernas con huevo duro Green beans with chopped boiled eggs	1.80
Manzana y apio Apple and celery	1.80
Lechuga y tomate Lettuce and tomatoes	1.75
Mixta (Lechuga, tomate y cebolla) Lettuce, tomatoes and onions	1.85
Especial (Lechuga, tomates, palmitos y espárragos Special (Lettuce, tomatoes, palm's hearts and asparagus)	2.75
Del Chef Chef's salad	4.85

Arroz y habichuelas	2.00
Salsa de setas Mushroom sauce	1.50
Papas fritas French fried potatoes	1.25

El Hotel Lina, en Santo Domingo, tiene uno de los más famosos restaurantes de la capital dominicana. Aquí está parte de su magnífico° menú.

APERITIVOS

Jugo de Tomate	0.90
Cóctel de Frutas Tropicales	1.25
Suprema de Toronja	1.00
Paté "Maison"	2.50
Entremeses Variados	5.00
Cóctel de Camarones	5.00
Cóctel de Langosta	7.00
Ostras Frescas en su Concha 1 Doc.	3.50
Queso de Cabeza de Jabalí	3.00
Jamón Serrano con Melón	7.00
Caviar Legítimo	16.00
Cazuelita de Callos a la Madrileña	3.00
Croquetas de Jamón y Pollo	2.50
Caracoles a la Borgoñona – 1/2 Doc.	5.00
Champignons al Ajillo	3.50
Hongos a la Segoviana Con tocineta y salsa en vino blanco	3.75
Salmón Ahumado	10.00
Camarones al Ajillo	4.00
Calamares a la Plancha	4.50
Calamares Fritos	4.50
Calamares a la Santanderina	4.50
Pulpitos de Roca a la Plancha	4.50

APPETIZERS

Tomato Juice	0.90
Tropical Fruit Cocktail	1.25
Grapefruit Supreme	1.00
Paté "Maison" (Home Fashion)	2.50
Hors D' oeuvres	5.00
Shrimp Cocktail	5.00
Lobster Cocktail	7.00
Oysters Half Shell – 1 Doz	3.50
Head Cheese	3.00
Spanish Cured Ham with Cantaloupe	7.00
Caviar Molosol	16.00
Tripe, Madrilenian Style, Small Casserole	3.00
Ham and Chicken Croquettes (fritters)	2.50
Escargots à la Bourguignon – 1/2 Doz	5.00
Sautéed Mushrooms with Garlic	3.50
Mushrooms Segovian Style With bacon and white wine sauce	3.75
Smoked Salmon	10.00
Sautéed Shrimp with Garlic	4.00
Broiled Squid Rings	4.50
Fried Squid Rings	4.50
Sautéed Squid Rings, Onions	4.50
Broiled Baby Octopus	4.50

NUESTRAS ESPECIALIDADES

Mero al Coco	9.00
Mero Lina	9.00
Mero a la Vasca	7.50
Chillo al Queso	13.00
Camarones a la Plancha	12.00
Langosta al Whisky	15.00
Zarzuela de Mariscos	12.00
Parrillada de Mariscos y Pescado	14.00
Mariscos al Jerez	14.00
Callos a la Madrileña	6.00
Paella a la Valenciana (30 Minutos)	7.00
Paella a la Marinera (30 Minutos)	8.50
Escalope de Ternera Cordon Bleu	8.50
Filete Tártaro (Carne Cruda)	9.00
Filete Roquefort	11.00
Filete a la Pimienta	11.00
Filete a la Mostaza	11.00
Filete al Orégano	11.00
Corazón de Filete "Gran Gastrónomo"	13.00

OUR SPECIALTIES

Sea Bass With Coconut Sauce	9.00
Sea Bass Flambé Au Brandy	9.00
Sea Bass, Basque Style	7.50
Red Snapper Sautéed With Cheese and Almonds	13.00
Broiled Jumbo Shrimp	12.00
Lobster Au Whisky	15.00
Mixed Seafood, in Casserole	12.00
Mixed Grill of Seafood and Fish	14.00
Seafood in Sherry Wine	14.00
Tripe, Madrilenian Style	6.00
Paella Valencian Style (30 Min.) Rice with Chicken, and Mixed Seafood	7.00
Paella of Rice and Seafood (30 Min.)	8.50
Veal "Cordon Bleu"	8.50
Filet Tartar (Raw Meat)	9.00
Roquefort Steak	11.00
Pepper Steak	11.00
Mustard Steak	11.00
Oregano Steak	11.00
The Superb Beef Tenderloin "Gran Gastrónomo"	13.00

Pretend you're going out to dinner at Che's Restaurant or the Hotel Lina. Choose a meal from the menus on these pages.

---

magnífico *great, splendid*

Receta

Black beans are a favorite dish of the Caribbean area. There are many variations of the basic dish—and a good cook will almost NEVER give out his or her recipe. Like most Caribbean dishes, black beans take much of their flavor from a sofrito, *which is made separately and added to the soup. The most popular way of eating black beans is over white rice, but they are also good with chopped hard-boiled eggs and sour cream—or by themselves.*

Following is an old Cuban recipe for black beans.

FRIJOLES NEGROS

1 lb. frijoles negros
10 tazas de agua
1 ají°

—Lavar° los frijoles.
—Poner los frijoles en agua, con un ají, por 3-6 horas.
—Cocinar° por 45 minutos—1 hora.

2/3 taza aceite de oliva°
1 cebolla°
4 dientes° de ajo°
1 ají
4 cdtas.° de sal
1/2 cdta. de pimienta
1/4 cdta. de orégano
1 hoja° de laurel
2 cdas.° de azúcar

Sofrito°
Picar° la cebolla y el ají—sin semillas°. Machacar° el ajo.
Freír° la cebolla, el ají y el ajo hasta dorar°.
Echar° 1 taza de frijoles aplastados° (con mucho cuidado°).
Cocinar por 5 minutos.

—Echar el sofrito en la cazuela° con los frijoles.
—Añadir° la sal, la pimienta, el orégano, el laurel y el azúcar.
—Hervir° por 1 hora.

2 cdas. vinagre
2 cdas. vino seco°
2 cdas. aceite de oliva

—Añadir el vinagre, el vino seco y cocinar a fuego lento° otra hora.
—Añadir 2 cdas. aceite de oliva antes de servir°.

Para 8 personas.

1. ¿Por cuántas horas ponemos los frijoles en agua?
2. ¿Cuáles son los ingredientes del sofrito?
3. ¿Para cuántas personas es la receta?

Write a simple recipe in Spanish for something you like to cook.

MAFALDA

receta *recipe* **ají** *bell pepper;* **aceite de oliva** *olive oil;* **cebolla** *onion;* **dientes** *cloves;* **ajo** *garlic;* **cdtas. (cucharaditas)** *teaspoonfuls;* **hoja** *leaf;* **cdas. (cucharadas)** *tablespoonfuls;* **vino seco** *cooking sherry;* **lavar** *wash;* **cocinar** *cook;* **sofrito** *sauté, seasoning;* **picar** *chop;* **semillas** *seeds;* **machacar** *crush;* **freír** *fry;* **hasta dorar** *until browned (golden brown);* **echar** *throw (in);* **aplastados** *squashed;* **con mucho cuidado** *very carefully;* **cazuela** *casserole;* **añadir** *add;* **hervir** *boil;* **cocinar a fuego lento** *simmer;* **antes de servir** *before serving* **mozo** *waiter;* **querida** *dear;* **santa** *holy;* **termita** *termite;* **qué** *what a;* **¡Bárbara!** *Great!*

Diversiones

In recent years, dancing has become one of the world's most popular leisure-time activities. Of course, there are many different ways of dancing—and some dancers manage to move even without a disco beat.

BALLETS DE SAN JUAN
PRESENTA EL MÁXIMO EVENTO ARTÍSTICO DEL AÑO. . .
FERNANDO BUJONES
ACLAMADO POR LA CRÍTICA COMO EL NUEVO NUREYEV,
¡EN UN PROGRAMA FORMIDABLE!
LA BAYADÈRE, SEGUNDO ACTO Y
ROMEO y JULIETA, PAS DE DEUX CON
FERNANDO BUJONES y
ANA MARIA CASTAÑÓN.
DON QUIJOTE, PAS DE DEUX Y
CONCERTINO, CON
MIGUEL CAMPANERÍA Y
MARI TERE DEL REAL.
ORQUESTA SINFÓNICA
DE PUERTO RICO
BAJO LA DIRECCIÓN DEL MAESTRO JOHN LANCHBERY
DIRECTORA ARTÍSTICA ANA GARCÍA
DICIEMBRE 10, 11 y 12 A LAS 8:15 P.M.
DICIEMBRE 13 A LAS 3:00 P.M.
UNA PRESENTACIÓN DE AMIGOS DE BALLET DE SAN JUAN Y
Administración para el Fomento de las Artes y la Cultura
BOLETOS $20 $25 Y $30 FECHA LÍMITE PARA RECOGER LAS RESERVACIONES NOVIEMBRE 27 EN EL CENTRO DE BELLAS ARTES 725-7353 725-7338 PRECIO ESPECIAL PARA JÓVENES HASTA 15 AÑOS $10 DOMINGO SOLAMENTE MATINÉE

Ballet Ecuatoriano de Cámara hoy en el "Sucre"

A las 19h00 de hoy se realiza en el escenario del Teatro Nacional Sucre, la presentación del grupo de danza "Ballet Ecuatoriano de Cámara", que dirige Rubén Guarderas. Colaborarán el grupo de danza de la Academia Giselle, dirigido por Camila Guarderas y los alumnos del Instituto Nacional de Danza.

El programa de hoy incluye: Las Sílfides, Dan-zón y la obra infantil Blanca Nieves.

Artículo de un periódico de Quito, Ecuador.

diversiones *amusements* **máximo** *greatest;* **aclamado por la crítica como** *by critical acclaim;* **formidable** *terrific;* **segundo** *second;* **bajo** *under;* **fomento** *patronage;* **boletos** *tickets;* **fecha** *date;* **recoger** *get;* **bellas artes** *fine arts;* **jóvenes** *young people* **19h00** *7:00 PM;* **se realiza** *is performed;* **escenario** *stage;* **dirige** *directs;* **colaborarán** *will collaborate;* **dirigido por** *directed by;* **incluye** *includes;* **sílfides** *sylphs (nymphs of the air);* **danzón** *popular Cuban dance;* **Blanca Nieves** *Snow White*

La
CIUDAD
se
DIVIERTE

Otra vez en la pantalla,
la No. 1 y mejor de todas:
ROY SCHEIDER
ROBERT SHAW
RICHARD DREY-
FUSS
En:
Tiburón

CANTINFLAS FILMS. S.A. Presenta a su artista exclusivo MARIO MORENO
CANTINFLAS
TOTALMENTE NUEVA
Hoy Miércoles en el teatro Cinerama Gran Premier a Beneficio de la Liga Puertorriqueña Contra el Cáncer
G
en EL BARRENDERO
MARÍA SORTE ÚRSULA PRATTS · EDUARDO ARCARAZ · ROXANA CHÁVEZ · ALBERTO CATALA · SARA GUASCH · CARMEN MORENO
Actuación especial de EVITA MUÑOZ "Chachita" y LINA MICHEL
Dirigida por MIGUEL M. DELGADO · Producida por JACQUES GELMAN · Fotografía de ROSALIO SOLANO
Música de GUSTAVO CÉSAR CARREÓN · Argumento de MARIO MORENO REYES y FERNANDO GALEANA · Diálogos Adicionales CARLOS LEÓN

Lux 4.
HOY
4.15-6.30 y 9.15 PM.
15 años - Adm. Q.1.50
4a. SEMANA DE EXITAZO ROTUNDO, ladrón, rey, gladiador, guerrero,
Conan
El Bárbaro

se divierte *has fun, amuses itself* **otra vez** *again;* **pantalla** *screen;* **tiburón** *shark* **Cantinflas** *Mexican comedian;* **barrendero** *street cleaner;* **producida por** *produced by;* **argumento** *plot* **exitazo rotundo** *whopping success, very big hit;* **ladrón** *thief;* **rey** *king;* **guerrero** *soldier;* **bárbaro** *barbarian*

Going to the movies is a favorite pastime for many people all over the world. There are many movies made every year in Spanish-speaking countries. Throughout the Spanish-speaking world, foreign-language movies are very popular—either dubbed in Spanish or else captioned with subtitles. And the names of the movies sometimes take unexpected turns.

Clasificación moral de las películas

ADULTOS

Lilí Marleen
La cobra satánica
Furia de las Ninjas
Frontera violenta
El hombre lobo en Londres
El vengador anónimo
Samurai asesino
Más allá del terror
Mi brillante carrera
La brigada del diablo
Conquistadores de Mongolia
La fuerza de los cinco
El día de la cobra

ADOLESCENTES

Carrera final
El último asalto
El increíble superperro
Serpiente emplumada
El planeta del terror
El cerebro
Regreso a la vida

TODOS

Cupido motorizado
Supermán
Futbolista fenómeno
Niña de la mochila azul
El escuadrón mosquito
Vacaciones misteriosas
Guerreros de acero
Contraataque de los valientes
Más allá del honor

Lista de películas en cines de Medellín, Colombia.

---

realidad *reality;* **merece** *deserves;* **premiada** *awarded a prize;* **dorados** *golden* **próximo** *next;* **tandas** *showings;* **únete** *join;* **suceso** *happening;* **películas** *films, movies;* **hombre lobo** *werewolf;* **Londres** *London;* **vengador** *avenger;* **asesino** *murderer;* **más allá de** *beyond;* **carrera** *career;* **diablo** *devil;* **fuerza** *strength;* **último** *last;* **asalto** *assault, attack;* **increíble** *incredible;* **serpiente** *serpent, snake;* **emplumanda** *plumed;* **cerebro** *brain;* **regreso** *return;* **vida** *life;* **futbolista** *soccer player;* **mochila** *knapsack, backpack;* **acero** *steel*

Conciertos en H.C.J.B.

LUNES 28

13h00 A.M. y F.M.—“El Cisne de Tuonela” de Sibelius, Sinfonía N° 6 en Fa Mayor “Pastoral” de Beethoven.

19h00 F.M.—Festival internacional de música.

21h00 A.M. y F.M.—Sonata N° 5 en Mi Menor para flauta, cémbalo y viola Da Gamba de J.S. Bach, Sonata para violín y piano K 304 de Mozart, Sonata N° 8 en Sol Mayor para violín y piano, Op. 30, N° 3 de Beethoven.

Programa de música clásica en una estación de radio de Quito, Ecuador.

EN

DISCOS 650*

SEMANA DEL 6 AL 13 DE DICIEMBRE

1.— NI SU HOMBRE, NI SU AMANTE.............. Lissette — (Odeon)
2.— ETERNAMENTE YOLANDA............ Haciendo Punto - (Artomax)
3.— MI PIEL........................... Conjunto Quisqueya - (Karen)
4.— PERICO LO TIENE................. Perico Ortiz - (New Generation)
5.— UN MAL NECESARIO........................... Jorge Char -)TH)
6.— UNA CANITA AL AIRE.......................... La Solución - (TH)
7.— A DÓNDE VAS.......................... Orlando Penn - (Combo)
8.— MUJER MUJER............................ Danny Rivera - (TH)
9.— DILEMA........................... Marco Antonio Muñiz - (RCA)
10.— QUIERO VIVIR POR TI....................... Los Vecinos - (Algar)

ESCÚCHELOS DURANTE 24 HORAS
LOS 7 DÍAS DE LA SEMANA

*Transmisión Simultánea en 98.1 MHZ, F.M. Stereo para el Área Metropolitana de Santo Domingo y la Zona Sur del País.

Canciones populares en la República Dominicana.

---

cisne *swan;* **flauta** *flute;* **cémbalo** *harpsichord* **sonido** *sound;* **noticias** *news* **ni . . . ni** *neither . . . nor;* **amante** *lover;* **haciendo punto** *stopping;* **piel** *skin;* **perico** *parakeet;* **mal** *evil;* **una canita al aire** *a little spree, some fun;* **vecinos** *neighbors;* **escúchelos** *listen to them;* **transmisión** *broadcast*

VUELVE UNA PELÍCULA
GRANDE ENTRE LAS GRANDES
BEN-HUR
TECHNICOLOR
MENUDO
La Película
COLOR

¿Cómo se llaman en inglés?
Here is a list of Spanish and English movie titles. Can you pair them up?

Lo que el viento° se llevó°
La zapatilla° roja
Los ladrones del arca perdida
De aquí a la eternidad
¡Fiebre!
Rebelde sin causa
¿Quién teme a Virginia Woolf?
Pinocho
Los Diez Mandamientos
Blanca Nieves y los siete enanitos
La Isla del Tesoro
La Cenicienta
Los tres mosqueteros
La vuelta al mundo en ochenta días
Las tres caras de Eva

The Red Shoes
Rebel Without a Cause
Raiders of the Lost Ark
Saturday Night Fever
Who's Afraid of Virginia Woolf?
Snow White and the Seven Dwarfs
Cinderella
Pinocchio
The Three Faces of Eve
Around the World in Eighty Days
The Three Musketeers
Treasure Island
The Ten Commandments
Gone with the Wind
From Here to Eternity

MAFALDA

I'M LOOKING THROUGH YOU, WHERE DID YOU GO...
¡LOS BEATLES!
546

¿CÓMO TE GUSTAN, SI NO ENTIENDES LO QUE DICEN?
¿Y?

A MEDIO MUNDO LE GUSTAN LOS PERROS, Y ¿QUIÉN ENTIENDE GUAU?
QUINO

---

vuelve *returns* **viento** *wind;* **se llevó** *carried off;* **zapatilla** *slipper* **medio mundo** *half the world;* **guau** *woof! (barking sound)*

deportes

Jugando básquetbol en Miami

Las muchachas hacen ejercicios de calistenia antes de empezar° a jugar.

Ellas también practican corriendo° con el balón.

¡Corre, corre!

Los equipos de los muchachos también practican.

---

jugando *playing* **antes de empezar** *before beginning;* **corriendo** *running*

Y UN POCO MÁS TARDE . . .

¿Quién va a ganar?

No importa.° Lo importante° es cómo juegan.

No importa. *It doesn't matter;* **lo importante** *the important thing*

MUNDIAL DE FÚTBOL

El Campeonato Mundial° de Fútbol es una serie° de partidos que establecen° el nuevo campeón del mundo. Los equipos son de diferentes países. En 1982, "el Mundial" fue° en España—y no hay otro hasta 1986.

ESPAÑA'82 por televisión

Calendario de juegos y transmisiones: 2a. fase.

FECHA	PARTIDO	GRUPO	JUEGO			HORA
Junio 28	1	D	Austria	vrs.	Francia	9:15
Junio 28	2	A	Polonia	vrs.	Bélgica	13:00
Junio 29	3	C	Italia	vrs.	Argentina	9:15
Junio 29	4	B	Alemania	vrs.	Inglaterra	13:00
Junio 30			Rusia	vrs.	Escocia*	21:30
Junio 30			Rusia	vrs.	Escocia*	22:00
Julio 1o.		D	Perdedor Partido 1	vrs.	Irlanda	9:15
Julio 1o.		A	Perdedor Partido 2	vrs.	Rusia	13:00
Julio 2		C	Perdedor Partido 3	vrs.	Brasil	9:15
Julio 2		B	Perdedor Partido 4	vrs.	España	13:00
Julio 3			Argelia	vrs.	Chile*	12:00
Julio 3			Brasil	vrs.	N. Zelandia*	14:00
Julio 4		D	Vencedor Partido 1	vrs.	Irlanda	9:15
Julio 4		A	Vencedor Partido 2	vrs.	Rusia	13:00
Julio 5		C	Vencedor Partido 3	vrs.	Brasil	9:15
Julio 5		B	Vencedor Partido 4	vrs.	España	13:00
Julio 6			Alemania	vrs.	Austria*	21:30
Julio 6			Alemania	vrs.	Austria*	22:00
Julio 7			Vencedor Partido 1	vrs.	Irlanda **	
			SEMIFINALES			
Julio 8	5		Vencedor Grupo A	vrs.	Vencedor Grupo C	9:15
Julio 8	6		Vencedor Grupo B	vrs.	Vencedor Grupo D	13:00
			FINALES			
Julio 10			Por 3o. y 4o. Lugar Perdedor Partido 5	vrs.	Perdedor Partido 6	12:00
Julio 11			Por 1o. y 2o. Lugar Ganador Partido 5	vrs.	Ganador Partido 6	12:00

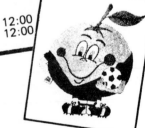

¡ITALIA CAMPEÓN...!

● POR TERCERA VEZ EN SU HISTORIA LA "SQUADRA AZZURRA" LOGRA EL TÍTULO, DERROTANDO A ALEMANIA 3-1

---

el (Campeonato) Mudial *World Cup (soccer championship);* **serie** *series;* **establecen** *establish;* **fue** *was* **Polonia** *Poland;* **Bélgica** *Belgium;* **Escocia** *Scotland;* **perdedor** *loser;* **Irlanda** *Ireland;* **Argelia** *Algeria;* **vencedor** *winner* **por tercera vez** *for the third time;* **logra** *gets;* **derrotando** *defeating*

El deporte también es progreso...

Los doce campeonatos

Italia y Brasil son los países que, con tres copas del mundo°, encabezan° la tabla° de los doce campeonatos mundiales.

Éstos fueron° los cuatro primeros de cada mundial:

AÑO	PRIMERO	SEGUNDO	TERCERO	CUARTO
1930	Uruguay	Argentina	Yugoslavla	E.Unidos
1934	Italia	Checoslovaquia	Alemania	Austria
1938	Italia	Hungría	Brasil	Suecia
1950	Uruguay	Brasil	Suecia	España
1954	Alemania	Hungría	Austria	Uruguay
1958	Brasil	Suecia	Francia	Alemania
1962	Brasil	Checoslovaquia	Chile	Yugoslavia
1966	Inglaterra	Alemania	Portugal	U.Soviética
1970	Brasil	Italia	Alemania	Uruguay
1974	Alemania	Holanda	Polonia	Brasil
1978	Argentina	Holanda	Brasil	Italia
1982	Italia	Alemania	Polonia	Francia

copas del mundo *World Cups;* **encabezan** *head;* **tabla** *list;* **fueron** *were;* **cuarto** *fourth;* **Suecia** *Sweden;* **U. Soviética = Unión Soviética**

Símbolos deportivos olímpicos

Fútbol

Béisbol

Básquetbol

Tenis

Ciclismo

Boxeo

Gimnasia

Judo

Natación

Esquí acuático

Vólibol

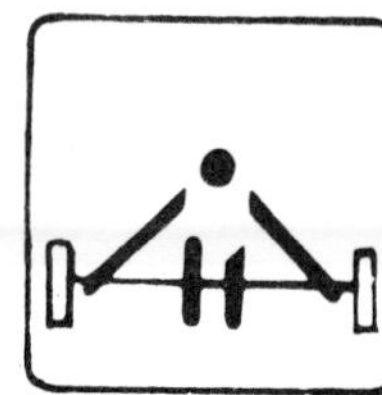
Pesas

International sports competitions provide artists with an opportunity for creating new symbols that represent the different sports activities—conveying a message that is the same in any language.

The following symbols were used in the Pan American Games of 1979, held in San Juan, Puerto Rico. Can you match the symbols with the appropriate sports?

1 
2 
3 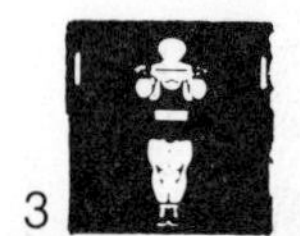
4 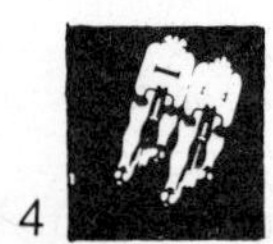
5 
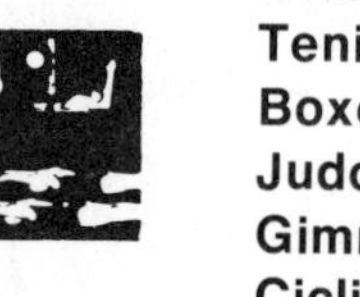
6
7 
8 
9 

Natación
Béisbol
Tenis
Boxeo
Judo
Gimnasia
Ciclismo
Pesas
Básquetbol

Look at the schedule of games on page 42. Using the names of the countries taking part in **España '82,** *make up teams for the continents represented. Based on the number of countries in each team, which one do you think would win the championship?*

...Y PARA DESPUÉS DE LOS PANAMERICANOS.

MINISTERIO
DEL DESARROLLO URBANO
Creando las bases para una vida mejor

---

 después de *after;* **ministerio** *ministry;* **desarrollo** *development;* **creando** *creating;* **mejor** *better*

Animales

En Miami

Los delfines son famosos por su inteligencia. Probablemente° el más famoso es "Flipper," que todavía podemos ver en la televisión cuando repiten los episodios de su serie. Hoy Flipper no está trabajando en televisión. Pero para una estrella como es él, es imposible estar retirado. Así que él hoy entretiene° a miles° de personas todos los días.

Los delfines saltan° muy alto fuera del agua y pueden° aprender a hacer muchas cosas divertidas. Cuando hacen su "trabajo" bien, quieren su recompensa.° ¡Cómo les gustan las sardinas!

probablemente *probably;* **entretiene** *he entertains;* **miles** *thousands;* **saltan** *jump;* **pueden** *they can;* **recompensa** *reward*

"Lolita," la ballena asesina

Las ballenas son los animales más grandes del mundo. Pero hay muchos tipos de ballenas. Lolita es una "ballena asesina." Comparada con las ballenas azules de los mares polares, Lolita es una "ballenita."

¡Aquí está Lolita!

No todas las ballenas tienen dientes.

Y no todos podemos montar° así.

Lolita puede° saltar fuera del agua.

 ballena asesina *killer whale;* **montar** *ride;* **puede** *can*

¡Qué alto salta!

Salta completamente fuera del agua.

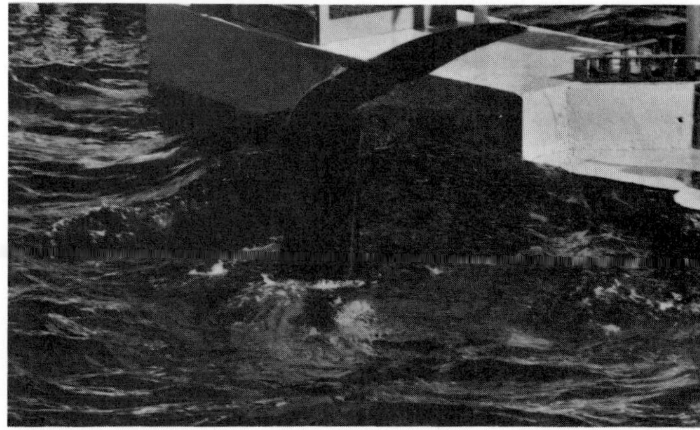

¿Adónde va ahora?

¿Qué dice el letrero?

¡Ay, sí, es importante leer los letreros!

En el parque zoológico

Los parques zoológicos son muy interesantes. En ellos podemos ver muchas clases de animales y observar cómo son y cómo viven.

Un cisne negro flota sobre el agua tranquila. Muchos cisnes son blancos, pero no todos.

Un cabrito° tiene hambre. La mamá cabra° da su leche.

Los flamencos son aves grandes y rosadas, con pescuezos° y patas° muy largas. Pueden estar en el agua y fuera de ella al mismo tiempo.

Los cocodrilos° y los caimanes° son diferentes. Cuando están entre piedras y vegetación, no es fácil ver dónde están.

El caballito tiene su cabeza° trabada° entre dos tablas°.

¿Qué dice la cotorrita°? "Galletita°, galletita." ¡Qué hambre tiene!

---

cabrito *kid, young goat;* **cabra** *goat;* **pescuezos** *necks;* **patas** *legs;* **cocodrilos** *crocodiles;* **caimanes** *alligators;* **cabeza** *head;* **trabada** *stuck;* **tablas** *boards;* **cotorrita** *little parrot;* **galletita** *cookie, cracker*

El pavo real no quiere fotografías hoy. —Por favor, pavito lindo° . . . ah, bueno, gracias.

¿El qué? *Oryctolagus cuniculos* es el nombre del conejo° en latín. (¿La palabra "conejo" viene de *cuniculos*?)

Pero, ¿dónde están los animales feroces°, las bestias exóticas, los leones, los tigres, los elefantes, las jirafas, las cebras, los rinocerontes, los. . . ? ¡Un minutito! ¿Qué clase de rey de qué clase de selva está aquí? Ah, es un leoncito° que es una fuente de agua para los niños.

lindo *pretty;* **conejo** *rabbit;* **feroces** *ferocious, savage;* **leoncito** *little lion*

La vida de los animales

DURACIÓN DE LA VIDA DE CIERTOS° ANIMALES*

Nombre	Duración (años)	Nombre	Duración (años)
Galápago gigante°	190	Oso negro	25
Tortuga	138	Tigre	25
Elefante	84	Gato doméstico	23
Ostra de agua dulce°	80	Leopardo	23
Búho°	68	Perro doméstico	22
Águila	55	Puma	20
Pelícano	51	Serpiente cascabel	20
Caballo	50	Vaca	20
Asno°	46	Oveja°	20
Mandril°	45	Castor°	19
Oso polar	41	Cabra	17
Chimpancé	37	Canguro°	16
Sapo°	36	Venado°	15
Gorila	33	Lobo	15
Gibón°	31	Coyote	14
Oso pardo	31	Pollo	14
Delfín	30	Conejo	13
León	30	Ardilla	10
Jirafa	28	Cerdo°	10
León marino°	28	Ratón blanco doméstico	3
Camello°	25		
Cebra	25		

* Datos° obtenidos° en cautiverio°.

¿Cuántos años tiene tu perro? ¿Tu gato? ¿Tu tortuga? Es una pregunta que puedes° contestar sin mucha dificultad°. Pero, ¿quién sabe cuántos años tiene una ballena o un elefante o un águila? La lista a la izquierda° compara la duración de la vida de diferentes animales. (No sabemos cuántos años una ballena puede vivir en el mar, pero Buffon, un naturalista francés del siglo° XVIII escribe° que las ballenas viven como° MIL años—lo que° es probablemente una exageración, pero en cautiverio viven como cien años.)

Make a list of animals and look up their Spanish names. Then, using an encyclopedia—or a big dictionary—look up the Latin generic name for the same animals. (A buffalo is a **búfalo** *is a "Bubalus buffelus.")*

Did you know that if you speak Spanish to your cat or dog, it will probably understand? (Okay, we won't push that one too far!) But do you know your pet's name in Spanish? ("Fido" is **Fido** [Fee'-do]; *don't lose too much sleep over this one.)*

MAFALDA

---

ciertos *certain;* **datos** *data;* **obtenidos** *obtained;* **cautiverio** *captivity;* **galápago gigante** *giant turtle;* **ostra de agua dulce** *fresh-water oyster;* **búho** *owl;* **asno** *donkey;* **mandril** *mandrill (large baboon);* **sapo** *toad;* **gibón** *gibbon (ape);* **león marino** *sea lion;* **camello** *camel;* **serpiente (de) cascabel** *rattlesnake;* **oveja** *sheep;* **castor** *beaver;* **canguro** *kangaroo;* **venado** *deer;* **cerdo** *pig, hog* **puedes** *you can;* **dificultad** *difficulty;* **a la izquierda** *on the left;* **siglo** *century;* **escribe** *writes;* **como** *about;* **lo que** *which* **no se admiten** *not allowed;* **moscas** *flies;* **analfabeta** *illiterate*

Madrid, Madrid, Madrid

Madrid es la ciudad capital de España. Tiene más de 4 millones de habitantes° y un área de 531 Km^2 (kilómetros cuadrados°). La ciudad, situada en el paralelo 40, ocupa el centro geográfico de la Península Ibérica. El suelo° está a 650 metros sobre el nivel del mar°.

El rey Felipe II hizo a Madrid la capital española en el año 1606. (En 1605 las prensas de Juan de Cuestas, en la calle de Atocha, en Madrid, publicaron° la primera edición de *Don Quijote,* el famoso libro de aventuras por Miguel de Cervantes y Saavedra.)

Madrid tiene un río Manzanares, con poca agua, mucha literatura y grandes puentes° históricos. (Toda capital europea tiene que tener un río: Viena tiene el Danubio, París tiene el Sena, Londres tiene el Támesis . . . pues Madrid tiene el Manzanares.)

Pero en la ciudad no encontramos° un solo° Madrid—hay muchos Madriles (bueno, así es el plural, ¿qué vamos a hacer?)—pues° la ciudad conservó° mucho de las diferentes épocas° de su historia en sus museos, en sus monumentos y en su forma de vivir°. El pasado°, el presente y el futuro, uno al lado del otro.

---

habitantes *inhabitants;* **kilómetros cuadrados** *square kilometers;* **suelo** *ground, land;* **sobre el nivel del mar** *above sea level;* **publicaron** *published;* **puentes** *bridges;* **no encontramos** *we don't find;* **un solo** *only one;* **pues** *because;* **conservó** *kept;* **épocas** *eras, periods;* **forma de vivir** *way of life;* **pasado** *past*

Museos de Madrid

Madrid es una ciudad con muchos museos que documentan la historia cultural, artística y social de España. La siguiente es una lista de varios museos madrileños de interés general.

EL PRADO
Es uno de los museos más importantes del mundo, en un espléndido edificio° del siglo XVIII. Pintura° española de los siglos XII al XVIII: El Greco, Velázquez, Ribera, Murillo, Goya. Pintura italiana: Fra Angélico, Rafael, escuela veneciana. Flamenco°: Bosco°, Rubens y Van Dyck. Escuelas alemana, holandesa°, inglesa. Escultura° clásica. Restaurante. Paseo del Prado. Teléfono 468 09 50.

Cuadros° de la colección del Museo del Prado.

El Greco (Domenicos Theotocópulos) (1541?-1614?): LA ADORACIÓN DE LOS PASTORES

Diego Rodríguez de Silva y Velázquez (1599-1660): LAS MENINAS

---

edificio *building;* **pintura** *painting;* **flamenco** *Flemish;* **Bosco** *Hieronymus Bosch (1450?-1516);* **holandesa** *Dutch;* **escultura** *sculpture;* **cuadros** *paintings* **pastores** *shepherds;* **meninas** *ladies-in-waiting*

MUSEO ESPAÑOL DE ARTE CONTEMPORÁNEO°
Pintura y escultura actuales°, española y extranjera°. Ciudad Universitaria, Avenida Juan de Herrera, 2. Teléfono 449 71 50.

MUSEO ROMÁNTICO
Colección de muebles° y cuadros del siglo XIX. San Mateo, 13. Teléfonos 448 10 71 y 448 10 45.

MUSEO ARQUEOLÓGICO
Colecciones de objetos prehistóricos y de las Edades Antigua y Media°. Numismática° y completa colección de cerámica de todas las épocas. Serrano, 13. Teléfono 403 66 07.

MUSEO DE AMÉRICA
Testimonios de las civilizaciones de Hispanoamérica. Ciudad Universitaria. Teléfono 243 94 37.

MUSEO MUNICIPAL
Objetos artísticos relacionados con° la historia de Madrid. Fuencarral, 78. Teléfono 221 66 56.

PALACIO REAL°
Dos siglos de historia. Porcelanas, tapices°, muebles, armaduras° y cuadros. Plaza de Oriente (entrada° por la Plaza de la Armería). Teléfono 248 74 04.

MUSEO DE CARROZAS°
Original colección de antiguos° coches de caballos°. Paseo Virgen del Puerto.

MUSEO DEL FERROCARRIL°
Interesantes maquetas° y documentos de la historia del ferrocarril. San Cosme y San Damián, 1 (Palacio del Duque de Fernán-Núñez). Teléfono 467 34 91.

Velázquez:
LA RENDICIÓN DE BREDA (LAS LANZAS)

Francisco de Goya y Lucientes (1746-1828):
LA FAMILIA DE CARLOS IV

---

contemporáneo *contemporary;* **actuales** *current, present-day;* **extranjera** *foreign;* **muebles** *furniture;* **Edades Antigua y Media** *ancient times and the Middle Ages;* **numismática** *numismatics (collections of coins and paper money);* **relacionados con** *related to;* **palacio real** *royal palace;* **tapices** *tapestries, carpets;* **armaduras** *suits of armor;* **entrada** *entered;* **carrozas** *coaches, carriages;* **antiguos** *old, antique;* **coches de caballos** *horse-drawn carts;* **ferrocarril** *railroad;* **maquetas** *scale models* **rendición** *surrender*

MUSEO DE CIENCIAS NATURALES
Colecciones de Zoología, Geología, Paleontología y Entomología. Paseo de la Castellana. Teléfono 261 86 07.

MUSEO ETNOLÓGICO ANTROPOLÓGICO
Objetos de las culturas primitivas. Alfonso XII, 68. Teléfono 239 59 95.

MUSEO MINERALÓGICO
Facultad° de Ciencias de la Universidad Autónoma.

MUSEO DEL EJÉRCITO°
Importantes colecciones de trofeos bélicos°. Méndez Núñez, 1. Teléfono 221 04 19.

MUSEO DE REPRODUCCIONES ARTÍSTICAS
Tiene una completa colección de reproducciones de obras de la antigüedad° clásica y renacentista°. Ciudad Universitaria. Edificio Museo de América. Teléfono 244 14 47.

MUSEO NACIONAL DE ARTES DECORATIVAS
Cerámica, muebles y otros elementos decorativos populares de todas las regiones españolas. Montalbán, 12. Teléfono 221 34 40.

MUSEO COLÓN DE FIGURAS DE CERA°
Representación de la España histórica y su actualidad°. Personajes° reproducidos en cera con absoluta fidelidad°. Paseo de Calvo Sotelo, 41. Teléfono 419 26 49.

MUSEO TAURINO°
Completa historia del toreo° en pinturas, estampas° y maquetas. Plaza de toros° de las Ventas. Teléfono 255 16 10.

TEMPLO° DE DEBOD
Templo egipcio°, de Nubia, del siglo IV antes de Cristo. Jardines° del General Fanjul.

MUSEO DE ESCULTURA
Debajo del puente de García Morato, en el Paseo de la Castellana.

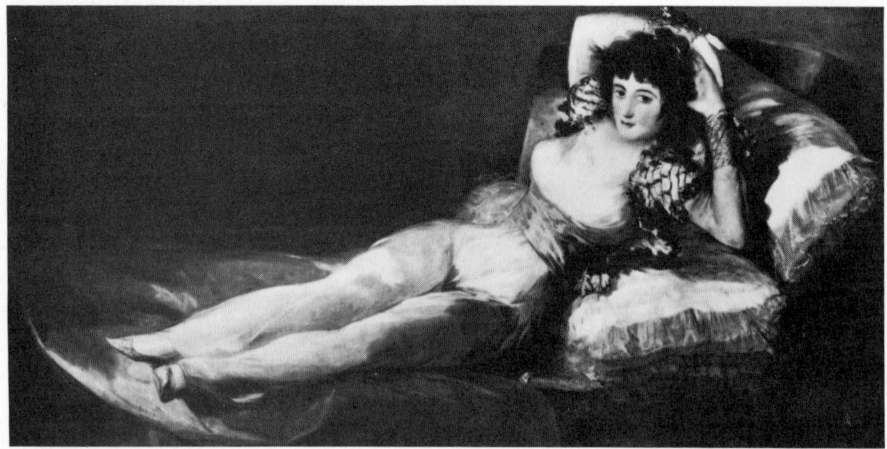

Goya: LA MAJA VESTIDA

1. ¿Qué tiene el Museo del Prado en su colección?
2. ¿Cómo es El Prado?
3. ¿Dónde hay una exhibición de objetos prehistóricos? ¿Y primitivos?
4. ¿Qué museo tiene objetos históricos de Madrid?
5. ¿En qué plaza está la entrada al Palacio Real? ¿Qué hay en el Palacio?

---

facultad *department;* **ejército** *army;* **bélicos** *of war;* **antigüedad** *antiquity;* **renacentista** *Renaissance;* **cera** *wax;* **actualidad** *present time;* **personajes** *characters, personalities;* **fidelidad** *faithfulness, authenticity;* **taurino** *bullfighting;* **toreo** *bullfighting;* **estampas** *prints, engravings;* **plaza de toros** *bullring;* **templo** *temple;* **egipcio** *Egyptian;* **jardines** *gardens* **maja** *lazy person;* **vestida** *dressed*

España

FRANCIA
San Sebastián
Bilbao
VIZCAYA
Oviedo
Covadonga
ASTURIAS
Santiago
GALICIA
Vigo
León
Burgos
NAVARRA
Pirineos
ANDORRA
Río Ebro
CATALUÑA
ARAGÓN
Zaragoza
Barcelona
Tarragona
Valladolid
Zamora
Río Duero
LEÓN
CASTILLA LA VIEJA
Salamanca
Segovia
Escorial
Ávila
Madrid
ESPAÑA
Cuenca
Toledo
Valencia
CASTILLA LA NUEVA
La Mancha
EXTREMADURA
Río Guadiana
Badajoz
PORTUGAL
Lisboa
OCÉANO ATLÁNTICO
Menorca
ISLAS BALEARES
Mallorca
Ibiza
Alicante
Murcia
Cartagena
Río Guadalquivir
Córdoba
ANDALUCÍA
Itálica
Sevilla
Granada
Almería
Málaga
Cádiz
Tarifa
Gibraltar
Estrecho de Gibraltar
MAR MEDITERRÁNEO

La música en España

La variedad de música folklórica de España es inmensa. Diversas° influencias formaron los caracteres de la expresión musical de las regiones españolas, y la música y la danza reflejan° las fuerzas° de su formación. El famoso flamenco andaluz es de la región de Andalucía, y su origen es gitano°. Ya decir gitano es decir internacional, pues los gitanos viajan° constantemente° en sus caravanas°. Pero dentro del mundo de la música flamenca también hay *malagueñas,* de la región de Málaga, y *sevillanas,* de la región de Sevilla. Podemos oír° la influencia árabe en la música del sur de España igual que° vemos la misma influencia en el arte y la arquitectura de la región.

Choose one of the Spanish painters mentioned in this chapter and prepare a report on his life and work—you'll be surprised with what you'll find out about him.

Which river goes through which capital? Potomac, Arno, Tajo, Danubio, Danubio. Lisboa, Budapest, Belgrado, Roma, Washington.

MAFALDA

---

diversas *different;* **reflejan** *reflect;* **fuerzas** *forces, influences;* **gitano** *gypsy;* **viajan** *travel;* **constantemente** *constantly;* **caravanas** *caravans (covered vehicles in which the gypsies live and travel);* **oír** *hear;* **igual que** *just as* **curioso** *strange;* **pensé** *I thought;* **era** *was*

Y de pronto...
¡Un nuevo mundo!

El 3 de agosto de 1492, Cristóbal Colón salió de Palos, España, con una tripulación° de 120 hombres en tres pequeños barcos de vela°, tres carabelas que cruzaron° el Mar Océano—que fue el nombre del Océano Atlántico en esa era. Cristóbal Colón pensó que la Tierra° era redonda° y que era posible ir a las Indias°, a Catay—que fue el nombre antiguo de China—y a Cipango—que fue Japón más tarde. Para° llegar a estas tierras exóticas y ricas, el gran navegante genovés decidió navegar en la dirección que el sol viaja por el cielo°—del este al oeste.

La expedición pasó dos meses en el Océano—día y noche, día y noche hacia el oeste. Pero, ¿dónde están las Indias? ¿Dónde está Catay? ¿Cipango? La tripulación demandó retornar° a España. Empezaron las erupciones de violencia a bordo°. ¿Un motín°?

El 12 de octubre de 1492, Rodrigo de Triana, miembro° de la expedición distinguió° algo en el horizonte° . . . ¡una isla! ¡Guanahaní! ¡San Salvador! ¡T I E R R A°!

El nombre indio de la islita donde Colón primero pisó° tierra en el Nuevo Mundo, Guanahaní, el Descubridor° cambió por *San Salvador.* (Hoy esta pequeña isla de las Bahamas se llama *Watling.*)

Y si llegó a las Indias, entonces las personas que viven aquí son . . . INDIOS.

¿Quién fue la reina Isabel?
¿Quién fue Cristóbal Colón?
¿De dónde salió Colón? ¿Cuándo?
¿Qué idea tuvo Colón?
¿Qué pasó?

---

tripulación *crew;* **barcos de vela** *sailing ships;* **cruzaron** *crossed;* **Tierra** *Earth;* **redonda** *round;* **Indias** *Indies;* **para** *in order to;* **cielo** *sky;* **retornar** *to return;* **a bordo** *on board;* **motín** *mutiny;* **miembro** *member;* **distinguió** *made out, saw in the distance;* **horizonte** *horizon;* **tierra** *land;* **pisó** *set foot on;* **Descubridor** *Discoverer*

Fechas de los descubrimientos

En su primer viaje, Cristóbal Colón descubrió San Salvador el 12 de octubre de 1492. El 27 de ocubre de ese año, la expedición llegó a la costa del noreste de Cuba. Colón llamó la isla—que por muchos años él pensó parte del continente y no una isla—**Juana.** (La° llamó Juana en honor de la hija de Isabel y Fernando, que más tarde fue reina de España y la historia llamó "Juana la Loca.") El 5 de diciembre de 1492 fue cuando Colón descubrió **Hispaniola,** isla que es hoy la República Dominicana y Haití. **Haití** fue uno de los nombres indios de la isla. Otro nombre fue **Quisqueya,** "tierra grande" o "madre de la tierra."

En su segundo viaje, Colón descubrió Puerto Rico, el 19 de noviembre de 1493. Llamó la isla **San Juan Bautista°,** pero más tarde este nombre fue el nombre que tomó la capital.

Pretend that you are on the Santa María, *on the first trip across the* Mar Océano, *and write a letter to a friend who stayed home in Spain. Describe your trip. (Don't worry about mailing the letter, though; it'll be a while before there are mailboxes aboard ships.)*

MAFALDA

---

la *it;* **San Juan Bautista** *Saint John the Baptist* **vino** *came;* **noticia** *news;* **resulta** *it turns out;* **eso** *that;* **¿Te das cuenta?** *Do you realize?;* **a mi maestra le falta** *my teacher is lacking;* **agilidad** *speed*

Al norte

Ponce de León

Juan Ponce de León acompañó° a Colón en el Segundo Viaje; en 1509 conquistó° a Puerto Rico y fue el primer gobernador° de esa isla. En 1513, buscando otra isla mencionada° en una leyenda india, descubrió la Florida. Ponce de León tomó posesión del nuevo territorio en el nombre del rey de España el 8 de abril de 1513, donde hoy aún está San Agustín: la primera ciudad de la *Isla* de la Florida. (La isla de la leyenda india tenía° una fuente de agua mágica: la Fuente de la Juventud°.)

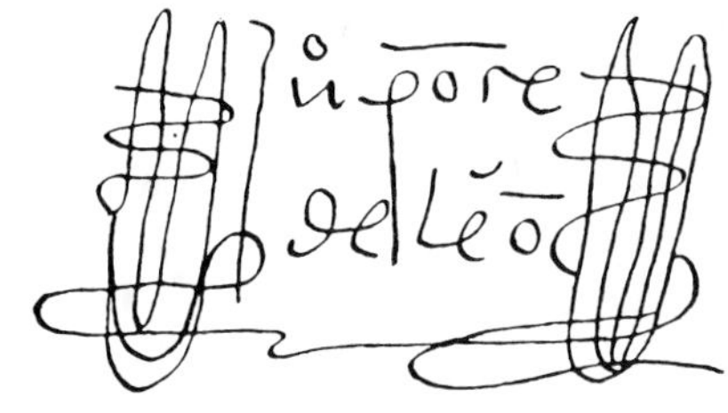

La Florida

En 1763, el Tratado° de París le da la Florida a Inglaterra. En cambio° Inglaterra devuelve° La Habana° a España.

Hoy, en muchas partes de la Florida, y especialmente en Miami, el inglés y el español son parte de la conversación diaria de muchas personas. Por toda Miami vemos letreros y señales° en español y en inglés.

Muchas de las personas que hablan español en Miami son cubanas y cubano-americanas. Pero en años recientes° más y más personas de otros países hispanoamericanos van a Miami por la atracción del clima° tropical y oportunidades culturales y económicas que son únicas°.

Mural en la Calle Ocho, en Miami.

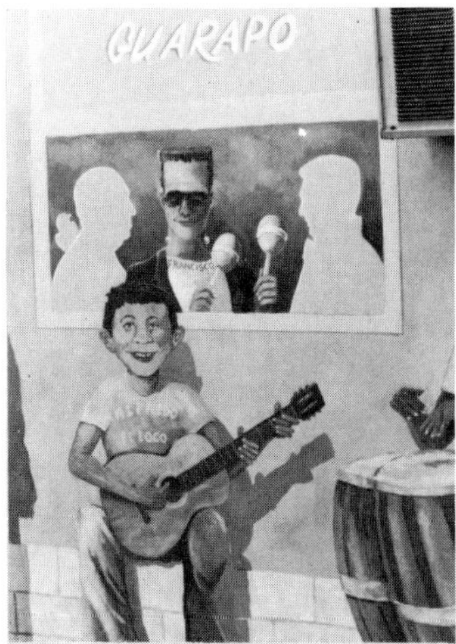

---

acompañó *accompanied;* **conquistó** *he conquered;* **gobernador** *governor;* **mencionada** *mentioned;* **tenía** *had;* *had;* **Juventud** *Youth;* **Tratado** *Treaty;* **en cambio** *in exchange;* **devuelve** *gives back;* **La Habana** *Havana;* **letreros y señales** *posters and signs;* **recientes** *recent;* **clima** *climate;* **únicas** *unique;* **guarapo** *sugar-cane juice*

Refranes españoles

A great wealth of folk wisdom is passed on in little sayings that develop over the years. These proverbs, adages, aphorisms are difficult to translate, but in a very few words, they hit the nail on the head—or put it all in a nutshell. Following is a short list of Spanish proverbs and their English translation (more or less).

No es oro todo lo que reluce.
All that glitters is not gold.

Lo que fuera sonará.
Whatever it was, we'll find out soon enough.

Las apariencias engañan.
Appearances are deceiving.

Escoba nueva barre bien.
A new broom sweeps well.

Saber es poder.
Knowledge is power.

Barriga llena, corazón contento.
Full belly, happy heart.

Haz lo que yo digo y no lo que yo hago.
Do as I say, not as I do.

Perro que ladra no muerde.
A dog that barks doesn't bite.

Cuando una puerta se cierra, otra se abre.
When one door closes, another one opens.

Más vale tarde que nunca.
Better late than never.

No hay mal que por bien no venga.
Nothing bad ever comes but for a good reason.

La envidia del amigo es peor que el odio del enemigo.
A friend's envy is worse than an enemy's hatred.

El que último ríe, ríe mejor.
He who laughs last laughs best.

En boca cerrada no entran las moscas.
Flies don't go into a shut mouth.

Poco a poco se va lejos.
Little by little, one goes a long way.

Expresiones del Caribe

The Caribbean area has come up with many colorful expressions. Read the following.

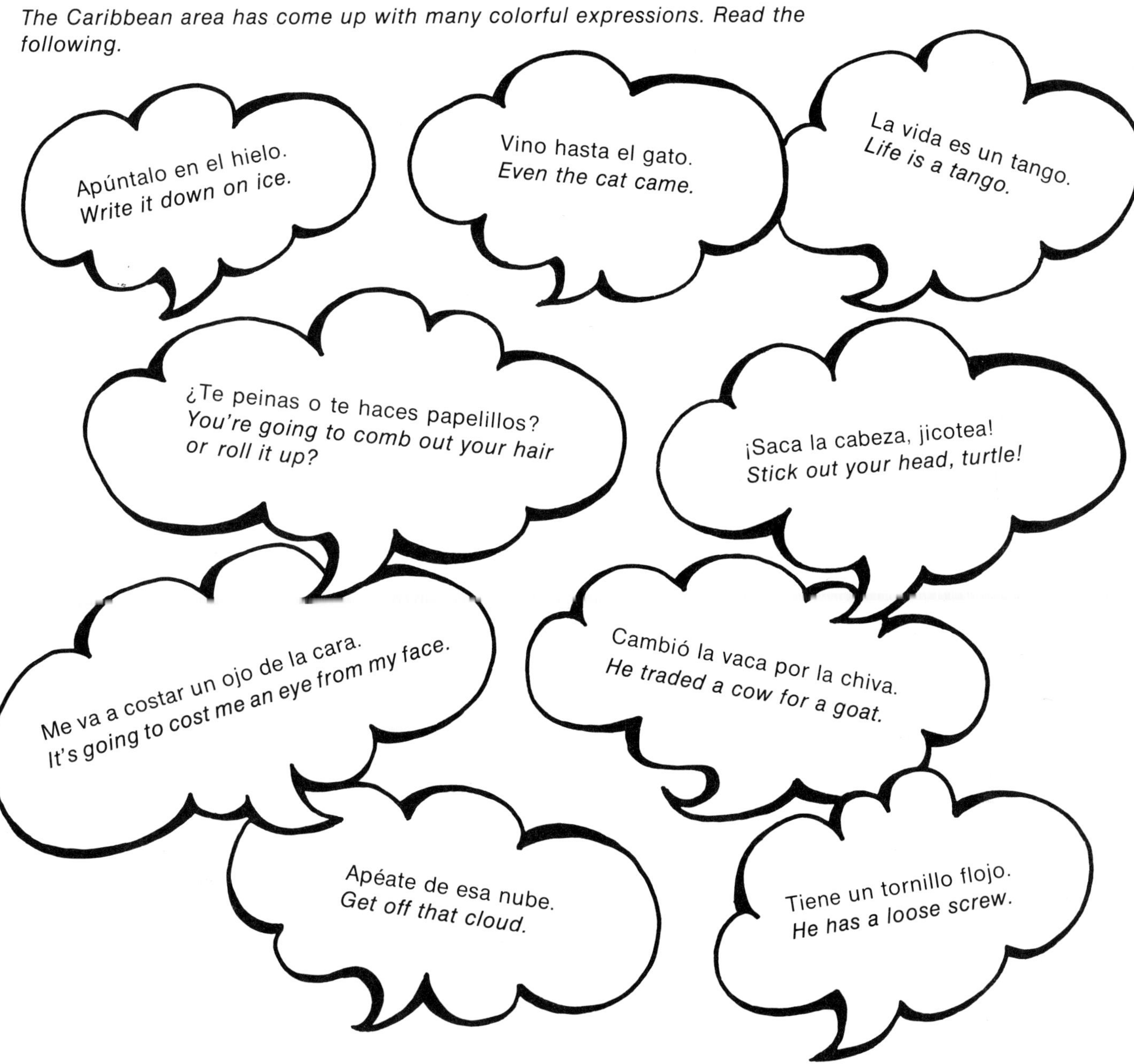

Apúntalo en el hielo.
Write it down on ice.
Vino hasta el gato.
Even the cat came.
La vida es un tango.
Life is a tango.
¿Te peinas o te haces papelillos?
You're going to comb out your hair or roll it up?
¡Saca la cabeza, jicotea!
Stick out your head, turtle!
Me va a costar un ojo de la cara.
It's going to cost me an eye from my face.
Cambió la vaca por la chiva.
He traded a cow for a goat.
Apéate de esa nube.
Get off that cloud.
Tiene un tornillo flojo.
He has a loose screw.

Many of the expressions on these two pages have English equivalents. Whether something costs an "eye" or "an arm and a leg," it's still expensive. We have to remember that the development of these expressions draws from the everyday experiences of a group of people—and it's very difficult to "argue apples and pears" when your garden is full of mangos and bananas.

Take a few of the sayings from these two pages and find an English saying that is similar—in wording or in meaning.

José Martí

(1853-1895) Autor y revolucionario cubano llamado "Apóstol de la Independencia."

Monumento a José Martí en Santo Domingo.

Cultivo° una rosa blanca,
en julio como en enero,
para el amigo sincero
que me da su mano franca°.
Y para el cruel que me arranca
el corazón° con que vivo,
Cardo° ni **ortiga**° cultivo;
Cultivo la rosa blanca.

Estatua de José Martí en Nueva York (Calle 59 y Avenida de las Américas).

cita histórica
—La conquista del porvenir ha de hacerse con las manos limpias. José Martí

Go to the library and find out what you can about other patriots who were leaders in the 19th century independence movements in the Spanish colonies. A good place to start is an encyclopedia, under Latin American history. Some key names are Bolivar, San Martín, O'Higgins, Sucre, Juárez.

---

cultivo *I grow;* **franca** *open, generous;* **me arranca el corazón** *tears out my heart;* **cardo** *thistle;* **ortiga** *nettle (plant)* **cita** *quotation;* **conquista** *conquest;* **porvenir** *future;* **ha de hacerse** *has to be done*

El Yunque

The Caribbean National Forest, El Yunque, *is one of the most popular areas in Puerto Rico for picnics, hikes, and camping.* El Yunque *is also a bird sanctuary and a center for ecological studies.*

BOSQUE NACIONAL DEL CARIBE

Este Bosque Pluvial comprende 28,000 cuerdas de terreno y se le conoce popularmente por El Yunque. Es el único bosque tropical en todo el Sistema de Bosques Nacionales de los Estados Unidos y tiene 240 especies de árboles, todos oriundos de esta región. Está formado por cuatro tipos de bosques claramente definidos; éstos son: el Bosque Pluvial, situado en las pendientes más bajas de las montañas, por debajo de los 2,000 pies de elevación; La Maleza Montana (también conocido como tipo Colorado), que se encuentran sobre los 2,000 pies de elevación; el Bosque de Palmeras, compuesto casi en su totalidad por la Palma de Sierra y localizado en las partes más elevadas de las montañas de Luquillo; y el Tipo Enano, que no crece más de 12 pies de alto y está limitado a las crestas de las montañas y picos más altos. Casi toda la vida silvestre que crece en el Bosque Pluvial es rara en otras partes de la Isla. Mientras que las culebras — que constituyen una amenaza en otros bosques — son muy raras aquí. El Servicio Forestal está a cargo del Bosque Nacional del Caribe. Se han reservado aproximadamente 2,100 cuerdas conocida como el Área Natural, Baño de Oro, para conservar en condiciones vírgenes los cuatro tipos de bosques originarios de esta región. El Bosque Nacional del Caribe ha sido como un refugio de pájaros para conservar aquellas especies que ya están casi extintas como resultado de la caza indisciplinada y la deforestación. El futuro del Bosque Nacional del Caribe descansa en las manos del Servicio Forestal y sus oficiales. Éstos dedican sus vidas a conservar la belleza natural y los recursos de este singular paraíso. El presente descansa en manos de cada visitante que pisa sus caminos y senderos. Ayúdenos a mantener su actual belleza poniendo de su parte para mantener limpio e intacto este paraje tan hermoso. Para más información escriba al Supervisor Forestal, Bosque National del Caribe,

CARIBBEAN NATIONAL FOREST

A precious 28,000 acres now comprise the Caribbean National Forest, more commonly known by its picturesque name — The Rain Forest. It is the only tropical forest in the entire U. S. National Forest System and boasts some 240 different tree species, all native to the area. Four distinct types of forest make up the Caribbean National Forest: THE RAIN FOREST, which is situated on the lower slopes of the mountains, below the 2,000 feet elevation mark; THE MONTANE THICKET, (also called The Colorado Forest), which is found above the 2,000 feet elevation point; THE PALM FOREST, made up almost entirely of The Sierra Palm tree, and located on the higher elevations of the Luquillo Mountains; and THE DWARF FOREST, with an average height of 12 feet, and limited to the highest peaks and ridges of the mountains. Most of the wildlife that flourishes in The Rain Forest is rare anywhere else on the Island, while snakes — which make other forests hazardous — are rare here. The Caribbean National Forest is managed by the Forest Service. They have set aside approximately 2,100 acres, known as the Baño de Oro Natural Area, to preserve in virgin condition the four types of forest indigenous to the area. The Forest has been established as a Commonwealth bird refuge to preserve those species which almost suffered extinction as a result of uncontrolled hunting and deforestation in earlier years. The future of the Caribbean National Forest rests in the hands of the Forest Service and its officers who devote their lives to preserving the natural beauty and resources of this unique paradise. The present rests in the hands of every visitor who travels its roads and walks its trails. You can help us to keep it beautiful today by doing your share to keep it clean. If you desire additional information about the Rain Forest you may write to the Forest Supervisor, Caribbean National Forest, Box AQ, Rio Piedras, Puerto Rico 00928.

Por las veredas de El Yunque

CATARATA° LA MINA

Puede llegar por dos rutas (1 hora):

1. Vereda de Árboles Grandes. Toma su nombre de los altos y robustos árboles que encontramos en ella.

2. Vereda La Mina. Sigue° el camino° del pequeño río que forma la catarata. Muchos tipos de bromelias° cubren los árboles de esta ruta.

ÁREAS DE JIRAS°

Si no tiene tiempo suficiente para explorar las veredas, tres áreas aquí ofrecen una muestra° de lo que es el bosque.

TORRE DE MONTE BRITTON

Torre de observación. 45 minutos por la Vereda Monte Britton, o 1 hora y 20 minutos por la Vereda El Yunque.

VEREDA EL YUNQUE

Pasa por cuatro tipos diferentes de bosques: Bosque Colorado, Palma de Sierra, Bosque Enano° y Bosque de Árboles Grandes. Toma dos horas para subir a su altura° de 3,496 pies sobre el nivel del mar.

ÁREAS DE RECREO → 3.0 KM
CENTRO DE LOS VISITANTES
RESTAURAN EL YUNQUE
VEREDAS A LOS PICOS
ÁREAS DE JIRAS

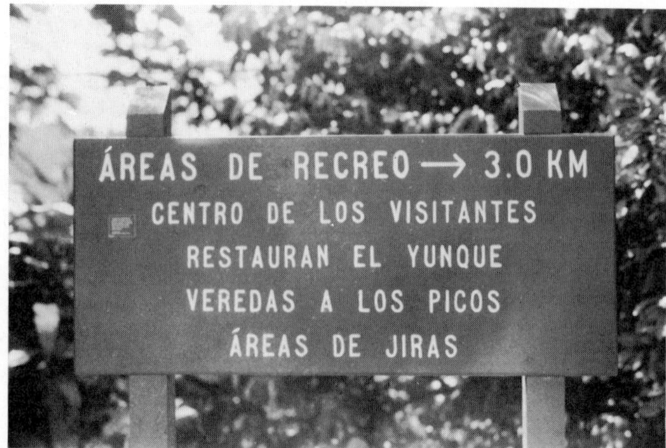

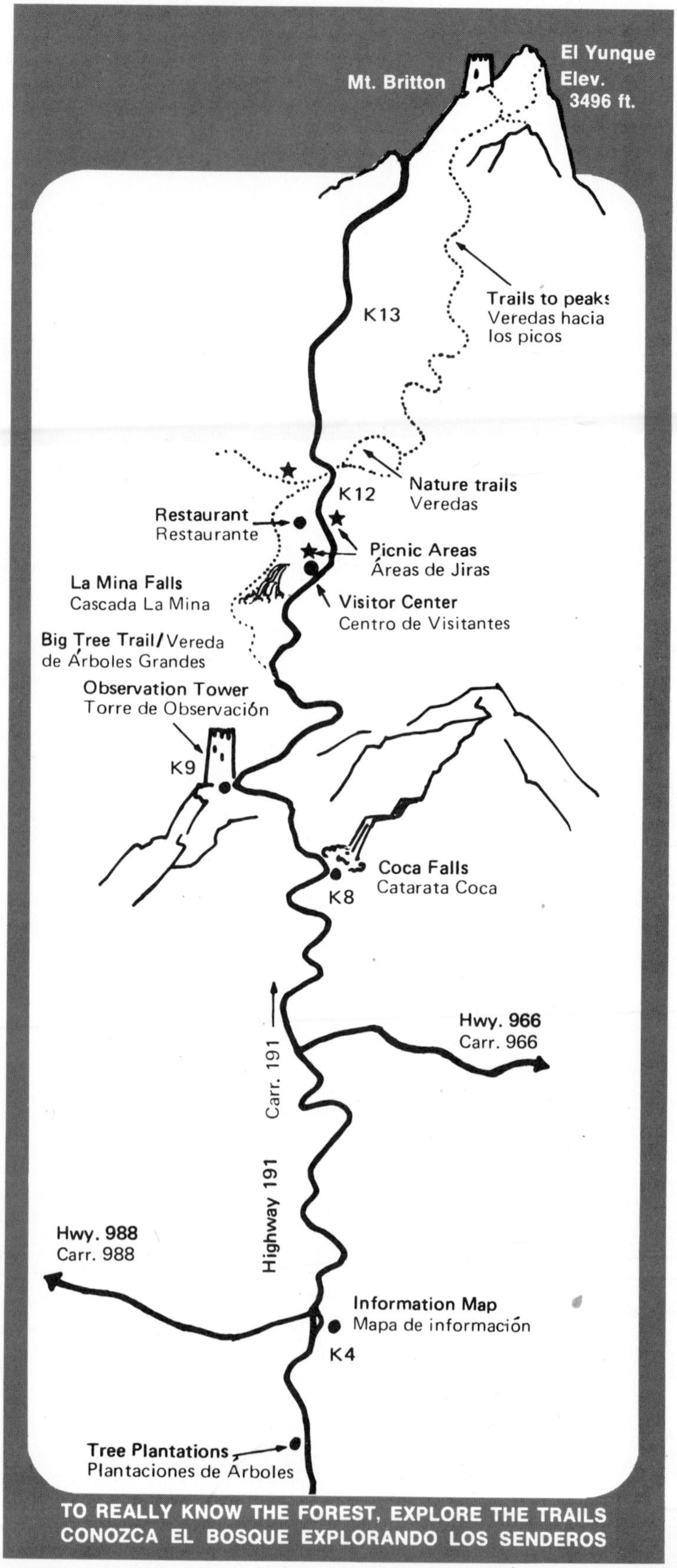

Mt. Britton
El Yunque
Elev.
3496 ft.
Trails to peaks
Veredas hacia
los picos
K13
Nature trails
Veredas
K12
Restaurant
Restaurante
Picnic Areas
Áreas de Jiras
La Mina Falls
Cascada La Mina
Visitor Center
Centro de Visitantes
Big Tree Trail/Vereda
de Árboles Grandes
Observation Tower
Torre de Observación
K9
Coca Falls
Catarata Coca
K8
Hwy. 966
Carr. 966
Carr. 191
Highway 191
Hwy. 988
Carr. 988
Information Map
Mapa de información
K4
Tree Plantations
Plantaciones de Arboles
TO REALLY KNOW THE FOREST, EXPLORE THE TRAILS
CONOZCA EL BOSQUE EXPLORANDO LOS SENDEROS

---

veredas *trails* **catarata** *waterfall;* **sigue** *follow;* **camino** *path;* **bromelias** *plants like Spanish moss;* **jiras** *picnics;* **muestra** *example;* **enano** *small, dwarfish;* **altura** *height;* **recreo** *recreation*

HELECHO GIGANTE Parece un delicado encaje verde puesto en lo alto de un pedestal de 40 pies, Pero el Helecho Gigante es en realidad un árbol. Se encuentra en abundancia en las húmedas pendientes de la montaña. Sus altos troncos no son otra cosa que un haz de raíces y están coronados por un penacho de fronda que se destaca contra el intenso azul del cielo tropical.

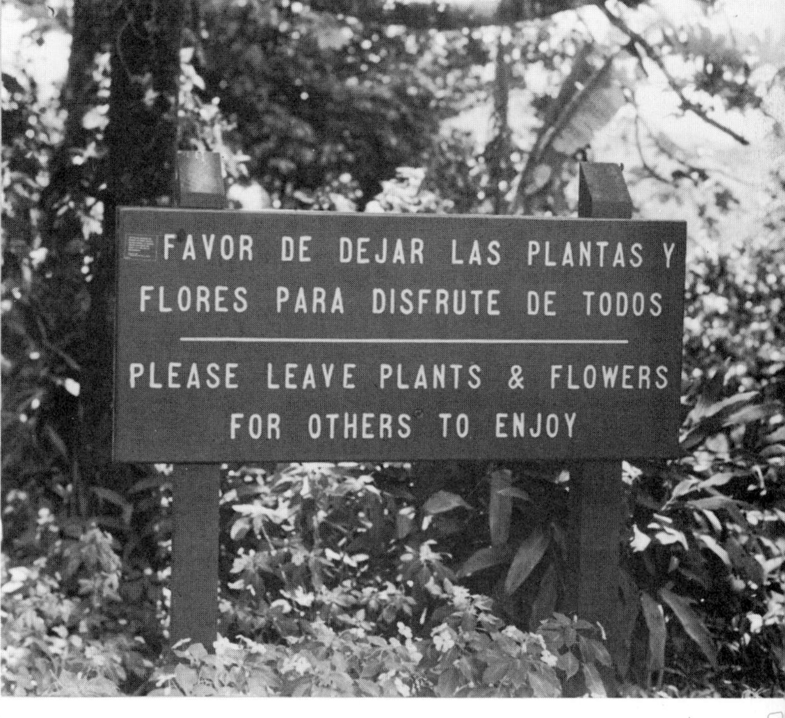
FAVOR DE DEJAR LAS PLANTAS Y
FLORES PARA DISFRUTE DE TODOS
PLEASE LEAVE PLANTS & FLOWERS
FOR OTHERS TO ENJOY

TREE FERN It looks like a delicate green plant perched on top of a 40-foot pedestal, but the Tree Fern is, in actuality, a tree! They can be seen in abundance on the sunny, moist mountain slopes. The very tall stems, which are actually bundles of roots, are crowned with wispy fronds which trace a lacy green pattern against the startling blue of the Caribbean sky.

EL COQUÍ No hay otro animalito más autóctono en Puerto Rico, ni más amado, que esta minúscula ranita de apenas una pulgada de largo que vive en los árboles. El Coquí suena más como un pájaro que una rana. Cada noche, cuando el Coquí se une al coro de millones de voces de la naturaleza, se puede distinguir claramente el cántico de dos notas, que le da su nombre – "CO-QUÍ, CO-QUÍ". Y como la luz del sol apenas puede penetrar la espesura del bosque, también se oye el Coquí, en pleno día, mientras uno sube por los senderos que conducen a la cima de la montaña.

THE COQUI No other species of wildlife is more endemic to Puerto Rico, or more loved, than this tiny one-inch tree frog. The Coqui sounds more like a bird than the usual "croaking" frog species. Every evening, as he joins his millions of companions in their nightly chorus, you can clearly hear him singing his name – "CO-QUI, CO-QUI". And because the rain forest is so heavily shaded in the daytime, you will also hear his musical greeting as you travel your way up the mountain roads and trails.

LA COTORRA PUERTORRIQUEÑA Una de las grandes tragedias ecológicas de nuestra isla es la desaparición, ya casi consumada, de esta rara ave que abundara una vez en toda la isla. Estos pájaros han tenido que buscar refugio en el bosque pluvial para protegerse de los cazadores sin escrúpulos. Ahora también se han convertido en víctimas del zarzal, que saquea sus nidos. Se están haciendo esfuerzos desesperados por conservar esta especie, aunque sea en cautiverio.

PUERTO RICAN PARROT One of the great ecological tragedies of our island is the threatened extinction of this very rare bird. Once found all over the island, they have had to seek sanctuary in the rain forest from undisiplined hunting. Now falling prey to nest-raiding thrashers, desperate attempts are being made to preserve the species in captivity.

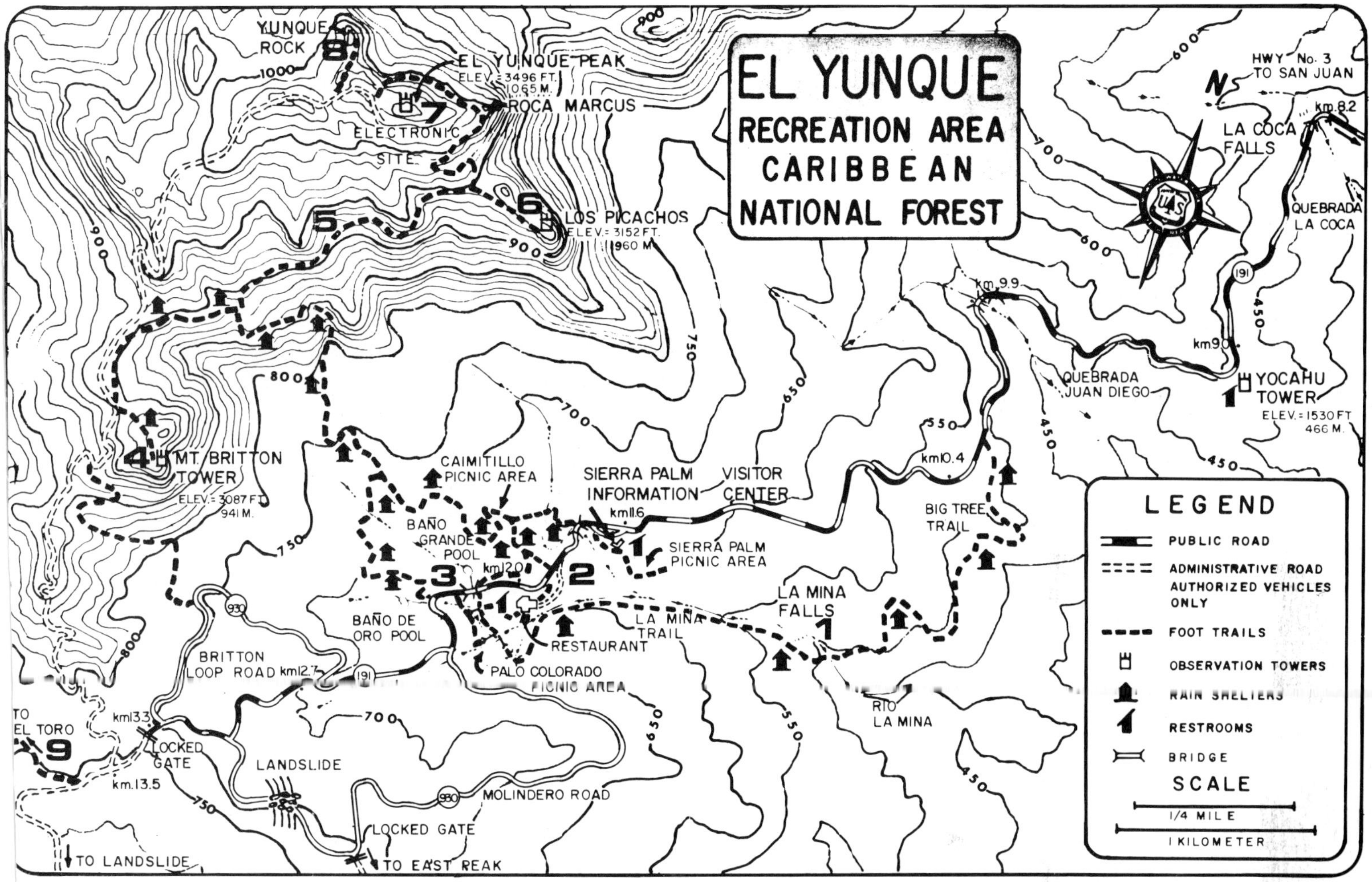

EL YUNQUE RECREATION AREA CARIBBEAN NATIONAL FOREST

YUNQUE ROCK
EL YUNQUE PEAK ELEV.= 3496 FT. 1065 M.
ROCA MARCUS
ELECTRONIC SITE
LOS PICACHOS ELEV.= 3152 FT. 960 M.
MT. BRITTON TOWER ELEV.= 3087 FT. 941 M.
CAIMITILLO PICNIC AREA
SIERRA PALM INFORMATION
VISITOR CENTER
SIERRA PALM PICNIC AREA
BAÑO GRANDE POOL
BAÑO DE ORO POOL
RESTAURANT
PALO COLORADO PICNIC AREA
LA MINA TRAIL
LA MINA FALLS
BIG TREE TRAIL
RIO LA MINA
BRITTON LOOP ROAD
TO EL TORO
LOCKED GATE
LANDSLIDE
MOLINDERO ROAD
TO LANDSLIDE
TO EAST PEAK
HWY No. 3 TO SAN JUAN
LA COCA FALLS
QUEBRADA LA COCA
QUEBRADA JUAN DIEGO
YOCAHU TOWER ELEV.= 1530 FT 466 M.

LEGEND

PUBLIC ROAD
ADMINISTRATIVE ROAD AUTHORIZED VEHICLES ONLY
FOOT TRAILS
OBSERVATION TOWERS
RAIN SHELTERS
RESTROOMS
BRIDGE

SCALE
1/4 MILE
1 KILOMETER

LIANAS Dondequiera que se mira en el Bosque Pluvial se ven estos largos tentáculos vegetales que van de árbol en árbol como gigantescas serpientes. Necesitan luz de sol, por eso, escalan los altos troncos tratando de salir de la enramada. Desde lo alto, las lianas envían raíces adventicias al suelo del bosque. Así se forman redes de lianas que trepan hacia el cielo en busca de luz y descienden al suelo en busca de sustento.

LIANAS Everywhere you look in the Rain Forest you will see these great woody vines looping like gigantic serpents from tree to tree. Their need for adequate sunlight forces them to scale the tall, dense trees in the forest. From their lofty, leafy heights, the Lianas send aerial roots to the forest floor forming interlacing networks with thousands of other vines which climb skyward for sunlight and earthward for sustenance.

Anuncios de ventas

The language of sales ads is florid, imaginative, and aggressive. The opportunity of a lifetime will be missed if one doesn't make it to the store in time for the sale. (Until the next sale, that is.)

venta general

Para toda su familia

¡Explosivas ofertas en todos nuestros departamentos!

¡No se lo pierda! Ésta es la oportunidad-cañonazo del año para toda la familia. Rebajas explosivas en moda para chicos y grandes... ¡Y toda una descarga de super-ofertas para el hogar!

¡Pura dinamita de oportunidades que ya comienza en nuestra VENTA GENERAL! Hoy mismo visite El Palacio de Hierro y convénzase por sí mismo de las estruendosas oportunidades en todos los departamentos.

Es muy fácil comprar a Crédito. Diariamente abierto de 10 A. M. a 7 P. M. Miércoles y Sábados hasta las 8 P. M.

el palacio de hierro

durango y centro

---

ofertas *offers;* **¡No se lo pierda!** *Don't miss it!;* **ésta** *this (one);* **cañonazo** *bombshell;* **rebajas** *discounts;* **moda** *fashion;* **grandes** *grown-ups;* **toda una descarga** *a whole discharge (volley, firing);* **hogar** *home;* **comienza** *begins;* **hoy mismo** *today, right now;* **visite** *visit;* **convénzase** *be convinced;* **sí mismo** *yourself;* **estruendosas** *deafening, noisy;* **diariamente** *daily*

ZAPATOS
Buenos y Baratos!..en
PAR-2
más barato no hay, no hay...!

¡OFERTAS DE LA SEMANA!

Q. 12.99 38001 más barato no hay, no hay...!
Q. 12.99 38002 más barato no hay, no hay...!
Q. 12.99 38003 más barato no hay, no hay...!
Q. 12.99 38013 más barato no hay, no hay...!
Q. 12.99 38014
Q. 12.99 38122 más barato no hay, no hay...!
Q. 9.99 38150 más barato no hay, no hay...!
Q. 7.99

zapaterías
PAR-2
más barato no hay, no hay...!

Centro Comerc
Centro Comerc
8a. Avenida 8-
7a. Avenida 9-
Novicentro Z

ALMACENES
FACOL

para Dama	
Faldas	$498.
Conjunto	598.
Vestido	398.
Blusa	298.
Slacks	468.
Vestido	1.198.
Baby doll	498.
Enaguas	268.
Interiores	78.
Vestido	998.
Camisa	448.

para Hombre	
Pantalón	$450.
Camisa	530.
Pantaloncillo	60.
Camiseta	150.
Pijama	580.

para niño	
Pantalón	$330.
Camisa	320.
Pijama	350.

para niña	
Vestido	$198.
Blusa	58.
Slacks	298.

Ricaurte Cra. 28 No. 12B-09 · Chapinero Cra. 16 No. 51-29 · Restrepo Cra 19 No 16-36 S. · 7 de Agosto Cra 24 No 63E-01 · Palermo Cra. 13 No 45-28

Prices in foreign countries are often confusing to the people who don't live there. Items that are imported from the United States, which are relatively inexpensive here, will be quite expensive because of import duties. Then, of course, there is the problem of converting the familiar dollar into pesos, soles, or quetzales. And in today's world economy, the rates of exchange vary constantly. Check with your local bank or in a newspaper for current rates or look at the table on page 88. These rates can—and often do—vary drastically overnight.

MAFALDA

Q. (quetzal) *monetary unit of Gualemala* **$498** *498 pesos (monetary unit of Colombia);* **conjunto** *suit, outfit;* **enaguas** *slips, petticoats;* **interiores** *underwear;* **pantaloncillo** *underpants;* **Cra. (Carretera)** *Highway* **¡Feliz día!** *Happy [Father's] Day!;* **che** *buddy (Argentina)*

17 Nuestra salud

A balanced diet, exercise, and sensible living habits are the best recipe for a good, long, healthy life. The human body is a machine that has to keep working for many, many years; and it works best when it is happy.

La campaña° contra fumar es una campaña mundial°. Desde los años de la colonización del Nuevo Mundo, cuando los europeos descubrieron el uso del tabaco—planta indígena° de las Américas—billones de personas de todos los países del mundo fuman. Y millones se enferman. Y mueren. Si no fumas, no empieces°. Y si fumas, no sigas°.

Deja de fumar

El uso del tabaco es una de las mayores° causas de enfermedades.

Dibujos usados° en Colombia en la campaña contra fumar.

Start your own classroom campaign against cigarette-smoking, drinking, or any other health-damaging habit you and your classmates feel is a problem.

---

campaña *campaign;* **mundial** *worldwide;* **indígena** *indigenous, native;* **no empieces** *don't begin;* **no sigas** *don't continue;* **deja de fumar** *stop smoking;* **mayores** *main, principal;* **usados** *used*

El clima

La temperatura y el estado del tiempo nos afecta a todos. Cuando es verano en el norte del mundo, es invierno en el sur. Los pronósticos° del tiempo son predicciones que a veces no se realizan°—pero otras veces nos ayudan a hacer planes. Y cuando viajamos debemos saber qué clase de tiempo podemos esperar°, porque a pocos° de nosotros nos gusta la playa cuando llueve.

el tiempo

Tiempo mayormente° bueno con aguaceros° aislados°. No hay sistemas atmosféricos importantes. Probabilidad de lluvia para San Juan, Ponce y Mayagüez: 20%. Vientos del sureste de 10 a 15 nudos°. Oleaje° cerca de 3 pies. Marejadas° del este de 3 a 5 pies.

el tiempo

Cielos parcialmente nublados con aguaceros y tronadas° aisladas. Probabilidad de lluvia: San Juan y Ponce: 30%, Mayagüez: 40%. Vientos del sureste de 10 a 15 nudos con ráfagas° ocasionalmente más fuertes. Oleaje cerca de 4 pies. Marejadas del este de 3 a 5 pies.

Clima Mundial

NUEVA YORK, 10 (AP) — Temperaturas y estado del tiempo en el mundo en las últimas 24 horas:

	C Mín.	F.	C Máx.	F.	
Amsterdam	20	68	26	79	Despej.
Atenas	18	64	28	82	Despej.
Barbados	26	79	33	91	Nublado
Beirut	20	68	25	77	Despej.
Belgrado	13	55	24	75	Nublado
Berlín	15	59	30	86	Despej.
Bogotá	8	46	18	64	Nublado
Bruselas	14	57	23	74	Nublado
Buenos Aires	5	41	12	54	Despej.
Caracas	20	68	28	82	Nublado
Chicago	14	57	29	84	Lluvia
Copenhague	14	57	22	72	Despej.
Curitiba	16	61	23	73	Nublado
Dublin	15	59	19	66	Nublado
El Cairo	23	73	35	95	Despej.
Estocolmo	17	63	26	79	Despej.
Francfort	17	63	31	88	Despej.
Ginebra	14	57	32	90	Despej.
Helsinki	13	55	25	77	Despej.
Hong Kong	27	81	30	86	Despej.
Honolulú	23	73	31	88	Nublado
Jerusalén	17	63	30	86	Despej.
Johannesburgo	5	41	18	64	Despej.
Kiev	14	57	22	72	Nublado
La Habana	23	73	27	81	Nublado
Lima	16	61	19	66	Nublado
Lisboa	16	61	27	81	Despej.
Londres	16	62	28	84	Despej.

	C Mín.	F.	C Máx.	F.	
Los Angeles	16	62	28	83	Despej.
Madrid	19	66	33	91	Despej.
México D.F	13	55	27	81	Despej.
Miami	18	64	30	86	Nublado
Montevideo	5	41	10	50	Nublado
Montreal	15	59	28	82	Nublado
Moscú	17	63	25	77	Despej.
Nueva Delhi	30	87	47	107	Nublado
Nueva York	24	75	33	91	Despej.
Nicosia	22	72	35	95	Despej.
Oslo	12	54	25	77	Despej.
París	19	66	32	90	Despej.
Pekín	21	70	31	86	Nublado
Río de Janeiro	17	63	29	84	Despej.
Roma	18	64	30	86	Despej.
San Francisco	11	53	20	67	Despej.
Santiago	6	43	12	54	Despej.
Sao Paulo	15	59	23	73	Despej.
Seúl	24	75	32	90	Nublado
Singapur	26	79	32	90	Despej.
Sydney	10	50	17	62	Lluvia
Taipei	25	77	33	91	Despej.
Tel Aviv	21	69	30	86	Despej.
Tokio	9	84	21	70	Despej.
Toronto	11	52	29	84	Nublado
Vancouver	13	55	24	75	Nublado
Viena	13	54	23	73	Despej.

EL TIEMPO HOY:

Parcialmente nublado con aguaceros bastante dispersos°. Vientos leves° y variables.

---

pronósticos *forecasts;* **no se realizan** *aren't fulfilled;* **esperar** *expect;* **pocos** *few* **mayormente** *mainly;* **aguaceros** *downpours, rainstorms;* **aislados** *isolated;* **nudos** *knots;* **oleaje** *wave heights;* **marejadas** *groundswells* **tronadas** *thunderstorms;* **ráfagas** *gusts of wind* **Atenas** *Athens;* **Estocolmo** *Stockholm;* **Ginebra** *Geneva;* **Lisboa** *Lisbon;* **Moscú** *Moscow;* **C. = centígrados;** **F. = Fahrenheit;** **Despej. (despejado)** *clear;* **lluvia** *rain* **bastante dispersos** *quite scattered;* **leves** *light*

Las vitaminas: fuentes y funciones

VITAMINAS FUNCIÓN	FUENTE
A..... mantiene los tejidos; aumenta la resistencia de piel y mucosas	hígado de res, pescado, espinaca, lechuga, tomate, zanahorias, mantequilla
B_1 (tiamina) favorece el metabolismo de los carbohidratos y la absorción de oxígeno por el cerebro	hígado de res, cerdo, leche, legumbres, maní, soya, pan integral, yema de huevo
B_2 (riboflavina) participa en la oxidación de compuestos y en la activación del nervio óptico	aguacate, almendras, pan enriquecido, espinacas, yogur, hígado
B_6 (piridoxina) esencial para metabolismo de carbohidratos y aminoácidos; estimula la actividad de los leucocitos	carne de res, zanahorias, maíz, huevos, jamón, extracto de malta, salmón fresco
B_{12}..... participa en el metabolismo de aminoácidos; es antianémica	hígado y riñón, leche, huevos, queso
C (ácido ascórbico) es antiinfecciosa, activa el metabolismo, conserva la substancia intercelular de sostén	verduras, naranja, limón, pimiento, col, bróculi
D..... regula la absorción del calcio y fósforo	aceite de hígado de bacalao, yema de huevo, leche, mantequilla
E..... es antioxidante, aumenta el metabolismo del fósforo en los huesos	semillas de cereales, aceites vegetales, yema de huevo, lechuga
K..... es antihemorrágica	levadura de cerveza, hígado, pescado, leche, legumbres secas

In Spanish, keep a diary for a week. Write down what you eat, what you do, how you feel, what the weather is like. At the end of the week, look back and read it all. Did you have a good week or one not so great? (Hint: Count the good things you wrote down and then the bad ones. If the good far outnumber the bad, that's your answer. Otherwise, better luck next week.)

MAFALDA

fuentes *sources* **mantiene** *maintains;* **tejidos** *tissues;* **aumenta** *augments, increases;* **mucosas** *mucous membranes;* **hígado** *liver;* **res** *beef;* **favorece** *aids;* **legumbres** *vegetables;* **maní** *peanut;* **soya** *soybean;* **pan integral** *whole wheat bread;* **yema** *yolk;* **participa** *takes part in;* **compuestos** *compounds;* **aguacate** *avocado;* **almendras** *almonds;* **enriquecido** *enriched;* **estimula** *stimulates;* **leucocitos** *white blood cells;* **carne** *meat;* **maíz** *corn;* **fresco** *fresh;* **riñón** *kidney;* **activa** *activates;* **conserva** *maintains;* **sostén** *support;* **limón** *lemon;* **pimiento** *pepper (vegetable);* **col** *cabbage;* **aceite de hígado de bacalao** *cod liver oil;* **huesos** *bones;* **levadura** *yeast* **lo mejor** *the best (thing);* **vejete** *ridiculous old man;* **anquilosado** *rusty, aging;* **veamos** *let's see*

De aquí y de allá

DATOS DE TECNOLOGÍA

Invenciones históricas

AÑO	*INVENCIÓN*	*INVENTOR*	*PAÍS*
650	el molino de viento°	Abu Lulua	Persia
725	el reloj mecánico	Yi Hsing	China
1440	la imprenta°	J. Guttenberg	Alemania
1590	el microscopio	Z. Janssen	Holanda
1593	el termómetro	Galileo	Italia
1608	el telescopio	H. Lippershey	Holanda
1644	el barómetro	E. Torricelli	Italia
1712	la máquina de vapor°	T. Newcomb	Inglaterra
1783	el globo°	J. y J. Montgolfier	Francia
1787	las conservas° en lata	N. Appert	Francia
1804	la locomotora	R. Trevithich	Inglaterra
1816	el estetoscopio	R. Laennec	Francia
1826-39	la fotografía	J. Mepce, L. Daguerre	Francia
1840	el telégrafo	S. Morse	Estados Unidos
1852	el dirigible aéreo°	H. Giffard	Francia
1850	el submarino	N. Monturiol	España
1860	la bicicleta	E. Michaux	Francia
1867	la máquina de escribir°	Ch. Sholes, Ch. Glidden	Estados Unidos
1867	la dinamita	A. Nobel	Suecia
1876	el teléfono	A. Graham Bell	Estados Unidos
1877	el fonógrafo	T. Edison	Estados Unidos
1879	la bujía° eléctrica	T. Edison	Estados Unidos
1884	la investigación submarina	I. Peral y Caballero	España
1884-1930	la televisión	varios	varios
1885	el automóvil	K. Benz, G. Daimler	Alemania
1888	la cámara portátil°	G. Eastman	Estados Unidos
1889-1896	el cinematógrafo°	T. Edison, A. Lumière, varios	varios
1895	los rayos X	W. Roentgen	Alemania
1897	el motor diesel	R. Diesel	Alemania
1902	la radio	G. Marconi, R. Fessiden	Estados Unidos
1903	el aeroplano	Orville y W. Wright	Estados Unidos
1907	el helicóptero	L. y J. Breguet	Francia
1914	el tanque° de guerra°	E. Swinton	Inglaterra
1922-35	el radar	Taylor, Young, Watson-Watt	varios
1942	el reactor atómico	E. Fermi	Estados Unidos
1944	la computadora° digital	H. Aiken	Estados Unidos
1945	la bomba atómica	A. Einstein, E. Fermi, V. Bush	Estados Unidos
1947	el transistor	Shockley, Bardeen, Brattain	Estados Unidos
1958	el rayo° láser	Ch. Townes	Estados Unidos

¿Cuáles países tuvieron más invenciones importantes?
¿Cuáles crees tú que fueron las invenciones más importantes? ¿Por qué?

---

molino de viento *windmill;* **imprenta** *printing press;* **máquina de vapor** *steam engine;* **globo** *balloon;* **conservas** *preserved food;* **dirigible aéreo** *dirigible, blimp;* **máquina de escribir** *typewriter;* **bujía** *light bulb;* **portátil** *portable;* **cinematógrafo** *movie projector;* **tanque** *tank;* **guerra** *war;* **computadora** *computer;* **rayo** *beam*

Horóscopo

What's your sign?

ARIES (21 de marzo al 19 de abril)
Cambios° importantes en tu casa, oficina o escuela. Debes pensar bien sobre el futuro. No hables° sobre cosas confidenciales.

TAURO (20 de abril al 20 de mayo)
Tienes que tener mucho cuidado°. Tu reputación está en juego°. No gastes° dinero en cosas que no necesitas.

GÉMINIS (21 de mayo al 20 de junio)
Las apariencias° superficiales no son suficientes para llegar a° una decisión inteligente.

CÁNCER (21 de junio al 22 de julio)
Un día muy productivo te espera° hoy. Encuentras la cooperación de tus amigos y asociados°.

LEO (23 de julio al 22 de agosto)
Puedes combinar negocios, viajes y amistades°. Grandes oportunidades para un romance.

VIRGO (23 de agosto al 22 de septiembre)
Una persona con mucha experiencia te ya a ayudar. Tienes gran suerte en negocios y finanzas.

---

cambios *changes;* **no hables** *don't talk;* **tener mucho cuidado** *be very careful;* **en juego** *at stake;* **no gastes** *don't spend;* **apariencias** *appearances;* **llegar a** *come to;* **espera** *awaits;* **asociados** *associates;* **amistades** *friendships*

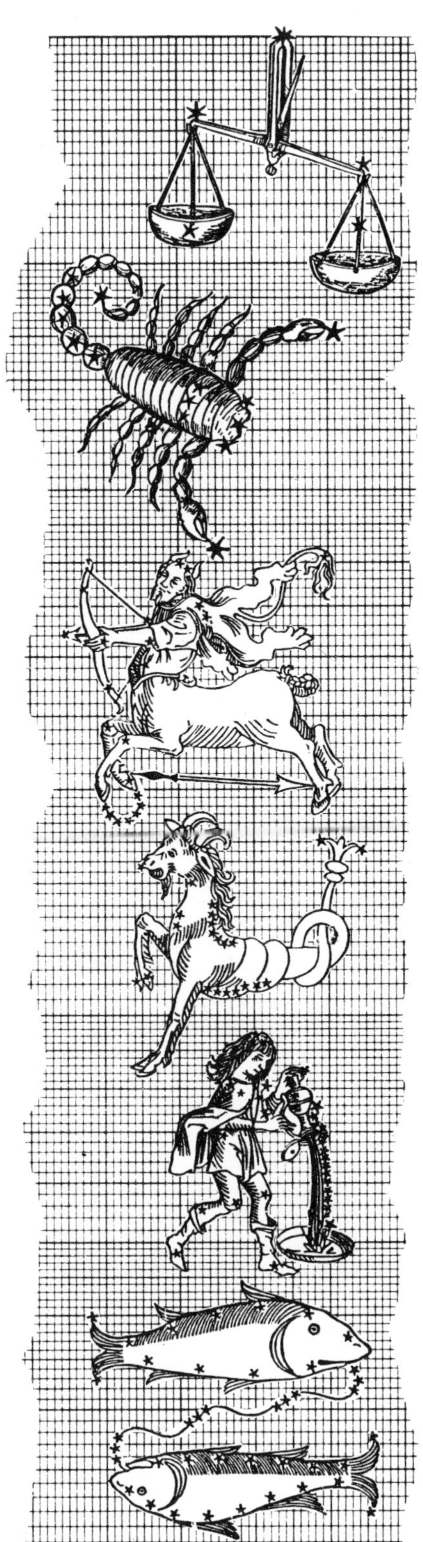

LIBRA (23 de septiembre al 22 de octubre)
La influencia de las posiciones planetarias es muy intensa. No pierdas tiempo° con detalles° insignificantes.

ESCORPIÓN (23 de octubre al 21 de noviembre)
Alguien° prueba° tu lealtad° y pasas con gran éxito. Encuentras la solución para un problema viejo.

SAGITARIO (22 de noviembre al 21 de diciembre)
La diversión no tiene que costar mucho. Tus amigos tienen mucho que decir sobre cómo pasar el fin de semana.

CAPRICORNIO (22 de diciembre al 19 de enero)
El presente es el mejor tiempo para hacer planes para el futuro. No prestes atención° a los rumores.

ACUARIO (20 de enero al 18 de febrero)
El tiempo es corto y tú tienes mucho que hacer. Un día magnífico para empezar proyectos° nuevos.

PISCIS (19 de febrero al 20 de marzo)
Tu imaginación está estimulada, pero no debes ir a extremos. Ayuda° a un amigo si puedes.

What is the astrological sign of your class? Make a list of everyone's birthday, find out what the astrological signs are, and see which one is the most common. (In Spanish, of course!)

---

no pierdas tiempo *don't waste time;* **detalles** *details;* **alguien** *someone;* **prueba** *tests;* **lealtad** *loyalty;* **no prestes atención** *don't pay attention;* **proyectos** *projects, plans;* **ayuda** *help*

El Titán de Bronce, Antonio Maceo

Antonio Maceo, el legendario Titán de Bronce, personificó la decisión del pueblo° cubano por conquistar° su independencia de España.

"La libertad no se mendiga°, se conquista° con el filo° del machete."

Maceo murió° en combate contra España durante la Guerra de Independencia, en la provincia de La Habana, el 7 de diciembre de 1896.

La Rogativa

En el Viejo San Juan hay una escultura que conmemora un hecho° histórico.

En 1797, los ingleses ocuparon la ciudad.
El obispo° de San Juan organizó una "rogativa," una procesión religiosa por las calles de la ciudad. Según la leyenda, cuando los ingleses vieron° la procesión, se asustaron° y se fueron de la isla.

MAFALDA

---

pueblo *people;* **conquistar** *win;* **no se mendiga** *is not to be begged for;* **se conquista** *it is won;* **filo** *cutting edge;* **murió** *died;* **hecho** *event;* **obispo** *bishop;* **vieron** *saw;* **se asustaron** *became frightened* **elegí** *I chose;* **tratar de** *try to*

Por los mercados

The markets of Spain and Latin America offer a great wealth of goods.

Éste es el mercado de Santo Domingo. Dentro de una gran estructura moderna, muchos tipos de vendedores, comerciantes° y artisanos° venden comestibles°, artículos de artesanía y muchas otras cosas.

Fuera del° mercado también hay puestos° donde podemos comprar frutas y vegetales.

comerciantes *merchants;* **artesanos** *craftsmen;* **comestibles** *food;* **fuera de** *outside;* **puestos** *stalls, booths*

Dinero, dinero, dinero

Argentina: peso

Bolivia: peso

Costa Rica: colón

Colombia: peso

Chile: peso

República Dominicana: peso

Ecuador: sucre

Guatemala: quetzal

Honduras: lempira

México: peso

Nicaragua: córdoba

Paraguay: guaraní

Perú: sol

El Salvador: colón

Uruguay: peso

Venezuela: bolívar

Cambiando el dinero

CAMBIO DE MONEDA

PAÍS	MONEDA NACIONAL	DÓLARES (EE. UU.)	CANTIDAD POR DÓLAR (EE. UU.)
Argentina	peso	.1043	9.59
Bolivia	peso	.00050	2000.00
Colombia	peso	.01359	73.58
Costa Rica	colón	.02000	5.00
Cuba	peso	1.1852	0.84
Chile	peso	.01276	78.37
República Dominicana	peso	1.0000	1.00
Ecuador	sucre	.02290	43.67
España	peseta	.006689	149.50
Guatemala	quetzal	1.0000	1.00
Honduras	lempira	.5000	2.00
México	peso	.00714	140.05
Nicaragua	córdoba	.1000	10.00
Panamá	dólar (EE. UU.)	1.0000	1.00
Paraguay	guaraní	.007937	125.99
Perú	sol	.0008	1250.00
Puerto Rico	dólar (EE. UU.)	1.0000	1.00
El Salvador	colón	.4023	2.48
Uruguay	peso	.02939	34.02
Venezuela	bolívar	.0850	11.76

Si tienes cien doláres y los cambias en Argentina, ¿cuántos pesos tienes?
Si tienes cincuenta soles en Perú, ¿cuántos dólares tienes?
¿Cuál peso vale° más?

MAFALDA

cambio de moneda *currency exchange rate;* **vale** *is worth* **aceitunas** *olives;* **¿Qué tal están?** *How are they?;* **ejecutivos** *executives;* **prueba** *try;* **imagen** *image*

En camino 

Most accidents happen near home—no matter where home happens to be.

TODO VIAJE EN CARRO PUEDE SER PELIGROSO. UNA GRAN CANTIDAD DE ACCIDENTES FATALES OCURREN DENTRO DE UN RADIO DE 25 MILLAS DE LA CASA. LAS DISTANCIAS CORTAS NUNCA SON GARANTÍA DE LA SEGURIDAD. PROTÉJASE, USE SU CINTURÓN DE SEGURIDAD.

UNA VÍA
DOBLE VÍA
UNA VÍA
RESPETE LAS SEÑALES DE TRÁNSITO

¡¡PARE!!

BICICLETAS

AUTOMOTO

NO DOBLE DERECHA

RESPETE LAS SEÑALES DE TRÁNSITO

---

cantidad *quantity, amount;* **radio** *radius;* **seguridad** *safety;* **protéjase** *protect yourself;* **use** *use;* **cinturón de seguridad** *seat belt* **¡Pare!** *Stop!;* **respete** *respect;* **no doble** *don't turn*

Altos de Chavón, República Dominicana

Al este de la ciudad de Santo Domingo, en la costa sur de la República Dominicana, está Altos de Chavón, una "aldea" para artistas y artesanos. Después de más de cinco años de construcción — pues toda la construcción es a mano° — el proyecto ya toma forma de una verdadera° aldea, con varias tiendas, restaurantes, galerías de arte, un museo, una discoteca, un hotel, además de los talleres° de educación artística.

La creación de este centro cultural fue para estimular el interés en el arte dominicano. La aldea es una réplica de una aldea medieval europea.

El símbolo de Altos de Chavón.

El Río Chavón.

La aldea presenta muchos conciertos.

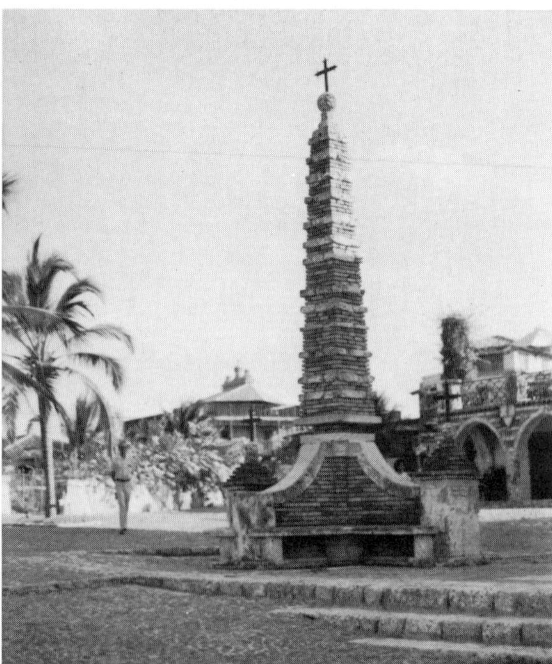

Frente a la iglesia° en la plaza central.

---

 a mano *by hand;* **verdadera** *true;* **talleres** *workshops;* **iglesia** *church*

Este edificio tiene un restaurante.

La iglesia de San Estanislao.

Entrada° a los jardines.

Fuente, de piedra de coral.

Construcción típica de la aldea.

GUANO
Coccotrinax
argentea
PALMAE

SALA DE
EXPOSICIONES
Y
CONFERENCIAS

ÁREA INVESTIGACIÓN
PROHIBIDO ENTRAR

JARDÍN BOTÁNICO Dr. RAFAEL M. MOSCOSO

El mar

The sea has been one of the favorite subjects for poets throughout history. Maybe it's because of the rhythmic patterns of the waves or the mystery of the great depths. The following poem, by a contemporary writer, is an example.

MAR

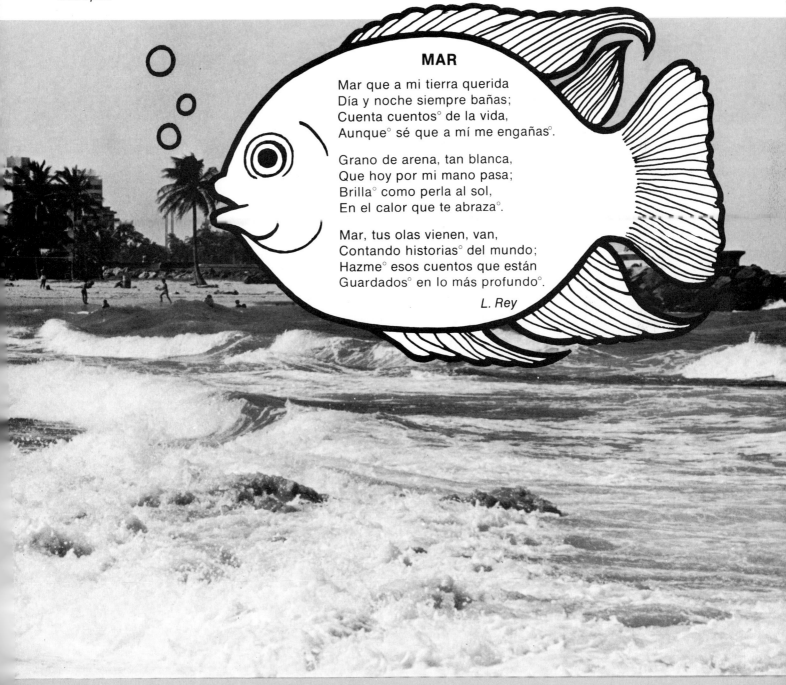

Mar que a mi tierra querida
Día y noche siempre bañas;
Cuenta cuentos° de la vida,
Aunque° sé que a mí me engañas°.

Grano de arena, tan blanca,
Que hoy por mi mano pasa;
Brilla° como perla al sol,
En el calor que te abraza°.

Mar, tus olas vienen, van,
Contando historias° del mundo;
Hazme° esos cuentos que están
Guardados° en lo más profundo°.

L. Rey

---

cuentos *stories;* **aunque** *although;* **engañas** *you deceive;* **brilla** *shine;* **abraza** *hugs;* **historias** *stories;* **hazme** *tell me;* **guardados** *kept;* **lo más profundo** *the deepest part*

El cielo

En el cielo vemos el sol  de día y la luna  de noche. También vemos muchas estrellas  y a veces las "estrellas" son planetas  o satélites 

El cielo también tiene nubes. Las nubes tienen humedad° que cae como lluvia nieve  o granizo  Las tempestades° traen truenos 

y relámpagos

además de mucho viento  y goteras  y malas condiciones para viajar y problemas para el tráfico  y resfriados 

Pero después de la tempestad sale° el arcoiris y todo sigue muy bien hasta la próxima vez.

ESTRELLAS BRILLANTES

Nombre y constelación	Magnitud	Distancia (años luz)
Sirio (Can Mayor)	−1,4	8.6
Cánope (Carina)	−0,7	900 (?)
Alfa Centauri (Centauro)	−0,3	4,3
Arturo (Boyero)	−0,1	41
Vega (Lira)	0,0	26
La Cabra (Auriga)	0,1	47
Rigel (Orión)	0,1	900 (?)
Proción (Can Menor)	0,4	10
Achernar (Eridano)	0,5	66
Beta Centauri (Centauro)	0,7	300

 humedad *moisture;* **tempestades** *storms;* **sale** *comes out*

El sol

El Sol es una estrella. Es el centro del Sistema Solar. La Tierra es el tercer planeta del Sistema Solar—en orden por distancia. La Tierra tiene sólo una luna, y la llamamos "Luna." Pero hay otros planetas que tienen varias lunas.

MERCURIO es el planeta más pequeño del sistema solar y el que está más cerca del Sol. No tiene atmósfera. Su temperature es 350°C. de día y −170°C. de noche. Un año en Mercurio dura° 88 días terrestres°.

VENUS es el planeta que está más cerca de la Tierra. Tiene atmósfera, pero es de dióxodo de carbón (97%). La temperatura en la superficie° de Venus es 460°C. Un año dura 225 días.

MARTE es el cuarto planeta del sistema solar. Su color es rojo, y la superficie tiene "canales" que son un misterio. La temperatura de Martes es −23° C. El año marciano dura 687 días. Marte tiene dos lunas.

JÚPITER es el planeta más grande del sistema solar (2½ veces la masa de los otros planetas juntos°). La temperatura es −150°C. Un año de Júpiter dura 11.86 años terrestres. Júpiter tiene dieciséis lunas.

SATURNO es el segundo planeta en tamaño°. Los anillos° de este planeta son la característica más conocida°. El viaje de Saturno alrededor del° Sol toma 29.46 años. Saturno tiene veintitrés lunas que conocemos hasta° hoy. La temperatura en Saturno es −180°C.

URANO fue el primer planeta que se descubrió usando un telescopio. Urano también tiene anillos y cinco lunas, pero sabemos muy poco de ellas. La temperatura en Urano es −210°C. El planeta toma 84 años para viajar alrededor del Sol.

NEPTUNO es el séptimo planeta del sistema solar. En 1846, J. G. Galle lo descubrió. Su temperatura es −220°C. El planeta toma 164.8 años en su viaje alrededor del sol. Tiene dos lunas.

PLUTÓN es el último planeta conocido. Su temperatura es −230°C., su año dura 247.7 años terrestres y tiene una lunas.

dura *lasts;* **terrestres** *earthly;* **superficie** *surface;* **juntos** *together;* **tamaño** *size;* **anillos** *rings;* **conocida** *well-known;* **alrededor de** *around;* **hasta** *up to*

La Tierra

Las Naciones Unidas

El 1º. de enero de 1942, Franklin D. Roosevelt, presidente de los Estados Unidos, usó el nombre "naciones unidas" en referencia a las veintiséis naciones aliadas° durante la Segunda Guerra Mundial. La Organización de Naciones Unidas (ONU) ratificó su carta° y oficialmente empezó su existencia el 24 de octubre de 1945. La Organización mantiene su sede° en su propio° edificio en Nueva York. Más de cien países son miembros hoy.

La Organización de los Estados Americanos

ORGANIZACIÓN DE LOS ESTADOS AMERICANOS

El 30 de abril de 1948, veintiuna repúblicas americanas formaron la Organización de Estados Americanos (OEA). La OEA es parte de las Naciones Unidas. Los objetivos de la Organización son el mantenimiento° de la paz y la cooperación entre los países miembros. La idea original fue de Simón Bolívar, que reunió a varios representantes en 1826, en el Congreso de Panamá.

MAFALDA

COMO SIEMPRE; APENAS UNO PONE LOS PIES EN LA TIERRA SE ACABA LA DIVERSIÓN

aliadas *allied;* **carta** *charter;* **sede** *headquarters;* **propio** *own;* **mantenimiento** *maintenance* **apenas** *hardly, scarcely*

La historia de Belinda

Había una vez, hace muchos años, en un reino muy lejano°, una princesa que se llamaba Belinda. Su papá, el rey Leoncio, estaba ya muy enfermo, porque tenía más de noventa años. Belinda no tenía mamá—la gran reina Celia había muerto° al nacer Belinda.

Belinda era la única hija del rey, y pronto iba a heredar° su trono°. Su belleza era muy grande—su piel suave° como la seda°, sus ojos como dos zafiros°, sus labios° rojos como el rubí—pero el rey temía por la vida de su hija, y ésta nunca salía del palacio, porque Leoncio temía que algo le iba a pasar a su querida hija. Un día, al anochecer°, Belinda miraba a la lejanía° desde su balcón del palacio real. Y allá, a lo lejos°, veía una luz que brillaba con gran fuerza. Mientras ella miraba esa luz, oyó que llamaban su nombre. Belinda supo° entonces que tenía que ir a encontrar esa luz. Esa luz que brillaba bajo la luna llena.

Era invierno, y los campos° del reino estaban cubiertos° de nieve. Y de pronto, en medio de° esta tranquilidad°, se vio la figura solitaria de la princesa Belinda, caminando fuera del palacio por primera vez en su vida. Vestida con° grandes pieles° y ricas joyas, ya no veía la luz que la llamaba. Pero ella seguía a la luna.

---

lejano *distant;* **había muerto** *had died;* **heredar** *inherit;* **trono** *throne;* **suave** *soft;* **seda** *silk;* **zafiros** *sapphires;* **labios** *lips;* **al anochecer** *at nightfall;* **a la lejanía, a lo lejos** *in the distance;* **supo** *knew;* **campos** *fields;* **cubiertos** *covered;* **en medio de** *in the middle of;* **tranquilidad** *tranquillity;* **vestida con** *dressed in;* **pieles** *furs*

De pronto Belinda se encontró con la primera persona que había visto° fuera del palacio. Era una niña que estaba llorando. Lloraba con tanto dolor que la princesa paró a preguntar qué le pasaba.
—¿Por qué lloras?—preguntó Belinda.
—Lloro por el frío que tengo. Íbamos toda la familia a casa de abuelita cuando vino° la nevada°.
—¿Y dónde están tus papás? ¿Por qué te dejaron?
—No, no me dejaron, princesita, no podíamos ver nada por la nieve y el viento. Oigo a mi mamá llorando, pero no puedo seguir, por el frío.
—Bueno, entonces toma mis abrigos de piel—. Y Belinda se quitó° las pieles que la envolvían°.—Corre a tu mamá; estas pieles te protegen del frío.
—¿Y usted, princesita?
—Yo no sé lo que es el frío.
Y Belinda siguió caminando bajo la luna llena.

Por° un camino solitario, Belinda se encontró con un niño que pedía limosna°.
-¿No me da algo, por favor?—le preguntó el niño.
Asombrada°, la princesa le habló al niño:
—¿Y por qué pides limosna en medio de la noche en un camino desierto°?
Y el niño contestó:
—La vida del limosnero° es cruel, princesita. Tanto puedo conseguir° en un camino desierto en medianoche como en la plaza llena de gente al mediodía.
El niño tenía tal° melancolía en sus ojos, que la princesa se quitó todas sus ricas joyas y sacó° las monedas° de oro que llevaba en su bolso°.
—Toma, niño, toma. Estas riquezas no me valen° nada, pues no sé nada de la vida.-Y con sus manos llenas de oro y piedras preciosas, el niño besó a la princesa y volvió a su casa.

---

había visto *she had seen;* **vino** *came;* **nevada** *snowfall;* **se quitó** *took off;* **envolvían** *were covering;* **por** *along;* **pedía limosna** *was begging;* **asombrada** *astonished;* **desierto** *deserted;* **limosnero** *beggar;* **conseguir** *get;* **tal** *such;* **sacó** *took out;* **monedas** *coins;* **bolso** *purse;* **no valen** *are not worth*

Ya era muy tarde, y la luna llena se perdía en el horizonte. La princesa estaba muy cansada°, pero también estaba muy alegre Por primera vez sentía el frío. Por primera vez sentía hambre.

La princesa se sentó° sobre una piedra, y en la completa oscuridad° de la noche, cerró sus ojos.

De pronto, Belinda sintió una mano sobre su cara. Y al mismo tiempo oyó la voz de una viejita a la cual no podía ver por la oscuridad.

—Hija, ¿qué haces tú sola en este campo desierto?

—¿Quién es? No puedo ver nada.

—Soy sólo una vieja pobre°, cerca del fin de mi vida. ¿Pero, qué haces tú aquí?—

Y entonces, en la oscuridad, la princesa le contó su historia a la viejita, quien la llevó a su choza°, donde no había ninguna° luz.

Las dos hablaron por horas en la oscuridad, pasando la noche como amigas nuevas. Y la viejita le hizo un cuento° muy largo de un rey y una reina y una princesa, hasta que° Belinda cerró sus ojos, dormida°.

Muy temprano por la mañana, cuando el sol salía°, los primeros rayos de luz entraron a la choza de la viejita. Y por primera vez Belinda vio la cara de su nueva amiga. Era una cara noble, que a pesar de° tantos años, no tenía arrugas°. Era una cara como la de Belinda. De pronto, la princesa todavía media dormida, llamó en su sueño°. —Mamá, mamá.

Y abriendo sus ojos completamente vio la sonrisa° en la cara de la viejita.

—Sí, hija.

Pero entonces Belinda también vio que la viejita que la cuidó° toda esa noche no veía. Detrás de sus párpados° no habían ojos. Y la princesa lloró por primera vez en su vida.

—No llores, hija mía,—dijo° la viejita–porque sin ojos no puedo llorar contigo. Yo soy tu madre; vieja y enferma. Ciega°, y según el resto del mundo, muerta°.

Y de repente°, la princesa llevó sus manos a los ojos . . . .

En ese momento oyó Belinda a alguien tocando en la puerta°, y con mucha sorpresa° abrió sus ojos y vio el rostro° de su mamá, que decía:

—¿Por qué comiste esas angulas° anoche tan tarde, hija? Mira qué pesadilla° tenías. Gritabas y llorabas como si te torturaban. Y ya es hora de levantarse para ir al colegio.

Y colorín° colorao°, este cuento se ha acabao.°

---

cansada *tired;* **se sentó** *sat down;* **oscuridad** *darkness;* **pobre** *poor;* **choza** *hut;* **ninguna** *no, not any;* **hizo un cuento** *told a story;* **hasta que** *until;* **dormida** *asleep;* **salía** *was rising;* **a pesar de** *in spite of;* **arrugas** *wrinkles;* **sueño** *dream;* **sonrisa** *smile;* **cuidó** *took care of;* **párpados** *eyelids;* **dijo** *said;* **ciega** *blind;* **muerta** *dead;* **de repente** *suddenly;* **sangre** *blood;* **mejillas** *cheeks;* **tocando en la puerta** *knocking on the door;* **sorpresa** *surprise;* **rostro** *face;* **angulas** *eels;* **pesadilla** *nightmare;* **colorín** *linnet (small songbird);* **colorao = colorado** *reddish;* **acabao = acabado** *ended (This little rhyme is a common ending for fairy tales.)*

Los días de los santos

A

ABELARDO	Febrero 9
ADELA	Septiembre 8
ADELAIDA	Diciembre 18
ADOLFO	Septiembre 27
ADRIÁN	Marzo 6
AGUSTÍN	Agosto 28
ALBERTO	Noviembre 15
ALEJANDRO	Febrero 26
ALFONSO	Agosto 1
ALFREDO	Enero 12
ALICIA	Junio 28
ALONSO	Octubre 31
ÁLVARO	Febrero 19
AMADEO	Marzo 31
AMBROSIO	Diciembre 7
AMALIA	Julio 10
ANA	Julio 26
ANASTASIA	Diciembre 25
ANATOLIO	Marzo 20
ANDRÉS	Noviembre 30
ÁNGEL	Mayo 5
ÁNGELA	Enero 27
ANSELMO	Abril 21
ANTONIA	Abril 20
ANTONIO	Junio 13
APOLONIA	Febrero 9
ARNALDO	Marzo 14
ARTURO	Septiembre 1
ASUNCIÓN	Agosto 15
AUGUSTO	Octubre 7
AURELIO	Julio 27
AVELINO	Noviembre 10

B

BALDOMERO	Febrero 27
BÁRBARA	Diciembre 4
BARTOLOMÉ	Agosto 24
BASILIO	Enero 2
BEATRIZ	Mayo 29
BEGOÑA	Octubre 11
BELÉN	Diciembre 25
BELTRÁN	Octubre 8
BENEDICTA	Octubre 8
BENEDICTO	Mayo 9
BENITA	Enero 14
BENITO	Julio 11
BENJAMÍN	Marzo 31
BERNABÉ	Junio 11
BERNARDINO	Mayo 20
BERNARDO	Agosto 20
BIENVENIDO	Marzo 22
BLAS	Febrero 3
BONIFACIO	Junio 5
BRENDANO	Octubre 20
BRÍGIDA	Julio 23
BRUNO	Octubre 6
BUENAVENTURA	Julio 15

C

CALIXTO	Octubre 14
CAMILO	Julio 14
CÁNDIDA	Septiembre 4
CÁNDIDO	Febrero 2
CARINA	Noviembre 7
CARLOS	Noviembre 4
CARMEN	Julio 16
CASILDA	Abril 9
CASIMIRO	Marzo 4
CASTOR	Marzo 28
CATALINA	Abril 29
CAYETANO	Agosto 8
CECILIA	Noviembre 22
CECILIO	Mayo 15
CELESTINO	Abril 5
CELINA	Octubre 21
CESÁREO	Febrero 25
CIPRIANO	Septiembre 16
CIRILO	Febrero 14
CLARA	Agosto 11
CLAUDIA	Marzo 20
CLAUDIO	Febrero 15
CLEMENTE	Noviembre 23
CLEMENTINO	Noviembre 14
CLOTILDE	Junio 3
COLETA	Marzo 6
CONCEPCIÓN	Diciembre 8
CONSTANCIO	Septiembre 23
CONSTANTINO	Julio 27
CORNELIO	Septiembre 16
COSME	Septiembre 26
CRISPÍN	Noviembre 19
CRISTINA	Marzo 13
CRISTÓBAL	Julio 10

D

DÁMASO	Diciembre 11
DAMIÁN	Septiembre 26
DANIEL	Enero 3
DARÍA	Octubre 25
DARÍO	Diciembre 19
DAVID	Junio 26
DELFÍN	Diciembre 24
DEMETRIO	Diciembre 22
DESIDERIO	Mayo 23
DIEGO	Noviembre 23
DIMAS	Marzo 25
DIONISIO	Octubre 9
DOLORES	Septiembre 15
DOMINGO	Agosto 7
DONATO	Febrero 25
DOROTEA	Octubre 30

E

EDGAR	Julio 8
EDMUNDO	Noviembre 16
EDUARDO	Octubre 13
EFRÉN	Junio 9
ELENA	Agosto 18
ELIAS	Julio 20
ELISEO	Junio 14
ELOY	Diciembre 1
ELVIRA	Abril 24
EMELIA	Mayo 30
EMILIANA	Enero 5
EMILIANO	Febrero 8
EMILIO	Mayo 28
EMMA	Febrero 29
ENGRACIA	Abril 16
ENGUELBERTO	Noviembre 7
ENRIQUE	Julio 13
EPIFANIO	Enero 21
ERASMO	Noviembre 25
ERMELINDA	Octubre 29
ERNESTO	Noviembre 7
ESCOLÁSTICA	Febrero 10
ESPERANZA	Diciembre 18
ESTANISLAO	Abril 11
ESTEBAN	Diciembre 26
ETHEL O AUDREY	Junio 23
EUGENIO	Febrero 20
EULALIA	Diciembre 10
EULOGIO	Enero 9
EUSEBIO	Agosto 2
EUSTASIO	Junio 2
EVARISTO	Diciembre 23
EXPEDITO	Abril 19
EXUPERIO	Mayo 2
EZEQUIEL	Abril 10

F

FABIÁN	Enero 20
FABIO	Julio 31
FABIOLA	Diciembre 27
FACUNDO	Noviembre 27
FAUSTINO	Febrero 16
FAUSTO	Octubre 13
FE	Agosto 1
FEDERICO	Julio 18
FELICIA	Mayo 16
FELICIANO	Junio 9
FELICIDAD	Marzo 7
FELICISIMO	Octubre 26
FELIPE	Mayo 3
FÉLIX	Mayo 29
FERMÍN	Julio 7
FERMINA	Noviembre 24
FERNANDO	Mayo 30
FIDEL	Abril 24
FILOMENO	Noviembre 14
FIRMILIANO	Octubre 28
FLAVIANO	Agosto 23
FLOR	Diciembre 31
FLORA	Noviembre 24
FLORENCIO	Mayo 23
FLORENTINA	Junio 20
FLORIÁN	Mayo 4
FORTUNATA	Febrero 21
FRANCISCA	Marzo 9
FRANCISCO	Octubre 4
FRUCTUOSO	Enero 20
FULGENCIO	Enero 14

G

GABRIEL	Septiembre 29
GEMA	Abril 11
GENARO	Septiembre 19
GENEROSO	Julio 17
GENOVEVA	Enero 3
GERARDINO	Julio 28
GERARDO	Septiembre 24
GERMÁN	Junio 15
GERTRUDIS	Noviembre 16
GIL	Septiembre 1
GISELA	Mayo 21
GODOFREDO	Noviembre 8
GONZALO	Noviembre 26
GRACIA	Mayo 5
GREGORIO	Septiembre 3
GUADALUPE	Diciembre 12
GUIDO	Septiembre 12
GUILLERMO	Junio 25
GUMERSINDO	Enero 13
GUNDELINA	Marzo 28

H

HERMÁN	Abril 7
HERMES	Agosto 28
HERMINIO	Abril 25
HILARIA	Agosto 12
HILARIO	Enero 13
HIPÓLITO	Agosto 13
HONESTO	Noviembre 28
HONORATO	Julio 10
HONORINA	Febrero 27
HONORIO	Septiembre 30
HUBERTO	Noviembre 3

Using this list, how many names of people you know can you find? Do you see your own name – or its Spanish equivalent?

	HUGO	Abril 1
	HUMBERTO	Julio 14
I	IGNACIO	Julio 31
	ILDEFONSO	Enero 23
	ILUMINADA	Noviembre 29
	INÉS	Enero 21
	IMMACULADA	Diciembre 8
	INOCENCIO	Marzo 12
	ÍÑIGO	Junio 1
	IRENE	Abril 5
	ISAAC	Octubre 19
	ISABEL	Noviembre 17
	ISIDORO	Abril 26
	ISIDRO	Mayo 15
	ISMAEL	Junio 17
	IVO	Mayo 20
J	JACINTO	Agosto 17
	JAVIER	Diciembre 3
	JEREMÍAS	Febrero 16
	JERÓNIMO	Septiembre 30
	JOAQUÍN	Julio 25
	JORGE	Abril 23
	JOSÉ	Marzo 19
	JUAN BAUTISTA	Junio 24
	JUANA	Diciembre 12
	JULIA	Abril 16
	JULIÁN	Enero 23
	JULIANA	Febrero 7
	JULIO	Julio 1
	JULITA	Junio 16
	JUSTINA	Mayo 14
	JUSTINO	Junio 1
	JUSTO	Mayo 28
L	LAURA	Octubre 20
	LÁZARO	Febrero 11
	LEA	Marzo 22
	LEANDRO	Noviembre 13
	LEOCADIA	Diciembre 9
	LEÓN	Noviembre 10
	LEONARDO	Noviembre 6
	LEONOR	Diciembre 29
	LEOPOLDO	Noviembre 15
	LIBORIO	Julio 23
	LIDIA	Agosto 3
	LIDUVINA	Abril 12
	LORENZA	Octubre 8
	LORENZO	Agosto 10
	LUCAS	Octubre 18
	LUCÍA	Diciembre 13
	LUCIANO	Enero 7
	LUCRECIA	Marzo 3
	LUIS	Junio 21
	LUISA	Marzo 15
	LOURDES	Febrero 11
M	MANUEL	Enero 1
	MARCELA	Enero 2
	MARCELO	Enero 16
	MARCIAL	Junio 30
	MARCOS	Abril 25
	MARGARITA	Noviembre 16
	Mª MAGDALENA	Julio 22
	Mª MICAELA	Junio 15
	MARIANO	Mayo 26
	MARINA	Julio 18
	MARTA	Julio 29
	MARTÍN	Noviembre 11
	MATEO	Septiembre 21
	MATÍAS	Mayo 14
	MATILDA	Marzo 14
	MAURICIO	Septiembre 22
	MAXIMILIANO	Marzo 12
	MÁXIMO	Enero 8
	MELANIA	Diciembre 31
	MELCHOR	Septiembre 7
	MERCEDES	Septiembre 24
	MIGUEL ARCÁNGEL	Septiembre 29
	MILAGROS	Noviembre 27
	MOISÉS	Noviembre 25
	MÓNICA	Agosto 27
	MONSERRAT	Abril 27
N	NARCISO	Octubre 29
	NATALIA	Marzo 16
	NÉSTOR	Marzo 4
	NICANOR	Junio 5
	NICOLÁS	Diciembre 6
	NINA	Diciembre 15
	NORBERTO	Junio 6
O	OBDULIA	Septiembre 5
	OCTAVIO	Noviembre 20
	OLAF	Julio 29
	OLIVA	Julio 2
	ORESTES	Diciembre 13
	OSCAR	Febrero 3
	OSVALDO	Agosto 5
	OTILIA	Diciembre 13
	OTO	Julio 2
P	PABLO	Junio 29
	PASCUAL	Diciembre 6
	PATRICIA	Marzo 13
	PATRICIO	Marzo 17
	PAULA	Enero 26
	PAULINA	Junio 8
	PEDRO	Junio 29
	PELAYO	Junio 26
	PERPETUA	Marzo 7
	PETRONILA	Mayo 31
	PETRONIO	Septiembre 6
	PÍA	Enero 19
	PILAR	Octubre 12
	PÍO	Abril 30
	PLÁCIDO	Octubre 11
	PLATÓN	Abril 4
	POLICARPO	Febrero 23
	PORFIRIO	Febrero 26
	PRISCILA	Julio 8
	PRÓSPERO	Junio 25
Q	QUINTÍN	Octubre 31
R	RAFAEL	Septiembre 29
	RAIMUNDO	Enero 7
	RAMIRO	Marzo 11
	RAMÓN	Enero 7
	RAÚL	Diciembre 30
	REINA	Agosto 22
	REINALDO	Agosto 4
	REMEDIOS	Febrero 3
	RICARDO	Abril 3
	RITA	Mayo 22
	ROBERTO	Septiembre 17
	ROCÍO	Octubre 17
	RODOLFO	Octubre 17
	RODRIGO	Marzo 13
	ROGELIO	Septiembre 16
	ROGER	Enero 4
	ROMANA	Febrero 28
	ROQUE	Agosto 16
	ROSA	Agosto 23
	ROSALIA	Julio 15
	ROSARIO	Octubre 7
	RUFINA	Julio 10
	RUFINO	Agosto 11
	RUFO	Abril 19
	RUPERTO	Marzo 27
S	SABINA	Octubre 27
	SALOMÓN	Marzo 13
	SALVADOR	Marzo 18
	SAMUEL	Febrero 15
	SANCHO	Septiembre 5
	SEBASTIÁN	Enero 20
	SEBASTIANA	Septiembre 16
	SEGISMUNDO	Mayo 1
	SERAFÍN	Octubre 12
	SERGIO	Febrero 24
	SEVERINO	Enero 8
	SILVESTRE	Diciembre 31
	SILVIA	Noviembre 2
	SILVIO	Abril 21
	SIMEÓN	Julio 1
	SIMÓN	Octubre 28
	SOFÍA	Septiembre 18
	SOLEDAD	Octubre 11
	SUSANA	Mayo 24
T	TATIANA	Enero 12
	TULA	Octubre 15
	TEODORA	Septiembre 11
	TEODORO	Abril 20
	TEODOSIA	Mayo 29
	TEODOSIO	Octubre 25
	TERENCIO	Junio 21
	TERESA	Octubre 15
	TIMOTEO	Enero 26
	TIRSO	Enero 24
	TITO	Enero 26
	TOMÁS	Julio 3
U	URSINO	Noviembre 29
	ÚRSULA	Octubre 21
V	VALENTÍN	Febrero 14
	VALENTINA	Julio 25
	VALERIA	Abril 28
	VALERIANO	Noviembre 28
	VERIDIANA	Febrero 1
	VERÓNICA	Julio 9
	VICENTE	Enero 22
	VÍCTOR	Mayo 8
	VICTORIA	Noviembre 23
	VICTORIANO	Marzo 23
	VICTORIO	Octubre 30
	VIDAL	Julio 2
	VIRGILIO	Marzo 25
	VISITACIÓN	Mayo 31
	VLADIMIRO	Julio 15
W	WENCESLAO	Septiembre 28
Y	YOLANDA	Diciembre 17
Z	ZACARÍAS	Marzo 27
	ZOA	Julio 5

Recuerdos de ayer

PRIMERAS DEFENSAS DE SAN JUAN **Después que los pobladores de Caparra se mudaron al islote de San Juan, los piratas acechaban continuamente al pequeño pueblo, y los indios caribes de las Antillas Menores devastaban las fincas de labranza. Por algunos años la única plaza fuerte lo fue Casa Blanca, construida en 1525, para ser habitada por los herederos de Ponce de León. Otra plaza fuerte, La Fortaleza, fue concluida en 1540, pero de su situación dentro del puerto, el Cronista Oviedo dijo: "Aunque la edificaran ciegos no la pudieron poner en parte tan sin provecho."**

Quizás el Castillo del Morro comenzó con la sugerencia de Oviedo de que el promontorio rocoso, o morro, al oeste de la isleta de San Juan era el sitio apropiado para fortificar el puerto. En 1539 se autorizan obras defensivas en este lugar, y la primera batería y torre se construyen hacia esa fecha. De esta manera comienza el largo proceso de construir fortificaciones en San Juan que duraría más de 350 años.

Los corsarios ya habían saqueado y quemado a la Habana, y en los años siguientes España sufrió otras innumerables pérdidas en tierra y mar. En 1586, por ejemplo, Sir Francis Drake devastó las ciudades de Santo Domingo, Cartagena, y San Agustín. Como medida defensiva, Don Juan de Tejeda y el ingeniero militar Juan Bautista Antonelli fueron enviados al Caribe a planear y fortalecer las defensas españolas.

Estos llegaron a San Juan en 1589 y aprobaron el lugar del Morro para construir un sólido fuerte. Antonelli diseñó una muralla en forma de hornabeque que cortaba el promontorio de norte a sur, para proteger al Morro contra un ataque por tierra. Para 1591 el hornabeque crecía lentamente con murallas de "tapiería," o sea, una mezcla de tierra, cascajo, cal y piedra caliza. Por primera vez El Morro empezaba a tomar la forma de una ciudadela o refugio.

FIRST DEFENSE OF SAN JUAN **After the settlers of Caparra moved to the islet of San Juan, pirates continually threatened the small town, and the Carib Indians of the Lesser Antilles ravaged the outlying farms. For years the only stronghold was Casa Blanca, built in 1525 as a home for the heirs of Ponce de León. Another stronghold, La Fortaleza, was completed in 1540, but of its location in the inner harbor, the chronicler Oviedo said: "Only blind men could have chosen such a site for a fort."**

Perhaps El Morro Castle began with Oviedo's suggestion that the rocky headland, or "morro," at the west end of San Juan islet was the proper place to fortify the harbor. In 1539 defensive works were authorized in that place, and the first battery and tower were built about that time. So began the long process of fort construction in San Juan that would continue for more than 350 years.

Corsairs had already sacked and burned Havana, and in the following years Spain suffered numerous other losses on land and sea. Thus in 1586 Sir Francis Drake devastated the cities of Santo Domingo, Cartagena, and St. Augustine. As a defensive measure, Don Juan de Tejeda and the military engineer Juan Bautista Antonelli were sent to the Caribbean to plan and strengthen the Spanish defenses.

They arrived in San Juan in 1589 and approved the El Morro site for building a strong fort. Antonelli laid out a hornwork (so-called because the wall resembled the horns of a bull) that stretched from north to south across the promontory to protect the headland against land attack. Four hundred laborers began work in 1591, and the hornwork slowly rose, with walls of limestone and "tapieria," a mixture of earth, rock, and lime. For the first time El Morro began to take the form of a citadel.

El escudo de Puerto Rico

 recuerdos *souvenirs* **reino** *kingdom*

El Viejo San Juan

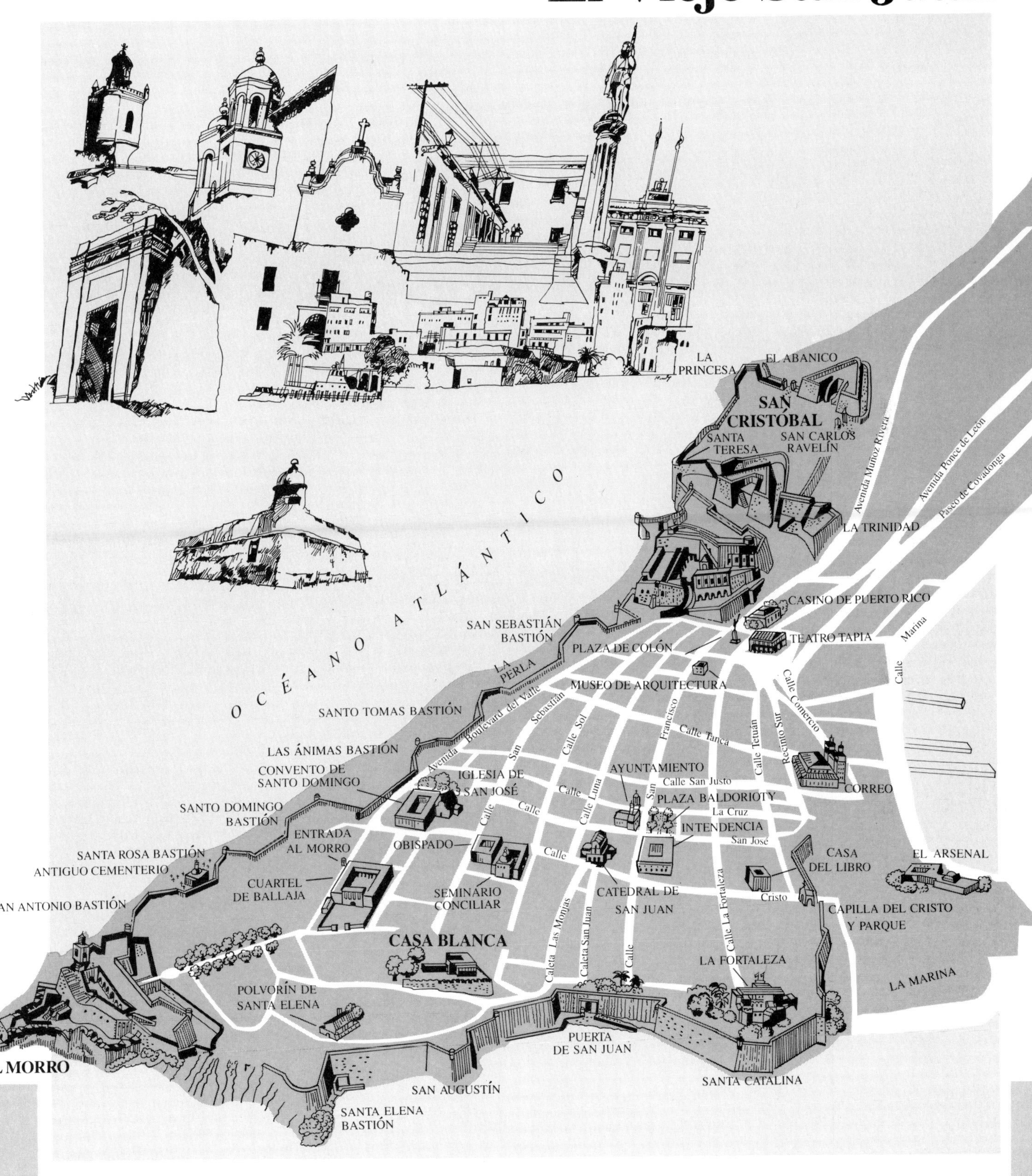

LA PRINCESA
EL ABANICO
SAN CRISTÓBAL
SANTA TERESA
SAN CARLOS RAVELÍN
Avenida Muñoz Rivera
Avenida Ponce de León
Paseo de Covadonga
LA TRINIDAD
OCÉANO ATLÁNTICO
CASINO DE PUERTO RICO
SAN SEBASTIÁN BASTIÓN
TEATRO TAPIA
PLAZA DE COLÓN
Marina
Calle
LA PERLA
MUSEO DE ARQUITECTURA
Calle Comercio
SANTO TOMAS BASTIÓN
Avenida Boulevard del Valle
Sebastián
Calle Sol
Francisco
Calle Tanca
Calle Tetuán
Recinto Sur
LAS ÁNIMAS BASTIÓN
CONVENTO DE SANTO DOMINGO
IGLESIA DE SAN JOSÉ
AYUNTAMIENTO
Calle San Justo
CORREO
SANTO DOMINGO BASTIÓN
PLAZA BALDORIOTY
La Cruz
INTENDENCIA
San José
ENTRADA AL MORRO
OBISPADO
Calle Luna
SANTA ROSA BASTIÓN
ANTIGUO CEMENTERIO
CASA DEL LIBRO
EL ARSENAL
CUARTEL DE BALLAJA
SEMINARIO CONCILIAR
CATEDRAL DE SAN JUAN
Cristo
CAPILLA DEL CRISTO Y PARQUE
SAN ANTONIO BASTIÓN
Calle La Fortaleza
CASA BLANCA
Caleta Las Monjas
Caleta San Juan
LA FORTALEZA
LA MARINA
POLVORÍN DE SANTA ELENA
PUERTA DE SAN JUAN
EL MORRO
SANTA CATALINA
SAN AUGUSTÍN
SANTA ELENA BASTIÓN

cuartel *barracks;* **ayuntamiento** *city hall;* **capilla** *chapel*

El Morro

EL CASTILLO DEL MORRO Frente al mar y dominando el puerto, las baterías superpuestas del Morro se elevan más de 140 pies sobre el nivel del mar. Originalmente llamado San Felipe del Morro, en honor al rey español Felipe III. La palabra "morro" significa promontorio o saliente. Una anchurosa colina abierta da acceso desde tierra al puente que cruza el profundo foso que rodea sus murallas. Éstas dominan todo el campo abierto y parte de la ciudad y costa del mar del norte. En su interior, el Castillo tiene aún todas las apariencias de una ciudadela viviente: cuarteles, cisternas, almacenes, calabozos, capilla, armería, y oficinas, a prueba de bombas y explosivos de aquella época. Rampas y escaleras intrincadas daban a las tropas rápido acceso a cualquier área de los altos murallones.

El Morro es el más antiguo de los castillos que formaban el centro del sistema defensivo de San Juan. Su misión era proveer un tipo de defensa vertical con niveles de fuego hacia la entrada del puerto. Su construcción se autorizó en 1539, comenzando con una torre abovedada en la punta del rocoso promontorio. La mayor parte de la obra se ejecutó entre 1589 a 1650. El Morro se terminó durante los años 1775 a 1787 y así ha existido hasta nuestros días.

CASTILLO
DE
SAN FELIPE DEL MORRO
A UNIT OF
SAN JUAN NATIONAL HISTORIC SITE

EL MORRO CASTLE The tiered batteries of El Morro rise more than 140 feet above the sea and command the harbor entrance. Originally named San Felipe del Morro, the fort honored King Philip III of Spain. (The word "morro" means headland or promontory.) On the landward side a broad grassy slope rises to the bridge that crosses the deep moat surrounding the walls. Inside, the castle has all the appearances of a living citadel: barracks, cisterns, supply and storage rooms, dungeons, a chapel, an armory, and offices—all bombproof against the explosives of past centuries. A network of ramps and stairways gave the defenders rapid access to the ramparts.

El Morro is the oldest and most strategic of the castles that formed San Juan's defensive system. Its mission was to close the harbor entrance with its firepower. Construction began in 1539 with the vaulted tower on the point of the headland. Most of El Morro was built between 1589 and the 1650's. As it stands today, the castle was completed during 1775 and 1787.

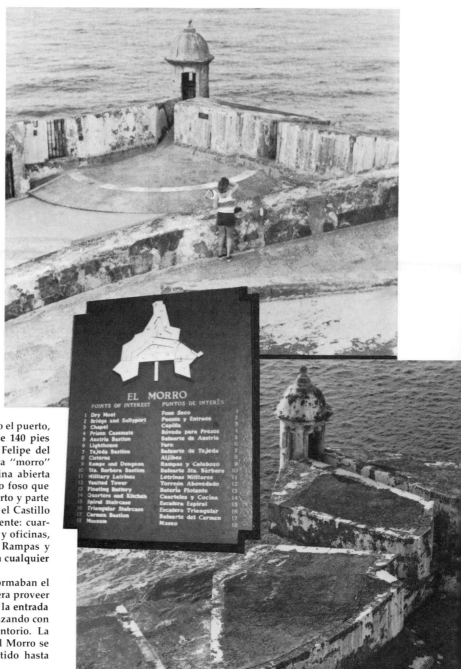

San Cristóbal

SAN CRISTÓBAL Esta poderosa fortaleza domina la antigua ciudad y todos los rincones de la isleta.

San Cristóbal, obra maestra de ingeniería militar del siglo XVIII, estaba compuesta de un complejo de estructuras sólidas e independientes de obras exteriores, que servían de unidades complementarias de defensa en profundidad. Esta fortaleza y sus obras exteriores eran el segundo baluarte defensivo de San Juan. El Morro era el otro. La misión principal de San Cristóbal era defender la ciudad de ataques terrestres, y en segundo lugar, proteger la costa norte. Las obras de este fuerte comienzan hacia 1634 como parte del proyecto de circunvalación. Un inesperado ataque inglés por tierra en 1598, y más tarde la quema de la ciudad por los holandeses (1625) demostró la necesidad de defensas por los lados este, sur, y oeste. Para el 1670 San Cristóbal era una ciudadela de tamaño regular, pero sus obras exteriores eran muy débiles. Esta fortaleza, como se conserva hoy, fue modernizada durante los años 1766 a 1783. Durante el asedio inglés de 1797, la poderosa artillería de San Cristóbal controló magistralmente todos los aproches orientales de la ciudad. De uno de sus cañones se disparó el primer tiro de la Guerra Hispano-Americana en Puerto Rico.

SAN CRISTÓBAL This powerful fortesss dominates every corner of the old city. A masterpiece of 18th-century military engineering, San Cristóbal was supported by a system of massive outworks which provided defense in depth. The fort's mission was to defend the city from land attacks and, secondarily, to protect the north coast. These works were started around 1634 as part of the project to surround the city with walls. An unexpected English land attack in 1598 and the burning of the city by the Dutch in 1625 showed the need for defenses to the east, south, and west. By 1670 San Cristóbal had reached its full size, but the outworks remained unfinished. The fort that we see today was finished between 1766 and 1783. During the British seige of 1797, San Cristóbal's powerful artillery masterfully controlled the eastern approaches to the city. A century later one of its guns fired the first shot of the Spanish-American War in Puerto Rico.

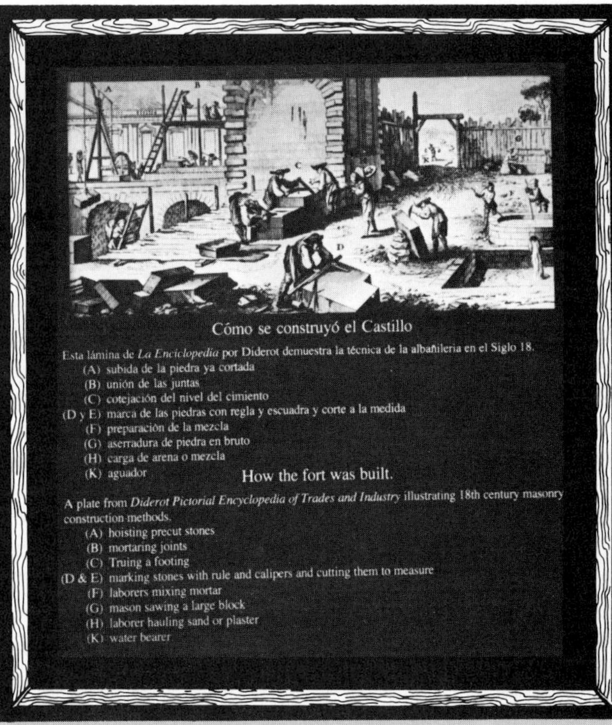

Cómo se construyó el Castillo

Esta lámina de *La Enciclopedia* por Diderot demuestra la técnica de la albañileria en el Siglo 18.
(A) subida de la piedra ya cortada
(B) unión de las juntas
(C) cotejación del nivel del cimiento
(D y E) marca de las piedras con regla y escuadra y corte a la medida
(F) preparación de la mezcla
(G) aserradura de piedra en bruto
(H) carga de arena o mezcla
(K) aguador

How the fort was built.

A plate from *Diderot Pictorial Encyclopedia of Trades and Industry* illustrating 18th century masonry construction methods.
(A) hoisting precut stones
(B) mortaring joints
(C) Truing a footing
(D & E) marking stones with rule and calipers and cutting them to measure
(F) laborers mixing mortar
(G) mason sawing a large block
(H) laborer hauling sand or plaster
(K) water bearer

Nuevas riquezas

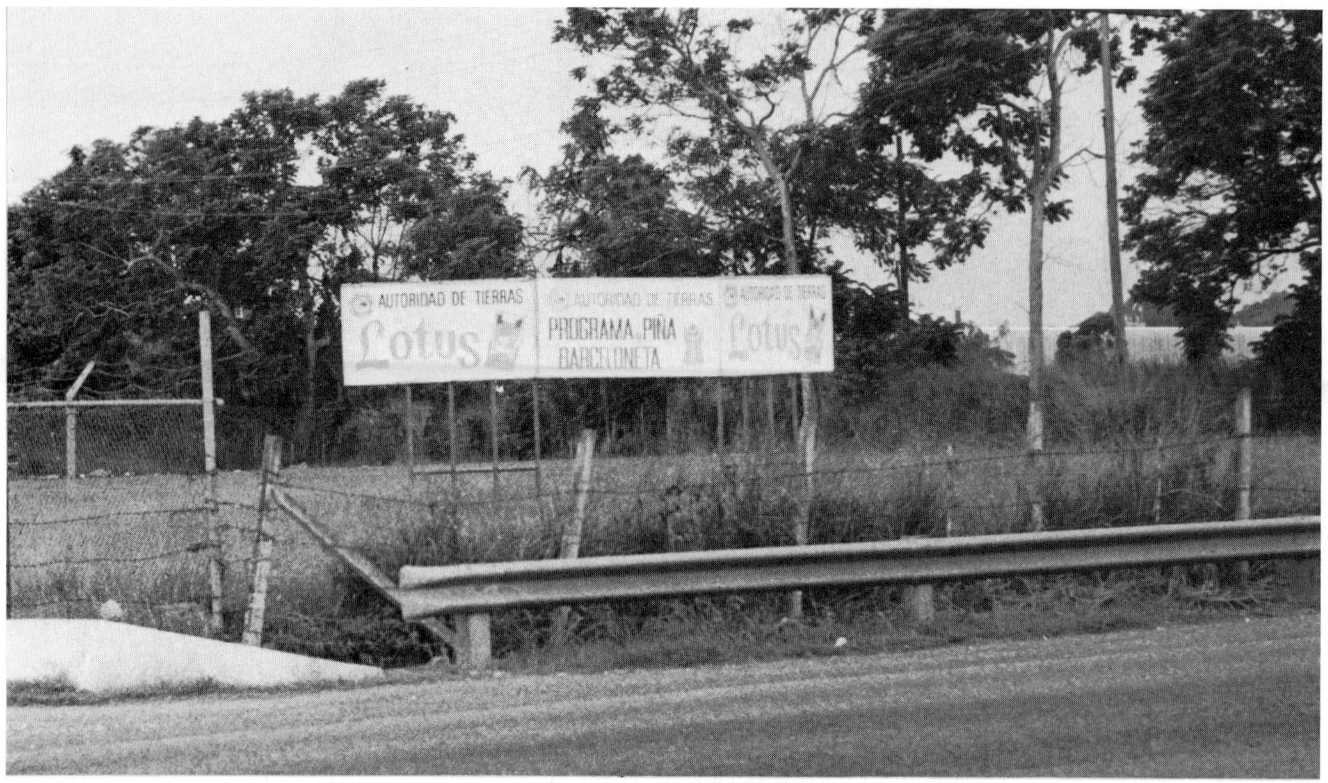

Entrada a la fábrica de piñas "Lotus," en Barceloneta, Puerto Rico.

Una plantación nueva. Después de dos años, la planta de la piña...

produce la fruta. Cuando ésta está madura°, la podemos comer.

---

 riquezas *wealth, riches* **madura** *ripe*

La maquinaria° de la fábrica quita° la cáscara° y el centro de la piña . . .

y pone la fruta en latas, y así la podemos comer fuera de estación.

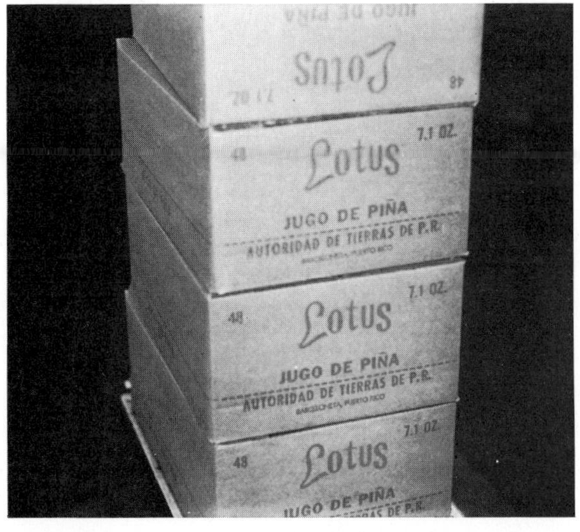

La fábrica también produce jugo de piña. ¡Y qué sabroso!

In Spanish, write your impressions of some historical or industrial place you have visited. What makes this place important historically or economically?

MAFALDA

¡EN ESTE DÍA DE LA MADRE, UN BESOTE PARA MI MAMÁ Y PARA TODAS LAS MAMÁS DEL MUNDO!
528

Y POR FAVOR,..... NO VAYAN A COMETER HOY *LA GAFFE* DE HACER SOPA

---

maquinaria *machinery;* **quita** *removes;* **cáscara** *outer covering* **besote** *great big kiss;* **no vayan** *I hope they aren't going to;* **"gaffe"** *blunder (French)*

La televisión, etc.

Desi Arnaz, líder de orquesta°, cantante° y actor. Su serie "Yo quiero° a Lucy" es uno de los mayores éxitos de la televisión.

Raúl Julia, actor. Estrella de la obra musical de Broadway, "Nueve."

Rita Morena, actriz de teatro, televisión y cine. Ganó un premio "Oscar" por su actuación en "Amor sin fronteras."°

 orquesta *orchestra;* **cantante** *singer;* **quiero** *I love;* **"Amor sin fronteras"** *"West Side Story"*

Priscilla López, actriz, bailarina y cantante. Ganó un premio "Tony" por su actuación en "Un día en Hollywood, una noche en Ukrania."

Plácido Domingo, tenor operático. Además de la ópera, también canta canciones populares y tangos argentinos.

Montserrat Caballé, soprano operática. "Una leyenda en su propio tiempo."

Every major city of Spain and Latin America has several television stations. Programming varies, but there is a wide variety of programs to suit the viewers' tastes. Many American shows are syndicated for Spanish-speaking audiences. Most of these shows are dubbed in Spanish.

TELEVISIÓN

VEA HOY POR
5
un hombre preocupado
La serie que lo pone al día sobre la realidad de nuestro ambiente

Anacaona

Una novela apasionante, cruda, realista. La vida de una nativa azotada por las circunstancias.

Anacaona es una versión libre, especialmente escrita para esta novela.

Desde el lunes 7 de diciembre a las 7 de la noche Rahintel por sus canales 7 y 11, transmitirá Anacaona, interpretada por Marilyn Pupo, Martín Lantigua y Luis Abreu, en los roles estelares.

Anacaona, de lunes a viernes a las 7 pm.

Es una producción de Venevisión de Puerto Rico.

---

vea *see;* **preocupado** *concerned;* **lo pone al día** *brings you up-to-date;* **ambiente** *atmosphere* **apasionante** *exciting;* **cruda** *raw;* **azotada** *beaten;* **transmitirá** *will broadcast;* **interpretada por** *performed by;* **estelares** *starring*

PROGRAMAS DE TV

10h30 Las travesuras de los Picapiedra
11h00 El Rey Arturo
11h30 El capitán escarlata
12h00 Mensaje
12h03 Follow me (sígueme) Eps. 34
12h15 Fútbol en acción
12h40 El safari "Los elefantes"
13h10 La familia Robinson
14h00 Viaje a lo desconocido
15h00 Matinée "Las calles de Los Angeles" con: Joanne Woodward y Fernando Allende
16h30 La Hechicera
17h00 La mujer maravilla
18h00 Enos
19h00 El show de Chespirito
20h00 Lo increíble
21h00 "30 minutos" Informativo dominical
21h30 Flamingo Road
22h30 Testamento de Juventud
23h30 Cuentos de misterio
24h00 Mensaje

09h30 Transmisión en diferido del partido N° 11 entre: "Checoslovaquia vs Kuwait
11h30 Ultra Siete
12h00 Tropa Loca
12h30 Ivanhoe
13h00 Los Bandidos
14h00 Transmisión en diferido del partido N° 8 entre "Inglaterra vs Francia
16h00 Lassie
16h30 Marvel Super Héroes
17h00 Bugs Bunny Show
17h30 Pinocho
18h00 Kroff Super Show
19h00 Cine Misterio "El Caimán Humano"
20h30 Lo mejor del Mundial
21h00 Centro Médico, presenta: "El Semidios"
22h00 Reprise partido N 36 "España vs I landa del Norte"

09h00 Fútbol Campeonato Nacional Serie A desde Quito
13h30 Domingo en el cine "La leyenda de la pistola de oro"
15h00 Los Monroes
16h00 Heidi
16h30 El Gato
17h00 Pequeña Lulú
17h30 Nuevo Circo
18h00 Pájaro Loco
18h30 El Pequeño Vagabundo
19h00 Buck Rogers
20h00 Estreno "En contra de la organización"
22h00 Una Hora
23h00 Sabor Latino

12h00 Fútbol en directo: Inglaterra vs Francia
14h00 Casa de Huéspedes
15h00 Popeye
15h30 Fútbol en diferido: Escocia vs. Nueva Zelandia
17h30 El Super simio
18h30 Dialogando
19h00 Mujer biónica
20h00 Teledeportes
20h30 60 super minutos
21h30 Jacques Cousteau
22h30 Matt Helm

10h25 Una luz en tu camino
10h30 Misa Dominical
11h00 Vida Nueva
11h30 Las Aventuras de Supermán
12h00 Chispitas
13h00 Ecuador
14h00 Arriba la Música
15h00 Asociación Ecuatoriana de Canales de Televisión, presenta en diferido desde España "Alemania vs Argelia"
17h00 Mi Familia
17h30 Siempre en Domingo
20h00 Noches Espectaculares, presenta: "No podrás escapar" con: Richard Benjamin, Paula Prentiss, Barry Sullivan
21h30 Chispazos
23h30 Una luz en tu camino

Find a couple of classmates to watch television with. Look at the program schedules on these pages and fight over which shows you are going to watch. (No hitting, and remember to do it in Spanish!)

---

travesuras *pranks, capers;* **los Picapiedra** *"The Flintstones";* **escarlata** *scarlet;* **lo desconocido** *the unknown;* **hechicera** *witch;* **La mujer maravilla** *"Wonder Woman";* **informativo dominical** *Sunday news report;* **transmisión** *telecast;* **en diferido** *delayed;* **Tropa Loca** *(Crazy Troop) "Hogan's Heroes";* **bandidos** *bandits;* **dios** *god;* **reprise** *repeat;* **pistola** *gun;* **circo** *circus;* **estreno** *premiere;* **sabor** *flavor;* **en directo** *live;* **simio** *monkey;* **dialogando** *conversing;* **Misa** *Mass;* **chispitas** *little sparks;* **arriba** *up with;* **chispazos** *big sparks*

FIN

Spanish-English

Vocabulary

VOCABULARY

All words in the text are listed in this vocabulary, with an English equivalent corresponding to the particular context in which they appear. Omitted are words in reading passages for which an English translation has been provided.

The following abbreviations are used:

adj	*adjective*	dim	*diminutive*	m	*masculine*	prep	*preposition*
adv	*adverb*	f	*feminine*	obj	*object*	pron	*pronoun*
com	*command*	fam	*familiar*	pl	*plural*	ref	*reflexive*
conj	*conjunction*	infin	*infinitive*	pol	*polite*	sing	*singular*

A

a *to, at, in;* **a crédito** *on credit*
abierto, -a *open*
abrazar *to hug*
el **abrigo** *coat*
abril *April*
abrir *to open*
absoluto, -a *absolute*
la **absorción** *absorption*
la **abuela** *grandmother*
el **abuelo** *grandfather*
acabao = **acabado, -a** *ended*
acabarse *to finish, end*
la **academia** *academy*
académico, -a *academic*
el **accidente** *accident*
la **acción** *action*
el **aceite** *oil;* el aceite de hígado de bacalao *cod liver oil;* el aceite de oliva *olive oil*
la **aceituna** *olive*
aceptamos *we accept*
aceptar *to accept*
el **acero** *steel*
el **ácido** *acid;* el ácido ascórbico *ascorbic acid*
aclamado, -a: aclamado, -a por la crítica *by critical acclaim*
acompañado, -a (con) *served (with)*
acompañar *to accompany*
la **activación** *activation*
activar *to activate*
la **actividad** *activity*
el **acto** *act*
el **actor** *actor*
la **actriz** *actress*
la **actuación** *performance*
actual *current, present-day*
la **actualidad** *present time*
la **actualización** *actualization, putting into effect*
Acuario *Aquarius*
acuático, -a *aquatic, living or growing in water*
la **adaptación** *adaptation*
además (de) *besides*
adicional *additional*
la **administración** *administration*
admirable *admirable*
el **admirador, -a** *admirer*
admitir *to allow;* no se admiten *(they are) not allowed*
el **adolescente,** la **adolescente** *adolescent*
¿adónde? *(to) where?*
la **adoración** *adoration*
el **adulto** *adult*
aéreo, -a *by air;* el dirigible aéreo *dirigible, blimp;* la línea aérea *airline;* por vía aérea *by air mail*
el **aeroplano** *airplane*
el **aeropuerto** *airport*
afectar *to affect*
África *Africa*
la **agencia** *agency;* la agencia de viajes *travel agency*
la **agilidad** *speed*
agosto *August*
el **agua** (f) *water;* la fuente de agua *water fountain;* la ostra de agua dulce *fresh-water oyster*
el **aguacate** *avocado*
el **aguacero** *downpour, rainstorm*
el **águila** (f) *eagle*
ahora *now*
el **aire** *air;* el aire acondicionado *air conditioning*
aislado, -a *isolated*
el **ají** *bell pepper*
el **ajo** *garlic*
el **ajuste** *adjustment*
al (*contraction of* **a** + **el**) *to the;* al salir *when leaving;* al venir *when arriving*
el **álbum** *album*
el **alcohol** *alcohol*
la **aldea** *village*
alegre *happy*
alemán, alemana *German*
Alemania *Germany*
la **alfabetización** *literacy*
el **alfabeto** *alphabet*
la **alforja** *saddlebag*
algo *something*
alguien *someone*
aliado, -a *allied*
el **almacén** *store*
la **almendra** *almond*
el **alojamiento** *lodging*
el **alquiler** *rental*
alrededor: alrededor de *around*
la **alternativa** *alternative*
alto, -a *tall; high;* lo alto de todo *the highest point*
la **altura** *height*
el **alumno, -a** *student, pupil*
allá *(over) there;* más allá de *beyond*
allí *there*
el **amante,** la **amante** *lover*
amar *to love;* me amó *he/she loved me*
el **ambiente** *atmosphere*
ambiente *surrounding*
América *America*
americano, -a *American*
el **amigo, -a** *friend*
el **aminoácido** *amino acid*
la **amistad** *friendship*
el **amor** *love;* "Amor sin fronteras" *"West Side Story"*
analfabeto, -a *illiterate*
ancho, -a *wide*
Andalucía *Andalusia, a region in southern Spain*
andaluz *Andalusian*
la **angula** *eel*
el **anillo** *ring*
animado, -a *lively*
el **animal** *animal*
el **aniversario** *anniversary*
anoche *last night*
el **anochecer** *nightfall;* al anochecer *at nightfall*
anónimo, -a *anonymous*
anquilosado, -a *rusty, aging*
la **antelación:** con antelación *in advance*
antes (de) *before*

antianémico, -a *antianemic*
la **antigüedad** *antiquity*
antiguo, -a *old, ancient, antique*
antihemorrágico, -a *anti-hemorrhagic*
antiinfeccioso, -a *antiinfectious*
antioxidante *antioxidant*
antropológico, -a *anthropological*
el **anuncio** *ad(vertisement);* los anuncios clasificados *classified ads*
añadir *to add*
el **año** *year;* el año luz *light year;* hace muchos años *many years ago*
la **apariencia** *appearance*
el **apartamento** *apartment*
apasionante *exciting*
el **apellido** *surname*
apenas *hardly, scarcely*
el **apetito** *appetite;* ¡Buen apetito! *Enjoy your meal!*
aplastado, -a *squashed*
el **apóstol** *apostle*
aprendemos: ¡Todos aprendemos! *We all learn!*
aprender *to learn*
aquí *here*
árabe *Arabic*
Aragón *Aragon, a region in northeastern Spain*
el **árbol** *tree;* el árbol genealógico *family tree*
el **arca** (f) *ark*
el **arcoiris** *rainbow*
la **ardilla** *squirrel*
el **área** (f) *area*
la **arena** *sand*
Argelia *Algeria*
argentino, -a *Argentine, from Argentina*
el **argumento** *plot*
la **armada** *armada, fleet of warships*
la **armadura** *suit of armor*
la **armería** *armory*
arqueológico, -a *archaeological*
la **arquitectura** *architecture*
arrancar *to tear out*
arriba *up with*
la **arruga** *wrinkle*
el **arte** *art;* las bellas artes *fine arts*
la **artesanía** *handicrafts*
el **artesano, -a** *craftsman*
el **artículo** *article*
el **artifacto** *artifact*
el **artista**, la **artista** *artist*
artístico, -a *artistic*
el **asalto** *assault, attack*
ascórbico, -a: el ácido ascórbico *ascorbic acid*
el **asesino, -a** *killer, murderer*
así *like that; so, thus*
la **asignatura** *subject*
el **asno** *donkey*
la **asociación** *association*
el **asociado, -a** *associate*
asombrado, -a *astonished*
asustarse *to become frightened*
Atenas *Athens*

la **atención:** no prestes atención *don't pay attention* (com)
Atlántico: el Océano Atlántico *Atlantic Ocean*
la **atmósfera** *atmosphere*
atmosférico, -a *atmospheric*
atómico, -a *atomic;* la bomba atómica *atom bomb;* el reactor atómico *atomic reactor*
la **atracción** *attraction*
aumentar *to augment, increase*
aún *still*
aunque *although*
auténtico, -a *authentic*
el **autobús** *bus*
el **automóvil** *automobile*
autónomo, -a *autonomous, independent*
el **autor, -a** *author*
autorizado, -a *authorized*
Av. = avenida *avenue*
avanzado, -a *advanced*
el **ave** (f) *bird*
Ave. = avenida *avenue*
la **avena** *oats*
la **avenida** *avenue*
la **aventura** *adventure*
el **aviso** *notice, announcement*
ayó (archaic) = **halló** *found*
la **ayuda** *help*
ayudar *to help;* ayuda *help* (com)
ayúdenos *help us* (com)
el **ayuntamiento** *city hall*
azotado, -a *beaten*
el **azúcar** (f) *sugar;* la caña de azúcar *sugar cane*
azul *blue*

B

el **bacalao:** el aceite de hígado de bacalao *cod liver oil*
las **Bahamas** *the Bahamas*
bailan *they dance*
bailar *to dance*
la **bailarina** *dancer*
bajo *under*
el **balcón** *balcony*
Baleares: las Islas Baleares *Balearic Islands*
el **balón** *ball*
la **ballena** *whale;* la ballena asesina *killer whale*
la **ballenita** *little whale* (dim)
el **ballet** *ballet*
el **banco** *bank*
la **banda** *band*
el **bandido, -a** *bandit*
bañar *to bathe*
el **baño** *bathroom;* el baño privado *private bathroom*
barato, -a *cheap, inexpensive*
bárbaro, -a *barbarian;* ¡Bárbaro, -a! *Great!*
el **barco** *boat, ship;* el barco de vela *sailing ship*
el **barómetro** *barometer*
el **barrendero, -a** *street cleaner*

la **base** *basis*
el **básquetbol** *basketball*
bastante *enough; quite*
bastar *to be enough;* basta *it's enough*
el **batido** *milkshake*
el **bebé** *baby*
el **béisbol** *baseball*
Belén *Bethlehem*
Bélgica *Belgium*
Belgrado *Belgrade, Yugoslavia*
bélico, -a *of war*
la **belleza** *beauty*
bello, -a *beautiful;* las bellas artes *fine arts*
el **beneficio** *benefit*
besar *to kiss*
el **besote** *great big kiss*
la **bestia** *animal, beast*
la **bicicleta** *bicycle*
bien *well*
los **bienes:** los bienes raíces *real estate*
bilingüe *bilingual*
el **billón** *billion*
biológico, -a *biological;* las ciencias biológicas *biological sciences*
biónico, -a *bionic*
la **bisabuela** *great-grandmother*
el **bisabuelo** *great-grandfather*
blanco, -a *white;* Blanca Nieves *Snow White*
la **blusa** *blouse*
el **boletín** *report, report card*
el **boleto** *(theater) ticket*
el **bolívar** *Venezuelan monetary unit*
el **bolso** *purse*
la **bomba** *bomb;* la bomba atómica *atom bomb*
el **bombero, -a** *firefighter*
bonito, -a *pretty*
el **bono** *bonus*
bordo: a bordo *on board*
el **bosque** *forest*
botánico, -a *botanical*
el **boxeo** *boxing*
Brasil *Brazil*
la **brigada** *brigade*
brillante *brilliant*
brillar *to shine*
el **bróculi** *broccoli*
la **bromelia** *bromeliad, plant like the pineapple and Spanish moss*
el **bronce** *bronze*
la **bruja** *witch*
Bs. = bolívares *Venezuelan monetary unit*
buen, -o, -a *good;* bueno (adv) *well, fine*
el **buey** *ox*
el **búho** *owl*
la **bujía** *light bulb*
buscar *to look for*

C

C. = centígrado(s) *centigrade*
el **caballero** *gentleman*
el **caballito** *little horse* (dim)

el **caballo** *horse*
la **cabeza** *head*
Cabo Cañaveral *Cape Canaveral, Florida*
la **cabra** *goat*
el **cabrito** *young goat, kid*
el **cactus** = el **cacto** *cactus*
cada *each*
caer *to fall*
el **café** *coffee*
el **caimán** *alligator*
el **cajero, -a** *cashier*
el **calcio** *calcium*
el **calendario** *calendar*
la **calificacción** *grade, mark*
la **calistenia** *calisthenics*
el **calor** *heat*
la **calle** *street*
la **cama** *bed*
la **cámara** *chamber; camera*
cambiar *to change;* cambie *change* (com)
el **cambio** *change, exchange, exchange rate;* en cambio *in exchange*
el **camello** *camel*
caminar *to walk*
el **camino** *path; way*
la **camisa** *shirt*
la **camiseta** *T-shirt*
la **campaña** *campaign*
el **campeón,** la **campeona** *champion*
el **campeonato** *championship;* el (Campeonato) Mundial *World Cup (soccer championship)*
el **campo** *field*
el **canal** *canal; channel*
Canarias: las Islas Canarias *Canary Islands*
Cáncer *Cancer*
la **canción** *song*
el **canguro** *kangaroo*
la **canita:** una canita al aire *a little spree, some fun*
cansado, -a *tired*
cantan *they sing*
el **cantante,** la **cantante** *singer*
cantar *to sing; to crow*
la **cantidad** *quantity, amount*
la **caña:** la caña de azúcar *sugar cane*
la **cañada** *ravine*
el **cañonazo** *cannon blast, bombshell*
la **capilla** *chapel*
la **capital** *capital*
el **capitán** *captain*
Capricornio *Capricorn*
la **cara** *face*
la **carabela** *caravel, sailing ship*
el **carácter** *character, characteristic*
la **característica** *characteristic*
la **caravana** *caravan (covered vehicle in which gypsies live and travel)*
el **carbohidrato** *carbohydrate*
el **carbón:** el dióxodo de carbón *carbon dioxide*
el **cardo** *thistle*
el **Caribe** *the Caribbean*
la **carne** *meat*
la **carrera** *career*
la **carretera** *highway*
el **carro** *car*
la **carroza** *coach, carriage*
la **carta** *charter*
la **cartera** *handbag, pocketbook, purse*
el **cartero** *mail carrier*
la **casa** *house, home;* la casa de huéspedes *guest-house*
el **cascabel:** la serpiente (de) cascabel *rattlesnake*
la **cáscara** *outer covering*
el **caso:** en caso de *in case of*
el **castellano** *Spanish, Castilian*
Castilla *Castile, a region in central Spain*
el **castillo** *castle*
el **castor** *beaver*
la **catarata** *waterfall; falls*
católico, -a *Catholic;* los Reyes Católicos *the Catholic Monarchs (Ferdinand and Isabella)*
la **causa** *cause*
el **cautiverio** *captivity*
la **cazuela** *casserole*
cda(s). = **cucharada(s)** *tablespoonful(s)*
cdta(s). = **cucharadita(s)** *teaspoonful(s)*
la **cebolla** *onion*
la **cebra** *zebra*
la **cédula** *I.D. card*
la **celebración** *celebration*
celebrado, -a *celebrated*
el **cémbalo** *harpsichord*
la **cena** *dinner, supper*
ceniciento, -a *covered with ashes, ash-colored;* la Cenicienta *Cinderella*
el **centenar** *one hundred;* centenares *hundreds*
centígrado(s) *centigrade*
el **centímetro** *centimeter*
central *central*
el **centro** *center*
centroamericano, -a *Central American*
la **cera** *wax*
la **cerámica** *ceramics, pottery*
cerca *near;* cerca de *near, close to;* más cerca *closer*
el **cerdo** *pig, hog*
el **cereal** *cereal*
el **cerebro** *brain*
cero *zero*
cerramos *we close*
cerrar (ie) *to close*
el **ciclismo** *cycling*
ciego, -a *blind*
el **cielo** *sky*
cien *one hundred*
la **ciencia** *science;* las ciencias biológicas *biological sciences;* las ciencias naturales *natural sciences*
cierto, -a *certain*
cinco *five*
cincuenta *fifty*
el **cine** *movies; movie theater*
el **cinematógrafo** *movie projector*
el **cinturón** *belt;* el cinturón de seguridad *seat belt*
el **circo** *circus*
la **circulación** *circulation*
la **circunstancia** *circumstance*
el **cisne** *swan*
la **cita** *quotation; appointment*
la **ciudad** *city*
cívico, -a *civic, of citizenship*
la **civilización** *civilization*
la **claridad** *clarity, clearness*
la **clase** *kind*
clásico, -a *classic*
la **clasificación** *classification*
clasificado, -a *classified;* los (anuncios) clasificados *classified ads*
el **clima** *climate, weather*
cm. = **centímetros** *centimeters*
la **cobra** *cobra*
la **cocina** *kitchen;* vajillas y utensilios de cocina *housewares*
cocinar *to cook;* cocinar a fuego lento *to simmer*
el **cocodrilo** *crocodile*
el **coche** *car;* el coche de caballos *horse-drawn cart*
la **col** *cabbage*
colaborar *to collaborate;* colaborarán *they will collaborate*
la **colección** *collection*
el **colegio** *school*
el **coliseo** *coliseum*
colombiano, -a *Colombian, from Colombia*
el **colón** *monetary unit of Costa Rica and El Salvador*
Colón: Cristóbal Colón *Christopher Columbus*
la **colonia** *housing development* (Mexico)
colonial *colonial*
la **colonización** *colonization*
el **color** *color*
colorao = **colorado, -a** *reddish*
el **colorín** *linnet (small songbird)*
¡combátala! *Fight it!* (com)
el **combate** *combat*
combatir *to fight*
combinar *to combine;* combine *combine* (com)
comen *they eat*
comenzar (ie) *to begin*
comer *to eat*
comercial (adj) *business*
el **comerciante,** la **comerciante** *merchant*
el **comercio** *business*
los **comestibles** *food*
cometer *to commit*
la **comida** *food*
comienza *he/she/it begins*

como *like, as; about*
¿cómo? *what?, how?;* ¿Cómo son? *What are they like?*
¡cómo! *how!*
cómodo, -a *comfortable*
la **compañía** *company*
comparado, -a (con) *compared (with)*
comparar *to compare*
el **compartimiento** *compartment;* el compartimiento de equipaje *baggage compartment*
compartir *to share*
completamente *completely, entirely*
completo, -a *complete*
la **compra** *purchase;* ir de compras *to go shopping*
comprar *to buy*
el **compuesto** *compound*
la **computadora** *computer*
comunicarse *to communicate*
con *with*
el **concierto** *concert*
la **condición** *condition*
conectarse *to be connected, plugged into*
el **conejo** *rabbit*
la **conferencia** *conference*
la **confianza** *confidence*
confidencial *confidential*
el **confort** *comfort*
el **congreso** *congress*
el **conjunto** *group, cast; suit, outfit*
conmemorar *to commemorate*
conocer *to know*
conocido, -a *well-known*
la **conquista** *conquest*
el **conquistador, -a** *conquistador, conqueror*
conquistar *to conquer; to win*
conseguir (i) *to get*
consentir (ie) *to consent*
la **conservación** *conservation*
conservar *to keep; to maintain*
las **conservas** *preserved food*
consiéntete *give your consent* (com)
consigo *with him/her/yourself (pol)*
constantemente *constantly*
constar de *to be composed of*
la **constelación** *constellation*
la **construcción** *construction, building*
consultar *to consult*
consúlteme *consult me* (com)
contar (ue) *to tell*
contemporáneo, -a *contemporary*
contestar *to answer*
contigo *with you* (fam)
el **continente** *continent*
continuar *to continue;* continúa *he/she/it continues*
contra *against;* en contra de *against*
el **contraataque** *counterattack*
el **control** *control;* el control remoto *remote control*

convencerse *to be convinced*
convénzase *be convinced* (com)
la **conversación** *conversation*
la **cooperación** *cooperation*
la **copa** *cup, trophy;* la copa del mundo *World Cup*
el **coral** *coral*
el **corazón** *heart*
el **córdoba** *monetary unit of Nicaragua*
corre *he/she/it runs*
el **correo** *mail;* por correo *by mail*
correr *to run*
corriendo *running*
la **cortesía** *courtesy*
la **cortina** *curtain*
corto, -a *short*
la **cosa** *thing*
la **costa** *coast*
costar (ue) *to cost*
la **cotorrita** *little parrot* (dim)
el **coyote** *coyote*
Cra. = carretera *highway*
la **creación** *creation*
creando *creating*
crear *to create*
la **creatividad** *creativity*
el **crédito** *credit;* a crédito *on credit;* la oficina de crédito *credit office;* la tarjeta de crédito *credit card*
la **crema** *cream*
Cristo: antes de Cristo *before Christ, B.C.*
la **crítica:** aclamado, -a por la crítica *by critical acclaim*
crudo, -a *raw*
cruel *cruel;* el cruel *the cruel (one)*
la **cruz** *cross*
cruzar *to cross*
cuadrado, -a *square*
el **cuadro** *painting*
¿cuál? *which?*
cualitativo, -a *qualitative*
cualquier, -a *any*
cuando *when*
¿cuándo? *when?*
cuantitativo, -a *quantitative*
¿cuántos, -as? *how many?*
el **cuartel** *barracks*
cuarto, -a *fourth*
cuatro *four*
cubano, -a *Cuban*
cubano-americano, -a *Cuban-American*
cubierto, -a *covered*
cubrir *to cover*
la **cucharada** *tablespoonful*
la **cucharadita** *teaspoonful*
la **cuenta:** darse cuenta *to realize;* ¿Te das cuenta? *Do you realize?*
el **cuento** *story;* hacer un cuento *to tell a story*
el **cuerpo** *part*
el **cuidado:** con mucho cuidado *very carefully;* tener mucho cuidado *to be very careful*

cuidar *to care for*
cultivar *to grow*
la **cultura** *culture*
cultural *cultural*
Cupido *Cupid*
Curazao *Curaçao*
curioso, -a *strange*
cursivo, -a *in script*
el **curso** *course*

CH

che *buddy* (Argentina)
Checoslovaquia *Czechoslovakia*
la **chica** *girl*
el **chico** *boy*
chileno, -a *Chilean*
el **chimpancé** *chimpanzee*
la **chinela** *slipper*
la **chispa** *spark*
el **chispazo** *big spark*
la **chispita** *little spark*
el **chocolate** *chocolate*
la **choza** *hut*

D

la **dama** *lady*
dan *they give*
el **Danubio** *the Danube (River)*
la **danza** *dance*
el **danzón** *popular Cuban dance*
dar *to give*
darse: darse cuenta *to realize;* ¿Te das cuenta? *Do you realize?*
los **datos** *data*
de *of, from;* de noche *at night*
debajo de *under*
deber *should*
decidir *to decide*
decir (i) *to say, tell*
la **decisión** *decision*
decorativo, -a *decorative, ornamental*
la **defensa:** la defensa civil *civil defense*
deficiente *deficient*
dejar *to leave behind:* no deja *don't leave behind* (com); dejar de (+ infin) *to stop:* deja de fumar *stop smoking* (com)
el **delfín** *dolphin*
demandar *to demand*
la **democracia** *democracy*
la **dentadura** *denture*
el **dentista,** la **dentista** *dentist*
dentro (de) *inside, within*
el **departamento** *department*
depender (en) *to depend (on)*
el **deporte** *sport*
deportivo, -a *sports;* la ropa deportiva *sportswear*
derecho, -a *right*
derrotando *defeating*
derrotar *to defeat*
el **desarme** *disarmament*

desarrollar *to develop*
el **desarrollo** *development*
el **desayuno** *breakfast*
la **descarga** *discharge, volley, firing*
desconocido, -a: lo desconocido *the unknown*
describe *describe* (com)
describir *to describe*
el **descubridor, -a** *discoverer*
el **descubrimiento** *discovery*
descubrir *to discover*
el **descuento** *discount*
desde *from*
desierto, -a *deserted*
despej. = despejado, -a *clear*
despejado, -a *clear*
el **desperdicio** *waste*
después *afterwards, then;* después de *after*
el **detal:** al detal *retail*
el **detalle** *detail*
detrás: detrás de *behind*
devolver (ue) *to give back*
devuelve *he/she/it gives back*
devuelven *they give back*
el **día** *day;* el día de la madre *Mother's Day;* de día *by day, during the daytime;* ¡Feliz día! *Happy [Father's] Day!;* todos los días *every day*
el **diablo** *devil*
dialogar *to converse*
el **diálogo** *dialog*
diariamente *daily*
el **diario** *daily (newspaper)*
diario, -a *daily*
el **dibujo** *drawing*
dice *he/she/it says*
dicen *they say*
diciembre *December*
el **diente** *tooth;* el diente de ajo *clove of garlic*
diesel *diesel*
diez *ten*
diferente *different*
diferido, -a: en diferido *delayed*
la **dificultad** *difficulty*
digital *digital*
digno, -a *dignified*
dijo *he/she said*
el **dilema** *dilemma*
la **dimensión** *dimension*
la **dinamita** *dynamite*
el **dinero** *money*
dio *he/she/it gave*
el **dios, -a** *god, goddess*
el **dióxido:** el dióxido de carbón *carbon dioxide*
la **dirección** *direction; address*
directo, -a: en directo *live*
el **director, -a** *director*
el **directorio** *directory*
el **dirigible:** el dirigible aéreo *dirigible, blimp*
dirigido, -a (por) *directed (by)*
dirigir *to direct*
dirigirse *to write (to)*
diríjase *write* (com)
el **disco** *record*
la **discoteca** *discothèque*
disfrutar *to enjoy;* disfrute *enjoy* (com)
disperso, -a *scattered*
disponible *available*
la **distancia** *distance;* larga distancia *long distance*
distinguido, -a *distinguished, high by comparison with others*
distinguir *to make out, see in the distance*
distribuido, -a (por) *distributed (by)*
la **diversión** *amusement*
diverso, -a *different, diverse*
divertido, -a *fun, amusing*
divertirse (ie) *to have fun, amuse oneself*
divierte: se divierte *it has fun, amuses itself*
doblar *to turn;* no doble *don't turn* (com)
doble *double;* doble vía *two-way (street)*
doce *twelve*
el **doctor, -a** *doctor*
el **documental** *documentary*
documentar *to document*
el **documento** *document*
el **dólar** *dollar*
el **dolor** *pain, suffering*
doméstico, -a *domesticated, tame*
el **domicilio:** el servicio a domicilio *home delivery*
dominar *to master*
el **domingo** *Sunday*
dominical (adj) *Sunday*
dominicano, -a *Dominican, from the Dominican Republic*
donado, -a (por) *donated (by)*
donde *where*
¿dónde? *where*
dorado, -a *golden*
dorar *to brown, fry golden brown*
dormido, -a *asleep*
dos *two*
dulce *sweet; fresh (water);* la ostra de agua dulce *fresh-water oyster*
el **duque** *duke*
durante *during*
durar *to last*

E

e *and*
la **ecología** *ecology*
económico, -a *economical, economic*
ecuatoriano, -a *Ecuadorian, from Ecuador*
echar *to throw (in)*
la **edad** *age;* la Edad Antigua *ancient times;* la Edad Media *the Middle Ages*
la **edición** *edition*
el **edificio** *building*
el **editorial** *editorial*
la **educación** *education;* la educación física *physical education, gym class*
EE. UU.: los Estados Unidos *the United States*
la **efectividad** *effectiveness*
los **efectos:** los efectos de oficina *office supplies, stationery*
egipcio, -a *Egyptian*
el **ejecutivo, -a** *executive*
el **ejemplo** *example;* por ejemplo *for example*
el **ejercicio** *exercise*
el **ejército** *army*
el *the*
él *he, it*
la **elección** *choice*
eléctrico, -a *electric*
la **electrónica** *electronics*
el **elefante** *elephant*
elegante *elegant*
elegir (i) *to choose*
el **elemento** *element*
ella *she, it*
ellos, -as *they; them*
la **emergencia** *emergency*
empacarse *to pack up*
empáquese *pack up* (com)
empezar (ie) *to begin*
empieces: no empieces *don't begin* (com)
el **empleo** *employment*
emplumado, -a *plumed*
en *in; at*
las **enaguas** *slips, petticoats*
el **enanito, -a** *little dwarf* (dim)
enano, -a *small, dwarfish*
encabezar *to head*
encantador, -a *enchanting*
encestar *to put in a basket;* enceste *put in a basket* (com)
encontrar (ue) *to find*
encontrarse (ue) (con) *to meet*
enero *January*
enfermarse *to get sick*
la **enfermedad** *illness*
enfermo, -a *sick*
engañar *to deceive*
enorme *enormous*
enriquecido, -a *enriched*
la **ensalada** *salad*
la **enseñanza** *teaching*
entender (ie) *to understand*
entiende *he/she understands*
entiendes *you understand* (fam)
la **entomología** *entomology (the study of insects)*
entonces *then*
la **entrada** *entrance; entrance fee*
entrado, -a *entered*
entrar *to enter*
entre *between, among*
entre: No entre *Do not enter, No Admittance*
entregarse *to hand over*
entretener (ie) *to entertain*
entretenido, -a *amusing, entertaining*
entretiene *he/she/it entertains*

el **envenenamiento** *poison;* el centro de tratamiento por envenenamiento *poison control center*
envolver (ue) *to cover*
el **episodio** *episode*
la **época** *era, period*
el **equipaje** *baggage*
el **equipo** *team; equipment*
la **era** *era, age*
era *he/she/it was*
la **erupción** *eruption*
es *he/she/it is*
esa *that;* esas *those*
la **escala** *scale, grading system*
escapar *to escape*
escarlato, -a *scarlet*
la **escena** *scene*
el **escenario** *stage*
Escocia *Scotland*
escolar *scholastic; student*
Escorpión *Scorpio*
escribir *to write;* la máquina de escribir *typewriter*
escrito, -a *written*
el **escuadrón** *squadron*
escuchar *to listen (to)*
escúchelos *listen to them* (com)
el **escudo** *coat of arms, shield*
la **escuela** *school*
la **escultura** *sculpture*
ese *that*
esencial *essential*
eso *that*
esos *those*
la **espada** *sword*
España *Spain*
el **español** *Spanish (language)*
español, -a *Spanish*
la **especia** *aromatic herb*
especial *special*
el **especialista,** la **especialista** *specialist*
especialmente *especially*
espectacular *spectacular*
el **espectáculo** *show*
el **espectador, -a** *spectator, observer*
el **espejo** *mirror*
esperar *to expect; to wait (for), await*
el **espía,** la **espía** *spy*
la **espinaca** *spinach*
el **espíritu** *spirit*
espléndido, -a *splendid*
esq. = esquina *corner; (on) the corner (of)*
el **esquí:** el esquí acuático *water-skiing*
la **esquina** *corner*
esta *this;* estas *these*
ésta *this (one);* éstas *these*
está *he/she/it is*
establecer *to establish*
la **estación** *season; station;* la estación de radio *radio station*
el **estacionamiento** *parking*
el **estado** *state*
los **Estados Unidos** *the United States*
el **estambre** *yarn*
la **estampa** *print, engraving*
la **estampilla** *stamp*
están *they are*
estar *to be*
la **estatua** *statue*
el **este** *east*
este *this*
éste *this (one)*
estelar *starring*
el **estetoscopio** *stethoscope*
el **estilo** *style*
estimulado, -a *stimulated*
estimular *to stimulate*
Estocolmo *Stockholm*
estos *these*
éstos *these*
la **estrella** *star;* la Estrella de Paz *star of Bethlehem*
el **estreno** *premiere*
la **estructura** *structure*
estruendoso, -a *deafening, noisy*
el **estudiante,** la **estudiante** *student*
estudiar *to study*
eternamente *eternally*
la **eternidad** *eternity*
etnológico, -a *ethnological*
Europa *Europe*
el **europeo, -a** *European*
europeo, -a *European*
Eva *Eve*
la **evaluación** *evaluation*
el **evento** *event*
la **exageración** *exaggeration*
exclusivo, -a *exclusive*
la **exhibición** *exhibition;* el salón de exhibición *showroom*
la **existencia** *existence*
el **exitazo** *big success, big hit;* el exitazo rotundo *whopping success, very big hit*
el **éxito** *success*
exótico, -a *exotic*
la **expedición** *expedition*
la **experiencia** *experience*
experimental *experimental*
el **experto** *expert*
explorar *to explore*
explosivo, -a *explosive*
la **exposición** *exposition, exhibition, show*
la **expresión** *expression*
la **expulsión** *expulsion*
extra *extra*
el **extracto:** el extracto de malta *malt extract*
extranjero, -a *foreign*
el **extremo** *extreme;* ir a extremos *to go to extremes*

F

F. = Fahrenheit *Fahrenheit*
la **fábrica** *factory*
fabuloso, -a *fabulous*
fácil *easy*
la **facilidad:** las facilidades de pago *easy payments*
fácilmente *easily*
la **facultad** *department (of learning in a university)*
Fahrenheit *Fahrenheit*
la **falda** *skirt*
faltar *to be lacking;* a él/ella le falta *he/she is lacking*
la **familia** *family*
familiar *familiar*
famoso, -a *famous*
fantástico, -a *fantastic*
fatal *fatal*
el **favor:** favor de *please;* por favor *please*
favorecer *to aid*
favorito, -a *favorite*
febrero *February*
la **fecha** *date*
federal *federal*
feliz (pl: **felices**) *happy;* ¡Feliz día! *Happy [Father's] Day!;* ¡Feliz Navidad! *Merry Christmas!*
femenino, -a *feminine*
la **feminidad** *femininity*
el **fenómeno** *phenomenon*
la **feria** *fair;* la feria mundial *world's fair*
feroz (pl: **feroces**) *ferocious, savage*
la **ferretería** *hardware (store)*
el **ferrocarril** *railroad*
el **festival** *festival*
la **fidelidad** *faithfulness, authenticity*
la **fiebre** *fever*
la **fiesta** *party, holiday*
la **figura** *figure*
Filadelfia *Philadelphia*
Filipinas: la República de Filipinas *the Philippines*
el **filo** *cutting edge*
el **fin** *end;* el fin de semana *week-end*
final *final, last*
financiar *to finance*
la **finanza** *finance*
la **física** *physics*
físico, -a *physical;* la educación física *physical education, gym class*
el **flamenco** *flamingo (bird); flamenco (music)*
flamenco, -a *Flemish; flamenco (music)*
la **flauta** *flute*
la **flecha** *arrow*
la **flexión** *bending*
florecer *to flower*
la **Florida** *Florida*
flotar *to float*
folklórico, -a *folkloric*
el **folleto** *brochure*
el **fomento** *patronage*
el **fonógrafo** *phonograph*
la **forma** *form, way;* la forma de vivir *way of life*
la **formación** *formation; development*
formar *to form*
formidable *formidable, terrific*
el **fósforo** *phosphorous*
la **foto** *photograph, picture*

la **fotografía** *photography; photograph*
francés, francesa *French*
Francia *France*
franco, -a *honest, open, generous*
la **franela** *flannel blanket*
freír *to fry*
frente: frente a *in front of*
fresco, -a *fresh*
el **frijol** *bean*
el **frío** *cold;* tener frío *to be cold*
la **frontera** *frontier;* "Amor sin fronteras" *"West Side Story"*
la **fruta** *fruit*
el **frutal** *fruit tree*
fue *he/she/it was*
el **fuego** *fire;* cocinar a fuego lento *to simmer*
la **fuente** *fountain; source;* la fuente de agua *water fountain*
fuera: fuera de *out of, outside*
fuera: como si fuera *as if it were*
fueron *they were*
fuerte *strong*
la **fuerza** *strength; force, influence*
fumar *to smoke;* deja de fumar *stop smoking* (com)
fume: no fume *no smoking*
la **función** *function*
fundado, -a (por) *founded (by)*
la **furia** *fury*
el **fusible** *fuse*
el **fútbol** *soccer*
el **futbolista,** la **futbolista** *soccer player*
el **futuro** *future*

G

la **"gaffe"** *blunder* (French)
el **galápago** *giant turtle (from the Galápagos Islands)*
la **galería** *gallery*
la **galletita** *cookie, cracker*
el **gallo** *rooster*
el **ganador, -a** *winner*
ganar *to win*
el **garaje** *garage*
la **garantía** *guarantee*
garantizado, -a *guaranteed*
el **gas** *gas*
gastar *to spend; to waste;* no gastes *don't spend* (com)
el **gato** *cat*
Géminis *Gemini*
genealógico, -a: el árbol genealógico *family tree*
el **general** *general*
general *general;* en general *in general*
Génova *Genoa, Italy*
genovés, genovesa *Genoese, from Genoa*
la **gente** *people*
la **geografía** *geography*
geográfico, -a *geographic*
la **geología** *geology*
la **gestión** *measure, step, action*
el **gibón** *gibbon (ape)*
gigante *giant, gigantic*
la **gimnasia** *gymnastics*
el **gimnasio** *gymnasium*
Ginebra *Geneva*
el **gitano, -a** *gypsy*
gitano, -a *gypsy*
el **gladiador** *gladiator*
el **globo** *balloon*
el **gobernador, -a** *governor*
el **golf** *golf*
el **gorila** *gorilla*
la **gota** *drop*
la **gotera** *drip, leak*
gracias *thank you*
gran *big; great*
grande *big; great;* los grandes *grown-ups;* en grande *on a big scale*
el **granizo** *hail*
el **grano** *grain*
gratis *gratis, free*
griego, -a *Greek*
gritar *to shout*
el **grupo** *group*
el **guano** *fan palm (tree)*
guapo, -a *handsome, good-looking, pretty*
el **guaraní** *monetary unit of Paraguay*
el **guarapo** *sugar-cane juice*
el **guardacostas** *coast guard*
guardado, -a *kept, guarded*
guau *woof! (barking sound)*
la **guerra** war; la Segunda Guerra Mundial *World War II*
el **guerrero** *soldier*
la **guía** *guide, directory;* la guía telefónica *telephone directory*
guiar *to guide*
la **Guinea Ecuatorial** *Guinea*
gustar *to like, to be pleasing to*
el **gusto:** al gusto *to order*

H

ha: ha de hacerse *it has to be done*
Habana: La Habana *Havana*
haber *to have*
la **habichuela** *bean*
la **habitación** *room*
el **habitante,** la **habitante** *inhabitant*
habla *he/she speaks;* se habla español *Spanish is spoken*
hablar *to speak, talk;* hablan *they speak;* no hables *don't talk* (com)
habrá *there will be*
hacer *to do, make;* hacer un cuento *to tell a story;* hace muchos años *many years ago*
hacerse: ha de hacerse *it has to be done*
hacia *toward, to*
haciendo: haciendo punto *stopping*
haga *make* (com)
Haití *Haiti*
el **hambre** (f) *hunger;* tener hambre *to be hungry*
hasta *until; up to; even;* hasta que *until*
hay *there is, there are*
hazme: hazme (un cuento) *tell me (a story)* (com)
el **hechicero, -a** *sorcerer, sorceress*
el **hecho** *event*
el **helado** *ice cream*
el **helicóptero** *helicopter*
heredar *to inherit*
el **hermano, -a** *brother, sister*
el **héroe** *hero*
hervir (ie) *to boil*
el **hierro** *iron*
hierve *he/she boils*
el **hígado** *liver;* el aceite de hígado de bacalao *cod liver oil*
el **hijo, -a** *son, daughter*
el **hispano, -a** *Hispanic*
hispano, -a *Hispanic*
Hispanoamérica *Spanish America*
hispanoamericano, -a *Spanish American*
la **historia** *story; history*
histórico, -a *historic*
el **hogar** *home*
la **hoja** *leaf*
Holanda *Holland, the Netherlands*
holandés, holandesa *Dutch*
el **hombre** *man;* el hombre lobo *werewolf*
el **honor** *honor*
honrado, -a *honest*
la **hora** *hour; time*
el **horizonte** *horizon*
el **horóscopo** *horoscope*
el **hospital** *hospital*
el **hotel** *hotel*
hoy *today;* hoy mismo *today, right now*
el **hueso** *bone*
el **huésped, -a** *guest;* la casa de huéspedes *guest-house*
el **huevo** *egg*
humano, -a *human*
la **humedad** *moisture*
Hungría *Hungary*

I

Ibérico, -a: la Península Ibérica *Iberic Peninsula*
la **ida:** (de) ida y vuelta *round-trip*
la **idea** *idea*
ideal *ideal*
idealizado, -a *idealized*
identificado, -a *identified*
el **idioma** *language*
la **iglesia** *church*
igual: igual que *just as, like*
la **imagen** *image*
la **imaginación** *imagination*
imaginar(se) *to imagine, think*
imagínese *imagine* (com)

el **imperio** *empire*
importante *important;* lo importante *the important thing*
importar *to matter;* no importa *it doesn't matter*
imposible *impossible*
la **imprenta** *printing press*
el **impuesto** *tax;* más el impuesto *plus tax*
inasisten. = **inasistencia** *days absent, absences*
la **inasistencia** *days absent, absences*
el **incienso** *frankincense*
incluido, -a *included*
incluir *to include*
incluye *it includes*
increíble *incredible, unbelievable*
la **independencia** *independence*
independiente *independent*
las **Indias** *the Indies*
indicado, -a *indicated, shown*
el **índice** *index, table of contents*
Índico: el Océano Índico *Indian Ocean*
el **indígena,** la **indígena** *native*
indígena *indigenous, native*
el **indio, -a** *Indian*
indio, -a *Indian*
la **influencia** *influence*
la **información** *information*
el **informativo** *news report*
informativo, -a *informative*
el **informe** *piece of information*
Inglaterra *England*
el **inglés** *English (language);* el inglés, la inglesa *Englishman, Englishwoman;* los ingleses *the English*
inglés, inglesa *English*
el **ingrediente** *ingredient*
el **ingreso:** la tarjeta de ingreso *tourist card*
la **inicial** *initial*
inicial *initial*
la **iniciativa** *initiative*
inmenso, -a *immense, huge*
insignificante *insignificant, not important*
la **instalación** *installation*
el **instituto** *institute*
integral: el pan integral *whole wheat bread*
la **integridad** *integrity*
la **inteligencia** *intelligence*
inteligente *intelligent*
intenso, -a *intense*
interactivo, -a *interactive*
intercelular *intercellular (between cells)*
el **interés** *interest*
interesante *interesting*
interior: la (ropa) interior *underwear*
internacional *international*
interpretado, -a (por) *performed (by)*
íntimo, -a *intimate*
la **investigación** *investigation*

el **invierno** *winter*
ir *to go;* ir de compras *to go shopping*
irse *to go away, leave*
Irlanda *Ireland*
la **isla** *island*
la **islita** *little island* (dim)
Italia *Italy*
italiano, -a *Italian*
el **itinerario** *itinerary, route*
la **izquierda** *left;* a la izquierda *on the left*

J

jamás *never*
el **jamón** *ham*
Japón *Japan*
japonés, japonesa *Japanese*
el **jardín** *garden*
la **jarra** *pitcher, jug, jar*
el **jazz** *jazz*
la **jira** *picnic, hike*
la **jirafa** *giraffe*
joven *young;* los jóvenes *young people*
la **joya** *jewel*
la **joyería** *jewelry*
el **judo** *judo*
el **juego** *game;* en juego *at stake*
jueves *Thursday*
jugando *playing*
jugar (ue) *to play*
el **jugo** *juice;* el jugo de piña *pineapple juice*
julio *July*
junio *June*
junto, -a *together*
Júpiter *Jupiter*
la **juventud** *youth*

K

el **kilo** *kilogram*
el **kilómetro** *kilometer;* el kilómetro cuadrado *square kilometer*
el **kiosko** *kiosk*
Km = kilómetros *kilometers;* Km^2 = kilómetros cuadrados *square kilometers*

L

la *the; her, it* (obj pron)
el **labio** *lip*
el **lado** *side;* al lado de *beside*
el **ladrón,** la **ladrona** *thief*
el **lago** *lake*
la **lanza** *lance, sword*
el **lapso** *marking period*
largo, -a *long;* larga distancia *long distance*
las *the; them* (obj pron)
el **láser** *laser;* el rayo láser *laser beam*
la **lata** *tin can*

el **latín** *Latin*
latino, -a *Latin American*
el **laurel** *laurel, bay leaf*
lavar *to wash*
le *(to, for) him, her, you (pol)* (obj pron)
la **lealtad** *loyalty*
la **leche** *milk*
la **lechuga** *lettuce*
leer *to read*
legendario, -a *legendary*
la **legumbre** *vegetable*
la **lejanía** *distance*
lejano, -a *distant*
lejos: a lo lejos *in the distance*
el **lempira** *monetary unit of Honduras*
lento, -a *slow*
León *León, a region in northwestern Spain*
el **león** *lion;* el león marino *sea lion*
el **leoncito** *little lion* (dim)
el **leopardo** *leopard*
les *(to) them, you (pol)* (obj pron)
la **letra** *letter*
el **letrero** *sign; poster*
el **leucocito** *white blood cell*
la **levadura** *yeast*
levantarse *to get up*
leve *light*
la **leyenda** *legend*
la **libertad** *liberty*
la **libra** *pound*
libre *free*
el **libro** *book*
el **líder,** la **líder** *leader*
la **liga** *league*
la **limitación** *limitation*
el **límite** *limit*
el **limón** *lemon*
la **limosna** *alms, charity;* pedir limosna *to beg*
el **limosnero, -a** *beggar*
la **limpieza** *cleanliness*
limpio, -a *clean*
lindo, -a *pretty*
la **línea** *line;* la línea aérea *airline*
Lisboa *Lisbon*
la **lista** *list*
listo, -a *ready*
la **literatura** *literature*
lo *it* (obj pron); *what is, that which is;* lo que *which*
el **lobo** *wolf;* el hombre lobo *werewolf*
loco, -a *crazy*
la **locomotora** *locomotive*
lograr *to achieve; to get*
la **lona** *canvas*
Londres *London*
los *the; them* (obj pron)
el **lugar** *place*
el **lujo:** de lujo *luxurious*
la **luna** *moon*
el **lunes** *Monday*
la **luz** *light;* el año luz *light year*

LL

la **llama** *flame*
llama: ¿Cómo se llama él/ella? *What's his/her name?*
la **llamada** *telephone call*
llamado, -a *called*
llaman: ¿Cómo se llaman? *What are their names?*
llamar *to call; to ring (the doorbell)*
llamarse *to be called, named*
llame *call* (com)
llegar *to arrive;* llegar a *to arrive at (in); to reach, to get to; to come to*
lleno, -a *full*
llevaban *they carried*
llevar *to carry, take along*
llevarse *to carry off;* se llevó *it carried off*
llorar *to cry*
llover (ue) *to rain*
llueve *it's raining*
la **lluvia** *rain*

M

m. = metros *meters*
machacar *to crush*
el **machete** *machete*
maderable *timber-yielding*
la **madre** *mother;* el día de la madre *Mother's Day*
maduro, -a *ripe*
el **maestro, -a** *teacher;* el maestro *maestro, great musician*
la **magia** *magic*
mágico, -a *magic*
magnífico, -a *great, splendid*
la **magnitud** *magnitude, size*
el **maíz** *corn*
el **majo, -a** *lazy person*
el **mal** *evil*
mal, -o, -a *bad*
la **malta** *malt*
la **mamá** *mother*
mami *mom, mommy*
el **mandamiento** *commandment*
mandar *to send*
el **mandril** *mandrill (large baboon)*
la **manera** *way, means*
el **mango** *mango (a tropical fruit)*
el **maní** *peanut*
la **mano** *hand;* a mano *by hand*
mantener (ie) *to maintain*
el **mantenimiento** *maintenance*
la **mantequilla** *butter*
mantiene *it maintains*
las **manualidades** *arts and crafts*
la **mañana** *morning;* por la mañana *in the morning*
mañana *tomorrow*
la **maqueta** *scale model*
la **máquina:** la máquina de escribir *typewriter;* la máquina de vapor *steam engine*
la **maquinaria** *machinery*
el **mar** *sea;* el nivel del mar *sea level*
la **maravilla** *wonder*
maravilloso, -a *marvelous*
la **marca** *brand*
marcar *to indicate, show*
marciano, -a *Martian*
la **marejada** *groundswell*
la **marimba** *marimba, xylophone*
marino, -a: el león marino *sea lion*
marítimo, -a *by sea*
Marruecos *Morocco*
Marte *Mars*
el **martes** *Tuesday*
marzo *March*
más *more; plus;* el/la más *the most;* más el impuesto *plus tax;* más de, más que *more than*
la **masa** *mass*
el **masaje** *massage*
las **matemáticas** *mathematics*
el **material** *material*
la **matinée** *matinée, afternoon performance*
el **matrimonio** *marriage*
max. = máximo, -a *maximum*
máximo, -a *greatest; maximum*
mayo *May*
mayor *main, principal; major;* el/la mayor *the largest, the biggest, the greatest;* al (por) mayor *wholesale*
mayormente *mainly*
me *me, to me* (obj pron)
mecánico, -a *mechanical*
la **medianoche** *midnight*
medicinal *medicinal*
el **médico, -a** *doctor*
médico, -a *medical*
medieval *medieval*
el **medio** *middle; environment;* en medio de *in the middle of*
medio, -a *half*
el **mediodía** *noon*
el **Mediterráneo** *the Mediterranean (Sea)*
la **mejilla** *cheek*
mejor *better;* el/la mejor *the best;* lo mejor *the best (thing)*
la **melancolía** *melancholy*
mencionado, -a *mentioned*
mendigar *to beg, beg for;* no se mendiga *it is not (to be) begged for*
la **menina** *lady-in-waiting*
menor *younger; minor*
el **mensaje** *message*
la **mente** *mind*
el **menú** *menu*
la **mercadería** *merchandise*
el **mercado** *marketplace*
Mercurio *Mercury*
merecer *to deserve*
el **merengue** *Caribbean dance*
el **mes** *month*
el **metabolismo** *metabolism*
el **metal** *metal*
el **método** *method*
el **metro** *meter*
metropolitano, -a *metropolitan*
mexicano, -a *Mexican*
México *Mexico*
mi(s) *my*
mí *me*
el **microscopio** *microscope*
el **miembro, -a** *member*
mientras *while*
el **miércoles** *Wednesday*
mil *a thousand*
la **milla** *mile*
el **millón** *million*
mín. = mínimo, -a *minimum*
el **mineral** *mineral*
mineralógico, -a *mineralogical*
mínimo, -a *minimum*
el **ministerio** *ministry*
el **minutito** *little minute* (dim); ¡Un minutito! *Just a minute!*
el **minuto** *minute;* ¡Un minutito! *Just a minute!*
mirar *to look at*
la **mirra** *myrrh*
la **misa** *Mass;* la misa dominical *Sunday Mass*
mismo, -a *same;* hoy mismo *today, right now;* sí mismo *oneself, yourself (pol)*
el **misterio** *mystery*
misterioso, -a *mysterious*
la **mochila** *knapsack, backpack*
la **moda** *fashion*
el **modelo** *model*
moderno, -a *modern*
el **molino** *mill;* el molino de viento *windmill*
el **momento** *moment*
la **moneda** *coin; currency, money*
montar *to ride*
el **monte** *mount, mountain*
el **monumento** *monument*
moral *moral*
moreno, -a *dark, dark-haired*
morir (ue) *to die*
el **moro, -a** *Moor*
la **mosca** *fly*
Moscú *Moscow*
el **mosquetero** *musketeer*
el **mosquito** *mosquito*
el **motín** *mutiny*
el **motor** *motor*
motorizado, -a *motorized*
el **mozo, -a** *waiter, waitress*
la **mucosa** *mucous membrane*
el **muchacho, -a** *boy, girl*
mucho, -a *much, a lot of;* muchos, -as *many, a lot of*
la **mudanza** *moving*
el **mueble** *(piece of) furniture;* los muebles *furniture*
la **mueblería** *furniture store*
muerto, -a *dead;* había muerto *he/she had died*
la **muestra** *example*
la **mujer** *woman*

mundial *pertaining to the world; (of the) world; worldwide;* el (Campeonato) Mundial *World Cup (soccer championship);* la feria mundial *world's fair;* la Segunda Guerra Mundial *World War II*
el **mundo** *world;* medio mundo *half the world;* todo el mundo *everyone*
municipal *municipal*
el **mural** *mural*
murió *he/she died*
el **museo** *museum*
la **música** *music*
musical *musical*
el **músico,** la **músico** *musician*
muy *very*

N

nacen *they are born*
nacer *to be born*
el **nacimiento** *birth*
la **nación** *nation;* las Naciones Unidas *the United Nations*
nacional *national*
la **nacionalidad** *nationality*
nada *nothing, anything*
la **naranja** *orange*
la **nariz** *nose*
la **natación** *swimming*
el **nativo, -a** *native*
el **naturalista,** la **naturalista** *naturalist*
el **navegante,** la **navegante** *sailor*
navegar *to sail*
la **Navidad** *Christmas;* ¡Feliz Navidad! *Merry Christmas!*
navideño, -a *(of) Christmas*
necesario, -a *necessary*
necesitar *to need*
el **negociado:** el Negociado Federal de Investigación *Federal Bureau of Investigation (FBI)*
el **negocio** *business;* los negocios *business (transactions)*
negro, -a *black*
Neptuno *Neptune*
el **nervio** *nerve*
la **nevada** *snowfall*
ni *nor;* ni . . . ni *neither . . . nor*
el **nido** *nest*
la **nieve** *snow;* Blanca Nieves *Snow White*
ninguno, -a *no, not any*
el **niño, -a** *child, little boy or girl*
el **nivel** *level;* el nivel del mar *sea level*
no *not*
la **noche** *night;* de noche *at night*
la **Nochebuena** *Christmas Eve*
Noé *Noah*
el **nombre** *name*
el **noreste** *northeast*
normal *normal*
el **norte** *north*
nos *us, to us* (obj pron)
nosotros, -as *we; us*
la **nota** *note*
la **noticia** *news;* las noticias *news*
la **novela** *TV serial, soap opera*
noventa *ninety*
el **novicio, -a** *novice, beginner*
noviembre *November*
la **nube** *cloud*
nublado, -a *cloudy*
el **nudo** *knot*
nuestro, -a *our*
Nueva York *New York*
Nueva Zelandia *New Zealand*
nueve *nine*
nuevo, -a *new*
numérico, -a *numerical*
el **número** *number*
la **numismática** *numismatics (collection of coins and paper money)*
nunca *never*
N. Zelandia: Nueva Zelandia *New Zealand*

O

o *or*
el **obispo** *bishop*
el **objetivo** *objective*
el **objeto** *object*
la **obra** *work*
la **observación** *observation*
observar *to observe*
obtenido, -a *obtained*
ocasionalmente *occasionally*
el **océano** *ocean*
ochenta *eighty*
octubre *October*
ocupado, -a *busy*
ocupar *to occupy*
ocurrir *to occur*
ocurrirse *to occur (to someone);* nunca se te ocurrió *it never occurred to you*
ocho *eight*
OEA: Organización de Estados Americanos *Organization of American States (OAS)*
el **oeste** *west*
la **oferta** *offer*
oficial *official*
oficialmente *officially*
la **oficina** *office;* la oficina de crédito *credit office;* los efectos de oficina *office supplies, stationery*
ofrecer *to offer*
oír *to hear*
el **ojo** *eye*
la **ola** *wave*
el **oleaje** *wave heights*
olímpico, -a *Olympic*
la **oliva** *olive*
ONU: la Organización de Naciones Unidas *the United Nations (UN)*
opcional *optional*
la **ópera** *opera*
el **operador, -a** *operator*
operático, -a *operatic*
la **oportunidad** *opportunity*
el **óptica** *optician*
la **óptica** *optics*
óptico, -a *optic*
el **orden** *order*
el **orégano** *oregano*
la **organización** *organization;* la Organización de Estados Americanos (OEA) *Organization of American States (OAS);* la Organización de Naciones Unidas (ONU) *the United Nations (UN)*
organizar *to organize*
el **orgullo** *pride*
el **Oriente** *the Orient, the East*
el **origen** *origin*
original *original*
el **oro** *gold*
la **orquesta** *orchestra*
el **orquideario** *area for orchids*
la **ortiga** *nettle (plant)*
la **oscuridad** *darkness*
oscuro, -a *dark*
el **oso** *bear*
la **ostra** *oyster;* la ostra de agua dulce *fresh-water oyster*
otro, -a *other, another;* otros, -as *others*
la **oveja** *sheep*
la **oxidación** *oxidation*
el **oxígeno** *oxygen*

P

el **pabellón** *pavilion*
Pacífico: el Océano Pacífico *Pacific Ocean*
el **padre** *father*
la **paella** *paella, a Valencian dish of rice, seafood, etc.*
pagar *to pay*
la **página** *page*
el **país** *country*
el **pájaro** *bird*
la **palabra** *word*
el **palacio** *palace*
la **paleontología** *paleontology (the study of fossils)*
la **palma** *palm (tree)*
el **pan** *bread;* el pan integral *whole wheat bread*
Panamá *Panama*
panamericano, -a: los (juegos) panamericanos *Pan-American games*
el **pantalón** *pants*
el **pantaloncillo** *underpants*
la **pantalla** *screen*
el **papá** *father;* los papás *parents*
papi *dad, daddy*
para *for; in order to;* ¿Para qué es? *What is it for?*
el **paralelo** *parallel* (geography)
parar *to stop;* ¡Pare! *Stop!* (com)
parcialmente *partially*

pardo, -a *brown*
París *Paris*
el **párpado** *eyelid*
el **parque** *park;* el parque zoológico *zoo*
el **parqueo** *parking*
la **parte** *part*
participar *to take part in*
el **partido** *game, match*
pasa: ¿Qué pasa? *What's happening?*
el **pasado** *past*
el **pasaje** *journey, fare*
el **pasajero, -a** *passenger*
el **pasaporte** *passport*
pasar *to happen; to spend (time); to pass;* pasar por *to pass through*
el **paseo** *boulevard*
el **pastor, -a** *shepherd, shepherdess*
la **pata** *leg (of an animal)*
el **pavo real** *peacock;* el pavito *little peacock* (dim)
el **payaso, -a** *clown*
la **paz** *peace*
pedir (i) *to ask for;* pedir limosna *to beg*
el **pelícano** *pelican*
la **película** *film, movie*
peligroso, -a *dangerous*
la **península** *peninsula*
pensar (ie) *to think*
pequeño, -a *small, little*
el **perdedor, -a** *loser*
perder (ie) *to lose; to waste (time)*
perderse (ie) *to miss*
perdido, -a *lost*
perfecto, -a *perfect*
el **perico** *parakeet*
el **periódico** *newspaper*
el **periodismo** *journalism*
el **período** *period*
la **perla** *pearl*
permiten: no se permiten *(they are) not allowed*
permitir *to permit, allow*
pero *but*
el **perro** *dog*
la **persona** *person*
el **personaje** *character; personage, personality*
personal *personal*
personificar *to personify*
Perú *Peru*
la **pesadilla** *nightmare*
pesar: a pesar de *in spite of*
pesar *to weigh*
las **pesas** *weight lifting*
el **pescado** *fish*
el **pescuezo** *neck*
la **peseta** *monetary unit of Spain*
el **pesimista,** la **pesimista** *pessimist*
el **peso** *monetary unit of several Latin American countries (See pages 86-87.)*
el **piano** *piano*
picar *to chop*
el **pico** *peak*
pida *ask for* (com)
el **pie** *foot*
la **piedra** *stone, rock*
la **piel** *skin; fur*
pierda: ¡No se lo pierda! *Don't miss it!* (com)
pierdas: no pierdas tiempo *don't waste time* (com)
la **pieza** *piece*
el **pijama** *pajamas*
la **pimienta** *(black) pepper*
el **pimiento** *pepper (vegetable)*
pinta *he/she paints*
pintar *to paint*
el **pintor, -a** *painter*
la **pintura** *painting*
la **piña** *pineapple;* el jugo de piña *pineapple juice*
la **piridoxina** *pyridoxine (vitamin B_6)*
pisar *to set foot on, step on*
la **piscina** *swimming pool*
Piscis *Pisces*
la **pistola** *gun*
el **plan** *plan*
el **planeta** *planet*
planetario, -a *planetary*
la **planta** *plant*
la **plantación** *plantation*
el **plato** *dish*
la **playa** *beach*
la **plaza** *plaza, square;* la plaza de toros *bullring*
el **plural** *plural*
Plutón *Pluto*
poblar *to populate*
pobre *poor*
poco: un poco *a little bit;* un poco más de *a little more*
poco, -a *little;* pocos, -as *few*
el **poder** *power*
poder (ue) *to be able, can*
polar *polar*
la **policía** *police (force)*
el **polo** *pole;* el Polo Norte *North Pole*
Polonia *Poland*
el **pollo** *chicken*
poner *to put;* poner al día *to bring up-to-date*
popular *popular*
la **popularidad** *popularity*
por *for; through; in; by; to; along;* ¿por qué? *why?*
la **porcelana** *porcelain, china*
el **porcentaje** *percentage*
porque *because*
portátil *portable*
el **porvenir** *future*
la **posesión** *possession*
la **posibilidad** *possibility*
posible *possible*
la **posición** *position*
practicar *to practice*
el **precio** *price*
precioso, -a *precious*
la **predicción** *prediction*
la **pregunta** *question*
preguntan *they ask*
preguntar *to ask*
prehistórico, -a *prehistoric*
premiado, -a *awarded a prize*
el **premio** *prize*
la **prensa** *press*
preocupado, -a *concerned, preoccupied*
la **presentación** *appearance; presentation*
presentar *to present*
el **presente** *present (time)*
el **presidente, -a** *president*
prestar: no prestes atención *don't pay attention* (com)
previo, -a *previous, former*
primer, -o, -a *first;* primero (adv) *first*
el **primero, -a** *the first one*
primitivo, -a *primitive*
la **princesa** *princess*
la **probabilidad** *probability*
probablemente *probably*
el **probador** *fitting room*
probar (ue) *to try; to test;* prueba *try* (com)
el **problema** *problem*
proceder *to originate, come from*
la **procesión** *procession*
la **producción** *production*
producido, -a (por) *produced (by)*
producir *to produce*
productivo, -a *productive*
la **profesión** *occupation, profession*
profesional *professional*
el **profesor, -a** *teacher, professor*
profundo, -a *deep;* lo más profundo *the deepest part*
el **programa** *program*
el **progreso** *progress*
prohibir *to prohibit;* Prohibido entrar *Keep out*
el **promedio** *average*
el **pronóstico** *forecast*
pronto *soon;* de pronto *suddenly*
propio, -a *own*
la **protección** *protection*
protegerse *to protect oneself*
protéjase *protect yourself* (com)
la **provincia** *province*
próximo, -a *next*
proyectar *to project*
el **proyecto** *project, plan*
el **proyector** *projector*
prueba *he/she tests*
el **psicoanalista,** la **psicoanalista** *psychoanalyst*
la **publicación** *publication*
publicar *to publish*
la **publicidad** *publicity, advertising*
el **público** *the public*
el **pueblo** *people*
puede *he/she/it can*
pueden *they can*
puedes *you can*
el **puente** *bridge*
el **puerco** *pig*
la **puerta** *door*
puertorriqueño, -a *Puerto Rican*
pues *well, so; because*
el **puesto** *stall, booth*
la **pulgada** *inch*

el **puma** *puma*
el **punto:** haciendo punto *stopping*
puro, -a *pure*

Q

Q. = quetzales *monetary unit of Guatemala*
que *that, which; who*
que: mas/menos . . . que *more/less . . . than*
¿qué? *what?; which?;* ¿por qué? *why?*
¡qué . . . !: *how (+ adj)! what a (+ noun)!*
querer (ie) *to want; to love*
querido, -a *dear*
el **queso** *cheese*
el **quetzal** *monetary unit of Guatemala*
quien *who; he/she who*
¿quién(es)? *who?*
quiere *he/she wants*
quiero *I want*
la **química** *chemistry*
la **quincallería** *housewares, notions*
quince *fifteen*
quitar *to remove*
quitarse *to take off*

R

el **radar** *radar*
la **radiación** *radiation*
el **radio** *radio; radius*
la **radio** *radio, broadcasting*
la **ráfaga** *gust of wind*
rápido, -a *fast*
el **rasgo** *trait, characteristic*
ratificar *to ratify*
el **ratón** *mouse*
el **rayo** *ray, beam;* el rayo láser *laser beam;* los rayos X *X-rays*
el **reactor** *reactor;* el reactor atómico *atomic reactor*
real *royal*
la **realidad** *reality*
realista (adj) *realistic*
realizar *to fulfill; to perform;* se realiza *it is performed*
la **rebaja** *discount*
el **rebelde,** la **rebelde** *rebel*
la **receta** *recipe*
reciente *recent*
recoger *to get*
la **recompensa** *reward*
la **recreación** *recreation*
el **recreo** *recreation*
el **recuerdo** *souvenir*
redondo, -a *round*
la **referencia** *reference*
reflejar *to reflect*
el **regalo** *gift*
la **región** *region*
regional *regional*
el **regreso** *return*
regular *so-so*
regular *to regulate*
la **reina** *queen*
el **reinado** *reign*
el **reino** *kingdom*
relacionado, -a (con) *related (to)*
el **relámpago** *lightning*
la **religión** *religion*
religioso, -a *religious*
el **reloj** *watch*
remoto, -a *remote*
renacentista *(of the) Renaissance*
la **rendición** *surrender*
el **rendimiento** *performance*
el **reparto:** de reparto *featured*
repente: de repente *suddenly*
repetir (i) *to repeat*
repiten *they repeat*
la **réplica** *replica, copy*
la **representación** *representation*
representado, -a *represented*
el **representante,** la **representante** *representative*
la **reprise** *repeat showing*
la **reproducción** *reproduction*
reproducido, -a *reproduced*
el **reproductor, -a** *reproducer*
la **república** *republic*
la **República Dominicana** *Dominican Republic*
la **reputación** *reputation*
la **res** *beef*
la **reserva** *reserve;* la reserva forestal *forest reserve*
la **reservación** *reservation*
reservado, -a *reserved, put aside*
el **resfriado** *cold (illness)*
la **residencia** *residence, home*
la **resistencia** *resistance*
respetar *to respect;* respete *respect* (com)
la **responsabilidad** *responsibility*
el **restaurant(e)** *restaurant*
restaurar *to restore*
el **resto** *rest*
resultar *to turn out, result;* resultar en *to result in*
retirado, -a *retired*
retornar *to return*
el **retrato** *picture*
la **reunión** *reunion*
reunir *to get together, assemble*
el **revolucionario, -a** *revolutionary*
el **rey** *king;* los Reyes Católicos *the Catholic Monarchs (Fernando and Isabel);* los Reyes Magos *the Magi, the Three Wise Men;* el día de los Reyes *Feast of the Three Kings, Epiphany*
la **riboflavina** *riboflavin (vitamin B_2)*
rico, -a *rich*
la **rifa** *raffle*
el **rinoceronte** *rhinoceros*
el **riñón** *kidney*
el **río** *river*
la **riqueza** *wealth, riches*
robado, -a *stolen*
robusto, -a *robust, strong*
rojo, -a *red*
el **rol** *role, part*
Roma *Rome*
el **romance** *romance*
romántico, -a *romantic*
la **ropa** *clothes;* la ropa deportiva *sportswear*
la **rosa** *rose*
rosado, -a *pink*
el **rostro** *face*
el **rubí** *ruby*
rubio, -a *blond*
el **rumor** *rumor*
Rusia *Russia*
la **ruta** *route*

S

el **sábado** *Saturday*
saber *to know;* saber (+ infin) *to know how to (+ infin)*
el **sable** *saber*
el **sabor** *flavor*
sabroso, -a *delicious*
sacar *to take out*
el **safari** *safari*
Sagitario *Sagittarius*
Sahara Español *Spanish Sahara*
la **sal** *salt*
la **sala** *room, hall*
salgan *they may leave*
la **salida** *exit*
salir *to leave; to come out; to rise (sun);* al salir *when leaving*
la **saliva** *saliva*
el **salmón** *salmon*
el **salón** *(large) room;* el salón de exhibición *showroom*
la **salsa** *Caribbean dance music*
saltar *to jump*
la **salud** *health*
San Agustín *Saint Augustine*
San Cristóbal *Saint Christopher*
la **sangre** *blood*
San Juan Bautista *Saint John the Baptist*
San Nicolás *Saint Nicholas*
el **santo** *saint's day, name day*
santo, -a *holy*
el **sapo** *toad*
la **sardina** *sardine*
satánico, -a *satanic*
el **satélite** *satellite*
Saturno *Saturn*
la **sección** *section*
seco, -a *dry*
el **secreto** *secret*
secreto, -a *secret*
la **seda** *silk*
la **sede** *headquarters*
seguir (i) *to follow, continue*
según *according to*
segundo, -a *second*
la **seguridad** *safety;* el cinturón de seguridad *seat belt*
seguro, -a *safe; sure*
la **selva** *jungle*
la **semana** *week;* el fin de semana *weekend;* toda la semana *all week long*

semifinal *semifinal*
la **semilla** *seed*
el **Sena** *the Seine (River)*
sentarse (ie) *to sit down*
sentir(se) (ie) *to feel*
la **señal** *sign;* la señal de tránsito *traffic sign*
la **señora** *woman; Mrs.*
separar *to pull out, remove;* separe *pull out* (com)
septiembre *September*
séptimo, -a *seventh*
ser *to be*
serán *they will be*
la **serie** *series*
la **serpiente** *serpent, snake;* la serpiente (de) cascabel *rattlesnake*
servicial *obliging*
el **servicio** *service;* el servicio a domicilio *home delivery;* el porcentaje de servicio *service charges*
servir *to serve*
Sevilla *Seville*
si *if*
sí *yes*
sí *oneself;* sí mismo *oneself, yourself (pol)*
siempre *always*
la **sierra** *sierra, jagged mountain range*
la **siesta** *siesta, afternoon nap or rest*
siete *seven*
sigas: no sigas *don't continue* (com)
el **siglo** *century*
significativo, -a *significant*
sigue *follow* (com)
siguiendo *following*
siguiente *following*
la **sílfide** *sylph (nymph of the air)*
la **silueta** *silhouette*
el **símbolo** *symbol*
similar *similar*
el **simio** *monkey, simian*
simple *simple*
simultáneo, -a *simultaneous*
sin *without*
sincero, -a *sincere*
la **sinfonía** *symphony*
sinfónico, -a *symphonic*
el **síntoma** *symptom*
el **sistema** *system*
situado, -a *situated*
sobre *on; above; about*
sobrepasar *to exceed*
sobresaliente *outstanding*
social *social*
la **soda** *soda*
el **sofrito** *sauté, seasoning*
el **sol** *sun; Peruvian monetary unit*
solamente *only*
solar *solar*
solicitar *to apply for;* solicite *apply for* (com)
solitario, -a *solitary*
solo, -a *single, alone*
sólo *only*
la **solución** *solution*
el **sombrero** *sombrero, hat*
el **sonido** *sound*
la **sonrisa** *smile*
la **sopa** *soup*
el **soporte** *support*
la **soprano** *soprano*
la **sorpresa** *surprise*
el **sorteo** *raffle*
el **sostén** *support*
soviético, -a: la Unión Soviética *the Soviet Union*
la **soya** *soybean*
su(s) *your* (pol), *his, her, its, their*
suave *soft*
subir *to go up*
el **submarino** *submarine*
submarino, -a *underwater*
la **substancia** *substance*
el **suceso** *happening*
el **sucre** *monetary unit of Ecuador*
la **sucursal** *branch office*
Sudamérica *South America*
sudamericano, -a *South American*
Suecia *Sweden*
el **suelo** *ground, land*
el **sueño** *dream*
la **suerte** *luck;* ¡Buena suerte! *Good luck!*
suficiente *sufficient*
la **suma** *sum;* en suma *to sum up, in short*
sup. = suplemento *supplement, section*
superficial *superficial*
la **superficie** *surface*
superior *superior*
el **superperro** *superdog*
el **suplemento** *supplement, section*
supo *he/she knew*
el **sur** *south*
el **sureste** *southeast*
el **suroeste** *southwest*

T

el **tabaco** *tobacco*
la **tabla** *list; board*
el **Tajo** *the Tagus (River)*
tal *such;* ¿Qué tal están? *How are they?*
el **taller** *workshop*
el **tamaño** *size*
también *also, too*
el **Támesis** *the Thames (River)*
tan *so (much)*
la **tanda** *showing*
el **tango** *tango*
el **tanque** *tank*
tanto, -a *so much, as much;* tantos, -as *so many*
el **tapiz** (pl: **tapices**) *tapestry, carpet*
la **tarde** *afternoon*
tarde *late;* más tarde *later*
la **tarifa** *rate*
la **tarjeta** *card;* la tarjeta de crédito *credit card;* la tarjeta de ingreso *tourist card*
la **tatarabuela** *great-great-grandmother*
el **tatarabuelo** *great-great-grandfather*
taurino, -a *bullfighting* (adj)
Tauro *Taurus*
el **taxi** *taxi*
la **taza** *cup*
te *you, to you* (fam obj pron)
teatral *theatrical, theater*
el **teatro** *theater*
el **tejido** *tissue*
tel. = teléfono *telephone number*
la **tela** *cloth, fabric*
telefónico, -a: la guía telefónica *telephone directory*
el **teléfono** *telephone; telephone number*
el **telégrafo** *telegraph*
el **telegrama** *telegram*
el **telescopio** *telescope*
la **televisión** *television*
el **televisor** *TV set*
temer *to be afraid;* temer a *to be afraid of*
la **temperatura** *temperature*
la **tempestad** *storm*
el **templo** *temple*
temprano *early*
tener *to have;* tener (mucho) cuidado *to be (very) careful;* tener frío *to be cold;* tener hambre *to be hungry;* tener que (+ infin) *to have to (+ infin)*
tenía *he/she/it had*
el **tenis** *tennis*
el **tenor** *tenor*
tercer, -o, -a *third*
terminar *to end*
la **termita** *termite*
el **termómetro** *thermometer*
terrestre *by land; earthly*
el **territorio** *territory*
el **terror** *terror*
el **tesoro** *treasure*
el **testamento** *testament*
el **testimonio** *testimony*
ti *you* (fam)
la **tiamina** *thiamine (vitamin* B_1*)*
el **tiburón** *shark*
el **tiempo** *time; weather;* no pierdas tiempo *don't waste time* (com)
la **tienda** *store*
la **tierra** *land;* la Tierra *Earth (planet)*
el **tigre** *tiger*
la **tinta** *ink*
el **tintero** *inkwell*
típico, -a *typical*
el **tipo** *kind, type*
las **tiras:** las tiras cómicas *comic strips*
el **titán** *titan (person of great size or power)*
el **título** *title*

TM: Teléfonos de México *Mexican telephone company*
el **tocacintas** *cassette player*
tocan *they play (music)*
tocar *to play (music);* tocar en la puerta *to knock on the door*
todavía *still*
todo, -a *all, all of, every; whole;* toda una descarga *a whole discharge (volley, firing);* todos los días *every day;* todo el mundo *everyone;* toda la semana *all week long*
todo (pron) *everything, all;* todos, -as *everyone;* ¡Todos aprendemos! *We all learn!*
tomar *to take*
el **tomate** *tomato*
tome *take* (com)
el **toreo** *bullfighting*
el **toro** *bull;* la plaza de toros *bullring*
la **torre** *tower;* la torre de control *control tower;* la torre de observación *observation tower*
la **tortuga** *turtle*
torturar *to torture*
el **tostón** *fried plantain*
total *total*
totalmente *totally*
trabado, -a *stuck*
trabaja *he/she works*
trabajar *to work*
el **trabajo** *work*
tradicional *traditional*
traer *to bring*
el **tráfico** *traffic*
el **traje** *costume*
la **tranquilidad** *tranquillity*
tranquilo, -a *calm, still*
el **transistor** *transistor*
el **tránsito** *traffic;* la señal de tránsito *traffic sign*
la **transmisión** *broadcast; telecast*
transmitir *to broadcast*
el **transportista**, la **transportista** *carrier*
el **traslado** *transfer*
el **tratado** *treaty*
el **tratamiento** *treatment*
tratar: tratar de *to try to*
través: a través de *by means of, through*
la **travesura** *prank, caper*
el **tren** *train*
tres *three*
el **trineo** *sleigh*
la **tripulación** *crew*
el **trofeo** *trophy*
la **tronada** *thunderstorm*
el **trono** *throne*
la **tropa** *troop*
tropical *tropical*
el **trueno** *thunder*
tu(s) *your* (fam)
tú *you* (fam)
el **tubo** *tube*
el **turista**, la **turista** *tourist*

U

Ud(s). = usted(es) *you* (pol)
Ukrania *the Ukraine*
último, -a *last*
un, una *a, an*
únete *join* (com)
único, -a *only; unique;* el único, -a *the only one*
unido, -a *united;* las Naciones Unidas *the United Nations*
el **uniforme** *uniform*
la **unión** *union*
la **Unión Soviética** *the Soviet Union*
unirse *to join*
universal *universal*
la **universidad** *university*
universitario, -a: la ciudad universitaria *university city*
el **universo** *universe*
uno, -a *one*
Urano *Uranus*
urbano, -a *urban*
la **urna** *urn, footed vase*
usa *he/she wears*
usado, -a *used*
usar *to wear; to use;* use *use* (com)
el **uso** *use*
U. Soviética: la Unión Soviética *the Soviet Union*
usted *you* (pol sing)
ustedes *you* (pol pl)
el **utensilio** *utensil*
utilizado, -a *used*

V

la **vaca** *cow*
las **vacaciones** *vacation*
el **vagabundo, -a** *vagabond, tramp*
la **vajilla** *dishes, china;* vajillas y utensilios de cocina *housewares*
valenciano, -a *Valencian, from Valencia*
valer *to be worth*
valiente *valiant, brave*
el **valor** *valor, courage; value, worth, price*
el **vapor:** la máquina de vapor *steam engine*
variable *variable*
variado, -a *varied, diverse*
la **variedad** *variety;* las variedades *variety show(s), entertainments*
varios, -as *several*
vayan: no vayan *(I hope) they aren't going to*
ve *he/she sees*
vea *see* (com)
veamos *let's see*
véase *see* (com)
veces: a veces *sometimes;* otras veces *other times*
el **vecino, -a** *neighbor*
la **vegetación** *vegetation*
vegetal *vegetable*
veintiséis *twenty-six*
veintiuno, -a *twenty-one*
el **vejete** *ridiculous old man*
la **vela** *candle*
el **venado** *deer*
el **vencedor, -a** *winner*
el **vendedor, -a** *seller*
vender *to sell*
veneciano, -a *Venetian, of Venice*
venenoso, -a *poisonous*
venga *come* (com)
el **vengador, -a** *avenger*
venir (ie) *to come; to arrive;* al venir *when arriving*
la **venta** *sale;* las ventas al detal *retail;* las ventas al por mayor *wholesale*
veo *I see*
ver *to see*
el **verano** *summer*
la **verdad** *truth;* de/en verdad *really*
verdadero, -a *true*
la **verdura** *green vegetable*
la **vereda** *trail*
la **versión** *version*
ves *you see* (fam)
el **vestido** *dress*
vestido, -a *dressed*
la **vez** (pl: **veces**) *time;* otra vez *again*
la **vía** *way;* por vía aérea *by air mail*
vía *via, by way of*
viajar *to travel*
el **viaje** *voyage, trip*
la **vida** *life*
el **viejo, -a** *old person*
viejo, -a *old*
Viena *Vienna*
viene *he/she/it comes*
el **viento** *wind;* el molino de viento *windmill*
el **viernes** *Friday*
vieron *they saw*
el **vinagre** *vinegar*
el **vino** *wine;* el vino seco *dry wine, cooking sherry*
vino *he/she/it came*
la **viola** *viola;* la viola da gamba *viola da gamba, an early stringed instrument*
la **violencia** *violence*
violento, -a *violent*
el **violín** *violin*
la **visa** *visa*
el **visitante**, la **visitante** *visitor*
visitar *to visit;* visite *visit* (com)
la **víspera** *eve*
visto, -a *seen;* había visto *he/she had seen*
la **vitamina** *vitamin*
vive *he/she lives*
vivir *to live*
el **vocero** *spokesman*
volar (ue) *to fly*
el **vólibol** *volleyball*
volver (ue) *to return*
la **voz** (pl: **voces**) *voice*
el **vuelo** *flight*
la **vuelta:** la vuelta al mundo *trip around the world;* (de) ida y vuelta *round-trip*

X

el **xilófono** *xylophone*

Y

y *and*
ya *already*
la **yema** *yolk*
yo *I*
el **yogur** *yogurt*
el **yunque** *anvil*

Z

el **zafiro** *sapphire*
la **zanahoria** *carrot*
la **zapatería** *shoe store*
la **zapatilla** *slipper*
el **zapato** *shoe*
la **zebra** = la **cebra** *zebra*
la **zona** *zone*
la **zoología** *zoology*
zoológico, -a: el parque zoológico *zoo*

Index

The following is a listing of topics featured in this reader and the pages where they appear.

A
B 5
C 6
D 7
E 8
F 9
G 0
H 1
I 2
J 3